Don't let them take your children

A practical guide to dealing with Social Services

Stuart Adams

2018

Contents

Acknowledgments

It all started a few years ago when circumstances introduced me to a retired writer and human rights activist–Brian Rothery. Brian was already actively involved in fighting miscarriages of justice, but his attentions had turned to what was becoming a modern day witch hunt of parents–child protection. Brian had established the Ectopia network, helping families who were fleeing UK social services by moving to Ireland.

Through supporting the network and the families who approached it challenges and strategies were developed, tested and employed. This led to the formal establishment of Prevent Intervention Now, a network of lay advocates to support parents. I began writing articles and commentaries for Brian's websites and we spent many hours examining how the system could be challenged. Brian's social commentaries inspired me to write this guide. Brian has overseen the development of the book and kindly edited parts of it. For so many reasons I will be forever in his debt.

My family have been a constant inspiration in writing this book. They have had to put up with my long hours working on cases for other families, often at the detriment of my family.

They have had to endure 'do not disturb' as the pages took shape and for their patience, encouragement and love I thank them all.

I also have to thank the many families who have trusted my strategies and worked alongside me to build their cases against the social workers. We have enjoyed many successes, and it is humbling that children are still with their natural families through the network's efforts.

I have enjoyed the wise counsel of a solicitor and a barrister who have tenaciously fought cases I have passed to them where the parents have needed the support of legal representation. I have learnt a lot from them and they have graciously supported my efforts in helping families. They know who are they and I thank them for all they have done.

I must also thank the excellent, but unpublished author Ben Capel for his psychological insights and critique of the 'expert witness' industry.

I must add that I am in not a 'writer'. Any typographical errors in the text belong to me and I can only apologise in advance should you find grammatical errors etc. I believe it is more important that this book is available to parents with perhaps a few errors, than it sat on my laptop awaiting the day I can afford a professional copy-writer. Thus I present it warts and all.

I must above all thank my long suffering partner, Sarah, who has been one of my editors, my best friend, a source of ideas and encouragement and a critical eye. Most important of all, she has been a mum to our children and supportive wife. Thank you for believing in me.

Finally thank you to my Mum and dear departed Grandma, who have always been there for me, through all the ups and downs of my life.

Foreword

Brian Rothery

When I retired, in the sense of not working for money, in my early Seventies, I began to use my apparent skills in certain human rights work, mainly in what I perceived to be miscarriages of justice and a slide towards state control and new forms of fascism. I had many years of experience, both in book writing and journalism and in technical positions, such as in IBM and in the public sector, which gave me an ability to examine legal documents and, in particular, the often dubious reports of so-called 'expert witnesses'. I set up a Ectopia.org website to support this work.

In 2013, after literally blundering into the subject of intervention by British social workers into the lives of families, I added a section on this subject to the website and the response was spectacular. Within a short period the website was entirely devoted to British families either losing their children or in dire danger of losing them because of what appeared to be heavy-handed intervention by social workers. I soon learned that one of the newest expressions of fascism was the ideology that the state, not parents, knows best when it comes to the protection of children. Indeed, parents were being seen as a threat to children.

The website and small amount of paralegal work quickly morphed into a network, or at least the foundations of one, spanning several countries, because families were fleeing from Britain, mainly to Ireland, in attempts to prevent their children being seized by social workers. I was soon out of my depth, not just in trying to assist families with accommodation but in giving them useful legal advice. The social workers were so arrogant and incompetent in their written reports that a certain amount could be done to slow them down, if not quite stop them in their tracks and reverse their decisions.

By 2013, I was seventy nine and no longer confident that I could cope with the demands of families crying out for help and asking for the legal advice that could save their children. The legal profession appeared to be disinterested (fortunately as discovered later with outstanding exceptions) and I was far from certain that I could acquire the legal knowledge that could help families to fight as litigants in person in the courts. I actually dreaded the thought that I might have to learn how to do it.

At this point, Stuart and his family came into my life. The other families spanned a wide social and educational range from window cleaner and cleaning lady to medical doctor and engineer and I had been aware of the potential of finding professional assistance within them. Stuart was the jackpot. He not only quickly learned all the legalities of turning the incompetent actions and, at times, illegality of what the social workers were doing to the advantage of families, but how to challenge them and reverse their decisions right up to the High Court.

When we finally managed to get parents into the High Court, we learned that we still lacked the ability and resources to continue to the next stages even after encouraging initial responses from the judges. At this point, a woman barrister and a solicitor began to assist Stuart. The result has been highly beneficial for the families seeking help and highly rewarding for us.

One result of the network's success, or indeed its existence, has been significant media response, especially on television, in the UK, Ireland, throughout Europe and internationally.

Over the years I have been asked several times on camera if I am not afraid that we are doing more harm than good. Because of Stuart and his legal colleagues, I have been able to reply that the High Court judges appear to agree with what we are doing.

'So far as I can discern from their public (published and spoken) statements, the architects of our current age of Child Protectionism, our Western Cultural Revolution, have never betrayed the slightest hint of doubt that their efforts are borne of anything other than pure righteousness. This, they may be somewhat perturbed to learn, they share with supremacists and fascists. Hitler and his sycophants were animated by identical certitudes; doubt is relegated by hardcore fascists, new cultural purifiers, who prefer to call themselves 'progressives', and psychotics alike to the status of contemptible soft-headedness or dangerous slipperiness (rather than, for example, a most precious and necessary check on human arrogance and delusion). The new revolutionaries of Child Salvation see themselves, uncannily, as engaged in a uniquely imperative struggle, a necessarily militant campaign, to flush out hidden child abusers wherever they may be and purge the world of their malignant presence.'

Ben Capel, unpublished <u>Notes from Another Country</u>

Preface

If you are reading this, it is more than likely that social workers or other child protection officials have entered your life. If they have not, you may not yet fully know how fortunate you are or what the potential threats are for you and your family.

You could be getting on with your life and enjoying your children, unaware that a referral has been made about you to social services, commonly referred to as 'SS'. A referral from a malicious neighbour, a nurse, doctor or teacher and that soon there will be a life-changing knock on your door by officials empowered under the law to make judgements about your abilities as a parent in the name of 'protecting children'.

You may think this only happens only to bad people, so if this book suggests to you that it could happen to you it will have served its purpose.

This is a self-help guide. It does not pretend to have all the answers, it is not proclaiming to be a full alternative to legal advice, nor is it a magic wand. The aim is to provide you with knowledge of the system, the methodology used against families and a range of options that *may* work in either preventing your children being removed from your care or in having children in care returned to you. I say *may* work because nothing can be guaranteed, but the information contained here is based upon the employment of such methods in real cases that have successfully challenged and beaten the system.

It will equip you with the knowledge of the professionals who will be involved, how they operate and the key things to be watchful for. It will provide you with a guide to the processes, the jargon and the dangers. Above all, it will give you a tactical advantage and a way to expose and fight the system that cares little for the best interests of your child and more for the break-up of often loving, caring and solid family units.

This book is for **all** parents, whether you have had Social Services at your door, are going through the system and aiming to protect your children, or are wise enough to equip yourself just in case. It is worth reiterating that no family is safe from the child protectionists and if not today, tomorrow it could be you.

A word of warning.

What you won't find in this book is pseudo-law, the *Freeman on the Land, Sovereign Citizen, Common Law not Statute law* and its ilk. The simple reason is that it does **not** work and no matter what the internet purveyors of this tell you, you will not protect your children or get them back from the system using any of the methods that the pseudo law advocates promote. In fact experience shows that those who do use this approach often end up not only losing their children but find themselves in contempt of court, or even prison. There are some legal remedies often over-looked by the legal professionals that you may find alluded to by the pseudo-law soothsayers which can be used, but the key is that they must be utilized within the law and legal/judicial rules.

Chapter ten inspects the pseudo-law approaches and examines why they can be such a dangerous path to tread.

The information and advice provided here has worked in England and Wales, Scotland, Northern Ireland and the Republic of Ireland. Although there are differences in child protection systems and court procedures the underlying advice can be adapted to which ever jurisdiction you are in.

In England and Wales 70,440 children were in the care of local authorities on 31st March 2016[i] and it is a number that is steadily increasing. Long term foster-care, adoptions and the influx of private corporations into the children's care home system shows what can only be described as a growing industry. This industry is fed by what the professionals call "Child Protection".

Before examining that system, a brief consideration of the outcomes for children who experience the State's *'Care'* paints a picture that should concern every parent, every so-called "child protectionist", every MP and you. Simple statistical outcomes will at this stage suffice and leave the reader in no-doubt that our current child protection system is just not working.

50% of prostitutes walking the streets came from the care system.

50% of Young Offender Institutes inmates have been in care.

80% of those selling the Big Issue (the magazine of the homeless) came from a care system background.

26% of the adult prison population have been in care.

25% of girls in care are pregnant by the time they leave the care system.

80% of care leavers find themselves unemployed within two years of leaving the care system.

50% of the girls in care are single mothers within two years of leaving the care system.

13% of children in care achieve the benchmark of 5 GCSE's compared to a rising figure of 58% of others.

9% of those in care achieve a university place compared to 47% of other young people.

7% of youngsters in care have a criminal conviction against just 2 percent of all under 18's.[ii]

Since the infamous 'Baby P' tragedy and more recently bolstered by the Daniel Pelka case and others, the numbers of children and families affected by Social Services intervention in their lives has risen dramatically and sadly the outcome has led to a substantial increase in the numbers of children being removed from their families. This has been encouraged by the government introducing legislation that has established a strict timetable of 26 weeks for cases to be resolved in the courts. Although the argument is as always, 'in the best interests of the child', the reality is an already pressured, under-funded, badly managed and poorly educated workforce of social workers are being placed under even more pressure to produce a result. The upshot of this is poor practice, cutting corners and widespread illegality to meet this artificial deadline.

It is notable since Baby P that the number of children taken into care for physical and sexual abuse or neglect has fallen as a percentage in the reasons for removal, yet the number of removals of children based on 'future emotional harm' has grown exponentially.

"Future emotional harm" is an accusation that has no defence. Equally, it has no requirement for evidence. It is crystal ball fortune telling at best, at worst it is an unevidenced opinion passed by a social worker or 'expert witness'. Your child can be taken from you on the basis that you may present some unsubstantiated and as yet an undefined risk to your child in the future. Even with no evidence of any harm but simply that there *could* be in the future, your family is torn apart.

Baby P is a red herring-the spin of social work-as an excuse for over-intervention and most heinous of all: a cover-up of the reality of the Baby P case. What happened to Peter Connolly was not a tragedy borne out of a lack of intervention by the state appointed child-protectors but a failure of those social workers to act with professionalism and diligence. Rightly the profession was called into serious question, but rather than learn the lessons that their failures were institutional, their focus was then misdirected. This case has led to an over-zealous approach by the social work profession. Now every child is at risk, no matter what the evidence (or lack of).

Whatever the reason for a social worker entering through your door they are now required to look for risks in a family even if their involvement was for benign reasons. Removal appears to be the fail-safe approach, or more accurately back-covering and a real loss of personal professional responsibility in favour of an agenda that lies in direct contradiction of the Children's Act 1989. At the heart of this Act is the objective of keeping families together. In fact all the research and evidence points to better outcomes for children where this occurs. Even where there may be problems with the parenting, keeping families together *still* produces better outcomes for those children than a life in care.

Yet it is this Act that is being used to tear families apart, often on the basis of flimsy or non-existent evidence. More frighteningly, the evidence used is often fabricated, backed by less than independent 'expert' witnesses and often the families are rail-roaded through a system where there is scant regard for protocol or procedures. In short, Social Services across the UK and generally across the English speaking countries (Republic of Ireland, USA, New Zealand, Australia) - are acting in an unaccountable fashion, destroying families on the basis of "better safe than sorry".

No doubt there will be some of you thinking "but they don't take children away from families without good reason". Sadly, this is exactly what Social Services do. Just consider for a moment the fact that there are over 70,000 children in the care system. Have there been thousands of convictions of abusive parents in the criminal courts for significant abuse of children? Have there been 70,000? Have there been 30,000? The simple answer is "no", the big question is "why not?". Why are there only a handful of such convictions in the criminal courts each year, yet large numbers of children are being removed on a regular basis?

The simple answer is the burden of proof–let's call it a 'legal loophole' peculiar to the Civil Courts, including the Court of Protection and Family Courts. This is the 'balance of probabilities'. In a criminal court your guilt must be proved beyond all reasonable doubt in the eyes of a jury of 12. In the family court a single judge decides based on a weighting of 51% to 49% that you are "guilty", "likely" or "possibly" "have" or "could" harm your child in some way, in the past, present or future. As long time anti-forced adoption campaigner Ian Josephs has said, there should be no punishment without a crime, yet this is exactly what the family court judges do. Without the evidence that would be required to convince a jury, a single judge can sentence you to a lifetime of punishment by ordering the removal of your child.

Introduction

I am going to be highly controversial here and suggest something that completely reverses the basis of child protection in the UK. The system is based and defended on the maxim of the "best interests of the child". Leaving aside that social services are darkly nicknamed as "SS", a nod to the Gestapo of Nazi Germany and the fact that Hitler himself was fond of the same phrase, I believe the basis for the phrase "best interests of the child" leads to abuse of children, not their protection.

Removing the rhetoric of the child protectionists and instead applying common sense and common humanity to the issues of children's welfare we must return to the basis of society that has held all aspects of human development together for millennia and that is the family and in particular parents. The nurturing of offspring does not have just a biological and psychological basis but was essential for the future survival of the family unit, small groups and even larger communities. The parents have had and always will have the most essential and crucial role in the care and development of their children. In times past some of that care was self-altruistic, more children were needed to help with the family work and survival and it may be argued that the large families of the industrial revolution era were instrumental in the success of that phenomenon. We can trace the original child protectionists back to this time with Parliament legislating against children working in mines, mills and other industries.

So parents and families were not just an insular part of our evolution but the key to the creation of our society and economy. Parents thus took central stage and the legal development of parental responsibility clarified this position. Mankind though is the most cruel of animals, prepared to destroy and wreak destruction on personal and societal levels and there can be no-doubt that parents can inflict cruelty upon a child; hence the development of child protection laws and ethics.

However, in the 21st century the basis of parents as the central core of family and protection of children has been usurped by the State. Parents are not seen as the core basis for the child in all aspects of the child's life but merely the biological means by which that life comes into being. Instead the state has created a sinister role for itself in attempting to control the child. Projecting this forward, we return to another of Hitler's favourite expressions, in that controlling the child is the key aspect to States controlling the future of society. Hence parental roles are being diminished in favour of ever increasing State control. Schooling is an important aspect of this, no longer is the rounded education of the child about the world into which they are growing, with all the attendant skills being provided, but schools have become factories of tick box, State determined curriculums that narrowly define what the child should know. Darker aspects of this include the criminalization of children expressing usual childhood traits, such as playground fall-outs or name calling. Schools have become an aspect of state control. If you don't believe this just try removing your children for a holiday in term-time or the even greater sin of home schooling.

This locking out of parents in important choices in their children's lives is then taken to its ultimate extreme when the child protectionists intervene in a family. The system is not focused on the help and support of any family who may just be struggling or going through a difficult patch, but seeks to find evidence of parental wrong-doing whatever the cost. Social workers have earned their nick-name of the "SS". Parents are often presumed guilty of any accusation and the social workers seek to find, create or even lie to make the parents appear to fit their perception.

They fail to see the parents as the most important constant in a child's life and appear completely unconcerned about their impact on a child and its family. The growing numbers of children being taken into care amply demonstrates this. Children are being removed in increasing numbers on increasingly spurious grounds, yet there is not the parallel increase in parents facing criminal trials. This largely because there has been no crime, yet even a parent found innocent of such an allegation in the criminal courts can still be 'found guilty' in the family courts on the hearsay, uncorroborated opinions of social workers and the "balance of probabilities". They then may face the ultimate sanction of losing their child to the care system.

So what is the answer? It is time to put parents back at the centre of children's lives, to work first from the presumption that parents know best and to apply the basic criminal presumption of innocence, before guilt has been proven beyond any reasonable doubt. Appreciating the role of parents and ensuring that the State steps away from trying to "model" society by this attack on the family and ultimately trusting that most parents will do what is best for their child is the only way that the deeply flawed child protection system can actually really help those children who need it, rather than the current model that seeks to find fault with any parent, from any walk of life.

As Hedley J. stated in Re L (Care: Threshold Criteria) [2007] 1 FLR 2050 *"society must be willing to tolerate very diverse standards of parenting, including the eccentric, the barely adequate and the inconsistent... it is not the provenance of the state to spare children all the consequences of defective parenting."*

So the "best interests can of the child" can only be properly addressed if the "best interests of the parents" are also placed at the heart of child-protection.

Chapter 1 Hope

The brown suitcase was old, slightly battered, but held a lot. It needed to, there was an awful lot to fit in it. Summer clothing, winter clothing, in fact any and all clothing. The kids two suit cases included the same, except for the odd cuddly toy and favourite bedtime story books.

In fact the lives of four people were reduced to four suitcases. The photos holding the happy memories, the heirloom furniture, threadbare, yet having a comfort that is only borne from memories and love left, with a heavy heart and yet an overbearing necessity.

The vehicle packed, all the nooks and crannies filled, to the extent that the rear axle sagged under the weight. With the children safely belted in the rear, the couple exchanged a look that confirmed they had all the necessities. It also expressed their fears and a deep sadness of having to leave the home they had built, nurtured and dedicated to their family.

The door key turned and the lock produced its usual, but soon to be forgotten, reassuring clunk of security. How ironic that the sound that had created so much peace of mind and security was now a signal of a step into the unknown for this family.

With another key the ignition was started and the vehicle took a quick, but assured, reverse off the drive and out onto the main road. This was not, as yet, an open road to the security sought. Unspoken, but shared, the couple's thoughts turned to those that sought to persecute them. Would they be watched and trailed? Would the authorities pull them over and ask to see proof they had the right to take that journey? Would their papers allow them passage or would this 'escape' be thwarted by those who attested to knowing best? Would their vehicle be sent out of the line at the border and their plan undone? Did they stand out as a frightened, persecuted family? Were they marked as "wanted" for doing nothing more than living their lives? The endless circle of these questions ate away at the souls of the two adults trying to escape from a draconian and biased system.

The two children in the back were oblivious. The whole story sold as a holiday and adventure. There was no need, at this stage to explain the system that sought to destroy the family and their lives. It was almost impossible to explain that some human beings could act with such fanaticism and blind obedience to a political mantra that was so discriminatory and destructive. They knew they had to protect the children from this pervasive and destructive force, not just in the physical sense, but in the emotional sense. They could not allow their children to grow up corrupted by this regime that allowed one human being to treat another in such a destructive manner.

To flee felt like the only option available. They had seen and read of destruction of others. They were determined that if the only way to prevent that was to run - then they would run.

As they drew close to the border and what they hoped was a gateway if not to freedom, but at least respite from the ever-encroaching authorities, their hearts grew glum. Here was the first test. Were they on a watch list? Was a uniformed, unthinking, rule follower about to stop them in their tracks? Again it was unspoken, yet shared by the hairs rising on their necks and the thin beads of perspiration appearing across their bodies. Despite the shared anxieties, neither raised such thoughts and feelings with the other. Both knew their roles: to protect their family they could not allow such fears to be openly manifested, yet the squeeze of each others' hand as they rolled up to the check-point confirmed that fear and their resolve.

They were through, though not out of the woods, as the next stage of their journey was about to begin. One hurdle was quickly replaced by another–a sign of the adrenaline flowing through their bodies. Would the authorities pull them out of line? 300 yards and they would be on the ferry, 25 minutes from departure. Could it all end before they rolled on to the super-structure of perceived freedom? No, they were on and soon sitting in the lounge, a lukewarm bitter coffee in their hands and the children sipping orange juice, excited by the boat ride and lands anew. A few hours time and they would be safe, at least for now. Still there were three hours and a whole new set of anxieties to be rode. Would the authorities there stop them and turn them back? Would they arrest them as fugitives and separate them from their children? Just what power did these authorities wield?

Driving off the ferry and onto land–the land of another country-their pulses racing again, another check point and the opportunity for the State to stop them in their tracks. Except nothing happened, and they passed through the check point unassailed. They had done it, at least for now, breathing space. The future may have held more difficulties, but the persecutors were now in another country and a new start was possible, a start that could offer the chance of a future for the children.

Was this Jews fleeing from Nazi Germany or the Russian Pogroms? No, this is here and now. This is the State that is persecuting families through the mantra of "Child-Protection" and the only recourse for many parents is to have to flee the country to protect their children against the horrors of the State's 21st Century witch hunt against parents and families.

A true story–names have been changed and the time-line condensed.

It appears to be a very Western phenomenon, yet has a long history within and between westernised societies. Australia has made apologies for the adoption policies it pursued as has Ireland in a much more subdued and controlled fashion. Yet the English and Welsh governments support the same policies with a gusto that borders on the insane. Ironically one of the countries that is experiencing an influx of the fleeing families is Ireland. Historically there may still be many unanswered questions about Ireland and adoption, but to the 21st Century refugee from Social Services in England and Wales it is an easily accessible (no passport required) option. This is backed by the fact that there is an active network of Good

Samaritans going above and beyond to help those fleeing from social services.

In the luxury and sunshine of the playboy mecca of Monaco there is an 86-year-old man by the name of Ian Josephs. A millionaire with a number of language schools across France, he appears to be the least likely to have an interest in the child protection system of the UK. Yet this octogenarian has been standing by the side of parents facing social services for over 50 years. It all began for him whilst serving as a county councillor in Kent. He was approached by a mother who had wrongly had her child taken into care, placed in an expensive private school owned by another local councillor and her child paid to sleep with the teachers. Ian Josephs took on this mother's case and, despite the authority's attempts at a cover up, the child was returned to his mother's care. The resultant widespread publicity brought other desperate parents to Ian Josephs' door and he took on their cases against the very authority in which he was a county councillor. He never lost a case, but this was to prove a heavy toll, both in his business and in his personal life, ultimately leading to the break-up of his first marriage. Probably to the dismay of many local parents, he gave up on the fight.

In 2003 a major case hit the headlines when Sally Clark, a British solicitor, had her conviction for the murder of her two babies overturned on appeal. The original prosecution had relied on the statistical analysis by the then celebrated paediatrician Professor Sir Roy Meadow. He had presented to the jury that the chance of two children dying from 'cot death' or sudden infant death syndrome in such a well-off family was statistically so unlikely that it could only be murder. His statistics of 1 in 73 million were the mainstay of the prosecution's case and the jury were led down the path of statistics-over-evidence. The Royal Statistical Society examined his claims and methodology and issued a statement that undermined Meadow's position, saying there was "no statistical basis" for the claims in Meadow's testimony. They went further and expressed concern at the "misuse of statistics in the courts".

Reliance on Meadow's statistical inaccuracies had convicted an innocent woman, but what the jury had not heard was that the prosecution had failed to disclose the pathologist's report that showed, in microbiological tests, that one of Clark's sons had more than likely died of natural causes. Clark was convicted in November 1999 and the convictions were upheld at appeal in October 2000, but overturned in a second appeal in January 2003. Unfortunately this tale did not have a happy ending: because of her ordeal, Sally Clark developed serious psychiatric problems and died in 2007 from alcohol poisoning.

In the same year, adoptions without parental consent also started to hit the headlines and Ian Josephs' sense of justice was once again fired enough for him to write to the Daily Mail regarding his experiences and express his concern that things had apparently got worse since his days of defending parents in Kent. This resulted in nearly 50 parents writing to him seeking his help. Although the type of support Ian had given in the past was no longer possible, due to the changes in the law, he set up a website called forced-adoption.com and offered guidance, support and advice through it. As a result Ian now helps over one thousand cases per year.

His support, whether just through the well-researched information on his website or via the phone, has been invaluable in helping many parents against the spectre of social services. Indeed, he has been instrumental in some key cases that have created legal precedents, such as the case of the family who fled to France to avoid having their unborn baby taken at birth. British social workers, though, are like dogs with the proverbial bone and they gained an order to remove the baby. However, with Ian's help and solicitors in France and England the family created the legal precedence for habitual residency, confirmed by the President of the family court division himself. The baby had to be returned to the parents in France.

Ian goes further in his help: if a parent contacts him he will call them back from Monaco at his own cost. He will also reimburse travel expenses for parents, in particular pregnant mums-to-be, who have fled the country. This is another aspect of the fight against social services-should parents flee the country to protect their children, from the social service net? If they do so, how do they survive? This brings us to a second individual whose own ire at the injustices being perpetrated against children and parents saw him take drastic action to help the desperate souls facing social services.

Brian Rothery is an Irishman, who, like Ian Josephs, had never had any dealings with social services in his family, but deplores the 'witch-hunt' that social services use against families. A retired author and investigative journalist, Brian has gone that one step further and co-ordinates a network of Good Samaritans that will not only offer support and advice, but actually provide safe-houses and a refuge for families to escape to. Brian may be a world away from the yachts and glamour of Monaco, but his contribution to parents is no less invaluable. Brian has investigated many miscarriages of justice and written extensively on the attack on vulnerable parents, but through his experiences of parents facing social services, particularly a very sad, home-grown tale, he came to the conclusion that decisive action was required.

On the evening of Saturday 16th April 2005, a young mother named Sharon Grace walked into the social services building in Wexford. She had with her two young daughters Mikahla (4) and Abby (3). She was desperate and needed help. I will let Brian take up the story from here:

"... [she] asked if she could see a social worker. The receptionist told her that the social worker worked Monday to Friday only and that there were no emergency contact numbers for social services. Ely House is situated spectacularly across the bridge from the historic waterfront of Wexford Town. Immediately across the road from the front entrance is a small beach where the River Slaney pours out under the bridge into the sea. With a child in each hand, Sharon left the building, crossed the road and went down over the short stony beach into the fast-flowing river. Fishermen recovered the three bodies.

At the inquest a year later the receptionist who had spoken to Sharon confirmed that, despite the tragedy, Ely House still had no list of emergency numbers for social services. That caused such a furore that today there is a new procedure for mothers in trouble. The police are called and the children are seized."

Having experienced similar treatment whilst trying to help a mother in need, Brian decided that he would have to help support parents and Ectopia network was born. This is the website that Brian runs with the aim to help those facing social services. Although the Sharon Grace story above is about the Irish social services, Brian deals mainly with cases originating in England and Wales.

Brian lives in the South of Ireland in a nineteenth century farmhouse that was restored by him and the outbuildings renovated into living accommodation. It is in these outbuildings that he began to offer a safe refuge for families fleeing the UK social services. Besides Brian's house is a converted barn which can comfortably sleep five, or even 6 or 7 at a push. It is totally self- contained with a fully equipped kitchen, bathroom, designated bedroom with room for four to sleep and a cosy lounge complete with log burner and internet access. It truly is a home from home. For a while this served as a safe house and refuge whilst families sorted their problems and were helped to find permanent accommodation. However, through the double edged sword of media coverage this refuge has had to be dropped due to its exposure in the national media covering the issue of forced adoption and social services. In its place is a network of Good Samaritans and supportive landlords that ensure that accommodation and refuge, be it short-term or permanent, is available. Inevitably Brian and Ian would soon join forces as Ian offered the financial means of escape, whilst Brian could help find accommodation for those who fled.

Brian developed contacts in countries other than Ireland where parents could flee and where he had recruited Good Samaritans to support a fleeing family. Hence at the time of writing the network of Good Samaritans extends from Ireland to Denmark, Belgium, France, Spain, Northern Cyprus and has family supporters in the UK who will offer overnight accommodation on route to the ferry or airports, or even safe-houses for a short stay for breathing space.

Within the fleeing families encountered by Brian were several individuals who wanted to take the fight back to the social services. They had often fled the UK, as many do in a panic, but soon learnt through research they had recourse to challenge social services and a number of parents began the fight back. Through their diligence and successes they could support the network, giving advice and help to parents, often preventing an unnecessary flight by the family.

The question of fight or flight will be dealt with below, but in January 2014 a serving MP, John Hemming, stated that families facing social services should, if they could afford it, flee the country as they would not find justice in the British family courts. That is a damning indictment of the system, ably abetted by the 'child-protectionists' who condemned Mr Hemming with the usual lines that his encouragement to flee was 'putting children at risk'. Despite many of the reports about Mr Hemming in the national press, he has consistently questioned the child protection system and the destruction of families by the courts on the flimsiest of evidence. He appears to be a lone voice in parliament against the horrors of social services. Although that is not strictly true, he was by far the most consistent and he runs Justice for Families–a legal advice and support company for parents facing social services.

John Hemming completes the triumvirate of successful campaigners. He started out as Ian Josephs did-as a councillor, being elected to represent Acocks Green ward in Birmingham in 1990. He became the leader of Birmingham Liberal Democrats and held the position of Deputy Leader of the City Council. He won election to parliament as MP for Yardley in 2005 and stood down from his council role in 2007. His role at the council gave him an insight into the funding of local authorities and could see first-hand the impact of the hypothecated funding that targets for adoptions had created. He helped to expose the adoption targets and was in no small way responsible for helping bring it to an end.

His Justice for Families campaign group was established to fight for the reform of public family law and has developed into a help and advice service to parents facing social services with McKenzie Friends who have helped parents represent themselves and even gained rights of audience in the family courts ranging from the county courts right up to the supreme court. Mr Hemming has presented several early day motions to parliament and frequently raised written and oral questions in the House of Commons. John Hemming lost his seat in the

2015 General Election and failed to be returned as the MP in the 2017 General Election. It is understood that he will again stand for parliament at the next General Election, so it can only be hoped that his voice is returned to the House of Commons.

It seemed almost inevitable that these three should develop a close working relationship, both on the long term strategy to expose and bring reform to the whole child protection system and in the day-to-day work of helping parents, often in times of family crisis. These three campaigners are not the only voices against this system, or the only source of help and support for parents and these others will be examined later.

For a number of parents, the core of this network lies in the Irish connection and Brian Rothery. It is Brian and the ectopia network that many parents turn to, in order to help them flee the UK social services and keep their children. Ireland has long been seen as the destination of choice for those fleeing social services. It is an English speaking country and many of its institutions and way of life reflect the UK. Perhaps an important determining factor in this choice is also the fact that Ireland is part of the Common Travel Area which means that a passport is not required to enter Ireland from the UK, but it is a separate jurisdiction and has not had the same over-zealous child removal approach as developed in the UK.

However, things are changing. Irish social services are moving towards the same harsh system and in 2012 Ireland held a Children's Referendum. The Referendum sought to establish if more adoptions should be considered for children in care. The referendum's outcome was in favour of the change, but was achieved on a very low turn-out and in 2013 a challenge was made to the bill. Although the challenge failed, leave for appeal was granted but the appeal failed.

Ireland still offers advantages to the fleeing family. As a result, over recent years the ectopia network has received a considerable number of families fleeing. Through the work of Good Samaritans and the coordination of Brian Rothery, families are supported in settling in Ireland. Many parents are referred to Brian by Ian Josephs, others find the ectopia website and the whole process often begins with an email from desperate parents. Sometimes the family is at a crisis level with unborn babies under threat of removal at birth, or facing threats and intimidation from the social services. Some parents just cannot function in the atmosphere of fear, suspicion and harassment and need to escape to safety for clarity of mind.

Where possible, families are identified by the level of risk to the children from social services and where it is felt that the family have a case to fight the local authority they are encouraged to stay and do so with the help of the network's lay advisors.

Critics may argue that providing such help for parents may place a child at risk of harm, but, just like Ian Josephs, where there is social work paperwork such as initial assessments, child protection meeting minutes or other reports, copies are requested to ensure that the network supports only those parents unfairly targeted, badly treated and who are victims of the child protection system. Parents are asked to evidence the counter position wherever possible. Where there is doubt over the safety of a child, or illegality or criminality, such as parents removing children subject to care orders, then the network will advise against fleeing and offer the support and advice of the lay advisors. The network will not aid or abet parents in breaking the law.

Brian retired from an active role in the network in early 2017, though he remains a vociferous critic of the system, but fortunately a few volunteers now coordinate the network. Once it is agreed that a family will take the option of fleeing, the network can help coordinate the best route, timings and what essentials they will need to bring and what will need to be sorted on arrival. Through a series of calls and emails, Good Samaritans carry out due diligence as to the genuineness of the case and all the logistics. Like some 1940's spy movie a rendezvous point is chosen for the family upon arrival in Ireland. It is an emotional and tragic experience. After what is often a long journey involving trains and ferries through the night, a family arrives at their destination station. There on the platform the family meet with one of the volunteers. Brian reflects on this experience, "... I can always identify the arriving family. It's not just the family laden down with suitcases and bags, juggling to carry those and hold tightly their children's hands, but the exhausted, bedraggled look, the confused faces and searching eyes, seeking out an unfamiliar, yet friendly, face. The children's faces equally confused, tired and disorientated, yet all of this quickly turns into relief as I catch their attention and utter their names followed by my introduction."

Families have expressed their own feelings of their experience. One couple succinctly expressed their experience on arrival as "relief, utter relief" and just for a short time no longer felt they still had to "look over their shoulder." Fleeing itself is not an easy borne ordeal. Such rituals have been played out at railway and bus stations, ferry ports and even airports.

The Good Samaritans are a close network of knowledgeable individuals, with useful contacts and information for the fleeing families. Shauna is one of these Good Samaritans. In fact all the Good Samaritans are women, for unfortunately these days it is the way it has to be. The suspicions against men, any man, when it comes to children has overwhelmingly shifted to seeing them all as possible abusers of children. Many airlines now will only sit unaccompanied minors next to female passengers and from surveys it is clear that many men would prefer to walk by a distressed child than turn to help for fear of what accusations may be made. It is a sad state of affairs that men have become such pariahs when it comes to proximity to children. This is in no small part due to the child protectionists and in particular the NSPCC, to whom we shall return later. The real irony is that women are equally responsible for abuse of children, yet that statistic, just as the fact that domestic violence is also perpetrated by women is often an untold story.

In the days and hours leading up to the arrival, Shauna will have been working hard, sourcing suitable accommodation for the family and, although a temporary expedient may have been found, the search will often be continuing for longer term accommodation once the family has arrived. On occasions Shauna, like the other Good Samaritans, will open up her home to the family whilst obtaining a permanent place of accommodation. The Samaritan's role does not end here: efforts may have to be made to try to secure access to benefits (a not altogether easy task), liaison with local charities who will help with food for the children, access to schools if appropriate and, the most important aspect–the empathetic listening ear. Shauna, like all the Good Samaritans, is a volunteer. None of them receives any payment-in fact they often have to put their hands in their own pockets as fuel is needed to transport families to their safe refuge and for calls made to landlords and charities.

Shauna is typical of the characters who volunteer. She is a mother of 6 children, working a full time job in the care sector. She has led a life that has not been without its own share of trials and tribulations, but one thing is clear-she is a fighter. Not just for her family, but for others too. Tall, with striking auburn hair and a strong spirit shining through, she cuts an authoritative figure you would prefer on your side rather than against you. Shauna became involved with the network after hearing a radio programme where Brian Rothery was being interviewed about the network, the injustices and extremes that families were facing in choosing to leave their homes, their extended family and all they know or own ensure the safety of their children. Shauna says, "It is a tragedy of immense proportions and I could not just sit back and watch a system destroy families based on an ideology. If parents were prepared to flee and leave everything behind to protect their children, then I had to do whatever I could to help them once they arrived."

Good Samaritans come from all walks of life and are not just centred on those who may have been aggrieved by social services. One example is the Belgian journalist Florence Bellone. Florence is the winner of the Lorenzo Natali special radio award for her exposé of the UK's child protection system:

"The Grand Jury distinguished the report for its investigative merit in highlighting a human rights issue occurring in a highly developed European Member State. The piece was characterised as 'a technically impressive, investigative report into shocking and relatively unknown human rights violations'."

Florence did not simply stop at her journalistic exposé but also took an active role in helping parents who fled to the continent, providing the same support and help as Shauna does in Ireland.

So the question is why do they do it? Why do these Good Samaritans put themselves out for families they do not know and have never met? The answer lies in truth and justice. Some Samaritans have decided to help and support because they have been the victim of the child-protection system, whilst some have become aware of the abuses and the travesty that are befalling innocent families and cannot just sit idly by watching generations of children being condemned to an inadequate care system. Despite exposé from journalists such as Florence Bellone, Christopher Booker and Sue Reid, the machinations of the child protection system and the aptly named 'secret courts' had largely escaped the wider public's view. With the President of the family division, Sir James Munby's call for greater transparency in the courts and the now wider reporting of family courts judgments, both the media and the public are becoming aware of the injustices and unethical practices of the social workers. As a result, not only are more cases now coming up for public scrutiny but the network is gaining positive media coverage with the BBC, ITV, Channel 4 and RTE in Ireland featuring the work they do along with major international media. This is a significant development and helps to bring to the wider public the real impact of social services on families' lives.

Of course the network is not the only place parents can turn for help. There are a plethora of groups and advisors, parental support services and McKenzie Friends. There is not the space here to list everyone and a short amount of searching on the internet will quickly bring to the attention of the parent a whole host of options and information. However a brief outline of some of the key organisations to whom parents can turn is provided.

McKenzie Friends are often used by parents facing the family courts. A McKenzie Friend is not a legally qualified person and technically cannot give legal advice, but they can be as knowledgeable, if not more so in some circumstances than the professionals who make their living from the system. Their role is to assist a person who is acting as a litigant in person, i.e. without formal legal representation. Generally, they quietly advise and suggest lines of questioning in cross examination, help with preparation of court paperwork, such as statements of truth and also provide experience of processes and procedures. They do not have any automatic rights of audience, so they are not able to speak on behalf of their client directly to the court and the judge; however this can be granted and a number of McKenzie Friends have been given a right of audience, even in the Supreme Court.

The recognition of the right to have a McKenzie Friend came from the McKenzie v McKenzie divorce case of 1970. Mr McKenzie was in divorce proceedings and originally had a legal aid representative. However, before the court proceedings began the legal aid was withdrawn and Mr McKenzie had to drop his solicitors, Geoffrey Gordon & Co., leaving him unrepresented. Geoffrey Gordon & Co. sent the case to an Australian barrister who was living in London, and though his Australian law qualification prevented him from practising in London, the idea was borne that this barrister - Ian Hanger–could sit with Mr Mckenzie and provide the quiet advice as outlined above. Frustratingly, the judge had different ideas and prevented the barrister from taking any active part, banishing him from the bar table and to the public gallery, limiting the advice he could give to adjournment time only. Mr Hanger, assuming his role had little value in the circumstances decided not to return for the second day of the hearing. The case went against Mr Mckenzie who appealed on the basis he had been denied representation. The outcome of the appeal was that the judge's intervention had deprived Mr McKenzie of assistance and ordered a retrial. Thus the basis for McKenzie Friends was established.

There are various groups and individuals who act as Mckenzie Friends, but as with any service there are some who are better than others. Generally, McKenzie Fiends act pro-bono, that is, without charge, bar travel and subsistence expenses. In recent years there has been a growing trend of Mckenzies who charge for their services, something that the Law Commission has become a little concerned about. Some McKenzie companies have sprung up, working very much on a profit basis and there are known to be a few less than scrupulous people charging fees that cost more than a qualified solicitor would, seeking to profit from the misery of families. Such a developing trend does give rise to concerns for desperate families seeking reassurance and support at a particularly vulnerable time. The answer is to do your due diligence and check out the person or the company: ask to contact past clients, look for people's experiences of them on the internet and ensure that you have a contract with set fees, just as you would with a solicitor. Of course, best of all is to find one who still offers free support. A McKenzie Friend is not a panacea for the rigours of court but they can be a helpful and knowledgeable support mechanism that means you are not alone in your fight.

Lay advisors can also be McKenzie Friends and vice versa. In general these are well researched, skilled and knowledgeable people, who have often been through the experience of social work intervention and may have developed actions that help stop the social workers or prevent your case going to court. They can of course offer no guarantees but their inside knowledge often gives you an advantage over those who face social services alone. Many of these lay advisors are within the networks highlighted above and on social media.

The author is one of the establishing members of **Prevent Intervention Now** (PIN- www.preventinterventionnow.org). Prevent Intervention Now's network of Lay Advocates has grown out of parents who through the Ectopia Network have successfully challenged social services. Their efforts in protecting their families have developed a deep knowledge base about family law and the courts. This was formalised into a lynchpin of effective support and making those skills and knowledge available to help parents facing social services. PIN is upfront about the fact it has to charge for its lay advocacy services as it is noted on the website: *"Many of our Lay Advocates started out as volunteers wishing to make a difference for families and doing cases free of charge. Taking on cases soon eats up time and resources. To do this effectively it soon becomes a full time process. Many of our Advocates work over weekends, bank holidays and in the evenings preparing paperwork and guidance for parents. Often in emergency situations they work through the night to have submissions ready for court the next day. Our lay advocates also take on your whole case, no matter how long it goes on for or how far you have to go through the courts–from Family Court to Appeal Court and beyond. They charge a one off fee for all of this. The fee reflects their experience, research and of course the huge number of hours it takes to consider reports, court documents, research appropriate case law and of course prepare documents for you. No-one can be expected to sustain this level of support for free, hence the advocates charge a small fee. This is not a commercial enterprise, but it is a dedicated and professional service to support parents directly. We will be hones –no one is getting rich off this, it is an honest day's work for a minimal fee by someone whose genuine desire is to help you and your family stay together."*

PIN works directly with parents but there are other places to turn to for support. Social media could become social services greatest enemy-the likes of Facebook and Twitter have allowed parents affected by social services to interact with each other, share experiences and, most importantly, ideas of how to fight back. Of course there is no way of confirming what is being exchanged is correct or admissible at law, but, because of the sheer numbers using it, the methods and procedures are quickly verified, questioned or corrected. There are a number of well known Mckenzie Friends and lay advisors on these sites who bring years of experience and understanding that help qualify much of what is shared. Groups such as 'UK Social Services', 'Families and children project' and 'Parents United' see parents from all walks of life sharing their experiences, knowledge and ideas. They also provide a campaigning front for families, with some choosing to advertise 'do not adopt my children' accompanied with pictures of the children and an outline of the social services and their partner agencies wrong-doing. It is a powerful tool as demonstrated by the attempts of the various local authorities to seek court orders to compel parents to remove their information. It is certainly becoming a starting point for many when social services begin an intervention.

There are now many avenues for affected families to seek support, advice and solace outside of the traditional legal representation, many times with better outcomes than placing sole reliance on a solicitor and barrister. Some of the support is ad hoc, found through conversations on social media, whilst others like the ectopia network and PIN provide hands on solutions and are highly organised across a number of countries.

Of course, we have to return to the simple question, why should such networks and support groups be needed? If the child protection system was ethical, professional and not based on ideology and profits then there probably would be no requirement for them at all, but the very fact they have originated, grown and developed to such a wide extent simply demonstrates that the system is flawed.

Chapter 2–The Child Protection System

Child abuse, exploitation, grooming, Satanic paedophilia: not a day goes by when these terms are not mentioned in the media. If the stories are to be believed, then there must be an increasing worry for parents about the safety and well-being of their children. But what if your child came to you and disclosed abuse, by a family member, teacher or even just a stranger? What would you do?

Every parent in the land would pick up the phone and call the authorities, but if parents think the horror of their child's disclosure is the most difficult thing they will have to deal with, then they had better think again as there is the ever-increasing likelihood that that disclosure will lead to the removal of all the children in the family.

It sounds unreal that, despite your child and hence by default you as parents are victims of the crime of abuse, it is likely that you as parents will be blamed by social services and they will apply to the courts to remove your children. The accusation will be that you have failed to protect them and therefore are not a fit parent. This happened to a mother we shall call Emily to protect her and her children's identity. After a tearful disclosure by her youngest daughter of familial abuse and absorbing its gravity, Emily's first reaction was to contact the local social services team. Never in her wildest dreams did she contemplate what the next twelve months would bring.

Through the lounge window she saw the squad car arrive and assumed that the two rather shabbily dressed women passengers were from social services, which actually gave her a sense of relief that help and direction were on hand. Their attitude, however, quickly changed her view of the situation which became one of fear and confusion.

She tried to explain her daughter's disclosure, still hoping for the help and support she had assumed would be central to any police or social worker plan. Instead, it swiftly became plain that all of these so called "professionals" appeared to be holding her in some kind of contempt.

She was told in no uncertain terms that her daughter would have to attend the police station to be interviewed. When she asked if she could bring her along later as she had to pick up her two older daughters from school, she was taken aback by the response-no the youngest daughter had to go now. The question and issue of the older siblings was brushed aside. Emily hid her thoughts: "But aren't you social services, aren't you supposed to have the resources to help families?"

Before this question had even had time to formulate from a thought to a verbalisation the "plan" was in place. The social workers would take the youngest to the police station and she would pick up her two daughters and she could then come along. This was all happening too fast. Emily protested that she wanted to be with her daughter, more importantly her daughter wanted to be with her mum. She tried reasoning- "She's only six, she's frightened, she wants her mum"–but it just seemed to fall on deaf ears and hard hearts. Her daughter clung to her waist seeking the envelopment of a mother's arms. In the mind numbing few minutes of these exchanges Emily had failed to notice that one of the women had left the room, only dawning on her as the woman re-entered the room with a coat for her daughter. From her daughter's wardrobe! The woman had just nonchalantly invaded her home.

"I'm sorry," the woman said without an ounce of remorse as evidenced in her tone and manner.

"We have to do this now." And with that she bent forward and attempted to pull the child from her. "No, Mummy, Mummy!" she screamed.

"Wait. I'll come," Emily said, cradling her daughter, but the woman kept a firm hold as her companion nonchalantly remarked, "No, you need to collect your children from school."

The next stage was a nightmare that would haunt Emily forever. She knew there was no further arguing, and it now fell to her to slowly and as reassuringly as possible push her own daughter from her and explain that she was to go with these nice ladies and policeman and she would be along soon, that they just wanted to talk to her and it would all be ok. She would forever regret telling her daughter that it would all be ok.

Her daughter was led by the social worker, screaming for Emily, to the car and even after the car door was closed Emily could hear her. Neighbours looked on. Suddenly they were gone.

Emily looked numbly towards the few watching neighbours and then went back into the house. What had just happened?

Looking back, she now realizes that it was at that point that her erosion as a mother and parent began. Her daughter would undergo what is called an ABE (Achieving Best Evidence) interview, recorded on video tape and the alleged perpetrator arrested soon after. Emily collected her other daughters from school, her head awash with worry, lost, question after question with no answers in her mind. She realized that she did not know which police station her daughter had gone to and that she had no names of the social workers. They probably had said their names but in the midst of it all she had forgotten or perhaps not even registered what they had said.

As time ticked by her worries grew and she decided to call the social services office. No one there would divulge any information and she was told to wait for the social worker to make contact. Around 9.30pm that evening, just after she had settled her daughters in bed, there was a knock at the door, on opening there stood the two social workers, but her youngest was not with them. Before she could even ask, one of the women said "We need to come in" and promptly walked through the door, almost pushing Emily aside in the process. Before Emily had even closed the door she was asked, "Where are your two daughters?" Emily's stomach cramped as the realization dawned of what could now be unfolding.

She explained that they were asleep and as she was doing so a piece of paper was wafted in front of her face. "We need you to sign this so we can arrange some respite for your daughters and give you some time to consider what has happened." Emily stuttered out that she didn't need respite, all she needed was her three daughters at home to provide the love, care and protection they needed. At this point the social worker dropped the bombshell.

"We believe that you knew about the abuse and failed to protect her." Either she signed the paper or they would call the police as they could not let the children stay in an 'un-assessed' environment. Despite Emily's best protests there was no shifting the social workers' view point. Even when she reluctantly signed the paper and asked to get the children some things together before she woke them, she was told there was no need, but just to get the children up.

The nightmare was now complete as around 10.00 PM she watched her confused, frightened and crying daughters disappear off into the night in the back of a social worker's car. That was the last time that any of her daughters were in their home. Over the next few weeks she only saw her daughters at a contact centre, twice a week for an hour at a time, but this gradually was eroded to once a week. She faced endless meetings with social services where her whole life was writ large, even the silly dare that had gone wrong when she was fifteen and she had been cautioned for shop lifting. As she sat in these meetings, she saw a picture emerge of her she could not recognise. Her GP, her daughters' teachers and a host of strange faces heard and reported about her and her parenting skills. She had to undergo a psychological assessment, interviews by the police and seek a solicitor as she saw the case against her being built. Nothing she said, or challenged seemed to be listened to. The social workers minds were made up.

Then the letter announcing legal action arrived. Although it was a shock, it was not a surprise. The local authority wanted to place the two older children in long term foster care and her youngest in adoption. She was accused of not being a fit parent, supposedly aware of the abuse but only acting once her daughter had made a disclosure in order to protect the perpetrator who ironically had been investigated by the police with no further action taken, because of a lack of credible evidence. Emily's solicitor advised her to accept the social services position, but to argue that she had seen the error of her ways and had changed after completing a parenting and child protection course. This he had argued was her best chance to get the children home, perhaps on a supervision order. Emily could not and would not admit to something she had not done, she had not known about the alleged abuse and when she did, reported it immediately. She had to tell the truth. From that moment on it was clear that the solicitor was not really fighting her case.

After a three day hearing, the judge summed up by accepting the local authority's position. That Emily must have known about the alleged abuse and only acted when she was forced into that position, so she had shown a disregard for her children and had failed to protect them. The children were placed on full care orders with the youngest being placed for adoption.

Three children were ripped from a loving mother and family, who did in fact do nothing wrong and did, in most sensible people's eyes, the right thing when faced with the disclosure. Yet if this is the way that parents are to be treated, if their child discloses abuse, then it is clear that parents will become reluctant to seek help and support. Thus allowing perpetrators of real abuse, to not only get away with their crimes but possibly go on and abuse others. This was a State intervention that was not only unwarranted but a grave attack on the position of parents as primary carers. Emily has evidence of lies, perjury and professional misconduct but the system does not want to hear it. It is a fight she has not given up on, but it is a salutary warning for parents that their children are in as much danger from the state as they are from any possible abuser.

A true story–names have been changed and the time -line condensed.

For most families affected by Social Services the moment that their lives can be transformed forever begins with a phone call, letter through the post or knock at the door. It is in this instant that the enemy reveals itself. Although the people standing on the doorstep may look like anyone else from any walk of life, the family will soon discover that behind the air of respectability and authority lies a dark and malicious system. It will soon be revealed that this sometimes smiling, but often expressionless individual will have a dogmatic and emotionless approach to the family unit.

It would be wrong to stereotype and take the above description of the social worker as applicable to all. There are many well-intentioned and genuinely caring social workers; however, from research and evidence of many families cases, they appear to be a rarity in the twenty-first century child protection system. Even these positive individuals present just as much danger to a family as the dark, vindictive character portrayed above, as the system and institutions of child protection are based upon a foundation of persecution. The system itself is highly politicised, profit hungry and removes children from families. The over-arching principles under which the system operates simply demonizes parents and assumes, quite incorrectly, when the outcomes are examined, that children are better served outside of the family and within the bizarrely named 'care system'.

The number of children entering the care system is growing with over 25,000 children a year being removed from their parents and official government statistics show a current total of over 70,000 children in care in England and Wales. Between 2008 and 2017 the number of children subject to a child protection plan has grown by ninety percent and court proceedings for care applications by one hundred and thirty percent[iii]. Adoptions are at their highest since recent records began in 1992 with 4000 placements being made between April 2012 and March 2013 and a Prime Minister calling for many more. In fact, the whole adoption drive has allocated over £170 million to local authorities and voluntary adoption agencies to drive up the number of prospective adoptive parents.

In December 2000, Tony Blair's New Labour introduced adoption targets for local authorities that required an increase of 50 percent in adoptions between 2000 and 2006. The basis and intention of this policy of targets was probably an honourable, if misplaced, one. For too long, large numbers of children had been languishing in the care system, moving from foster placement to foster placement and the well intentioned government wanted to provide those children with a permanency and security of placement. Perversely this is not the reality of what has actually occurred and the policy created a demand for younger children to feed these targets as the older children were much more difficult to place.

Perhaps the darkest aspect to arise out of this well intentioned but flawed policy was the increasing numbers of babies taken, some literally within moments of birth. The basis for these removals is more often than not the 'risk of future emotional harm'. There is no way to evidence this and, more importantly, no real defence for a parent to use against it. Babies are of course much easier to place for adoption than older children, making the targets easier to meet. Ironically, many of these mothers or mums-to-be were raised in the care system themselves and this is one of the indicators social services use in assessing unacceptable risk of parenting. Thus the system is not only self condemning but self perpetuating. Above all, the simple conclusion that must be drawn is that the system does not work.

Startlingly, local authorities were to be paid huge financial rewards for meeting these targets. Thus the flood gates were opened. Here was a chance for local authorities to make money from the misery of families and where an authority did not have the numbers of children to meet the target, they simply went out and found them. Many families, whose social services involvement would previously not have got past a paper exercise, suddenly found they were under investigation instead of the referrals being sensibly dismissed at an early stage. Social work managers under pressure from their bosses clearly placed undue pressure on front line staff to ensure that the targets could be met and, as a result, not just bad practice but highly questionable practices crept in. Although these targets were officially abandoned in 2008, the corruption had become ingrained-social work and the system had moved onto a much more persecution-based platform. The legacy of which was reinforced by the Baby P case and the myth that grew from it; this affects many families today. The financial reward system for adoptions completely changed the basis of child protection and a few examples will demonstrate just why this change occurred. Between 2004 and 2007, 30 councils received substantial sums, for example:

Sheffield City Council were paid a reward grant of £1,025,000

Northamptonshire County Council received £1,119,115

Hampshire received £1,675,619

Kent County Council received £2,156,583

Essex County Council was granted £2,469,200

Despite the financial incentives being officially scrapped in 2008, the drive to increase adoptions remains with targets largely hidden in plain sight such as Ofsted's ruling that only councils who get all proposed adoptions placed within 12 months can receive the top inspection rating and David Cameron at the 2013 Conservative party conference effectively gloating at the 4000 adoptions achieved in 2012-13 but promising a substantial increase on that figure. The government approach to adoptions has not changed since that time, although it must be noted that adoption numbers have slipped recently, largely attributed to Justice Munby's-President of the Family Courts Division- ruling in a case referred to as Re B-S[iv]. (We shall return to this later.)

Foster care is similarly being promoted with large posters adorning various sites advertising the financial incentives for potential carers with an average offering of £350[v] per week per child, though often higher in some local authority areas.

This is a big money business. On the other side of the coin, private fostering and adoption companies charge up to £65,000[vi] to carry out placement and support for an adopted child. The biggest single indicator of profit to be made from children's lives is the move into the care homes market by the outsourcing company G4S, who now have 10 homes established. G4S had a revenue stream of £6.8 billion in the financial year 2016 and with share holders to recompense this is clearly a company that does not suddenly operate in non-profit areas or out of the goodness of their hearts. Children's homes must be a profitable and growing market for the company. Children have become a valuable trading commodity, and the protection is not about neglect or abuse, it is about profit.

G4S are not the only large private company hugely benefiting from this child and family exploitation. Although there are many such companies, one of the biggest is Core Assets. Core Assets is a multi-faceted 'care' company offering its services to local authorities It carries out fostering placements, assessments and advice through its own social workers and independent experts. In 2013 Core Assets had a turnover of £138,098,000.00 with an annual profit of £4,790,000.00. The most sinister aspects of this company is not just the extent of its 'services' and profits but a huge conflict of interest. In 2012 Core Assets acquired Carter Brown Associates, a major UK family expert witness company. Carter Brown provides expert witness services to local authorities and the legal profession and ultimately the courts. Thus, the very company who provides the placements for children in fostering or adoption also now controls the expert witnesses who advise the family court judges on a removal of a child. So the big question is: who are Carter Brown's experts actually working for? If the experts recommending removal are working for the very firm that will place and therefore earn huge sums of money from those children how can any Carter Brown expert witness be truly independent?

It is not just the fostering and adoption aspect that is such a lucrative business. To be completely technically accurate, it is not social workers who remove children from families, but the British justice system. It is not unusual for a family case going through the courts to cost upwards of £500,000. At an average cost of around £70,000 per day for the legal aid solicitors and barristers, it quite clear to see why this system is self perpetuating. Add in to this the £2000-£3000 (substantially more in some instances) per expert witness report and even to the casual observer the basis for the current system of child protection can be simply understood.

The child protectionists in the local authorities are ably abetted in perpetuating the myth of the system by the large children's charities, whose emotive adverts and campaigns promote the impression that the UK is awash with abused children, whereas the facts simply do not support this subliminal message that is being forced on the public. The fund raising that results from these emotional appeals is rarely seen by any of the children they purport to help; instead the vast majority is spent on even more campaigns and lobbying and of course the vastly inflated remuneration for their executives.

This largely unaccountable system is practically unique to England and Wales and the methods and ideology practised by the social workers are some of the most extreme and damaging in Europe. It is fair to say that child protection social workers are some of the most far removed practitioners of the true meaning of social work.

Social work in England and Wales grew out of the need to support the poorest in society. Originating in church charity and alms this developed into the formal 'Poor Law' and the establishment of the workhouse. The real driving force behind the development from a simple relief of poverty into a wider social sphere was the advent of the Industrial Revolution and the social change that accompanied the economic changes. The first social workers were the hospital almoners, based in medical institutions. These workers assessed those presenting for free treatment on the basis that were 'deserving enough' of the service. This role slowly began to move into other social spheres and by the turn of the twentieth century the roles were overseen by the establishment of the Hospital Almoners Council.

Modern day social work grew out of this philanthropic activity and has been consistently incorporated into government policy and legislation, whereby the state has granted itself powers through the social work profession to intervene in ever increasing aspects of an individuals life. It can be argued that this is not necessarily a negative development as many people require help and support at varying times in their lives. However, what has occurred is no longer philanthropy.

Social work is supposed to uphold social justice, reduce society's inequalities and promote human rights by improving the quality of life of the unfortunate people and to aid their realisation of the potential within them. Forcibly removing children where no crimes have been committed by the parents, where parenting is deemed inadequate because it does not fit the opinion of a social worker or upon anonymous reports where hearsay and not evidence is all the social worker has to go on is no longer social work, but an abuse of authority and power.

The child protection system parents face today is far removed from social support and any of the philosophies of social work. The real irony is that those parents whose children may have significant and complex needs have to fight for any real support and funding. Children's services often claim they do not have the resources to provide the necessary services that a child needs.

Yet in the sphere of child protection it would appear that money is simply no object when it comes to the persecution of families.

Chapter 3 What to expect. The procedures and protocols of child protection.

Where does it all start? How do those people hidden away in the local authority offices become interested in your family and move from their nonentity to looming large on your doorstep?

It all starts with a referral. In effect what this means is that someone and that could be anyone: from your neighbour, the police, a teacher, a medical professional or a complete stranger on the street who has raised some sort of concern about your children with the social services. That concern may have no basis in fact or reality, but it is enough for the social services to spring into action.

Herein lies the first problem. Many things that would once have had common sense applied and the referral simply recorded with no further action are now taken out of all proportion. Your toddler is tired and creates a little scene in the supermarket because you have just said no to that chocolate bar. You firmly admonish the child and move on. This suddenly taken out of all context because someone witnessed just the end of the escapade and merely sees you "tell your child off" and their tears and perhaps continuing tantrum. This kindly stranger reports you to the social services for your completely natural parenting. Yet where sense would once have prevailed with such a referral these days it is a serious child protection issue. Instead of applying the sensible view that such behaviour by a toddler is hardly out of context for any number of toddlers accompanying their parents shopping in a supermarket, it is instead seen as an indicator of child abuse, most likely emotional abuse. A perfectly innocent trip to do your shopping could be the catalyst for a full blown investigation into your family.

The above may appear a little like scaremongering, but in April 2013 Kiya Ask, a 20-year-old mother from Skegness in Lincolnshire, found social services on her doorstep after visiting a branch of Boots with her fifteen-month-old Amelia[vii]. Whilst in Boots Kiya gave her daughter the medicine for the bronchial infection she had. Amelia started coughing, and a pharmacist went completely overboard. "She's choking!" and "Someone get her some oxygen." Amelia was just struggling to swallow the pills she had been prescribed. Ten days later social workers appeared after a referral from the Boots employee. They went through Kiya's house, looking in cupboards, the fridge-freezer, all her daughter's drawers and checked for safety guards on all the plugs. They then sat and watched Kiya with Amelia for an hour. Luckily the case was then closed, but not without the effect of instilling fear into Kiya both at the time and for her future. Boots felt the action of their staff was entirely justified.

Why were such drastic measures required? A fifteen-month-old may have a little problem swallowing prescribed tablets, but the incident was taken out of all context and the referral could have sparked a much more draconian response than the unpleasant one that this mother was subjected to. Her daughter was ill, she had done the responsible thing and sought medical attention and was trying to administer medicine to alleviate the problem, yet instead of this being a non-incident, with no harm to any child, the mother was immediately investigated as some sort of abuser. This was a lucky escape from the social services clutches for Amelia and her mother as on another day with another social worker the whole incident may have had far worse consequences. The local authority's comment was interesting in itself. Lincolnshire county council said it "had a duty to investigate all complaints." It is the use of the word "complaint" that rings alarm bells. This suggests that Lincolnshire county council were using the definition of the word in its legal context as the other definitions do not fit the incident. So the referral right from the beginning was being viewed as some sort of breach of the law. Such interpretations applied to child protection can only lead to a prevailing culture of incrimination within the social services working practices. This is borne out by many parents who feel that they are seen as guilty until proved innocent. It is into this climate of presumed guilt that most referrals are now viewed.

Referrals are usually handled by designated call centre staff and depending on the nature of the referral and the presumed risk or need then allocated to the relevant social work team for investigation. Each local authority works slightly differently in how it organises its resources, and the names given to the various teams, but the essential elements that follow will be common to them all.

A duty social worker will then begin to gather information on the child and the family. This will be carried out through a number of methods. There may be further discussions with the referrer. Records will checked for the child or any other family members to see if there is any existing information held by the social work department. A check will be specifically made to see if the child is already subject to a child protection plan or if there are any other assessments on record, such as a common assessment (CAF-Common Assessment Framework). Other agencies deemed appropriate will be involved, such as the police if an offence has been or may be suspected of having been committed or the probation service if the child is viewed as at potential risk of harm from an offender. A new record will be created in respect of each child in the household and if there is a child from another family involved, then another referral will be completed in respect of that child. Investigation is carried out into the risk that there may be to the parents–particularly young parents from the situation.

From this the social worker creates an initial record that includes the nature of the concern; why and how the concern has arisen; what appears to be the needs of the family; whether the concern involves abuse or neglect and the basis for those concerns and whether immediate action is required to protect the child or any of the children in the family household. This process cannot be "stepped down" without the agreement of a social services manager.

All of this is carried out without reference to the parents or the family. Further information may be gleaned from other agencies. The big danger here for parents is not just the referral and the system rapidly creating labels for your children, but data held by many agencies on the public is often incorrect, out of date or sometimes compromised by poor recording. It is not unknown for the police to have erroneous data about an individual on their systems, for example. In the atmosphere of modern child protection it is often the case that the veracity of the information collected is not confirmed and double -checked and hence parents are often shocked when reports from social workers land on their doormat full of untruths, distortions and inaccuracies.

Where referrals are made in the evening, weekends or public holidays the referral is usually dealt with by the EDT–The Emergency Duty Team. The EDT follow the same procedures, ascertaining the nature of the referral and acting accordingly. Where there are child welfare concerns the member of staff dealing with the referral will consult with the manager on duty, carry out enquiries with all other available agencies and check the records. The manager may then initiate a Section 47 enquiry, call a strategy discussion and decide upon appropriate action–we shall return to this later.

Where the referral is to be handed over to the day staff all appropriate records have to be sent to that team for their attention the next working day.

By the time the allocated social worker makes contact with the parent all the above information has been gathered and a "picture" already formed by the social worker of the child, the family and the concern. Perhaps this is one of the greatest failures and criticisms of modern day child protection social work. The "picture" formed is frequently adhered to by the local authority in spite of any rebuttal evidence or explanations that parents may be able to offer. It is often said that social workers will not admit that they have got things wrong, and parents can find themselves in a never ending spiral of claim and counter-claim. This approach often results in the social workers seeking "evidence" of their pre-conceived ideas, rather than maintaining an open and enquiring mind. It is not unusual for evidence to be misrepresented, distorted or even fabricated. Recently there have been a number of social workers struck off the HCPC register for their fabrications[viii], changing of records or unsubstantiated allegations. I would suggest not nearly enough. With the above in mind it is easy to see why so many families are ending up in the courts under the threat of having their children removed.

The outcome of an investigation into a referral may be: no further action at that point, although a common assessment may be completed; an initial assessment of needs though this may be largely overlooked if there is a decision to instigate a Section 47 enquiry; the provision of services; a strategy meeting; a core assessment or even emergency protection. The impact for the parent is that they may never know they have been "investigated" until the police and social workers arrive on their doorstep. What is clear and as we progress through the processes what becomes increasingly obvious is that parents are not deemed a significant "witness" within these proceedings.

For many parents it is the initial phone call or knock on the door that is that moment when life will never be the same again. The social workers will want to come into your home. They will want to meet and observe your children. They will ask to see the children's bedrooms. They will want a "chat" with you and maybe your children–sometimes alone. The smiling persona that greets you and the request for a little "chat" is far from either. This little chat is actually them gathering evidence, not just about you but about your home.

Is it clean and tidy? How are your children presenting? Are they clean, looked after? If you haven't washed up the kitchen pots, or the children are still in their pyjamas mid morning, or you are still in yours, even if your curtains are closed when they arrive – all of this will be used against you. Your privacy has just been invaded and may continue to be for a long time.

The social worker will then produce an initial assessment, identify if any services are "required" or decide if your child is a child in need or if a more detailed core assessment is to be undertaken. Most referrals will generate an initial assessment unless there is a view from the beginning that the case will require an immediate Strategy Meeting. Any common assessment that has already been completed will be used to inform the Initial Assessment. There is a strict deadline of seven days from referral for this, any delay has to be reviewed by a manager and take into account the welfare of the child.

Where a common assessment has been completed, this information should be used to inform the Initial Assessment. Action is then planned about who will undertake what. Considerations will cover whether your children should be spoken to alone or with you, when interviews with you and other family members should take place, what concerns should be relayed to you or the children, what contributions, both historical and contemporary, can be made by other agencies and whether information may be required from other local authorities or even abroad.

This information seeking should not be done without the parents permission, but it often is on the basis that to seek permissions may be prejudicial to the child's welfare or a criminal investigation, aggravate the parental behaviours or would be seen to increase the risk to a child. Frequently none of the aforementioned is a genuine reason, but social workers will hide behind such, in order to ensure the parent is as little informed as possible.

The outcome of this Initial Assessment should be focused on the welfare of the child and inform and plan the next steps to be taken which may be: a section 17 enquiry for a child in need, or if there is reasonable cause to suspect that the child is suffering, or is likely to suffer, significant harm, a section 47 enquiry. As above there could be no further action, a plan to deliver support, a core assessment for the section 17 enquiry or a strategy meeting for the section 47 enquiry. Of course, as always at any stage in social services investigations emergency protection could be the outcome. The assessment should be provided to the parent in written form and discussed with them, but the latter frequently does not always happen.

Section 17 of the Children's Act 1989 defines what constitutes a child in need. Where a child is "unlikely to achieve or maintain a reasonable standard of health or development without the provision of services by a local authority; or their health or development is likely to be significantly impaired, or further impaired without the provision of such services; or they are disabled."

If it is decided that the threshold for a child in need is met a meeting will be held within twenty-eight days of the completion of the Initial Assessment, followed by a review of the agreed child in need plan decided at that meeting within three months and then further reviews every six months unless there arises a need for an earlier review. The allocated social worker or team leader usually chairs such a meeting and it is attended by all direct and relevant agencies, such as health, schools and the like. At the heart of the meeting should be the child and the family, whose views and wishes should be represented, even if they cannot attend.

The meeting should clearly analyse the needs, concerns and

difficulties, design a plan to address these and define the non universal services to be provided and desired outcomes within an expected timescale. Copies of the plan are sent to parents and child where it is appropriate and to all involved professionals within ten working days of the meeting. Where the plan cannot be progressed or if it fails to meet the child's needs, then an earlier review meeting may be convened.

Core Assessments are multi-agency, in-depth assessment of a child's developmental and /or welfare needs, and the parents' capacity to ensure the child can be kept safe from harm. Core assessments are usually triggered when: an Initial Assessment recommends further assessment; a strategy meeting or discussion initiates a section 47 enquiry; or when new information is obtained on an open case. The core assessment procedures are based on the Common Assessment Framework and it has to be completed within thirty five working days of the referral.

These assessments often see the commission of specialist assessments such as reports from the child and adolescent health services. Core assessments must include direct communication with the child alone, using their preferred language or method of communication to ascertain the child's views and wishes, which should be taken into account. As we shall see later, the latter is often paid lip service and frequently dismissed should the case come before a court. The children must have been visited at home and their bedrooms inspected. Similarly the parents should be approached in the same manner with the same outcomes. A full analysis should have been completed and, most importantly, clear evidence should be presented to qualify the decision of the chosen services to be delivered. If needed a child in need plan may also be implemented. Core assessments are updated on an annual basis. Core assessments are also separate to any section 47 report.

When considering making a referral to Children's Social Care, practitioners are normally expected to discuss any concerns with the family and seek their agreement for a referral to be made. However, discussing with the parent the intention to refer should only be done where such discussion will not place a child at risk of significant harm, or increased risk of significant harm, or put any other person at risk of harm.

The above assessments generally focus on the needs of the child and the services that can be offered to ensure that the welfare of the child is being met. A section 47 enquiry is more encompassing of the serious issues of direct child protection. This is perhaps the most onerous of the "assessment" regime that a family can be faced with–it usually means that the family are facing very serious allegations in relation to the welfare of their child. The Children's Act 1989 places a "duty to investigate, where there is reasonable cause to suspect that a child is suffering, or likely to suffer significant harm" and to decide if there should be any action undertaken to safeguard and ensure the welfare of the child. Although the statutory duty falls upon the local authority to make necessary enquiries any criminal allegations must be investigated by the police in a parallel enquiry to the section 47 one. All the major agencies also have a statutory duty to help the local authority in its enquiries and be part of the meetings and processes that underpin the enquiry.

A section 47 enquiry can be initiated at any point during the social workers' consideration of any case that has come before them. It can be started at the point of the referral, at the information gathering stage or at any time during the assessments. However, a section 47 enquiry can only be started after a strategy meeting or discussion. A strategy discussion brings together the multi-agencies to consider the concerns and the next course of action, which could be emergency protection, the obtaining of an Emergency Protection Order (EPO) or the exercise of the police powers of protection. Whoever is tasked with this safeguarding move must visit the child and make the decision as to how best to protect them. Although this section of the legislation was clearly designed by parliament to be used in the most serious and drastic of cases, a creeping extension of the use of this section is clearly bringing many more families into the child protection regime that in the not too distant past would not have appeared on this radar. This move is in no small due to the vagueness of the threshold criteria applied and the interpretation of those words.

An example of the Threshold Response Table.

Criteria for strategy meeting	Section 17 Assessment
Any allegation of abuse or neglect or any suspicious injury in a pre/non	Allegation of physical assault with no visible or only minor injury (other than to a pre- or non-mobile child)

mobile child.	
Two or more minor injuries in pre-mobile or non-verbal babies or young children (including disabled children).	Any incident / injury triggering concern e.g. a series of apparently accidental injuries or a minor non-accidental injury
Allegations or suspicions about a serious injury/ sexual abuse to a child	Repeated expressed minor concerns from one or more sources
Repeated allegations or reasonable suspicions of non-accidental injury.	Level 3 Domestic Abuse
The child has been traumatised, injured or	Allegation concerning serious verbal threats

neglected as a result of domestic violence.	
Repeated allegations involving serious verbal threats and / or emotional abuse	Allegations of emotional abuse including that caused by minor domestic violence
Allegations / reasonable suspicions of serious neglect.	Allegations of periodic neglect including insufficient supervision; poor hygiene; clothing or nutrition; failure to seek/attend treatment or appointments; young carers undertaking intimate personal care.
Medical referral of non-organic failure to thrive in under fives	Suspicions of sexual abuse (e.g., sexualised behaviour, medical concerns or referral by concerned relative, neighbour, carer).
Direct allegation of sexual abuse made by child	No available parent, child in need of accommodation and no specific risk if this need is met.

or abuser's confession to such abuse	
Any allegation suggesting connections between sexually abused children in different families or more than one abuser.	
An individual (adult or child) posing a risk to children.	
Any suspicious injury or allegation involving a child already subject to a child protection plan or looked after by a local authority.	

No available parent / carer and child is left vulnerable to significant harm e.g. an abandoned baby	
Suspicion that a child has suffered or is at risk of significant harm due to fabricated / induced illness.	
Children subject of parental delusions.	
An unborn baby who is considered at risk of significant harm.	
A child at risk of sexual exploitation or	

trafficking.	
Registered sex offender or convicted violent subject of MAPPA moving into a household with under 18 year olds.	
Pregnancy in a child under 13.	
A child at risk of FGM, honour based violence or forced marriage.	

The clear issue here is that the criteria are open to many interpretations by social workers and other agency representatives. The requirement for substantial evidence can clearly be brushed aside in favour of opinion. Add to that the culture of social work as already described, and it becomes easy to understand why so many children are falling into the child-protection trap.

After the strategy meeting there may be the decision to take immediate protection action. This does not always equate to the obtaining of an emergency protection order or the use of police powers to remove a child. It could mean for instance: the removal of an alleged abuser from the household, application of a Section 20 voluntary agreement to move the child into care, a temporary move of the child to extended family, and is only undertaken as an immediate action to protect the child. It is not necessarily the long-term strategy that will be finalised by a court.

It is interesting to note that police powers of removal should only be used in exceptional circumstances, approved by an independent officer of at least Inspector rank and must not be used in place of an application for an EPO in most circumstances. Frequently- and the High Court has ruled upon the unacceptability of this - social workers seek to utilise the police power of protection to circumvent the need for an EPO application.

Where an EPO is obtained, time is of the essence for social workers as the order can only last for eight days (with an extension available for a further eight days), so they must ensure that a section 47 enquiry and assessments are quickly underway and that a decision on whether to apply for a care order or allow the EPO to lapse is taken. What this can mean for parents is that they are very quickly served with court proceedings seeking to remove their children for much longer. Within days of the issue of an EPO or use of a police protection the parents are faced with a judge and a list of allegations against them. Bewildered, unprepared and frequently badly represented, if at all, the system will soon consume them completely. Not all families face these draconian measures just because a section 47 enquiry has been started, but it shows the precarious position that families are faced with once the social services net draws them in.

Parents and children (where age appropriate) should be involved in contributing to section 47 enquiries and their views and wishes obtained, however this again can be merely lip service and what is said by parents distorted or ignored. It is fair to warn parents that any discussions with social workers are not undertaken to obtain the parents' explanations or defences, but simply to gather as much evidence as possible to use against them. Parents who have undergone such horrors of the system frequently complain of lies, misrepresentations, fabrications, along with tales of intimidation and harassment.

The reports of parents are too consistent and with too many similarities to be dismissed. A short internet search and examination of social media groups quickly demonstrates the sheer scale of the problem that parents have to face.

It is upon seeing these reports that parents quickly lose any and all trust in the people that they have to deal with. Social services are supposed to ensure that they handle things sensitively, openly and with as much transparency as possible, as long as that does not jeopardise the welfare or safety of the child, but this rarely happens. Section 47 enquiries will often require further specialist assessments, paediatric examinations or other investigations–all with one purpose to gather as much evidence as possible against the parents and to verify the original referral whether or not there was a genuine basis.

Parents may be invited to a Child Protection Conference. This can be a hugely intimidating and frightening experience. Although the parents may bring along a legal representative or advocate, they are not allowed to speak on their behalf, as it is not a "legal meeting," however this position is frequently broken by the local authorities who bring along a member of their legal team, who will be allowed to speak at the meeting. The parents will be faced with a panel of "professionals" from the various agencies and as there could be as many as twelve plus it takes a strong parent not to feel that each of them is sitting in judgement, often reading from reports that contain blatant fabrications or misrepresentations. Obviously parents are mere passengers on a journey over which they have little control because decisions about the outcome of the conference may have already been submitted by the social workers in their reports. The meeting simply rubber stamps their recommendations.

It is here that the parents will also meet a representative of another agency. The chair of the conference will supposedly be an independent member, from the Local Child Safeguarding Board (LCSB). It is a misnomer to call this person independent. They are employed to be part of the board by the local authority, they work hand-in-hand with social workers and, although they give the impression they are there to provide a balance to the meeting and are independent, they are simply another element in the child protection regime. They work from the same hymn sheet and rarely question the veracity of the story painted by the investigating social workers. Indeed some of them deliberately do not let the parents speak, or actually remove them from the meetings.

Overall the dice are stacked firmly against the parents, regardless of their innocence or guilt.

The child protection conference will establish a plan which will involve the social workers seeing your children at regular intervals and there may be further assessments, courses or particular expectations of parents prescribed. The plan will initially be reviewed every three months and may run for up to twelve months. At any point where it may be seen that the plan is failing, any of the removal measures may be considered against the parents. In between these meetings there will be Core Group meetings where a smaller team headed by the social worker will also review progress. Effectively social services will bring a level of interference into a family's life that can actually stop the family functioning as a secure unit, causing stress, upset, anxiety and worry. The parents may split up and the split could be encouraged by the social workers. Upon reaching the third review conference, social workers are expected to liaise with their managers and legal services to decide upon the way forward. If a child has been on a protection plan for more than two years and significant changes have not taken place then discussions will begin as to the required action, which generally means the beginning of court proceedings and the likely removal of the child.

Section 47 enquiries also usually require some sort of "risk assessment" of the family. This will examine: the causes for concern; the family's strengths; the ability to protect; family history; all previous records; protective factors, such as full time schooling, extended family and how any risk may be minimized. Sometimes specialist risk assessments are required, such as in cases of allegations of sexual abuse, or a past history of mental health conditions.

Of course not all section 47 enquiries lead down such draconian routes. There are a number of possible outcomes as defined by the protocols. For each child involved, one of the following outcomes is to apply:

Concerns are unfounded;

Concerns remain for workers but no real evidence to substantiate;

Concerns are substantiated but the child not judged to be at continuing risk;

Child judged to be at continuing risk of significant harm.

Where the concerns are unfounded, generally the assessments will end and the provision of any services assessed and provided, but the case will be closed. Where there is a lack of evidence to substantiate the concerns, the enquiry is likely to be stepped down to a section 17 child in need provision. Where the concerns are founded, but the child is not deemed to be at continuing risk, then a child protection plan will still be put into action and a decision of the action to be taken should the plan not be followed by the parents. There may not be a child protection conference to undertake the planning aspect, and again it is likely to be dealt with under a section 17 child in need plan. Where there is any judgement of a continuing risk of harm, then a Child Protection Conference will be called following the procedures outlined above.

The time line for section 47 enquiries expects that a strategy meeting will take place within three days of the referral and the assessment concluded within forty five working days from the point of referral. An initial Child Protection Conference must be instigated within fifteen working days of the strategy meeting. Again, the strict timetables push parents headlong into a world that they had probably never envisioned, even in their worst nightmares, as there is a widely held belief that such things happen to other people and not to nice parents like them.

The final assessment process to examine is perhaps one of the most pernicious and cruel and this is the pre-birth assessment, particularly for a first time mother. Where an unborn child is thought to be at risk, social services will step in, usually with a view to removing the child at birth. The removal of new born babies is increasing exponentially, usually on the main criteria of future risk as opposed to any actual harm caused. In the case of a first time mother, there can be no actual harm caused unless there is substance abuse whilst pregnant, which is the case in only a small minority of mothers. The main issue here is the concept of future risk. Like the threshold table above, there is a long and practically non-exhaustive list of "indicators" that social services apply to label a baby at risk of future emotional harm or neglect. A few examples should suffice to show the range and breadth that bring social workers into the lives of pregnant mothers. Where there are concerns about the parenting capacity; where alcohol or substance abuse may be affecting the health of the baby; very young mothers to be; where a child in the family has been previously removed; where there may be mental health problems or learning difficulties with the parents; where a person who has been convicted of an offence against a child or is simply believed to have by the child protection professionals and even where parents are making informed decisions to have a home birth, free birth or are choosing not to consent to medical professionals demands.

Pre-birth assessments follow a similar pattern to the assessments outlined above, with multi-agency meetings, child protection plans, section 47 enquiries or provision of services similar to a section 17 child in need assessment. The difference at this stage is that no orders can be placed on an unborn child as it does not become a legal entity until birth. Once born, EPOs or police protection can be utilised to remove the newborn, often within hours, sometime minutes of its birth. It has not been unknown for social workers and police officers to be in attendance in the delivery room.

Such instances are not the worst excesses of the over intervention by the child protectionists. In 2014, front page news was made by the courts ordering the forcible sedation and then a caesarian section of an Italian woman to remove her baby, which was then placed for adoption. The lady in question wasn't even a national of the UK, yet social services sought, and a judge in the court of protection agreed to, an order to carry out this dystopian action. If this case does not demonstrate the almost totalitarian way that social services operate, it is difficult to imagine what would.

The final stop on the journey that any of the above interventions can bring is the family courts, to which we shall later return. What is evidentially clear is that the processes and procedures of child protection work relatively quickly and although in the realm of protecting children this seems apposite, it also means that innocent parents have little time to learn what they can do to help protect their children from the often unwarranted interference of social services.

A quick guide is provided below:

Referral	Often the starting point of social services becoming involved in your family. Someone makes a report to them about your child. It could be a teacher at your child's school, a medical practitioner, a police officer, a neighbour, even a member of your family. Quite often they are anonymous, sometimes purely malicious, but whoever and whatever its nature it will start the wheels of investigation into YOUR life turning.

Initial Assessment	Usually performed by a duty social worker without any reference to you or your family. Local Authority records will be checked for any past involvement, enquiries made of other agencies such as the police, possibly your child's school. The outcome of this assessment can be No Further Action and you are unlikely to even be aware that it has happened. Allocation to a Social Worker to carry out further investigations and assessments or even immediate 'protective measures' such as removal of the child.
Common Framework Assessment: (CAF)	This is a process for gathering and recording information about a child for whom a practitioner has concerns in a standard format. It aims to identify the needs of the child and how to meet those needs. It is a shared assessment and planning framework for use across all children's services and all local areas in the UK.

The CAF consists of:

- A pre-assessment checklist (helps decide who would benefit from a common assessment)
- A process (enables practitioners to undertake a common assessment and then act on the result)
- A standard form (record the assessment) |

	• Delivery plan (and a review form) • Standing alone (a consent statement) This is a voluntary assessment and requires consent at the start of the process with the full knowledge of what will happen. When completed, the child and or parent/carer must give their consent again for the information to be stored and shared with other services.
Strategy Meeting	A multi-agency meeting without parental or the child's input. The purpose of the meeting is to: i. Share information amongst agencies; ii. agree the conduct and timing of a criminal investigation; iii. decide whether a Section 47 inquiry should be instigated and if it is; iv. plan how the section 47 inquiry should be carried out–who does what and when–including the timing of any police investigations or medical examination; v. agree what action may be needed to ensure the immediate protection and safeguarding of the welfare of the child; vi. determine what information should be shared

	with the family so long as it does not place the child at further risk or prejudice any ongoing police investigation; vii. determine if any legal action is required to protect the child.
Section 47 Inquiry	This is an inquiry under the Children's Act 1989 whereby Section 47 places a duty on Local Authorities to makes enquiries and circumstances relating to a child where: • the Local Authority has already obtained an Emergency Protection Order in relation to the child or • Where the Local Authority is informed that a child who lives or is found in its area is the subject of an Emergency Protection Order, is in Police Protection or has contravened a ban imposed by a curfew notice under s.14 of the Crime and Disorder Act 1998 and has reasonable cause to <u>suspect that a child who lives or is found within its area is suffering, or likely to suffer significant harm.</u> The results of that assessment will form part of the LA's evidence if it commences proceedings for a Care or Supervision Order.

Child Protection Conference	Following a Section 47 inquiry if the Local Authority believe the concerns about the child are substantiated a Child Protection Conference may be called. It is a multi-agency meeting and parents attending may be met by an array of representatives, some familiar, some not so. It can be a daunting and intimidating environment. It should take place within 15 working days of the last strategy meeting. The purpose of the Child Protection Conference is:

- To bring together and analyse in an inter-agency setting the information that has been obtained about the child's developmental needs and the parents' or carers' capacity to respond to these needs to ensure the child's safety and promote the child's health and development within the context of their wider family and environment;

- To consider the evidence presented to the conference and taking into account the child's present situation and information about his or her family history and present and past family functioning, make judgements about the likelihood of the child suffering significant harm in the future and decide whether the child is continuing to, or is likely to, suffer significant harm; and

	● To decide what future action is needed to safeguard the child and promote his/her welfare, how that action will be taken forward, and with what intended outcomes.
	If the Conference attendees decide that that the child has suffered harm and is likely to suffer significant harm in the future and that the child will require inter-agency help, assistance will need to be delivered through a formal child protection plan. The Chair will then need to determine which category of abuse or neglect the child has suffered or is likely to suffer i.e. physical harm, emotional harm, sexual abuse or neglect and this will be recorded on the Child Protection Plan. The attendees at the Conference will put together an outline of the Child Protection Plan to safeguard and promote the welfare of the child.
Child Protection Plan	A child protection plan should must set out what work needs to be done why and by whom and should: ● Describe the identified developmental needs of the child and what therapeutic services are required to meet these needs; ● Include specific, achievable, child-focused outcomes intended to safeguard and promote the child's welfare;

	• Include realistic strategies and specific actions to bring about changes necessary to achieve the planned outcomes; • Set out when and in what situations the child will be seen by the lead social worker, both alone and with other family members or caregivers present; • Clearly identify and set out the roles and responsibilities of each professional involved with the child; • Include a contingency plan to be followed if circumstances radically change • Set out when the plan is to be reviewed and how any progress is to be measured. The plan must be as "workable" as possible for the family. The Local Authority often also ask the family to enter into a written agreement after finalising the child protection plan so the expectations on the family are very clear. The child protection plan should also take into account the child's wishes and feelings and should be explained and agreed with the child as far as is possible in view of the child's age.
Child Need	In section 17 of the Children Act 1989 defines a child as being in need in law if: • He or she is unlikely to achieve or

111

	maintain or to have the opportunity to achieve or maintain a reasonable standard of health or development without the provision of services from the LA; ● His or her health or development is likely to be significantly impaired, or further impaired, without the provision of services from the LA; ● He or she has a disability. Any Child that is assessed as a Child in Need is entitled to services from the Local Authority. Assessment is usually carried out under the Framework for the Assessment of Children in Need and Their Families (2000)
Framework for the Assessment of Children in Need and Their Families (2000)	This provides a systematic way of analysing, collecting and understanding information to help professionals make an informed judgement about how to help a child and their family and promote the child's welfare. The assessment may include a Common Framework or 'core' assessment, section 47 inquiries or strategy meetings too.
Section 20	Under S20 of the Children Act 1989 a Local Authority has a duty to provide accommodation for a child in need who appears to require it in the following circumstances:

- where there is no one with parental responsibility for him;
- where he is lost or abandoned;
- where the person caring for him is prevented from providing him with suitable accommodation or care, for whatever reason and for however long;
- where he is over 16 and the LA considers his welfare is likely to be seriously prejudiced without the provision of accommodation.

Any child accommodated under section 20 or under a Care or Emergency Protection Order is considered to be "looked after" by the LA. This has been one of the most widely misused 'powers' by social services–to the extent that the courts have issued guidance around its use. Parents are often cajoled into signing a section 20 allowing social workers to take their children on a 'voluntary' basis rather than seeking a court order. Parents should never sign these as doing so makes it easier for social workers to take your child(ren) without having to prove their case in court. It is often an indicator that the social worker does not have enough evidence to obtain the said court order.

A child can be removed at any time by their parent from section 20 accommodation.

Legal Planning Meeting	When the Local Authority holds concerns about a child and believes that the Threshold Criteria might be met for an application for a Care or Supervision order under Section 31 of the Children's Act 1989, it will convene a Legal Planning Meeting. This will be with the Local Authority's solicitors and they will determine if legal action is required. Parents are not invited to this and the minutes of the discussion are considered 'legally privileged' and so remain confidential to the Local Authority.
Public Law Outline (PLO)	The procedure for taking a case to court. Parents are issued with a letter informing them that the local Authority is planning to apply to court for an order. The letter will invite parents to a pre-proceedings meeting, which is a last chance to effect a plan to prevent the escalation to court proceedings. This plan will have specific targets and a defined time-frame. Sadly this action is often overlooked, and the meeting decides to go directly to court.
Threshold Criteria	A judge must decide if 'threshold is met before they can make any order. The child is either suffering or is at risk of suffering significant harm. Significant harm can be caused by what the parents are doing or failing to do for their children. It may also be found to be met if the child is deemed

	beyond parental control.

Chapter 4 The Villains

As the judge closed the hearing with a confirmation of yet another interim care order on their children, the Cafcass officers stood to address the judge. It was an intervention in the proceedings that pushed the border of politeness. Full of her own self ego and clear rapport with the judge through far too many appearances before him she cut him down mid-sentence. 'Judge there is another issue!' He turned towards her, peering over the top of his half rimmed spectacles. His expression a curious mix of annoyance and geniality towards her.

' Yes, Miss Cathcart?'

She proceeded, 'I have concerns your honour, these children are subject to care orders due to alleged sexual abuse by a sibling. The teenager in question has been seen to be overly familiar with the Mother and it is reported the mother referred to the teenager as 'daddy' when discussing the baby. It is not beyond consideration that there may have been an incestuous relationship by which the child was born and may account for her disabilities.'

The whole court froze, even the judge seemed taken aback. The mother looked at the Father, her eyes clearly saying 'is this for real?'

Miss Cathcart did not pause though,

' Your Honour, I believe that you should order a DNA test!'

Both the mother and father's solicitor's jumped to their feet, but before they could even begin to stutter into words their objections at the suggestion, the judge concluded:

'So be it, I agree that DNA testing be so ordered.'

As the mother's solicitor meekly tried to raise an objection, the judge waved his hand and said:

'The court has made its orders.' and began to rise from his seat, the clerk cried 'All rise!' and the hearing ended.

As the parties began to gather their things and leave the court, the mother caught the Cafcass officer smirking wildly at the social worker who smiled smugly back at her.

Now not only had their child being charged with sexual assault, but the mother was under suspicion for incest. It was clear that the so called 'professionals' were building their case in whatever underhand way they felt they could.

Her solicitor reassured her, that such a test would help in the long term as such suggestions, whilst clearly ridiculous could lead to appeal points for unfair procedures and bias of the court.

Although the testing proved that the allegation was a complete fabrication, it had done enough to blacken the character of the mother in court. In spite of all the evidence that demonstrated the Mother had acted appropriately when faced with the disclosures from her daughter, the court still placed all of her children in long term foster care under a care order.

A true story–names have been changed and the time -line condensed.

Although it may be provocative to entitle this chapter the villains, it is a reflection of how parents feel after interactions with social services and their associated agencies. Social media, newspaper reports and the general feedback about social workers and their child protection companions rarely presents them in a positive light. There is a simple reason for this: there are few good news stories to emerge from their activities. If their actions of "child stealing" are not being exposed, more often than not their failings are being highlighted. To say social workers and child protectionists have a fairly bad press is an understatement. Such a widely held reputation does not just appear from nowhere, so there must be a basis for it.

When parents first come into contact with the social services, the array of people who suddenly become involved can be bewildering. Why is a probation officer invited to a child protection meeting when you have never even had a parking ticket, never mind being charged with a crime? It all came about through the introduction of inter-agency working. Major social work failures in the past, such as the Victoria Climbie case, highlighted the insular workings of the various agencies that had been involved and as a result the public enquiry lead by Lord Laming recommended that child protection required closer integration and sharing of information between agencies, resulting in the multi-agency platform of child protection that greets parents caught in the system.

The more the parents understand and appreciate the role of some of these key agencies, the more prepared they can be to deal with them. Hence this chapter examines who these people are and the part they may play in destroying your family. Although this will not necessarily be an exhaustive list and you may find titles used by 'officials' vary, it will give an overview of the individual roles you may come across.

The named or lead Social Worker in your case. This social worker will be in charge of your case, under the auspices of their manager, will make the major decisions about its progress, decide what assessments are to be carried out (if any) and write reports on you and your family. They will want to talk with you, with your child/ren and 'inspect' your home. They will often be accompanied by another social worker, just to make their authority (bullying) complete. It is best to assume that from the initial meeting that the social worker has already made up their mind about you, whatever the nature of the referral. It does not matter that you may have asked them for help on a single issue, because when a social worker enters your home they are tasked with undertaking a risk assessment, even if the point of them being there is completely benign. So effectively they are actively seeking to find issues with your family, your home, your circumstances, in other words looking to 'pin' something on you. Long gone are the days of a social worker being there to help and support: they are there largely to assess if they can build a case to remove your child. Now that may seem an extreme accusation, but it is now their modus operandi[ix] and social workers have become so risk averse that common sense has been jettisoned. All parents are a risk.

The <u>Social Worker's Manager.</u> This person oversees the social worker's activities and is the one most likely to make the decisions about your family. It may be that they have never met you or your family although you may meet them at a Child Protection meeting or PLO. Their decisions about your family will be based on the narrow and probably highly biased reports provided by the social worker. So immediately your position is compromised by the fact that the decision maker has a blinkered view of the situation. Even if decisions go up to even more senior managers–the same tainted and largely unevidenced opinions will be the basis for their actions. Thus the system is endemic and self-reinforcing. If the lie is repeated oft enough, it becomes easy for them to believe it as the truth. You will often hear parents say that social workers will never admit that they are wrong, even in the face of unequivocal evidence. It is, sadly, generally true. The social workers reports and assessments, even if they are mainly opinion and lacking clear facts, become the 'truth' regarding your case as far as the social services are concerned. Of course this repetition to other professionals at meetings and in reports also becomes their 'truth'. Even when parents object to what is written about them, no-one listens, because, after all, you are just parents and the social workers and their managers are 'professionals.'

The Director of Children's Services. This individual may only come into play if you direct a complaint about the social workers at them. This is a statutory position–i.e. it is governed by legislation, namely: Sections 18 (7) (Director of Children's Services) and 19(2) (Lead Member for Children's Services) of the Children Act 2004. This means that local authorities must have regard to it and, if they decide to depart from it, they will need to have clear reasons for doing so.[x]

According to the guidance 'The Children Act 2004 requires every upper tier local authority to appoint a Director of

Children's Services and designate a Lead Member (this means a local councillor) for Children's Services.' Their role is to discharge 'the education and children's social services functions of the local authority. This includes (but is not limited to) responsibility for children and young people receiving education or childrens' social care services in their area and all children looked after by the local authority or in custody (regardless of where they are placed).'[xi]

The Director has a professional responsibility including all operational matters (hence why you should complain to them about social workers practice) to ensure improving outcomes for children. It is the last part of that sentence that I would say has become completely lost, as the individual child has become a case number, a statistic in a social engineering sociological experiment that has gone drastically off the rails. Where the role of the Director becomes increasingly useful to parents is in the specific responsibilities outlined in Section 18 of the Children Act 2004 and in the State's guidance that clearly states:

'The DCS is responsible for securing the provision of services which address the needs of all children and young people, including the most disadvantaged and vulnerable, and their families and carers. In discharging these responsibilities, the DCS will work closely with other local partners to improve the outcomes and well-being of children and young people. The DCS is responsible for the performance of local authority functions relating to the education and social care of children and young people. The DCS is responsible for ensuring that effective systems are in place for discharging these functions, including where a local authority has commissioned any services from another provider rather than delivering them itself. The DCS should have regard to the General Principles of the United Nations Convention on the Rights of the Child (UNCRC) and ensure that children and young people are involved in the development and delivery of local service.'[xii]

The words underlined are of immense importance as the UK signed the UNCRC on 19 April 1990, ratified it on 16 December 1991 and it came into force on 15 January 1992. Thus all the rights enshrined therein can be utilised by parents on behalf of their children. We shall return to these rights in greater detail later. In Ireland the Convention has not been fully incorporated into domestic law, so although it can still be used, its legal standing in the courts is not as powerful as in the UK.

Health Workers often feature heavily in child protection issues, from GPs to Health Visitors through to specialist consultants. All of these may be invited to child protection meetings and asked to provide reports. As one of the most insidious experiences of many families arises from the role of Health Visitors, we will focus on that role here.

Interestingly the government does not recognise any legal standing of the Health Visitor or its title. This distinct long standing 'profession' was removed from the statute books in 2001 and is not found in the Nursing and Midwifery Order of 2001. Let that sink in. A health visitor is not a recognised legal health professional. Thousands of families are letting a health visitor into their homes supposedly to provide support and guidance to their new born and toddlers. Weighing, measuring, advice about feeding and yet the government does not recognise them professionally. Just who are these families letting though their door? Well it must only be fair to say that many of them are qualified health practitioners who could provide excellent support for new mums and dads and families with young children. I don't doubt that there are many out there that fulfil this role superbly. However, behind this philanthropic support is a much darker agenda.

Primary Care Trusts require that health visitors screen all new parents for a likely risk of child abuse. Of course the health visitors don't tell the parents that they are doing this or that a record is being established about their family. A label of possible concern placed on a family could have devastating consequences if that family turns up at a hospital with a toddler after a minor accident. Access to that record at the hospital may raise suspicions that would not have been there had it not been for this surreptitious record and opinion of a health visitor.

So what is in this screening process? The health visitor is noting 'risk factors' such as: mother's age, marital status, education, was the baby premature or in special care, do the parents have any history of mental illness, violence or criminality[xiii]. Equally such risk factors relate to poverty so being labelled 'poor' places a family in the higher risk categories in many instances.

Of course these 'issues' get revisited at case conferences. According to AIMS, "At many case conferences, false allegations have been spread like Chinese whispers to so many agencies that they are believed simply because of repetition, not good-quality investigation. Other researchers have pointed out that risk-assessment measures are increasingly used to "pass judgements and used retrospectively to justify past decisions and actions".

And as Dr Walter Barker, Director of the Child Development Programme at Bristol University, pointed out: "The very fact of suspicion that someone may abuse their child creates subconscious barriers and hostile feelings for most people who work with such families." (Barker W. Practical and ethical doubts about screening for child abuse. Health Visitor, 1990; 63: 14-7) whilst Goddard C et al. in 'Structured risk assessment procedures: Instruments of abuse? 'Child Abuse Rev; Openmarket pointed out:

'Risk-assessment measures are increasingly used to pass judgements, and exploited retrospectively to justify past decisions and actions.'

It is summed up perfectly by this quote:

'This increasing involvement in child protection threatens the ethical basis of health visiting.' (Taylor. S and Tilley. N)[xiv].

Thus we can see that health visiting is driven not by the health aspect but by the child protection agenda. Of course what is important here is that health visiting is a service and as it is not mandatory you do not have to engage. Simply put, it would appear that the modern day health visitor is a Trojan horse of child protection. Similarly, the locality safeguarding nurses and school nurses play out parallel roles in this risk assessment culture.

So if we have the social worker, the health visitor and the nurses all looking at families through the window of child abuse first and foremost, no wonder that so many children are being taken into care and adopted against their parent's wishes.

The Police: like the Local Authority, have a duty under the Children's Act 1989 (in Ireland the Child Care Act 1991) to work with other services to safeguard and secure the welfare of children within their area who are suffering or likely to suffer significant harm. As a result they must assess the risk of harm to a child, interview children and judge how to keep the child safe moving forward. They are also duty bound to refer children to the local children's services. In the context of child protection conferences the police will provide information, both from the police national database and any 'soft' intelligence about the parents/family. It is usually representatives from the Public Protection Units that will attend meetings (if they actually bother to turn up).

Sadly the police resources are often misused by the social workers, utilizing their presence to force parents into signing Section 20s, obtaining access to homes on false pretences, executing removal orders-the list is long and it must be said that it is an unholy alliance of the State ranged against parents.

Head-teachers / School Teachers/ Attendance Officers are also invited to conferences and asked to submit reports. It will generally be those staff who have a safeguarding duty. Do not be deceived, no matter how good a relationship you my have had with these individuals as they are there simply to play one role-that of supporting the Local Authority's position. It is unlikely that these individuals will raise their heads above the parapet and stand up for you and your child. A few may, but do not count on it. It would be very unusual for any of them to go against the social worker's recommendations and although they may not be championing the Local Authorities' cause they will simply go along with it as the fear of 'getting it wrong' means they will quietly acquiesce. Of course, like the modern day health visitor, teachers have become increasingly 'child protectionist', not that they do not have a role in the welfare of the youngsters in their care, (they do and always have) but they are effectively developing into 'spies' for social services. Being late for school, days off, term time holidays have all moved from 'normal' to a basis for reporting to social services. Finally, for the vast majority of parents their children will be in the state school system and despite changes to how schools are run and funded in recent years, the vast majority are still run by the Local Education Authorities. In other words, the Head-teachers and teachers are employed by the Local Authority. Where do you think their loyalties may lay? Simply put, (as previously) do not trust them.

Independent Conference Chair (usually from Local Safeguarding Board and may also be an Independent Reviewing Officer) is the person who chairs Child Protection Conferences / Child in Need meetings. The most important note with this role is that despite the name they are far from independent. They are in fact part of the employ of the Local Authority through the Safeguarding Board or a person employed by the local authority to undertake the role. The independence is claimed because they are not directly working on the case, but at the end of the day they are just another Local Authority employee. Worse is that the majority are ex social workers or social care employees–so in other words hewn from exactly the same stone. Their role is to:

- To meet with the family prior to the conference, to ensure that they are clear about the purpose and process of the conference and their role in it;
- To agree issues of attendance and participation of family members, including exclusions where necessary;
- To ensure that there was evidence that the child's voice was heard;
- To ensure consideration is given to any cultural needs or learning disability;
- To ensure that facilities for disabled participants are available;
- To chair the meeting, setting out its purpose for all participants and to ensure that participants are given adequate opportunity to express their views;
- To ensure the family understands what is being said and make sure they are included in the planning;
- To respond to issues of dissent and to make the final decision about child protection plans;

Where it is decided that the child should be subject to a child protection plan, the IRO needs to assist in formulating a child protection plan that addresses identified risks; N.B. This should form the main part of the meeting and should be outcome focused.

To ensure that expectations of parents and the outcomes required to achieve the ending of the child protection plan are clear to all parties;

To identify core group members, including timescales for meetings, and with whom case responsibility lies;

Where insufficient information is available at an initial conference to make decisions about a child protection plan, to decide whether the conference should be reconvened when a fuller assessment has been completed.

Where the criteria for a child protection plan are not met but support services are required, to lead the formulation of a Complex Child in Need Plan;

To ensure the electronic record is updated in light of the conference decision;

To ensure appropriate arrangements are made for the child to be informed about the outcome of the conference. Usually the social worker will be the best person to do this, having already discussed the child's views with them before the conference.[xv]

As can be seen, a lot of responsibility lies with the Chair, and sometimes with that comes a super ego too. Effectively there is another social worker sitting in and running the meeting. They have never met you till you arrive for the first meeting and they will want to meet you prior to the start of the meeting, to explain how it will be run. It's almost guaranteed that if your social worker has recommended a Child Protection Plan, then that is what is going to happen. Do not expect that the Chair will have a different view to the social worker's position or lay much store by what you have to say. It is fair to presume that the outcome of the conference is decided before you set foot in the room.

Cafcass officer/ Guardian ad Litem

Cafcass is the Children and Family Court Advisory and Support Service. Its role is to serve the interests of children in the family courts. It is supposed to be independent of social services and the courts (although it works within the family court rules), but in all reality it is far from independent. Its officers are generally made up of social workers. They may not be in the employment of a local authority, but their training, outlook, experience and approach to child protection comes from the same ideological background.

Cafcass officers produce reports for the court in private law proceedings and act as Guardian ad Litem in care and adoption proceedings. In the latter, they will often 'side' with the local authority's stance, or sometimes even wish to go beyond what the local authority plan. For instance the local authority may be happy to have a Supervision order, whilst the Guardian pushes the court for a full care order. They are supposed to represent the interests of the child: appointing solicitors and barristers for them, listening to their wishes and feelings and ensuring that the child's welfare remains paramount. There are as many complaints by parents about Cafcass officers as there are about social workers.

Cafcass is an executive non-departmental public body and as many public bodies have found their funding has been cut drastically over the last few years leading to officers devoting less time to each individual case as the number of cases they each have to deal with has increased. Frequently they will meet with each parent and the child/ren only once before producing a report. That report is likely to rely heavily on the social work reports and thus, even unintentionally perhaps, take on the bias of the local authority case. That said, the importance of the Guardian should not be underestimated. Judges frequently follow their recommendations. It does not hurt to cultivate the relationship with the Guardian as far as possible, no matter how briefly you may meet them.

MAPPA, MASH & other such associated abbreviations.

MAPPA : the Multi Agency Public Protection Arrangements. Often referred to as a safeguarding hub. Tt is the collection of the agencies that work in managing sexual and violent offenders. There is a frequent link to child protection through such actions as: information sharing, disclosures, domestic violence victims and perpetrators information, as well as risk assessments of offenders within a family.

MASH: Multi Agency Safeguarding Hubs. Multi-agency safeguarding hubs are designed for information-sharing and multi-agency decision-making. Sometimes that means bringing the staff together from social services, the police and health practitioners in one central location. In practice though it is usually more of an umbrella term for the agencies working closely together.

Multi agency working has been deemed the key to early and effective identification of risk, improved information sharing, joint decision making and coordinated action. Various reports and reviews over the years have featured the failure to work effectively together as a reason why children have slipped through the child protection net. The advent of these hubs are designed to prevent such failures.

You may hear references to such 'bodies' if facing child protection actions. In effect it is putting together all the villains in one theoretical place where they can concoct their cases. The problem is that they all share an ideological belief and may act as a simple reinforcement of each other's beliefs about a family. I am not criticising the multi agency working, I do believe it can have a positive effect in protecting children who need it. However I do believe, the self reinforcement that such 'hubs' create, can cause much damage to innocent families.

Other 'officials' you may come across at Child Protection level are Probation Officers. If you have had dealings with them, they will provide information on how you engaged with your probation period, what level of risk they assigned to you and what level of risk they believe you may pose now.

This list is not exhaustive by any stretch, but it is given to give a glimpse into the range of professionals who may be arranged around a table, talking about you and scaling your level of risk to your children. If your child is in care, then you will also come across Independent Reviewing Officers who are again in the employ of the Local Authority / Safeguarding Boards and have a responsibility to ensure that children looked after by the Local Authority have regular reviews to consider the care plan and placement. They should not only listen to, but give proper consideration to the child's views and make certain that the Local Authority is fulfilling its duties and functions. You may find that the independence of reviewing officers is a little more real, but again, by and large, they also tow the line of the Local Authority.

Chapter 5: How to Fight Back

(1) Key Strategies

As stated at the outset, there is no panacea or magic wand for dealing with Social Services, however what follow are some strategies that have reaped rewards for parents in preventing their children being removed or helped in having their children rehabilitated to the family. These are tried and tested, but as always there can never be any guarantees. The key point is that it is easier to try to stop social services in their tracks by challenging them from the initial contact than it is once a child has been removed. There are some basic rules to follow that help you bolster your position. What you must not do, though, is give up. You need to be as tenacious as social workers are in executing your plans because they will be relentless unless you stop them.

Despite the belief (largely held by social workers themselves) that social workers have considerable legal powers, the reality is that they actually possess very few. They do not have the right to enter your home and you are within your rights to refuse them entry. First off, you need to decide whether you will 'engage' with them. Either way you decide, neither offers any guarantees, but the over-riding factor you must be aware of is that there is no such thing as a friendly 'chat' by a social worker. Right from the start they are there to collect evidence against you. Anything you say will be used against you, twisted, misrepresented or even be presented as a downright lie about what you said. If a social worker calls you or writes asking to meet to discuss a 'referral or concerns', do not talk to them about anything but ask them to put in writing what the issues are; forewarned is forearmed.

Do not let a social worker in your home without an appointment. When that appointment is arranged, ensure that your children are elsewhere with a family member or a trusted person. This is mainly for your benefit; it allows you to focus fully on the social worker and their 'concerns'. It is a good idea to have family or friends with you, not just for moral support, but as witnesses who can provide testimony as to what was said. Someone should take notes, but most importantly:

RECORD everything, either voice, video or both. You do not have to inform the social worker that you are recording though you may wish to and if they refuse to be recorded then the question has to be why? Any professional undertaking their job properly, within the law should have no reason to wish to avoid being recorded. You can offer them a copy, indeed you can suggest that they may like to record it too (most people now have smart phones that include voice recorders, so it is likely that they have the means on their person). Recording ensures that there is a 100% accurate record of the meeting.

There are often discussions about the legality of recording either openly or surreptitiously-the law is clear and simple-you can record anyone in your home regardless of whether they consent or not. In fact the only place where you cannot record is the court room (and even there it is possible to apply to the judge to request the opportunity to record).

In fact recent case law in the UK saw a parent's recording not only accepted into court but the entire case turned on it.

In Re L (A Child) [2015] EWFC B148 a mother made covert recordings of the abusive and racially insensitive foster carer who she was living with along with her baby, and until the recordings were played, she had been disbelieved. The court relied on the recordings and made findings against the foster carer who was clearly heard verbally abusing the mother.

In Ireland, P.H. & Anor -v- The Child and Family Agency [2016] IEHC 106 established the same right whereby it was noted in the judgment that:

'Permitting persons the subject of the agency's attentions to record interactions with the agency is the least that can be done as a first step to attempt to redress the imbalance as between parties in such a situation. The agency should cease to object to recording by persons in such situations.'

Recording by a person for their own use, does not breach any criminal or civil legislation and in fact such is specifically exempted from the Data Protection Act, (as opposed to an organisation which is required to follow the act) in addition, the LA or its agents/ employees may also commit an offence if they stop a person from doing so under the prevention from harassment act.

Protection from Harassment Act 1997

Section 1 (1A) as amended by s125 Serious and Organised Crime Act 2005.

s1 Prohibition of harassment.

(1) A person must not pursue a course of conduct-

(a) which amounts to harassment of another, and

(b) which he knows or ought to know amounts to harassment of the other.

(1A) A person must not pursue a course of conduct -

(a) which involves harassment of two or more persons, and

(b) which he knows or ought to know involves harassment of those persons, and

(c) by which he intends to persuade any person (whether or not one of those mentioned above)-

(i) not to do something that he is entitled or required to do, or

(ii) to do something that he is not under any obligation to do

(2) For the purposes of this section, the person whose course of conduct is in question ought to know that it amounts to or involves harassment of another if a reasonable person in possession of the same information would think the course of conduct amounted to or involved harassment of the other.

(3)Subsection (1) or (1A) does not apply to a course of conduct if the person who pursued it shows-

(a) that it was pursued for the purpose of preventing or detecting crime,

(b) that it was pursued under any enactment or rule of law or to comply with any condition or requirement imposed by any person under any enactment, or

(c) that in the particular circumstances the pursuit of the course of conduct was reasonable.

Having an accurate recording of social workers can open up avenues to challenge the social worker, possibly if their actions are unlawful, to bring 'Fitness to Practice' cases or even private prosecutions. It means that you can raise issues at Child Protection meetings and say "but you said...A, B, C not X, Y, Z and I have the recording to prove it..." It can mean that you keep control as to the accuracy of what appears in reports, but more importantly can raise the issue of the credibility of the social worker in front of other so called 'professionals'. If you put the credibility of the social worker into question, then your chances of undoing their allegations may increase.

Never sign anything–ask for a copy of it to consider and to seek legal advice. If they are desperate and pressuring you to sign something immediately without being able to take advice, it is generally a strong indication that that what they are asking of you is either to your detriment, outside of standard protocols, a coercion tactic or even illegal. Quite often the social worker in these situations will have police officers with them or will even call them. It is a tactic to make you submissive to their demands. The police can only initiate their police powers to remove a child if there is an immediate risk/danger to the child and that must be imminent. It must also be sanctioned by a senior officer of at least Inspector level in the UK.

You must, politely, but firmly, ask them to confirm what is the imminent danger,? Have they obtained the authority of a senior officer and most importantly inform them that if there is no real imminent danger, bar what may be the hearsay of a social worker (who you can point out was asking you to 'voluntarily' sign/agree to something and thus there was no mandatory issue at stake) then inform them that their any actions could be subject to a Judicial Review. We shall return to this powerful legal action later. It should be noted that in the UK a social worker can request the police to exercise their power only in situations where a child is at immediate risk of harm or abuse. Section 46 of the Children Act 1989 does not give police the right to force an entry to remove a child, and thus they require a warrant, but the Police and Criminal Evidence Act 1984 allows police to enter a property to save life or limb. This is often misused where there is no threat to life or limb; yet is utilised to effect entry. A child can be only kept in police protection for a period of up to 72 hours.

In Ireland the law is very similar. Under the Child Care Act 1991-Section 12 only confers powers to remove where "a member of the An Garda Siochana has reasonable grounds for believing that-

(a) there is an immediate and serious risk to the health or welfare of a child, and

(b) it would not be sufficient for the protection of the child from such immediate and serious risk to await the making of an application for an emergency care order by a health board under section 13..."

Again the same approach applies: ask the Garda to verify the immediate and serious risk and inform them that by acting where no such risk exists that their actions will be subject to a Judicial Review in the High Court.

A short note here is that Judicial Review has been particularly effective for families who have faced such situations in Ireland and as a result in some areas the local police force has become much more circumspect in its dealings with families. Judicial

Review can be a powerful tool if used correctly.

Do not make any agreements verbally or otherwise and above all NEVER agree to a Section 20 agreement. This is voluntarily allowing your children to be taken into care of the Local Authority. It has long been used as a way of the Local Authority taking your children without having to go to the courts (usually as they have no recourse to do so at that point). If your child has been taken under a Section 20, then as it is a voluntary agreement you can legally remove them at any time. Doing this would probably force the social workers hand into going to court for an emergency order. You should be notified of this and it gives you an opportunity to challenge their actions in front of a judge or magistrates. Remember that an emergency order can only be granted if there is an <u>immediate risk or threat</u> to the child. Do not be intimidated by this threat. If you revoke the Section 20, you have an opportunity to bring your child home and it is not necessarily a given that any application by the Local Authority for an emergency order will be granted, particularly if you have your legal arguments ready.

In Ireland a similar section is under Section 4 of the Child Care Act 1991 whereby '4 (2) Without prejudice to the provisions of Parts III, IV and VI, nothing in this section shall authorise a health board to take a child into its care against the wishes of a parent having custody of him or of any person acting in *loco parentis* or to maintain him in its care under this section if that parent or any such person wishes to resume care of him. '

So the basic rule is do not agree. If you are threatened with court simply say that you are happy to test their evidence in front of a judge. Agreeing to a Section 20 or voluntary care can be a major disadvantage for parents because agreeing is tantamount to accepting that there is an issue or concern that requires the removal of your child/children from you. It can pretty much be guaranteed that sooner rather than later, any agreement to let your children go into voluntary care will be followed by an application on behalf of the Local Authority to place your children formally in foster care under a court order. It is better to challenge the whole basis from the outset, attending court if necessary rather than giving an advantage to the social workers from the outset. This is not idle speculation but based upon the experience of parents who have followed such advice and succeeded in preventing their children being removed.

Diarise everything. One of the best ways to keep on top of your case is to keep a diary: of every event, meeting and piece of correspondence. Your aim is to develop a detailed day by day account that can be referenced in the future. This can be invaluable when challenging social workers. As we shall see, they become so caught up in their lies and fabrications that they will often deny saying something, or even deny sending a letter. They may even say they have sent letters when they haven't. A simple day by day account of: the date, who said what (cross-referenced with your recordings), letters received— the sender, the date of the letter, the date received, the contents thereof. By doing this you will have a comprehensive record to utilise against the social workers. Remember you are just one case in many they have, many they are applying the same methods with, and thus being able to produce cross-referenced evidence can have a considerable impact.

Do not split from your partner unless there is clear evidence of domestic violence that cannot be denied, such as a conviction. Social workers often attempt to 'divide and conquer', promising that the children won't be removed if you leave the partner. Unless there is a clear and undeniable threat from your partner, do not engage in their demands. Ask the social worker to <u>verify with evidence</u> the clear and direct threat that your partner poses. Do not accept their opinion or possible 'future' risks as a genuine reason to part. Social workers will often say that they have 'concerns' but 'concerns' are not enough as they must prove their assertions to a court, so it is not unreasonable to ask them to prove them to you. Where you have evidence to the contrary, i.e. they say there is a conviction for domestic violence and there is none, ask for the date, the convicting court, the sentence, the probation officer's name. Apply to the police for police records (more on this later) and tell them you are/have done so. You are stronger together, so fight it together–again if you split on the social workers recommendation it will be used against you in any court proceedings. Frequently parents report that they split on a social worker's say so in order to protect their children from removal and the social services still removed their child.

Following on from the above, submit a Subject Access Request (Freedom of Information Request In Ireland). Under the Data Protection Acts you are entitled to see what social services have on record about you. It is worth making this application for your entire family as it can not only bring to light glaring errors, but you have a right to have inaccurate information corrected. It also fires a nice 'warning shot across the bows' that you are aware of your rights (and clearly some law) and are not prepared to take what they say about you at face value. An application is simple and can and should be done, not just to Social Services but to your GP for your medical records, the police to ensure that they don't hold any erroneous data on you (one applicant found that the police had a string of convictions listed against him, yet he had never been arrested or been to court, not even so much as for a parking fine). You are entitled to have inaccurate data corrected. The Data Protection Act obliges organisations to keep information that is factually accurate. You cannot alter or remove opinions, including medical diagnoses, <u>unless those opinions themselves are based on inaccurate factual information</u>. There is no requirement to fill in any official forms and it can be done with a simple letter as below.

Your Names
Address
Child Services Data Controller
(local council address)

(Date)

Dear Sir,

Subject Access Requests in relation to the following:
(your   name)
(partner's   name-if   applicable)
(children's names)

Of (home address)

Please send me the information which I am entitled to under section 7(1) of the Data Protection Act 1998 in relation to Case (case numbers for children), currently being run by (lead social worker on your case), further I require all the information un-redacted as per Section 35 of the DPA.

(Section 35 (2) Where the disclosure is necessary:

for the purpose of, or in connection with, any legal proceedings (including prospective legal proceedings); or for the purpose of <u>obtaining legal advice</u>; or

is otherwise necessary for the purposes of <u>establishing, exercising or defending</u>

<u>legal rights</u>, personal data are <u>exempt from the non-disclosure provisions</u>.)

Please include:

1. Copies of all records, handwritten AND computerised.
2. Copies of all e-mails, faxes, letters etc.
3. Copies of all telephone messages, transcript and original recordings.
4. Copies of all internal memo's, and external correspondence. Whereby Third parties need to give permission for this, please seek that permission and obtain the relevant records.
5. Copies of all 'Running Sheets'.

If third party data is included please obtain the necessary permissions for its release.

Please would you also advise me of the logic involved in any automated decisions taken by you about me pursuant to section 7(1) (d) of the Data Protection Act 1998.

If you need further information from me, or a fee, please let me know as soon as possible. If you do not normally handle these requests for your organization, please pass this letter to your Data Protection Officer or another appropriate officer without delay.

This letter has been sent via Recorded Delivery. You have 40 Calendar days in which to respond to this request.

Yours faithfully

(your   name)
(partner's name- if applicable)

Where you make an application to the police, add in 'Copies of Officers Notebooks.

Generally, Subject Access Requests are returned with large areas redacted i.e. blacked out. That is why you include the Section 35 notice, in an attempt to obtain the reports un-redacted.

If they fail to respond, deny you the paperwork or fail to provide it un-redacted, then you can make a complaint to the ICO– nformation Commissioner Office.

If you do find inaccurate information on your paperwork, then you should first raise the issues with the organization in question. The ICOs are very useful in giving guidance, they provide example letters. An example of a concern letter is below[xvi].

[Your full address]
[Phone number]
[The date]

[Name and address of the organization]
[Reference number (if provided within the initial response)]

Dear [Sir or Madam / name of the person you have been in contact with]

Information **rights** **concern**
[Your full name and address and any other details such as account number to help identify you]

I am concerned that you have not handled my personal

information properly.

[Give details of your concern, explaining clearly and simply what has happened and, where appropriate, the effect it has had on you.]

I understand that before reporting my concern to the Information Commissioner's Office (ICO) I should give you the chance to deal with it.

If, when I receive your response, I would still like to report my concern to the ICO, I will give them a copy of it to consider.

You can find guidance on your obligations under information rights legislation on the ICO's website (**www.ico.org.uk**) as well as information on their regulatory powers and the action they can take.

Please send a full response within 28 calendar days. If you cannot respond within that timescale, please tell me when you will be able to respond.

If there is anything you would like to discuss, please contact me on the following number [telephone number].

Yours   sincerely,
[Signature]

If the organization fails to respond or refuses to correct

inaccurate information, then the ICO is your next port of call. They say:

'If the organization has been unable, or unwilling, to resolve your information rights concern, you can raise the matter with us. We will use the information you have provided, including the organization's response to your concerns, to decide if your concern provides an opportunity to improve information rights practice. If we think it does provide that opportunity, we will take appropriate action. This could take a variety of forms.

You should raise the matter with us within three months of your last meaningful contact with the organization concerned. You can follow the advice on this page, or you can raise your concern with us[xvii].'

There is a right to claim compensation from an organisation if you have suffered damage because they have breached part of the Act. The guidance currently given by the ICO is that you can only make a claim for distress if you have also suffered damage. However, in 2015 the Court of Appeal ruled, in the case of Vidal-Hall v Google, that compensation under the DPA could be awarded for distress alone. Google appealed this aspect of the judgment to the Supreme Court, but the appeal was withdrawn following an agreement being reached between the parties. The ICO is currently amending the guidance to reflect the ruling. In the cases of social service interventions, damages and distress could well be the loss of your children / family life.

The advice of the information commissioner is:

'You do not have to make a court claim if an organisation agrees to pay you compensation. If you cannot reach an agreement with them, you can apply to a court for compensation alone or you can combine your claim with an action to put right any breach of the Act....If you fail to reach an agreement, you should write to the organisation before you start court proceedings, to tell them that you intend to take the matter to court. If you do not, the court may penalise you. You should send the letter by recorded delivery and address it to the person you have been dealing with, or the company secretary. In some cases, this may help prompt the data controller to settle the dispute.'

If your child is in care, and you have contact, ensure that your contact is completely focused upon your child. It is not an environment to make criticisms to contact workers or use your child as a conduit to raise issues. Use the time wisely ensuring that your child's needs are met. Any negatives are recorded and fed back to the social work team and will be used in court against you. Keep your contact time positive. I appreciate this seems like common sense and what you would expect any parent to do. But from experience, I can assure you that some parents have created unnecessary issues at contact that has done them no good in the longer term. Sometimes it is wiser to bite your tongue and play by their rules to effect a better outcome for your family. It may seem counter-intuitive, but record any issues you see and at the end of the session report them to the contact supervisor. Don't raise them in front of your child. Remember you are building a case against them, just as they are trying to build one against you.

Unless ordered by a court, do not undertake any assessments with 'experts' chosen by the Local Authority. There is a reason why social services like to choose who they want to undertake any assessments of you–these 'experts' are the paid assassins of social services. Parents are neatly labelled with problems such as 'borderline personality disorder', 'failure to prioritise the children's needs over their own', 'lack empathy or insight ' and the list just goes on. If your case is turning on having to undertake some form of 'expert' assessment, then demand someone of your choice and ensure that the Local Authority pay for the report. If the assessment is truly required and is open and transparent, then no social service department should have any issue with paying for an 'expert' that you put forward. Surely it is the assessment by an 'expert' that is important, not the who.

Expert witnesses to the court can be paid very substantial sums of money, so it is definitely not in their interests to upset a Local Authority by going against the thrust of their case. This is often markedly seen in the 'remit' that an 'expert' is given by the Local Authority, i.e. what it is that the LA want them to look at about you. There cannot be an even playing field when the so called expert begins their work, not by meeting with you in an objective, open minded, neutral way, but by reading all the social workers' and other reports. Thus, immediately, the agenda is set, ideas become fixated, and the assessment is framed by the expert to conclude that you have some deep set issue or other that will usually require extensive counselling or therapy that will take far too long to allow your children to stay with you or be returned to you. It's so simple, the social worker, though having no professional training or qualifications in for example medicine, psychology, or psychiatry, will slip into a report that they believe you are 'depressed', or have a 'mental health issue', or that your 'concerns that you believe your child may be autistic are actually fabricated'. These points are the road map for the expert so that they simply focus on these issues which make for a biased, unfair assessment. Suddenly the report they produce illustrates a person you do not recognise as you. You have 'traits' of this, that or the other. The problem is that having traits of something does not mean that you are suffering from or have those conditions. We all have traits of various conditions, but a genuine professionally qualified, ethical expert would not diagnose you with the condition simply because of this. Yet time and again this has been enough to remove children from a loving family.

Of course the assertion of this underhand collusion will be dismissed by defenders of the system. They will state that the court / local authority has to give the expert an insight for them to be able to undertake an effective assessment. Whilst there may be a need to offer such insights, the relationship between these local authority picked experts and social workers can and does at time border upon conspiracy. In

2014 the Court Of Appeal published a scathing judgment that highlighted this unethical and unfair collusion.

In the case Re NL (A Child) (Appeal: Interim Care Order: Facts and Reasons) [2014] EWHC 270 (Fam)[xviii] the justices' removed a baby from its mother based on the pivotal evidence of the clinical psychologist. The Clinical Psychologist had concluded that the child was at risk of physical and emotional harm if the mother failed to maintain her sobriety. The psychologist in question was Dr van Rooyen[xix]. The appeal court found that Van Rooyen's report on the mother had been researched and written in a day and that Van Rooyen had neither spoken to the mother or the medical and psychological experts with whom the mother and baby were living. Instead, Dr Van Rooyen had relied on documents and a phone call to a social worker. Mrs Justice Puffley's judgment noted:

'[34] I am gravely troubled by the speed, the manner and the ambit of Dr van Rooyen's involvement. It simply cannot be right, fair or reasonable to commission an expert to provide what may turn out to be the pivotal evidence justifying separation of a neonate from his mother in the way that happened here.

[35] It surprises and alarms me that Dr van Rooyen was asked, and was prepared, to provide a report during the course of a single working day, a terrifyingly tight timeframe, and on the basis of papers supplemented by a telephone conversation with a local authority professional who had never met the mother. I struggle to understand how Dr van Rooyen's apparently firm opinions, adverse to the mother, could have been formed given the complete absence of any kind of discussion with her or, indeed, any communication with [the resource].

[36] To my mind, it is quite simply unacceptable for an 'independent' expert to be instructed in the way Dr van Rooyen was-to conduct such a scant inquiry in preparation for a hearing which was to have such wide ranging consequences for the child.[xx]

This is one case where the perpetrators were exposed but it would be unwise to assume that this was a one off or something unusual. Such collusions do still happen. There are probably many more just like Dr van Rooyen who are happy to collude and effectively mislead a court in order to effect the removal of a child. Van Rooyen boasts on her website that she does about 150 of these reports a year for the courts. You do the math: even if the fee for each case is just a thousand pounds (and it is common knowledge that the fees are much, much more) then no wonder Dr van Rooyen is happy to oblige a social workers requests.

The quality of expert witnesses was researched and exposed by Professor Jane Ireland. Her report Evaluating Expert Witness Psychological Reports: Exploring Quality' 2012 highlighted major shortcomings in the experts providing Psychological reports on parents to the courts.

Particular areas of concern were noted:

An over-reliance on psychometrics, use of defunct assessments, and using assessments with no validity;
The under-use of recognised methods to assess risk in cases involving domestic violence, general violence and sexual violence;
a proportion of experts commenting on mental health and yet having no indicated background in that area.

And the Family Justice Council (who had commissioned the report) noted that:

'The report points to serious issues both with the quality of reports and the qualifications of those carrying them out. We are not surprised in view of the concerns we heard expressed throughout our work about the quality of reports generally. We recommend that studies of the expert witness reports supplied by various professions be commissioned by the Interim Board, subsequently the Family Justice Service.

Agreed quality standards for experts in the family courts are clearly needed and we recommend that they should be developed. The FJS should lead this work. Meeting the standards could be a requirement for payments to be approved by the LSC. Criteria could include adherence to set timescales, membership of appropriate professional bodies and completion of specified court focused training, peer review and continuing professional development.'

This must have rattled many of the powers that be because Professor Ireland was accused of producing a report that *reached conclusions that were not justified by the data and threatening fellow psychologists with legal action if they did not withdraw complaints about her research.*

However all the charges against Professor Ireland were dismissed. Whatever the reports shortcomings it certainly raised the issues that still affect the expert witness industry today, to the extent that the Children and Families Act 2014 did attempt to put clear limitations on the use of expert witnesses, not least that an expert should only be instructed by the court where it is necessary in order to resolve the case justly.

Remember that a psychological assessment is nothing more than opinion, therapies come and go as do 'disorders'. As one scientist puts it: 'Much of psychological science consists of studies of topics so nebulous that any statistical analysis is pro forma and cannot lend weight to the study's conclusions. And more, psychological research is rarely replicated or even examined in any depth by other workers, which opens the door to the possibility of outright fraud.[xxi]

As I am no expert on nuances of the psychological assessments used and their flaws, I have turned to an expert in the field Ben Capel, to provide us with an in depth consideration of the problems with reliance by the courts upon psycho-babble.

'Experts and Charlatans: A guide for the perplexed by Ben Capel.

"The concept of the unconscious has long been knocking at the gates of psychology and asking to be let in. Philosophy and literature have often toyed with it, but science could find no use for it."

Sigmund Freud (1940)

What kind of psychological expertise is drawn upon by the Family Courts when they decide to forcibly remove children from their biological parents? Is it "scientific?" Is it trustworthy? Is it capable of providing Court decision-makers with rigorously truthful evidence?

In what follows in this introduction to Stuart Adams' timely and urgently necessary book, I seek to address these questions. In so doing, I hope to demonstrate that much of the psychological expertise these courts rely upon is, in fact, highly questionable. Tragically for the children and parents affected by this expert witness testimony, the answer to each question is, far too often, simply "No."

Medical expertise and diagnostics at work

A six-month-old baby with a chesty cough takes a turn for the worse in the evening. He seems to be struggling to breathe, is hot and clammy and, although very sleepy, is breathing in a curiously laboured and rapid manner. His frightened young parents immediately phone the on-call doctor, who arrives at their home within an hour.

He examines the baby's breathing pattern, listens to his chest with a stethoscope, and takes his temperature. Calmly, he tells the parents that their little boy's chesty cough has become exacerbated by infantile asthma, possibly brought on as a result of the common infection which is afflicting many babies in the area. The baby is showing signs of paradoxical breathing, where the chest contracts during inhalation and expands upon exhalation – a classic sign of infantile asthma.

He administers a small dose of bronchodilator syrup (salbutamol) by dripping it gently into baby's mouth with a sterile plastic syringe, and leaves the bottle and syringe with the parents. Within minutes, baby's breathing returns to normal and he slips into a peaceful sleep, much to his worried parents enormous relief.

The young doctor in this real scene (I was one of the young parents and the baby boy was my firstborn, now happily a healthy young adult free from asthma and significantly taller than me) is an expert in a traditional sense. He is learned in an established medical knowledge that has repeatedly demonstrated universal regularities with respect to the aetiology of common (and not so common) illnesses. That knowledge is able to make clear distinctions between illness and health.

Significantly, he uses instruments to assist him: the stethoscope, the thermometer. From his observations, he makes a diagnosis and provides a curative treatment, which returns the little patient to the state he was in before the illness struck (the "status quo ante").

There's a kind of circularity at work here: the physician observes, gathers symptoms together and recognises an objectively generalised syndrome (a medical term for a recognisable, recurrently observed condition characterised by several symptoms occurring consistently together): in this instance, most notably the paradoxical breathing of infantile asthma, which distinguishes the condition from a simple respiratory tract infection. The established medical knowledge he draws from is able to make clear distinctions between health and illness, allowing him to make a diagnoses and prognosis with the assistance of reliable and accurate medical instruments.

Now let's examine an altogether different case of pathology: psychopathology. As we shall see, medical diagnostics and clinical psychodiagnostics are radically discontinuous. I have borrowed what follows from the Belgian psychoanalyst and clinical psychologist Paul Verhaeghe, who cites it in his illuminating, award-winning work of 2004, *On Being Normal and Other Disorders*.

Clinical psychodiagnostics and the problem with psychological expertise

Can you identify syndromes from psychological symptoms?

In our example of the baby with infantile asthma, the attending physician recognised a series of signs or symptoms that, occurring together, regularly, if not invariably, form a recognisable, diagnosable syndrome. Can the same be said of psychological symptoms, as argued by the architects of the American Psychiatric Association's *Diagnostic and Statistical Manual of Mental Disorders* (the DSM for short), the most widely used psychiatric classification system in the world, currently in its fifth edition?

A teenage joyrider's tale

A fifteen-year-old and his worried parents consult a psychologist after he has been apprehended by the police while joyriding. His mother and father aren't simply seeking a diagnosis; they want corrective treatment urgently. This isn't the first time the boy has taken an illegal excursion in someone else's car and the juvenile court is now threatening to take much more punitive action, possibly a custodial sentence.

During the first interview, the psychologist discovers more information. The boy's car-stealing pursuits have a curious signature: he always chooses Mercedes. Once behind the wheel, he schlepps around aimlessly on his own, eventually leaving the car undamaged in another part of the country before hitchhiking back home. When the psychologist asks why the car has to be a Mercedes, the boy seems a little baffled and can only say that he especially likes that make of vehicle.

Can a diagnosis yet be made from these symptoms: car theft, aimless driving, only stealing Mercedes vehicles, leaving the car unharmed? Maybe "joyriding" is about as far as we can get at this point, although it's not in the DSM. Where is the universalised syndrome, the psychological equivalent of infantile asthma? Can more information yield more symptoms that might enable a syndrome to be reliably recognised?

In the second interview, the psychologist explores family relationships and dynamics. Our teenage joyrider is an only child. His parents, once drawn to each other's differentness (father's origins are working class, mother's prosperous), are currently in the midst of a marital crisis. The mother is having an affair, while the father is burying himself in work for … Mercedes.

Intriguingly, it emerges in this interview that the region where the boy leaves his stolen car isn't random: it's the place where his mother was born.

Symptom gathering is running into complexities and enigmas not encountered by the physician in the infantile asthma scenario. Whose symptoms are we dealing with anyway? The son's behaviour isn't a quirk or a 'disease' located in his body; it's impossible to understand outside of its context, as he appears to be caught in some way between his parents' problems.

A psychoanalytic hypothesis begins to suggest itself: the boy is in some as yet obscure way responding to the conflicted, possibly dying, desire between his parents, as though he is trying to answer an impossible series of questions in relation to it. Questions like, how can I find a solution to the agony of my parents' estrangement, of their love turning sour, of what will happen if the estrangement worsens; can I save my parents' relationship, or at least buy time, by deflecting their attention onto me and away from one another?

A short psychoanalytic detour

The boy is barely conscious of the role the troubled desire of his parents is playing in his strange compulsion to joyride. His consciously-available rationales for his actions are plainly insufficient and impoverished, and quickly turn to bafflement, not because he is being obstinate or dishonest, but because the motivating elements in his behaviour are largely unconscious and by definition not accessible to simple self-reflection.

The French psychoanalyst Jacques Lacan once summed this kind of knotty conundrum up succinctly: "The unconscious is the discourse of the Other." We find ourselves composed of thoughts, words and messages that are not strictly our own, but have come to us from the first "Others" in our lives: our parents.

And that's just the beginning; unless we're writing or discussing something like a set of instructions for assembling flatpack furniture, much of spontaneous human speech (and writing for that matter) is ambiguous and open to interpretation (come to think of it, if you've ever tried to assemble flatpack furniture, you'll have discovered that this usually applies to the instructions, too). We all encounter human speech and its hallmark propensity for equivocation and ambiguity everywhere we go beyond the family of infancy. That's rather a lot of puzzlement to contend with while growing up (and, I should add, during adulthood), especially when it comes from those privileged and influential sources we regard as authorities (teachers, adults, "experts", etc).

To compound matters, parents and other adults may not be aware that we have overheard them (and possibly misheard them), and may themselves be unaware of the meanings of some of their behaviours and comments, all of which get received by children as *messages* of a peculiarly significant kind: irreducibly enigmatic messages. This is especially true of messages conveying forms of desire – e.g., parental dreams of who we ought to become, negative desires such as fears of who we ought *not* to become and, perhaps most enigmatically of all, parental love for us.

For psychoanalytic thinkers such as Lacan and Jean Laplanche, parental love is both a necessity and a mystery. We want it, we crave it, our survival depends on it. Yet it can be painfully impoverished. It can also rapidly become smothering, even devouring. As a form of desire, it evokes an unanswerable set of tormenting questions: why does/doesn't he/she love me and what does he/she want of me? And can I deliver that anyway?

Our inability to comfortably understand these inherently puzzling messages is in fact one of the most powerful motives for pushing them out of conscious awareness: what baffles us torments us. But they don't cease to exist when removed from consciousness. They continue to exert an insistent yet ineffable influence on our lives, our moods, our actions, our interpretations of our experiences.

Back to clinical psychodiagnostics

What this example of the joyriding teenager makes abundantly clear is that, unlike medical diagnostics, clinical psychodiagnostics cannot be confined to the individual. The boy's parents are, in sense, joyriding with him, or at least they're in his mind when he takes his little jaunts.

Psychic, as opposed to psychological, identity includes the unconscious dimension of the mind. Psychology should perhaps more properly be called "egology," as Professor Verhaeghe suggests, because it confines itself purely to the consciously available mind (the "I" or "ego") and systematically ignores the unconscious as though it doesn't exist. "Psyche" (soul) encompasses both unconscious and conscious mental dimensions.

As this 15-year-old shows us, psychic identity, along with its potential or actual psychopathologies and aberrant behaviours, can only be understood as a relation with an 'other', almost always a composite figure made up of all those others who have fed us our most insistent and enduring enigmatic messages during our lives. The unconscious, as the distinguished psychoanalyst Eric Laurent (2014) has recently put it, cannot be reduced to learning; it's more associated with what *eludes* learning, with what we cannot comprehend, with what we fail to domesticate with conscious understanding. This unconscious yet potently motivating 'other' is of equal importance to the individual him or herself, strangely intimate and eerily familiar, yet external to conscious cognitive comprehension (Lacan's witty neologism for this external intimacy was, aptly, "extimacy").

But in addition to this inherently relational aspect of psychic identity (and therefore of diagnostics), there is another radical difference with medical assessment. It is a fundamental error to suppose that one can, like a physician, identify a number of distinct symptoms that have already been recurrently observed in other psychologically 'ill' patients and then tie them together into an objective, universalisable syndrome.

In fact, what happens far more typically in clinical psychodiagnostics is the exact opposite. For the physician, the more information he or she collects, the clearer the objective diagnosis becomes. For the psychologist, the more information he or she acquires, the more unique the situation becomes, rendering generalisability all the more elusive, if not impossible. We can take the easy way out, and shoehorn our observations into an ever-expanding and continually changing list of syndromes, a la the DSM, or into prefabricated statements in psychometric tests (more on this later). Or, like psychoanalysts, we can explore these peculiarities without seeking to diminish them or prematurely wrap them up in pre-emptive (and therefore fake) "expert understanding."

The key distinction: from signs to signifiers

Why, contra medical diagnostics, does psychological assessment tend in this direction from general/vague to idiosyncratic? Because in physical medicine, symptoms are *signs* indicative of underlying malfunctioning, whereas in clinical psychodiagnosis they *signifiers* that embody a continually shifting penumbra of meanings that present different aspects in different interactions between patient and clinician, or at different times in the same individual. We are never exactly identical to ourselves for any significant length of time, and different people are inclined to mobilise sometimes widely different aspects or versions of ourselves despite our fantasies of consistency. Some people can encourage you to feel relaxed, erudite and conversational, while others make you feel your fly might be open or you've got a bogey on your cheek.

Paul Verhaeghe explains the difference between signs and symptoms with admirable clarity:

"A sign always points to a fixed meaning: a red traffic

178

light means stop. A signifier refers to an underlying, ever-changing signified, with the result that it is impossible to talk about a fixed meaning. Meanings are determined by the larger linguistic and sociocultural context in which this particular signifier is used. (Compare the difference of the signifier "sheaf" in these two quotations: "His sheaf was neither miserly nor spiteful" and "Alas! How many would sooner steal their brother's whole shock than add to it a single sheaf!")."

Verhaeghe, Paul. *On Being Normal and Other Disorders: A Manual for Clinical Psychodiagnostics* (p. 18). Karnac Books. Kindle Edition.

To return to our troubled adolescent and his parents, the signifier "Mercedes" will never hold the same meaning in any other clinical scenario as it does here. Whereas the number ("N") of infants showing more or less identical signs of infantile asthma runs into tens of thousands, in clinical psychodiagnostics, "N" all too frequently = 1.

While medical diagnostics starts with the specific (the symptom) and progresses toward the general (the syndrome), clinical psychodiagnostics begins from the vague and obscure (the incipient complaint) and progresses to the specific, where N=1. To do justice to their patients, psychologists should ask not so much "What disorder does this patient have?" but "To whom or what do these particular symptoms refer? What are their unique meanings to this patient, and what specific predicament or conundrum do they relate to in his or her life?"

Another significant difference: whereas physicians use instruments such as stethoscopes, ophthalmoscopes, X-rays, functional Magnetic Resonance Imaging (fMRI), Positron Emission Topography (PET) scans, CT scans, etc., to arrive at their diagnoses, the psychoanalyst (though not necessarily the clinical psychologist) relies upon the spontaneous speech of the patient. Medical instruments detect the presence of abnormality; listening to speech often discerns the elusive, the enigmatic, the omitted.

We often resist speaking truths that we fear may cast us in an unfavourable light, or which frighten us or overexcite us or humiliate us. No stethoscope or scan technology can detect what spontaneous, freely-articulated speech, with its equivocations and ambiguities, invariably intimates: that which we are studiously (or at least recurrently) failing or refusing to utter. The points at which speech and smooth narratives alter and fail (as in the baffled teenager who could find no words for his need to joyride in Mercedes cars) are the points that interest the psychoanalyst. The psychometrician views them as useless verbal garbage.

Technological instruments, and psychological instruments such as psychometric assessment tools are no exception, will systematically fail to detect these critical aporia – aporia that, when pursued through free association (the unique method of psychoanalysis – speaking as freely and truthfully as possible without self-censorship) yield the unique singularity of the speaking person's desires, fears, unintegrated experiences. In other words, the opaquely ciphered and as yet unspoken heart of the individual's unique psyche.

The clear distinctions physical medicine can make between illness and health, which arise from an established, widely-tested knowledge-base whose findings are commonly replicated (e.g., fever begins at 37 or 98.6 degrees), are largely unavailable in clinical psychodiagnostics. Where does individual idiosyncrasy end and abnormality begin? If it is true that psychological symptoms result in suffering – people approach psychoanalysts because they are in unmanageable psychic pain – is this suffering measurable and quantifiable like abnormal temperature or elevated blood pressure?

We are now in approaching the so far implicit critique of the kind of psychological "expertise" routinely drawn upon in those closed tribunals we call the Family Courts.

The Great Family Court Expert Witness Fallacy

At huge cost to the public purse, Family Courts rely heavily on paid expert testimony to make life-changing decisions about the families that come before them. I should clarify that I am focusing here on the nature of the *psychological* expertise they overwhelmingly draw upon when seeking to determine the right course of action to ensure a child's emotional, psychological, physical and social wellbeing.

In the light of the distinctions made in the previous paragraphs between medical and clinical psychodiagnostics, I will not be including medical expertise in what follows, not because medical opinions are incontestable, but because the assessments and prognostications of, say, a paediatric oncologist or endocrinologist or neurologist arise from the established, tried and tested knowledge base referred to earlier, with its reliance on signs and its progression from the specific to the generalisable.

No such established knowledge base exists for psychology: there are humanistic, psychoanalytic, analytical-psychological, cognitive-behavioural, personal construct, person-centred, neuropsychological, neurolinguistic-programming, varieties (and many more), each distinct from one another and each with very different (and often antagonistic and mutually exclusive) emphases on what matters most in therapy. To nail my colours to the mast, I stand in the psychoanalytic paradigm and privilege the thought of the Lacanian school, although I consider Sigmund Freud, Carl Jung and Melanie Klein of indispensable importance and value.

Determining psychological suffering is radically different to diagnosing medical illness. And importing a methodology derived from medical diagnostics will generally, if not invariably, result in "findings" and "recommendations" that are little more than pseudo-scientific mummery dressed up as objective truth.

Many of the psychological experts contributing to the Family Courts (while extracting princely fees from the public purse) are clinical psychologists schooled in methods derived from the cognitive behavioural therapies (CBTs), the dominant toolkit for most chartered clinical psychologists practising in the United Kingdom.

Some Family Court expert witnesses are not really experts in any meaningful sense at all, but are rather fake experts: typically, civil servants (social workers) who set themselves up as freelancing "masters" of nebulous, recently-concocted and continually expanding "disciplines" such as "child abuse" and "child safeguarding/protection," which have become so insanely elastic as to include much of what would once have been considered normal parental authority and discipline.

The distinguished American political scientist, Stephen Baskerville (1997, 2017) has exhaustively catalogued the incompetence, dishonesty, fallaciousness and ruthless financial avarice of this mercenary army of official inquisitors, who have caused incalculable anguish and irreparable harm to countless US families in the Family Courts. These "feminist tribunals" (Baskerville's meticulously-evidenced term) have colluded in the effacement of due process protections observed in criminal courts and willingly used the testimony of these baloney entrepreneurs-often pertaining to alleged events they did not witness and were never party to-to erroneously remove children from parents or to remove fathers, blameless of any wrongdoing, from their families and their homes.

To return to the CBT-schooled experts: whether or not they declare themselves adherents of CBT, a hallmark indication that they share its presuppositions (which I will seek to demonstrate are ideological, not scientific) resides in their routine use of standardised psychometric tests to reach exceedingly dubious conclusions. As CBT-indoctrinated psychologists, they wholly ignore the critical role of unconscious influences as well as the crucial distinctions outlined earlier between medical and clinical psychodiagnostics. All, it has to be said, at a frankly inestimable cost in anguish to the unfortunate families who may be, and often are, forcibly torn asunder as a consequence of their recommendations.

But why are standardised psychological tests, which must be meticulously refined and re-tested during the piloting phase for reliability and validity before publication, so dangerous and unreliable in the Family Court context?

"Standardisation" and the critical role of context

Standardised psychometric tests have become very much in

vogue in a range of disparate settings. Many candidates for jobs in major companies, for example, will have been subjected to them prior to or during the interview process. And they positively abound in clinical psychology, psychiatry and other "professions" such as social work and probation.

While there may be other ways of distinguishing psychometric tests from one another, there are really three broad types: those, like IQ tests, that purport to measure performance (potentially useful if one is, say, attempting to get a handle on the pace of cognitive decline in a patient with an aggressive form of dementia); those, like the Minnesota Multiphasic Personality Inventory (MMPI) or the Rorschach, purporting to measure psychological "traits," and those like the Beck Depression Inventory (BDI) or the Millon Clinical Multiaxial Inventory (MCMI), purporting to measure subjective (pathological) "states."

Each of these categories are premised on deeply dubious assumptions. The tester simply assumes that the quantification exercise he or she is conducting on a living human subject is actually measuring some underlying, relatively static "thing." A "thing" which is assumed to be simply sitting there in "nature," in the subject's mind, like a mushroom in a forest, unmediated by the human language used to describe it. This is, as the Melbourne-based psychoanalyst David Ferraro has demonstrated, an exercise in crude reification rooted in a kind of naïve scientific realism.

Where, for example, is the universally agreed definition of "personality" or "trait" in psychology? There isn't one, an absence which doesn't deter psychometricians from devising tests to measure it. They are instead testing a series of hypothetical constructs that they themselves have concocted but ignoring the personal speech of the subject being tested. A depressed patient's personal speech, for example, is constitutive of the specific form of the deep subjective misery he or she is experiencing. To ignore it is to ignore the subjective heart of the suffering.

The reification Ferraro refers to is typically undergirded with statistics apparently demonstrating correlations (these are the various forms of reliability and validity). And yet correlation is no proof of causation.

The trouble with standardisation: human beings aren't standard

These assessments purport to yield objective measurements

(psycho-*metrics*) of enduring psychological attributes. And because they use standardised questionnaires or "probes" involving lists of pre-devised statements (like the BDI, or the MMPI or the MCMI, and so on) and involve number crunching, they appear "scientific" to those unschooled in the radical distinctions between medical and clinical psychodiagnostics.

Verhaeghe puts his finger deftly on the core fallacy of psychometrics:

> "To measure something, one needs an objective unit of measurement: cm, kilos, grades, and so on. Yet in clinical praxis such an objective unit of measurement is missing. What would depression's unit of measurement be, what would an average "depressive quotient" look like? While it is true that contemporary psychodiagnostics has a number of scales through which we try to measure anxiety, depression, and other states, in the final analysis such measurements come down to the counting of words or expressions against which patients can measure the extent of applicability to themselves."

Verhaeghe, Paul. *On Being Normal and Other Disorders: A Manual for Clinical Psychodiagnostics* (p. 7). Karnac Books. Kindle Edition.

The last sentence repays careful consideration. These assessments never attend to the patient's own freely chosen words. Instead, they list a series of statements or questions devised by the test's designer(s) to which the patient is invited to attribute the extent of his or her agreement or disagreement. Sometimes this takes the form of a Likert scale (e.g., 0 for "does not apply to me", 1 for "applies slightly", 2 for "moderately", 3 for "mostly", 4 for "strongly", etc.). At other times, respondents simply tick the boxes (always a dubious exercise) marked "does not apply" "slightly" "moderately" etc. Sometimes the only options are simple binary opposites (yes/no, true/false, applicable/inapplicable). These responses are then composed by the tester into scores claiming to represent the respondent's underlying (and enduring) psychological reality.

Illusions masquerading as facts: the psychometric disavowal of the unconscious

Numbers often seem more convincing than words, because

they create the illusion of objectivity and solidity. But nothing could be further from the truth. When it comes to human subjectivity, as we have already seen with the inapplicability of the physician's instruments to the psyche, the numbers relate to answers to a questionnaire or responses to a series of statements. The presupposition here is that mental suffering is caused by the presence of some pathological entity: cognitive-behaviourists, for example, like to talk about "cognitive distortions" which they believe are actually existing mental "things" equivalent to a congenitally malformed heart valve or an abnormal tissue mass. Conceived of as "errors of thinking," these imaginary entities render the task of the physician-mimicking psychologist is to identify them and then panel-beat them into alignment with "normal" cognitions.

There are several massive and vitiating presuppositions at work in this enterprise. To begin with, who can claim to be an expert on psychological normality? From a psychoanalytic point of view, as soon as you scratch the surface of an apparently "normal" individual (someone who publicly observes the customs and conventions of his or her culture, perhaps) you rapidly discover myriad eccentricities. For a psychoanalyst, there's nothing more "normal" than individually-specific private peculiarities. A CBT practitioner will see these as aberrations to be eradicated through a form of benevolent indoctrination, whereas for a psychoanalyst they are ciphered keys to the patient's unique but repressed truth.

Despite what they claim in their journals and conferences, no psychologist has ever "seen" or captured a "cognition", any more than they have captured an angel dancing on the head of a pin or a pixie at the bottom of the garden. The term "cognition" is a linguistic inference, a construction (the same applies to "personality" or "trait"). The only material the psychologist has had access to is the patient's speech.

But the psychometrician isn't interested in the patient's spontaneous speech. And that's because it's invariably loaded with inherently messy phenomena that resist standardisation, like slips of the tongue, unexpected verbal associations to an issue under discussion, defensive digressions, daydreams, bungled speech acts, and elements of fantasy (we often fill voids in knowledge, like how our parents felt about us when we were babies, with fantasies of what we imagined they felt: fantasy begins where knowledge ends).

This disregard for the ambiguity and equivocation of ordinary spontaneous human speech leads the psychometrician to coerce speech instead: the only thing that matters to the psychometrician who seeks to measure or identify "personality traits" or "cognitive distortions" are a series of refutable, propositional statements. When seduced by the collective fantasy of counting "cognitions", that's all that matters.

To the psychoanalyst however, it's precisely the multiple equivocations, fantasies, daydreams, digressions, etc., that matter, because psychoanalysts are interested in freely articulated human language, not illusory constructs like "cognitions." All these fundamentally "unstandardisable" elements of language are precisely the features of speech that indicate the fleeting emergence of truths that aren't yet available to conscious introspection. Or rather, they locate a momentary failure in the process of repression, which aims to keep the words that disturb or baffle us out of conscious discourse. We can only identify repression, which is utterly silent when operating smoothly (in a sense, it IS silence, or at least omission), when it transiently falters, allowing repressed verbal material to leak into conscious speech as if by accident.

Secondly, the presumption that it's possible to access this enigmatic, obscurely-ciphered, person-specific truth – the truth that forms the kernel of the individual's psychological symptoms - through a "standardised" set of questions or refutable statements takes it as read that people are perfectly transparent to themselves. The adolescent joyrider we met earlier, from this point of view, is simply being obstinately uncooperative with the nice helpful psychologist when he can't explain why he steals Mercedes cars.

This denial of an unconscious part of the mind can and does rapidly become savagely punitive in psychologies that ignore it: "can't," after all, isn't the same as "won't." Yet the latter is the likely judgment when the psychological ideology you are using has pretensions to being an empirical science. A science on the hunt for the presence of abnormalities. Rather than, say (as with psychoanalysis), an ethical practice allowing time and space for the emergence of hitherto consciously inaccessible signifiers that could lend meaning to an otherwise bizarre or incomprehensible symptom (or array of symptoms).

The perplexed boy would, in the absence of a viable concept of the unconscious in is "expert" examiner, find that his sincere bafflement would rapidly be redescribed by a CBT practitioner or psychometrician as deliberate evasiveness or obstructiveness.

Psychoanalysis helps people to notice what is absent in their narratives and rationalisations. And it encourages them to pursue these missing signifiers using their own words, while "egologies" regard psychological symptoms as essentially worthless cognitive errors that need to be removed through re-education.

For the psychoanalyst, the human subject is a sentient, intelligent being with unique "blanks" or voids in their conscious narratives – a being who can be encouraged to speak (make consciousness) psychic truths that have hitherto remained unarticulated. For the egologist, the suffering human being is a kind of dimwit, a twerp who has made cognitive errors and needs corrective coaching from an expert in normality.

This is frankly authoritarian and coercive, pressuring patients into silence or, worse, into acquiescence with the psychologist's definitions of what normal "cognitions" ought to be. Telling a terrified patient, for example, that she is "catastrophising" (a favourite term of CBT technicians working with anxious or traumatised patients) is little more than a sneering and contemptuous belittling of her truthful experience.

We have yet, however, to consider another pseudo-scientific illusion: the notion that human beings are repositories of more or less static information that can be reliably "mined", irrespective of the context of the mining operation.

The disavowed role of context: Minds are not "databanks"

There is, for example, an immense (and incommensurably unbridgeable) difference between piloting a trial-run of a psychometric test with volunteer undergraduates in a university psychology department and conducting the same test, despite its apparent credentials for reliability and validity, in a Family Court assessment. In the former setting, students have freely chosen whether or not to participate. They can be reasonably assured that the tester intends them no harm and that there will be no distressing consequences for them, like being expelled from their courses, merely for participating in the test.

The same is generally true of patients consulting a psychologist in a mental health/clinical setting. The psychologist has an ethical obligation to demonstrate beneficence at all times to his or her patients; in other words, bone fide chartered psychologists in clinical settings must never knowingly conduct themselves in such a way as to bring additional distress or damage to a patient and must act at all times to work in the interests of their patients' wellbeing.

How can this possibly pertain in a Family Court setting, where the expert administering the psychometric assessment to a parent may use its findings to recommend the forced removal of beloved children? Where is the beneficence? Is it remotely possible to collect reliable "data" from a terrified, indescribably stressed parent? Or might, just might, the terror and stress taint and vitiate the validity and reliability of the responses?

The supposition that human beings are walking databanks, with minds like computer hard drives loaded with 'information' that can be accurately and reliably accessed with a 'probe' like a questionnaire that may take no more than 30 minutes to administer, and irrespective of the context, is frankly delusional. And an exceedingly dangerous delusion at that, at least to those captive victims who feel obliged to undergo the ordeal for fear of turning the Court against them.

The conditions under which these tests are conducted on sentient, intelligent human beings make all the difference to the results they yield. Terrified and hyper-stressed people fearing the loss of their children do not respond identically to themselves when they are experiencing trust and psychological safety. They are not data warehouses waiting to be mined, but living beings with continually evolving minds whose mental representations, interpretations, perceptions and beliefs are in a ceaseless state of flux.

Finding psychopathology or producing it?

The assessment may iatrogenically produce what comes out of it. I communicate not merely to share data, like a robot, but to engage in exchange. When I am talking with a trusted friend, I let my thoughts and verbal associations to what we are discussing roam freely and easily. When I am feeling probed, I am inclined to resist; if I fear my interlocutor, I will spontaneously tailor my speech to a danger setting. What I say won't be "data" but human speech, riddled as it invariably is with involuntary aporia, equivocation and ambiguity as well as the defensive utterances (including hostility, resistiveness, attempts at placation, and so on) called forth by the nature and purpose of the conversation itself.

Hostility and fear are wholly intelligible and probably

unavoidable responses to any setting where one senses one is in great danger. And they are inevitably produced, not merely found, in psychometric assessments conducted in the context of the ultimate threat to a parent, where the prospect of the forcible and potentially permanent removal of one's children is under active consideration by the tester and the Court which appointed him or her.

All of this is ignored by standardised psychometric instruments, which as we've seen never let respondents speak in their own voices but force them instead to submit to prefabricated questions and statements devised by an "expert" who knows nothing about the unique particularities of their lives - and never will if they rely on tests like this, which are almost designed to exclude the uniquely subjective singularity of the individuals tested.

A psychoanalysis, by contrast, will typically take several years, with the assessment phase itself lasting as long as is necessary – usually many hours – to form a provisional diagnosis, which remains under review as treatment proceeds, and with both assessment and treatment privileging the patient's speech, not the analyst's.

Do standardised tests test subjectivity, or merely what the tests test?

The obsession with standardisation in contemporary clinical psychology, which many of its practitioners, it has to be said, seek to humanise with warmth, humour and kindness (at least in clinical settings), does not, as it claims, "objectively" measure that which is not subject to objective measurement: individual human subjectivity. Because it can't. It *objectifies* subjectivity instead, converting human psychic life from a dynamically evolving process into a static "thing." In other words, these assessments distort what they "access" or "measure" beyond recognition.

If we sense that someone is mired in some variety of subjective misery – fear, bleak melancholic withdrawal from life, acute grief, even physical pain – why should we assume that that suffering has no validity unless we "verify" it in some kind of "objective" form (a number on Likert scale, a biomarker in a blood test, an overall rating from a psychometric scale)?

If two mothers who have lost an adolescent child to suicide give different numerical scores to the extent of sadness, loss, anger, etc. they are experiencing, does that mean that one is suffering less than the other? Even if they give the same numerical ratings, do the numbers mean they are experiencing identical subjective states? My toleration of sadness may lead me to grant it a relatively low numerical rating, even though it is infernally intense, because it's become part of life's wallpaper, while someone less familiar with the mood may attribute a much higher number to it. Is one of us in more pain than the other? Or two people may give the same score to their sadness in a Beck Depression Inventory. But if one is suffering a psychotic depression and the other a reactive depression occasioned by a bereavement, the identical "score" will wholly obscure crucial clinical distinctions.

A polygraph test, preposterously referred to as a 'lie detector' test, actually 'objectively' measures highly contestable physical *proxies* for deceit, such as sweat, electrical conductivity of the skin, heart rate, etc. To assume that this furnishes an objective measure of the quantity of truth being emitted by the subject is to fall into absurdity: an experienced, psychopathic liar will remain unperturbed throughout and appear virtuously honest, whereas a nervous, neurotically guilt-prone but entirely innocent person will perspire and heart-thump his way to a "pants on fire" verdict.

The agony of bereavement is no less real for being impossible to quantify, and in fact the language of objective measurement simply devalues the speech of the suffering person.

Why the spontaneous, idiosyncratic speech of the suffering subject matters: a clinical example from psychoanalysis

A middle-aged man who has recently experienced a double trauma – the loss of his ambivalently-loved father after a short but aggressive illness, followed shortly afterwards by the collapse of his once-thriving business, which he'd spent his entire adult life building – is drowning in despair that he can barely articulate. He just wants to die and is fighting what seems like a losing battle: the struggle against the siren-like desire to end it all, as the anguish of being has become intolerable.

A year or so after his father's death, he recounts to his analyst a dream that he'd had the previous evening:

He is walking along a bleak but beautiful and deserted beach. With great suddenness, the sky darkens with massive, slate-grey clouds. The wind starts to roar and howl, and droplets of rain from the now-blackening, lightning-streaked heavens turn rapidly into a violently torrential deluge. Most disturbing of all, the once-calm sea surges and rises with mountainous waves, coal-black but glistening in the night-like darkness, streaked with foam as they swell and crash. The demonic waters draw menacingly toward him and he begins to sense that he will shortly be swallowed irretrievably by them. Instead of feeling "At last, my life is ending," he feels afraid.

At this point he notices a wooden shack on the beach, and rushes toward it. There is a key in the lock of the door, which he frantically turns. He is able to enter and close the door behind him. The shack (the man actually says "shed" this time) has a large window facing the sea. As he stands before it, a colossal, black wave smashes into the shed and he hears the glass shatter as he turns away in horror. He is convinced he is done for and expects icy sea water to engulf him and drag him out to oblivion. But to his astonishment, the glass has not broken. It has shattered, yes, but all the pieces remain intact, even though it has bowed inwards under the impact of the wave. Outside, to his relief, the waves are receding.

After a pause of a few moments, his analyst asks him why he referred to the shack as a shed. He hardly needs to think for long: "It was a rather solidly-constructed shed that my father built in our garden when I was a boy. He let me help him, and I used to like going in there to read after it was built. I felt at peace and safe and cosy there."

Much of the analysis to date had been taken up with the man's complicated and often troubled relationship with his father. He had grown up feeling that he had disappointed his father, and that his father disliked him beneath a veneer of dutiful fatherly love. His father could be verbally harsh, but was never physically violent. Even so, the patient felt that his father hadn't "been there" when he needed him as an adolescent, especially when he was unhappy at school and struggling to cope with being bullied.

And yet: being within a shed constructed by his father made him feel safe and secure. He spoke the question now forming in in his mind out loud, "Was I underestimating my Dad?"

The analyst quietly suggested, "Perhaps you were more protected by your father's love than you thought. His shed saved you in your dream. Maybe you have more of his strength that you knew."

The man begins to silently cry. He begins to speak of his

sudden realisation that he had simply failed to appreciate and even notice his father's quiet but steady devotion to him throughout his boyhood and adulthood, had failed to appreciate that his father was refusing to pretend that the world could be made safe and was instead encouraging his son to become tougher and braver to withstand it. A profound sense of gratitude came over him.

These words of his brought a new perspective to the relationship that had never occurred to him before. The depression began to lift from that day onwards, recurring every so often in relation to contingent life stresses, but less severely. Several years later it was completely absent.

The pivotal importance of the patient's speech

As the American-born Lacanian psychoanalyst Bruce Fink has lucidly argued, what had dispelled this dangerous, suicidal depression wasn't the cleverness of the analyst or "expert", who in this instance merely offered a brief, provisional suggestion, but the ensuing words of the patient. He began *to bring to speech truths that had never been spoken before*, and the effects were transformative.

This process – bringing to speech truths that had never been spoken before (and therefore never made conscious) - would never have been permitted to arise in either a standardised psychometric assessment or a standardised-manualised treatment such as CBT, both of which flatly and brutally disregard subjective, idiosyncratic speech (and certainly dreams, no matter how crucial they feel to the patient) in favour of propositional statements devised by an "expert."

In conclusion

If you are asked to undergo a psychometric assessment by a Family Court-appointed psychological "expert", you may be well advised to insist on another means of assessment, one that takes full account of your own chosen words and descriptions. It is exceedingly easy for the Court to hear none of this when perusing a psychological expert's report. They will see instead what he or she has concluded based on your responses to questions and statements that were not your own, but imposed on you by the test. And these experts will dress their subjective and erroneous interpretations, based on their own erroneous hypothetical constructs, in the language of scientific objectivity, replete with correlational statistics to complete the illusion of validity.

I will leave the last words to the psychoanalyst and clinical psychologist David Ferraro:

"If your psychological 'therapy' is one that a court could or does order, then it isn't a therapy at all, but an ideological program; and you are not a 'therapist', but rather, a kind of cop."

https://melbournelacanian.wordpress.com/2016/01/30/notes-on-ethics-and-psychoanalysis/'

Wherever possible seek out your own choice of an expert for any assessments.

Do not approach any solicitors firm that is on the list given to you by Social Services. Often when social workers tell you they are considering care proceedings or have issued a Public Law Outline (PLO) to you they will give you a list of local family law solicitors. In either of the previously mentioned circumstances you are entitled to legal aid. Although the local authority will not tell you, these solicitors firms are often frequently employed by the local authority. One day they can be in court supposedly representing you–the next day acting in a case for the local authority. The simple adage here is that those solicitors firms are not going to 'bite the hand that feeds them'. Your case and the paltry legal aid fees are nothing compared to the full professional fees that can be earned working on behalf of the local authority. It follows that a solicitor who fights hard for parents and wins against the local authority is soon going to find that their lucrative contracts with them will dry up.

If approaching a solicitor look for one in the neighbouring counties or even further afield. If there are no links with your local authority then the solicitor may just put up a reasonable fight for you. Always remember though that as a Litigant in Person you can say exactly what you wish, but with a solicitor you may lose that opportunity.

The system in the UK will not let a couple, even if you are man and wife, have the same representative. In many ways that makes sense, as you want someone dedicated to your aspect of the case, particularly if you are seen as the cause of concern or are being alleged to have been a perpetrator of domestic violence or some other allegation. Not by your partner I may add, but by the social workers (it is amazing the number of cases where I have couples telling me that such incidents have never occurred, yet the social worker has it as a key concern). However, what the system does by this position is very similar to the advice outlined above regarding being pressured to split from your partner–it offers the opportunity of divide and rule. Your solicitor may say you are not the issue so by condemning your partner you will get the children or similar. Generally that is a ruse, because agreeing that your partner has done something they haven't doesn't necessarily bring the children to you but the courts find that yes the partner has done X, Y or Z and you have failed to protect, so you are not safe to have your children either. The best course of action is for one of you to have a solicitor/barrister and the other to self represent-that way you can maintain a unified position.

These seemingly small but significant issues can be the making or breaking of your case. You will always be stronger together.

Do not trust any professional involved with child protection. It has been said previously but it is worth repeating. Your midwife, health visitor, GP, or your child's teachers may have had a brilliant relationship with you, but child protection is so emotive a subject that no one wants to get anything 'wrong'.

Hence you should be wary of these professionals, as they soon become the eyes and ears of social workers, effectively acting like a modern day Stasi and reporting back everything to the social workers. They will be looking more closely, seeking issues where none were even considered before. They will judge you, assess you (unofficially) and then you will find these very professionals arranged around a table at a social services meeting. Again, be wary of what you tell these people, as nothing is ever 'off the record.'

The final generalised rule is seek help and advice–do not be taken in by a social worker telling you that you cannot discuss your case with anyone. You are entirely free to seek advice, whether it be from a legal advisor, lay advocates, other parents, or your family. There is a lot of information out there, sadly some of it can be inaccurate, lead you down pseudo law paths (Freeman, Sovereign citizen,) conspiracy theories (such as social workers are paid a bonus for each removed/adopted child–they aren't and never have been) and although well meant, at times given without any real knowledge of the system. Always seek a range of advice and information and make up your own mind. Remember the only way to beat the system is to use the system. The law doesn't just work for social workers, it works for you too.

Those are just overview, generalised rules that will set you up to be in a far stronger position to deal social services intervention. We will now turn to more in-depth strategies that can stop the social workers in their tracks and move on to easier targets. I do not wish to sound derogatory by that last remark but those who take the time to research and fight back at every opportunity have the greatest chance of removing these people from their lives. This section is really the backbone of this text and our aim here is to avoid having to deal with the contents of the Chapter 7-The Courts.

Chapter 5: How to Fight Back

(2) Complaints

As a parent facing social services, it is likely that you have sought advice, through the world-wide web, family, friends and the legal profession. One piece of advice you may receive, is do not complain as this will just make the situation worse, but work with the social workers and it will all be okay. Well, the advice here may be out on a limb, but I say complain, complain to as wide a range of people, organisations, regulators and authorities as possible.

The basic reason–if you don't complain about something that is incorrect, inaccurate, not done to procedure or even illegal and you try to raise that later you will be simply met with the 'wall' of 'well you raised no issues about that, you accepted that' and so forth. In my humble opinion, but based upon the success of many cases, you need to challenge every tiny aspect of their dealings with you, even points you may think are just niggling or trivial-let nothing go. You are in a war of attrition and your attack and defence strategies are to have as many 'fronts' open as possible. You want to tie these people down to having to respond to your issues with their actions. Remember these people are 'Public Servants' and thus owe duties to the public they serve. Make them adhere to the rules.

(i) Children's Services (the Social Services)

Complaints about the way your case is being handled, the actions of the social workers, the reports they write, the methods they use in engaging with you, just about every aspect falls under the auspices of Section 26 of the Children's Act 1989. The key sections are below:

Section 26

(3)Every local authority shall establish a procedure for considering any representations (including any complaint) made to them by—

(a)any child who is being looked after by them or who is not being looked after by them but is in need;

(b)a parent of his;

(c)any person who is not a parent of his but who has parental responsibility for him;

(d)any local authority foster parent;

(e)such other person as the authority consider has a sufficient interest in the child's welfare to warrant his representations

---

being considered by them,

about the discharge by the authority of any of their [F9qualifying functions] in relation to the child.

[F10(3A) The following are qualifying functions for the purposes of subsection (3)—

(a) functions under this Part,

(b) such functions under Part 4 or 5 as are specified by the [F11Secretary of State] in regulations.

(3B) The duty under subsection (3) extends to representations (including complaints) made to the authority by—

(a) any person mentioned in section 3(1) of the Adoption and Children Act 2002 (persons for whose needs provision is made by the Adoption Service) and any other person to whom arrangements for the provision of adoption support services (within the meaning of that Act) extend,

(b) such other person as the authority consider has sufficient interest in a child who is or may be adopted to warrant his representations being considered by them,

about the discharge by the authority of such functions under the Adoption and Children Act 2002 as are specified by the [F12Secretary of State] in regulations.]

[F13(3C) The duty under subsection (3) extends to any representations (including complaints) which are made to the authority by—

(a)a child with respect to whom a special guardianship order is in force,

(b)a special guardian or a parent of such a child,

(c)any other person the authority consider has a sufficient interest in the welfare of such a child to warrant his representations being considered by them, or

(d)any person who has applied for an assessment under section 14F(3) or (4),

about the discharge by the authority of such functions under section 14F as may be specified by the [F14Secretary of State] in regulations.]

(4)The procedure shall ensure that at least one person who is not a member or officer of the authority takes part in—

(a)the consideration; and

(b)any discussions which are held by the authority about the action (if any) to be taken in relation to the child in the light of the consideration

[F15but this subsection is subject to subsection (5A).]

[F16(4A)Regulations may be made by the [F17Secretary of State] imposing time limits on the making of representations under this section.]

(5)In carrying out any consideration of representations under this section a local authority shall comply with any regulations made by the [F18Secretary of State] for the purpose of regulating the procedure to be followed.

[F19(5A)Regulations under subsection (5) may provide that subsection (4) does not apply in relation to any consideration or discussion which takes place as part of a procedure for which provision is made by the regulations for the purpose of resolving informally the matters raised in the representations.]

(6)The [F20Secretary of State] may make regulations requiring local authorities to monitor the arrangements that they have made with a view to ensuring that they comply with any regulations made for the purposes of subsection (5).

(7)Where any representation has been considered under the procedure established by a local authority under this section, the authority shall—

(a)have due regard to the findings of those considering the representation; and

(b)take such steps as are reasonably practicable to notify (in writing)—

(i)the person making the representation;

(ii)the child (if the authority consider that he has sufficient

> *understanding); and*
>
> *(iii)such other persons (if any) as appear to the authority to be likely to be affected, of the authority's decision in the matter and their reasons for taking that decision and of any action which they have taken, or propose to take.*
>
> *(8)Every local authority shall give such publicity to their procedure for considering representations under this section as they consider appropriate.]*[xxii]

It is worth examining the text because there are several aspects of the duties placed upon the local authority regarding the complaints system that infrequently get translated into the reality of how complaints are dealt with by the local authority. Knowing what they should be doing as opposed to what they may tell you they are doing in handling a complaint offers the possibility of widening the whole nature of your complaint, perhaps even to the level of a legal challenge.

The legislation states that under *'Section 26 (4)The procedure shall ensure that <u>at least one person who is not a member or officer of the authority</u> takes part in—*

(a)the consideration; and (b)any discussions which are held by the authority about the action (if any) to be taken in

relation to the child in the light of the consideration

[F15but this subsection is subject to subsection (5A).]'

So let's look at a typical LA complaint procedure. This examination focuses on the example of Somerset County Council's process[xxiii].

The standardised format you will get from most local authorities follows a 'three stage process' and when you delve into it, you find that the initial stages of any complaint are processed in a manner that is contrived to close the complaint down as soon as possible.

The first step is 'Informal Resolution.' It means sorting out the problem 'locally' i.e. with your social worker or their manager. So we will ask the very people we are complaining about to resolve the problem. That is we will ask them to investigate themselves! Call me cynical, but how many social workers will say they have got it wrong? Your complaint will fall at the first hurdle. Notice here that no person who is 'not a member or officer of the authority' is involved. This is allowed under *'(5A) Regulations under subsection (5) may provide that subsection (4) does not apply in relation to any consideration or discussion which takes place as part of a*

217

procedure for which provision is made by the regulations for the purpose of resolving informally the matters raised in the representations.'

So it is fair we may conclude that the informal resolution process will fail.

The next step is 'Stage 1 Local Resolution.' This is the actual start of a formal complaint being logged. According to our example local authority this process 'is an investigation by the service'.

We are still dealing with the same people as at the informal stage. We may get someone else within the service, but it is still the same department investigating itself. If you have labelled your complaint as being under Section 26, then there should be an external person appointed, but again this is missing. There is a time limit of 10 days to reply, a limit that will probably be breached. In fact they are likely to respond that they need more time and will give you a new date. If you haven't cottoned on yet, your complaint has now taken several weeks and still you have got nowhere.

In all likelihood there is unlikely to be any findings in your favour and you will be fobbed off with the fact they have 'concerns' and they have a legal duty to investigate. But, don't be down-hearted as we can go to 'Stage 2 Formal investigation.'

Stage 2 is where we finally get our so called independent investigator in. However look at how Somerset word their description:

'*A Stage 2 investigation is carried out by someone who is independent from the service.*' From experience this means it is probably someone who is still in the employ of the local authority but not in the Social Services Department, possibly someone from the authority's complaints team. This means that the LA are actually violating the law. The legislation specifically stipulates that there should be at least one member who is not a member or officer of the authority. This of itself means that you can jump start the process directly to the Local Government Ombudsman. You can escalate your complaint based on the fact that the LA is effectively acting *ultra vires* (outside of the law) and as a result your rights are being violated. We shall turn to the Local Government Ombudsman shortly, but for now we shall return to the next stage of the complaint process.

Under Stage 2 any investigation under the statutory process (which is what all complaints should be made under i.e. section 26 of the Children Act 1989) should be completed within 25 working days, but this may 'where necessary be extended to a maximum of 65 working days'. Again as you can see the time-line is constantly slipping. However, this can benefit you, as anything you have challenged that continues to arise in reports or at Child Protection meetings/Core groups and the like can be put in question and that no reliance may be made upon such information, as it is the subject of a complaint.

If the outcome of the Stage 2 process does not achieve what you were seeking, the final process is Stage 3. You have 20 working days to arrange a meeting with the Service Director to discuss his or her response and to move to Stage 3. This time the complaint is examined by a panel of three individuals who should be completely independent of the local authority. A date will be arranged for the panel to meet to review your complaint within 30 working days. The panel will have copies of all the complaints files and you should also summarise your complaint to it and detail why you feel the complaint has not been resolved. Specify what action you expect the authority to take to resolve the complaint.

A panel hearing will discuss the case and you are free to take along someone to support you or speak on your behalf. The panel then produces a report with any recommendations they see the LA could take to resolve the complaint and you should have this within five working days of the hearing. The LA will respond within fifteen working days. As always, be prepared for slippage and the extension of the timetable. This is the end of the line with the LA. If your complaint is not resolved, you have the option of complaining to the Local Government Ombudsman

The Local Government Ombudsman

PO Box 4771

Coventry

CV4 0EH 47

Tel: 0300 061 0614

Fax 024 7682 0001

Website: http://www.lgo.org.uk

The Local Government Ombudsman (LGO), is one of a set of organisations I have nick-named 'toothless wonders'. They describe themselves as 'the final stage for complaints about councils, all adult social care providers (including care homes and home care agencies) and some other organisations providing local public services. We are a free service. We investigate complaints in a fair and independent way-we do not take sides.' What is interesting is that although you are told by the LA that you can go to the Local Government Ombudsman at any point during your complaint the Ombudsman themselves expect that you should have gone 'through all stages of their complaints procedure'. They further stipulate that you must bring any complaint within twelve months. If you look back over the stages, it can be seen that it is very easy for the LA to drag their heels and ensure that you actually fall outside of this time frame. Thus, you must not let the complaint(s) drag on, because any failure to move things ahead after the Stage 1 complaint should have you considering moving it to the LGO.

Generally, the LGO will look at service failures such as:

- Delay
- Poor record keeping

- Failure to take action
- Failure to follow procedures or the law
- Poor communication
- Giving out misleading information
- Failure to investigate
- The organisation not doing what it said it would

So as you compile your complaint the above is a little aide memoir as to the issues you need to focus upon. A quick glance through that list pretty much sums up exactly what social workers do wrong most of time. It is appalling that they get away with it day in and day out. It is interesting to note though that Children's and Education Services complaints were upheld in 63% of the cases referred. I would say that it is a telling statistic of how often social workers and children's departments step out of line.

However, even if the LGO upholds your complaint what can you expect?

'We will make one of the following decisions:

- *Uphold your complaint and recommend how the organisation should put things right*
- *Uphold only part of your complaint*

- *Uphold your complaint but not make any recommendations because the organisation may have put things right by the time we decide your complaint*
- *Uphold your complaint but not make any recommendations as we consider the fault didn't have a significant effect on you*
- *Not uphold your complaint*
- *We cannot or will not investigate your complaint*

&

We might ask the organisation to:

- *apologise to you*
- *provide a service you should have had*
- *make a decision it should have done before*
- *reconsider a decision it did not take properly in the first place*
- *improve its procedures so similar problems do not happen again*
- *make a payment'*

Ultimately the value of having a complaint upheld is that it gives you leverage against the LA, however any court proceedings do not necessarily have to acknowledge any of the LGO's findings, but they may. If the LGO fails you you do have the option of undertaking a Judicial Review of the LGO's findings. However, I would suggest that the LGO is not the body you really want to be dragging into court, your sights should be firmly set on the Children's Services Department of the local authority and as we shall see it is this organisation that a Judicial Review will be most effective against.

This is clearly a bureaucratic process, that is time-consuming, but throughout the process you must remember that you are creating extra pressure and work for the social services team. They will need to provide their own responses to the complaints, they can be asked to clarify points by the independent reviewers. Of course there is no limit to the number of complaints you can raise, though it makes sense to choose each complaint wisely so no one can say that you are simply being vexatious, and thus you must ensure that what you chose to complain about are valid concerns that relate to practice, procedures and rights.

To really make your complaint have some weight behind it, it is important to spread the complaint to the widest possible audience of possibly 'interested' parties. Send a copy to:

Director of Children's Services

The Leader of the Council,
CEO of the Council
Local Councillor
Councillor responsible for Families and/or Children (Lead Member)

Opposition Councillor spokesperson or Families and/or Children

The County Solicitor
The Complaints Manager
Social Worker & SW Team leader/Area Manager (if known)
Ofsted
Department for Education

The Minister for Children
Local MP.

Provide a cover letter asking the person to investigate the wrongs and although it is highly unlikely, with some not responding at all, some may and may also ask questions of the service. This is what you want. Social Services are effectively a closed shop and you need to get people shining a light on them and their practices. This is particularly effective with Local Councillors, the lead member and their shadow cabinet opposite number, because you can point out that all councillors are vicariously liable for what is undertaken in their names. They are in effect corporate parents.

I have outlined the complaint process in the LA and, when you review it, it looks on the surface to be a rather long-winded pointless exercise. However by making a formal complaint and escalating it you are getting your issues with the Children's Services department officially recorded. That could become exceptionally useful later.

You can of course make official complaints about the individual *fitness to practice* of social workers. It is often a good idea to run such a complaint in parallel to the LA complaint.

In the England the regulatory body is the Health & Care and Professions Council (HCPC). (The Children and Social Work Act 2017 was granted Royal Assent on Thursday 27 April 2017 and the act sets out that the new regulator will be called Social Work England and will set standards for social workers and ensure public protection. At the moment no timetable is set for this change).

In Wales, Social Care Wales is the regulator, in Northern Ireland the Northern Ireland Social Care Council and the Scottish Social Services Council (SSSC) for Scotland. Although they are devolved to the regions of the UK they all operate under a Memorandum of Understanding. In the Republic of Ireland CORU is the regulator for social workers.

Any social worker working or wishing to work in any of those countries **must** be registered with the appropriate regulator. Further Social Worker is a designated title, which makes a person who claims that title must be qualified to do so. Anyone who uses it and is not registered and/or who misuses a designated title is breaking the law and may be prosecuted. Each regulator holds a register, and it is possible to check if your Social Worker is registered.

In all the regions anyone can raise a concern about a registrant. This includes members of the public, employers, the police and other health and care professionals.

The fitness to practise concern is a high bar to cross in terms of making a complaint stick. It generally means that the registrant is 'impaired' in their ability to practise effectively or safely.

One off 'mistakes' or unprofessional conduct/behaviour won't really be pursued by the regulator, but if you can show a litany of poor practice and/or unprofessional conduct, then there is a greater chance of a full investigation and possible fitness to practice hearing. In other words as far as the regulators are concerned the bar is set exceptionally high before they will act and that means in reality that a social worker can get away with many instances of unprofessional conduct, poor behaviour and poor practice, because not every family they are acting in this way with will actually make a complaint. Therefore anyone who does make a complaint is likely to be dismissed as a lone voice and the issue seen as a one-off and relatively minor. I say it is a poor way to regulate any profession. Any complaint made, must be thorough in its execution.

The way to do that is to examine the codes of professional conduct and ethics[xxiv] that social workers must abide by, in order to continue to be registered. The codes are far too long to include here so they are reproduced in full in Appendix A for the HCPC (which pretty much can be read for the whole of the UK) and in Appendix B for the Republic of Ireland. By carefully matching the issues you have with a social worker's conduct to the standards, you can build a case that demonstrates how they have failed in their basic duties under the standards. Below is an example of a real letter (individuals redacted) that demonstrates the use of the standards to make a complaint.

Dear xxx

I wish to make a **formal complaint** about xxx, Senior Social Worker.

On 13/04/2016 I sent an E mail to xxx with regard to the undertaking of an assessment. This E mail simply, politely and lawfully set out my request to have the assessment undertaken in the jurisdiction of Ireland rather than in the UK (where I currently reside) and my reasoning thereof.

It appears I was then copied in to a reply to this E mail which had been sent by xxx to xxx in which xxx exclaimed **"Omg he is a pompous git! C u after lunch."**

You can imagine my utter dismay that a so-called *'professional'* would not only refer to a service user/client in such a derogatory fashion, but that they would use this language and descriptors to another colleague.

This is not only unprofessional and unethical but abusive. It is clear that when professionals speak like that to each other about a service user/client that they are failing not only in good practice but clearly have an opinion that will colour and bias any dealings that that professional and their team will have with the particular individual. In this case the individual is me. All trust in professional standards, objectivity and transparency has now been destroyed and leads me to believe that I would never be able to obtain a fair and transparent, honest or unbiased hearing at the hands of this so called professional.

The Standards of Ethics, Conduct and Performance expected of Registered Social Workers states clearly what is expected of a Social Worker:

"To protect the public, you must comply with this Code of Professional Conduct and

Ethics.

The social work values informing this code are

Respect for the inherent dignity and worth of persons

Pursuit of social justice

Integrity of professional practice

Confidentiality in professional practice

Competence in professional practice."

Immediately it can be seen that xxx has failed on all the core values. It is clear that xxx has no respect for my dignity or worth, no social justice can be achieved whereby a social worker can describe a service user as a 'pompous git', her integrity is highly questionable and she has no respect for confidentiality as if she can make such a basic error as sending her disgusting comments to me as well as her colleague, then one has to question what other basic errors of confidentiality she has or is likely to make. Of course all the above goes to the heart of her competence to practice.

According to the code she should be upholding human rights in her practice, by:

'respecting the right to self-determination; promoting the right to participation and

treating each person in a caring and respectful fashion.' Evidently I am not to be afforded any of those by xxx.

By belittling my requested actions in my email with her squalid outburst she has failed in 'Respecting service users' relationships

In your practice, you should respect service users' relationships with their families and other

caring relationships. You should also show respect for colleagues and others working to help *service users.'* Her failure is not just at me but also in respect of her colleagues.

She further fails on the integrity guidelines which clearly state that she should be:

'Carrying out your duties professionally and ethically

a) To protect the public you must: carry out your duties and responsibilities in a professional and ethical way; always behave with integrity and honesty.

b) Your practice should benefit and not harm others. Often difficult decisions must be made that

may be perceived as harmful by a service user. If there is a conflict of interests between the

service user and the safeguarding of children or other vulnerable people, safeguarding should

take precedence.'

I do not believe that such a comment made by xxx can be said in any way to fulfil her obligations. Her practice is certainly not benefiting me and clearly due to her biases I am likely to suffer harm by her in that I will not and cannot obtain a fair, honest and unbiased consideration by her and her team.

It is clear that she is failing to act in the best interests of service users as required by the code:

'You must: treat service users as individuals; respect diversity, different cultures and values and not condone, facilitate or collaborate with any form of discrimination; respect and, where appropriate, promote or advocate the views and wishes of service users and carers;

support service users' rights to take part in all aspects of the service and to make informed choices about the service they receive; ' again all this is sadly lacking.

Perhaps of greatest concern is that such actions by xxx brings the service into disrepute.

She has not '*Maintained high standards of personal conduct.'*

She has caused *'abuse, harm or neglect service users, carers or colleagues;*

behaved in a way that would call into question your suitability to work in health and social care

professional services; and engaged in conduct that is likely to damage the public's confidence in you or in her profession. '

There are a range of other competencies and issues that can be called into question in the code, which I am sure you are well aware of and it is clear that xxx actions brings into question her fitness to practice. Thus I am obligated to report xxx actions to CORU.

I expect that xxx and her team are removed from our family case forthwith. That a thorough investigation is carried out and disciplinary action is undertaken and that you will also report this violation of the code and raise a fitness to practice complaint yourselves with CORU.

There can be no excuse or explanation for this completely unacceptable action. I do not think that anyone with a shred of integrity or intelligence would deem my email anything but polite, clear and based upon sound logic and law. Pompous it certainly was not. As for being a 'git'–I actually wonder if xxx even knows what that means. The OED states it is *'An unpleasant or contemptible person.'* Clearly that is xxx view of me and as such being the holder of such discriminatory and unethical views she should be suspended immediately as her relationship with service users is likely to cause abuse or harm. There can be no hiding behind the fact that the email was sent inadvertently to me, what it does is demonstrate the way that xxx views and treats service users. I suspect that I am not the only one who has been on the receiving end of her contempt. Highly unprofessional.

xxx email of 17.41 today, xx/xx/16 -does not suffice as any apology – this is clearly back-covering- it is unequivocal that her email, sent to xxx WAS referencing me as it was a direct response to xxx forwarding my email regarding the assessment she had sent to her. I will not be fobbed off or accept this inappropriate apology – at least she should have had the decency to admit that she was referring to me and made a sincere apology on that basis, though that would not suffice for the clear lack of professionalism and breaking of the vast majority of the code of conduct as outlined above. I expect that there will be genuine consequences for this major public policy failure.

I look forward to your swift reply and how you intend to bring an effective remedy to this situation.

Yours faithfully

As can be seen, fitting the issue to the action builds the severity of the complaint. Although we have said the bar is high, and it is very difficult to get the regulators to issue fitness to practice proceedings the very fact that you issue such a complaint brings pressure on the individual and the department.

Most importantly it demonstrates that you are aware of their obligations and your rights. Look at it as a warning shot across their bows that you are onto them and that you will be focused on ensuring that they do everything to the letter. Making them abide by their obligations and most importantly the law can have a major effect on how your case progresses. If they cannot get away with being unprofessional or deceitful, then you have a good opportunity of stopping the case in its tracks sooner rather than later.

Complaining about the Police.

Frequently parents find themselves having confrontations with the police who for various reasons accompany social workers on visits. They are of course, they part of the multi-agency working and provide information about parents to Child Protection and other meetings. Often there is a mis-use of police powers to ensure a child is removed without a court order being in place (to which we shall return). So there can be a myriad of reasons that it may be necessary to make a formal complaint about the police.

It is best to complain directly to the police force in question before looking to the IPCC or Garda Ombudsman and it can be done by either attending at a police station, filling in a complaint form which are usually available on their websites, by a letter to the Chief Constable/the Police Complaints Department or even through your MP/TD who can make a complaint on your behalf. Make your complaint immediately; don't allow too much time to pass.

You will find that most complaints are dealt with by what is called Local Resolution and although you may object to this, the police do not have to acquiesce to your objections and may continue at that level. Any outcome of a complaint that you aren't happy with can then be passed to the IPCC/ Ombudsman.

Again the purpose of the complaint is not necessarily to get findings in your favour as to be honest such internal investigations are unlikely to find their officers at fault because the institutional nature of the organisation will definitely 'look after their own.' However you are again raising issues about failures to adhere to policy, procedures, the law and of course your rights. It is these areas that you need to focus on in your complaint, to demonstrating how the officers actions have violated each aspect. It is certainly a good idea to copy your complaints in to your Police and Crime Commissioner (England and Wales) and your local MP.

Complaints about NHS Staff.

As we have seen, there is a myriad of health professionals who may be involved in your case, despite some of them never even having met your children or you previously. It matters not which health professional it is that is causing you an issue you can make a complaint about them and their actions to the NHS[xxv] and to their regulators.

Every NHS organisation has specific complaints procedure and you can ask the particular service, i.e. GP, Midwife, Health visitor for a copy of the complaints procedure, however it is also perfectly acceptable to address the complaint to the manager at the particular health centre location where the health care professional is based. From there it will be passed to the correct person for investigation. You can complain by making a complaint in writing, by email or by speaking to the individual.

If you speak to them, they may be able to resolve your concerns without you having to go through the formal complaints process. There is a local resolution available, which effectively means raising the issue with the provider and them sorting it out, however that is unlikely to happen where child protection is involved. Thus the formal complaint is generally required.

As with the previous advice, make your complaint as soon as possible especially as there is a time limit for NHS complaint- 12 months from the date the event happened, or 12 months from the date you first became aware of the issue. If you need help with making a complaint, you can approach your local patient Advice and Liaison Service (PALS) and/or The NHS Complaints Independent Advocacy Service. The Process itself is summarised by the Government as thus:

'Making a complaint:

If you would like to make a complaint you can go either directly to the organisation that provided your care (the 'provider') or to the relevant organisation that bought the service you received (the 'commissioner').

If your issue is resolved, then there is no further action.

If your issue is not resolved then you can refer your complaint to the 'Parliamentary and Health Service Ombudsman' for further investigation.'

As can be seen if you are unhappy with the response to your complaint then you escalate it to the Parliamentary and Health Service Ombudsman[xxvi].

You can complain about a professionals conduct, reports they write (if they are inaccurate, defamatory or go beyond their professional remit), their failure to provide a service and any inappropriate behaviour. Once again the focus is on the policy, procedure and your rights.

These are probably the key bodies that you may find yourself needing to make a complaint to about their staff. These are also the individuals you will probably find facing you and writing reports on you for child protection conferences. So where there is a reason to complain, you should as it is powerful to sit in a conference and be able to raise the fact that a number of people opposite you are actually the subject of a complaint. It is possible to argue that reports should be withdrawn or at least have no reliance placed upon them whilst the author of that report is under investigation. If the chair disagrees or allows decisions to be made on the basis of those questionable reports, then it opens up the basis for a considerable complaint against the legitimacy of the meeting's decisions and not least the possibility of legal action.

Finally of course, do not make complaints where there is no legitimacy in your complaint. You need to have your complaint based on facts and evidence paired to the policies, procedures, the law and your rights. Fortunately the vast majority of cases have at least some aspect of these issues, but to pursue frivolous complaints can do your case no good in the long term, so your complaint must be based on genuine breaches.

Chapter 5: How to Fight Back

(3) Knowledge is power

To be able to make effective complaints you need to know four key areas about child protection.

(i) Children's and Child Protection Law. This is a huge area and far more wide ranging than a book such as this could encompass. However, there are some fundamental areas that you need to be aware of and of course where to look for further information to grow your knowledge.

(ii) The guidelines that social workers use. The most important being 'Working Together' (England), 'Children First' (Ireland), Regional Policies and Procedures (N. Ireland), 'All Wales Child Protection Procedures' (Wales) and National Guidance for Child Protection (in Scotland). These all lay out the procedures adopted and how social workers should manage child protection cases. In some instances the material has a legislative basis whilst in others it is national guidance and good practice.

(iii) Your rights and your children's rights, which includes the European Convention on Human Rights, the United Nations

Convention on Rights of the Child. You will also see we cover some other important conventions, which are often ignored in cases of child protection.

(iv) The Codes of Standards, Practice and ethics by which each professional must adhere, as well as their public expectation as a public servant.

It must be noted that this isn't exhaustive, for example, if you want to complain about a health visitor you need to know the standards by which they must adhere. Equally police conduct needs careful examination of the law that attributes powers to them, to know if they are acting legally in their actions. What follows will give you an extensive framework upon which you can build and hopefully provide you with the confidence to challenge the system.

The Law.

Often when you are the victim of social work intervention you are ground down by the system. Social workers will tell you that they have to investigate, because that's the law, they will refer to 'statutory' (i.e. legal) visits to see your children, that they have a legal right to enter your home (they don't). To you, it seems like the law is simply stacked against you and that you are drowning under their onslaught. The law however works for you too, it provides you with protections and rights. It's time to turn the tables on the social workers. To do this, you must understand the basic precepts of the law under which they are operating.

The over-riding child law in the UK is the Children Act 1989, we have already alluded to it a number of times. This is the law that both private proceedings and public (i.e. usually care proceedings) fall under in England and Wales. Scotland and Northern Ireland have their own versions and in the Republic of Ireland it is the Child Care Act 1991 with which we are concerned. We shall come back to the other laws that supplement and build on this pivotal law.

The Children's Act 1989 provides the framework surrounding the care and protection of children. It supposedly puts the welfare of the child centre stage in matters pertaining to parental responsibility, safeguarding as well as inter agency cooperation. It confers powers upon the Local Authorities, Police and other agencies in matters pertaining to child protection. We shall examine the most frequently used sections of this act that parents will hear about and face.

Section 1 of the act covers the 'Paramountcy Principle' that essentially makes the welfare of the child the most important aspect of all decision making when it comes to the upbringing of a child. Courts should always apply the no order principle, which means that the court should only make an order when it is better for the outcomes of the child than not making an order. The child's wishes and feelings should be taken into account by the court (where the child is mature enough) and perhaps most importantly and perhaps most ignored–that <u>every effort should be made to preserve the child's home and family links.</u>

The latter point is often completely ignored by social workers, who it would appear seem hell bent on removing children from their family and distancing them as much as possible from their kin. Knowing this at the outset of your dealings with the social workers is crucial. This allows you to put the onus back on to the local authority to demonstrate how they are working with you, providing the support they perceive you need and acting within Section 1 at all times. The preservation of family does not just suddenly appear within court proceedings, it is there and relevant from the social worker ringing your door bell. That allows you to ensure that you make it known to the social worker that you expect them to uphold this piece of law.

You can question their every action in the context of 'How does this further the aim to ensuring that the family stay together?' Effectively you take very opportunity to make them qualify what they are doing or asking of you. For example if they suggest or demand that you put your children into Section 20 respite care for a short while, then you need to ask them, preferably in writing to demonstrate how this is beneficial to your family and how it fits into the principle of preserving the family unit. Ask them to specify what are the alternatives: what supports could be put in place to effect the same outcomes, what are the negative impact upon children removed from their parents' care in these instances, what work do they propose with either you or your child, in that period that they see will effect a longer term positive outcome for the family? Whatever they want or ask to do must have a beneficial purpose for you and your children so make them stand upon their requests/demands.

Equally if they begin talking about possible court applications, removals, section 20's or PLO then again you can challenge what efforts they have made to ensure their compliance with

Section 1, point out their deficiencies in providing support to mitigate the concerns they have (they rarely provide the support they should). Section 1 does not standalone in a sort of legal vacuum in the courts of England and Wales but is enforced and verified by European Case law. For example: In KEEGAN v. IRELAND-16969/90 [1994] ECHR 18 (26 May 1994) paragraph 50:

'According to the principles set out by the Court in its case-law, where the existence of a family tie with a child has been established, the State must act in a manner calculated to enable that tie to be developed and legal safeguards must be created that render possible as from the moment of birth the child's integration in his family..... In this context reference may be made to the principle laid down in Article 7 of the United Nations Convention on the Rights of the Child of 20 November 1989 that a child has, as far as possible, the right to be cared for by his or her parents. It is, moreover, appropriate to recall that the mutual enjoyment by parent and child of each other's company constitutes a fundamental element of family life even when the relationship between the parents has broken down.'

Where social workers fail in their duties and obligations under this law, it is possible to challenge such issues via a judicial review.

Section 17 of the Children Act is the next key section. Section 17 deals with Children in Need. A child in need is defined as *'a child who is unlikely to achieve or maintain a satisfactory level of health or development, or their health and development will be significantly impaired, without the provision of services; or a child who is disabled.'* What is important to remember about this section is that it is entirely voluntary, yet is often used by social workers as a 'soft' option to interfere in a family where child protection measures are a largely unsubstantiated option. Social workers focus their assessments on a child's special educational needs, disabilities, or if a child is a carer, or because they have committed a crime. This assessment is also be used for children whose parents are in prison and for children seeking asylum. The type of services provided under section 17 may include providing accommodation, giving assistance in kind, or sometimes though rarely, in cash.

The correct use of a Section 17 is actually about assessing the services that need to be provided to ensure the best outcomes for a child, whether that be universal services, such as GP,

Schools, Health Visitor, or more specific services provided by specialist providers. The upper tiers of children in need are where it is statutorily deemed that multi agency services should be involved, such as children being placed for adoption, or in local authority care. At this level the children's social care department become the lead agency for delivery of services.

However Section 17 is often used for a 'stepping down' from child protection plans, but still provides a way for social workers to intervene. Unless there is speciality / multi-disciplinary service actually required, then a child in need plan is not an appropriate tool to continue social services involvement. This could be a legally challenge-able action. If this is a route that your social worker seems to be travelling, then you need to challenge the basis for it. If there is none other than universal services (i.e. services anyone can access, such as GP, school) recommended, then it is important that you again challenge the basis of the intervention. Why does there need to be social work involvement if they are not going to be bringing any specialist services? Question the position around the voluntary nature of this section. The important thing, is stand on your rights. You do not have to consent and if they threaten you with any escalation because you do not consent, then utilise the power of Article 8 of the ECHR, i.e., what basis does the state have to arbitrarily interfere in your private family life if they are not offering specialised services?

Section 47 creates a duty to investigate to local authorities where there is reasonable cause to suspect that a child is suffering, or likely to suffer, significant harm and to make enquiries, to enable it to decide whether it should take any action to safeguard and promote the welfare of the child.

The police, health service, education and other services are statutorily obliged to help social services carry out their enquiries and provide information to them. Needless to say when a section 47 has been initiated then parents are powerless to affect any part of the process. If you withhold consent for access to medical files for example, then the social workers can circumvent that in the name of child protection. It is not good practice, there may be no basis for such disclosures at that point in their enquiry, but it frequently happens. As stated before you may not even be aware that a section 47 is taking place until after the event and the decisions of a strategy meeting.

You can only effectively challenge the section 47 after the event. Despite the powers conferred on the local authority, the inception of a section 47 enquiry must be based upon a realistic premise, that the local authority have good cause to believe that a child is suffering, or likely to suffer, significant harm. Thus in dealing with any referral that may lead down this path, then the local authority must ensure it has carried out its due diligence. It is not a protocol that can be hid behind to cover failings prior to its inception. If a section 47 enquiry and its outcomes i.e. child protection conferences/ plans are based upon flawed, inaccurate or incorrect information then the basis for the enquiry and the actions thereof can be legally challenged. It is at this juncture where action based on flawed disclosures have been most successfully challenged by PIN and its advocates on behalf of families.

Section 46 deals with Police Powers. This confers powers on a police officer who has reasonable cause to believe that a child could otherwise be likely to suffer significant harm, then the officer may:

- remove the child to suitable accommodation; or
- take reasonable steps to ensure that the child's removal from any hospital, or other place in which the

child is then being accommodated is prevented.

It is very important to note that no child may be kept in police protection for more than 72 hours. This power is often misused, often at the behest of a social worker who being unable to get a parent to agree to a voluntary section 20 accommodation of a child, or suspecting or knowing that the information they hold; would not cross the threshold for an emergency protection order in a court, seeks to obtain a child through the use of police powers. Thus once this is accomplished then the likelihood of an emergency protection order being granted thereafter, as the court will see or even hear from a police officer that they felt they had to act, is greatly increased. This power is also often abused by the fact that the use of such power is threatened to a parent by either a police officer social worker or both, in order to pressure that parent into giving their child up into local authority care by means of a Section 20.

It is draconian, and parliament surely meant this as a purely emergency power in times of dire need, not as an alternative to the proper court processes.

Home Office circular 017 / 2008 *The duties and powers of the* police under *The Children Act 1989*[xxvii] laid out the guidelines for officers in particular it noted:

'To understand and establish significant harm it is necessary to consider:

a) the family context

b) the child's development within the context of their family and wider social and cultural environment

c) any special needs, such as a medical condition, communication difficulty or disability that may affect the child's development and care within the family

d) the nature of harm, in terms of ill-treatment or failure to provide adequate care

e) the impact on the child's health and development and

f) the adequacy of parental care.

It is important always to take account of the child's reactions, and his or her perceptions, according to the child's age and understanding.

23. *Under section 31(9) of the Children Act 1989: (as*

amended by the Adoption and Children's Act 2002)

'harm' *means ill-treatment or the impairment of health or development, including, impairment suffered from seeing or hearing the ill-treatment of another.*

'development' *means physical, intellectual, emotional, social or behavioural development*

'health' *means physical or mental health; and*

'ill-treatment' *includes sexual abuse and forms of ill-treatment which are not physical.*

24. Under section 31(10) of the Act:

- *Where the question of whether harm suffered by a child is significant turns on the child's health and development, his/her health or development shall be compared with that which could reasonably be expected of a similar child.'*

With all due respect to Her Majesty's Officers, is is unlikely that such a comprehensive appreciation or knowledge of the law and guidance is present when making such decisions. It is more likely they will be guided by a social worker's entreatment to utilise their powers. It is also worthy of note that the circular specifically points out that:

'A constable does not have the right to enter and search premises to remove a child without a warrant. However, in practical terms a constable is likely to find a child in an emergency situation where other powers are being exercised for entry to dwellings, for example, under section 17 of the Police and Criminal Evidence Act, to arrest someone for an arrestable offence or a breach of the peace, or to save life or limb. An officer may use reasonable force in the execution of his or her duty. Reasonable force has been defined in case law as 'such force as is reasonable in the circumstances'.

This is particularly relevant because officers may attend at your home with a social worker, but they have no right to enter and you have no need to open the door to them. Present yourself and your children at a window to demonstrate they are well. Stay polite, and do not give them reason to believe that there is a risk to life or limb, or that a crime is proceeding. Tell the officers to come back with a warrant or a court order. Once you let them in they can effect pretty much what they choose no matter what your protestations.

Further in R v Syed - Power of Entry to Save Life & Limb, the court made a significant ruling 'The court agreed with a previous case Baker v Crown Prosecution Service [2009] EWHC 299 (Admin), that the term danger to life or limb was outdated but nevertheless indicated that it was a serious matter and that there should be a fear that something has happened or may happen which would involve serious injury to a person.' The court agreed with the findings in the Baker case which stated:

"The expression 'saving life or limb' is a colourful, slightly outmoded expression. It is here used in close proximity with the expression 'preventing serious damage to property'. That predicates a degree of apprehended serious bodily injury. Without implicitly limiting or excluding the possible types of serious bodily injury, apprehended knife injuries and gunshot injuries will obviously normally be capable of coming within the subsection."

The court held that concern for welfare was not sufficient to enter properties using section 17, it was too low a threshold. The court did sympathise with police and took the view that they would be damned if they did and damned if they did not. If something serious had happened, or was about to happen, and they did not do anything about it because they took the view they had no right of entry, no doubt there would have been a degree of criticism after the event. However Parliament had set the level high as it was a very serious matter for a citizen to have their house entered by the police without a warrant.'xxviii

Once gain we look to the European jurisprudence that states ' *Circumstances must be confirmed and alternatives to taking in care must be exhausted, impact on parents and children must be assessed P, C and S v United Kingdom (2002) 35 EHRR 31, [2002] 2 FLR 631 para 116 "116. The margin of appreciation so to be accorded to the competent national authorities will vary in the light of the nature of the issues and the seriousness of the interests at stake. While the authorities enjoy a wide margin of appreciation in assessing the necessity of taking a child into care, in particular where an emergency situation arises, the Court must still be satisfied in the circumstances of the case that there existed circumstances justifying the removal of the child, and it is for the respondent State to establish that a careful assessment of the impact of the proposed care measure on the parents and the child, as well as of the possible alternatives to taking the child into public care, was carried out prior to implementation of a care measure (see K and T v Finland [2001] ECHR 25702/94 at para 166; Kutzner v Germany [2002] ECHR 46544/99 at para 67).'*

Thus it is clear that police protection even in cases of 'emergency' must be proportional to the circumstances and justified in the actions that the state takes. Further the Eriksson v. Sweden judgment of 22 June 1989, (Series A no. 156, p. 24, para. 58), stated emergency removal and orders are only allowed if danger is actually established. Thus the say so of a social worker does not amount to the necessary bar to be crossed for a police officer to effect such powers, they must be clearly able to identify an imminent danger. One of the worst examples of this use of police protection has been in labour wards and the removal of newborns. Again it is difficult to argue that whilst a Mother and baby are in a hospital setting with the attendant medical staff and supervision that an immediate danger presents itself, yet babies have, and are been taken, by the misuse of police powers.

So armed with the laws and protocols, any parent can establish a reasonable case against the instigation of police powers where no identifiable imminent danger is present. That's not to say that arrogance of the authorities will be defeated and a child not taken. It often happens, however once again it is possible to make a legal challenge on this.

Under the Child Care Act 1991, the Garda (Irish police force) have similar powers as the UK Police, under Section 12. Section 12 states:

'(1) Where a member of the Garda Síochána has reasonable grounds for believing that—

(a) there is an immediate and serious risk to the health or welfare of a child, and

(b) it would not be sufficient for the protection of the child from such immediate and serious risk to await the making of an application for an emergency care order by a health board under <u>section 13</u> ,the member, accompanied by such other persons as may be necessary, <u>may, without warrant, enter (if need be by force) any house or other place</u> (including any building or part of a building, tent, caravan or other temporary or moveable structure, vehicle, vessel, aircraft or hovercraft) and remove the child to safety.

(2) The provisions of subsection (1) are without prejudice to

any other powers exercisable by a member of the Garda Síochána.

(3) Where a child is removed by a member of the Garda Síochána in accordance with subsection (1), the child shall as soon as possible be delivered up to the custody of the health board for the area in which the child is for the time being.

(4) Where a child is delivered up to the custody of a health board in accordance with subsection (3), the health board shall, unless it returns the child to the parent having custody of him or a person acting in loco parentis, make application for an emergency care order at the next sitting of the District Court held in the same district court district or, in the event that the next such sitting is not due to be held within three days of the date on which the child is delivered up to the custody of the health board, at a sitting of the District Court, which has been specially arranged under section 13 (4), held within the said three days, and it shall be lawful for the health board to retain custody of the child pending the hearing of that application.[xxix] '

The key difference between the two is that a Garda do not require a warrant to enter any house or other place, but the point to be remembered is that the same requirements as to imminent danger are still required. Where fleeing families have faced removal of their children under Section 12, PIN has successfully prevented such occurring by speaking to the Garda or the parent relating the information passed to them that there must be established 'imminent danger' and if that cannot be shown to be the case and the Garda act, then a judicial review will launched against the Garda in the High Court. This has prevented the Garda from acting illegally and where they have, a number of judicial reviews against their actions have been successfully granted by the High Court.

In both instances it is the duty of the police to place the child in a secure environment, which generally means passing the child to social services care. Unless there is a plan to return the child to its parent, then the local authority or the Child and Family Agency (in Ireland) must apply for either an emergency protection order or interim care order without delay.

Which brings us neatly on to Section 44–Emergency Protection Orders (in Ireland Emergency Care Orders, Section 13 of the Child Care Act 1991). A court may only make an emergency protection order under section 44 of the Children

Act 1989: if it is *'satisfied that there is reasonable cause to believe that a child is likely to suffer significant harm if the child:*

- *is not removed to different accommodation provided by the applicant; or*
- *does not remain in the place in which the child is then being accommodated.'*

In Ireland Section 13 of the Child Care Act 1991 makes similar provision:

'(1) If a justice of the District Court is of opinion on the application of a health board that there is reasonable cause to believe that—

(a) there is an immediate and serious risk to the health or welfare of a child which necessitates his being placed in the care of a health board, or

(b) there is likely to be such a risk if the child is removed from the place where he is for the time being, the justice may make an order to be known and in this Act referred to as an "emergency care order".

(2) An emergency care order shall place the child under the care of the health board for the area in which the child is for the time being for a period of eight days or such shorter period as may be specified in the order.'

An emergency protection order (EPO) may also be granted, if the local authority enquires made under section 47, are being frustrated by access to the child being unreasonably refused to a person authorised to seek access. And the applicant has reasonable cause to believe that access is needed as a matter of urgency. An emergency protection order gives authority to remove a child, and place the child under the protection of the applicant. An EPO may last for a maximum of 8 days. (That includes any period of police protection.) The court may extend the period for a further 7 days thus giving a maximum time of 15 days. In this time the Local Authority / CFA must decide if they are going to proceed to make an application for a care or supervision order.

Emergency Protection orders are often made *ex-parte*-that is without notice to you that the court hearing is actually happening, therefore you are unable to make representations. You can make an application to discharge the order if it was granted without you being present, but such an application cannot be made until the expiration of 72 hours since its inception. Scarily, there is no right to an appeal regarding any decision to make, refuse to make or discharge an EPO. The only method of review currently available would be judicial review, which is unlikely to be of value as the order will have lapsed before you are actually granted an actual judicial review hearing.

The bar for such applications is high, but in all reality such orders are granted without much reservation or proper consideration of the facts. Indeed there is a propensity in most child care proceedings to prefer the word of social workers over parents' evidence, indeed I have been present at the granting of Emergency Care Orders in the District Court in Ireland, where the parents were not even heard or their submissions read. It is unsurprising that many aggrieved parents say that the courts are corrupt.

If you are given notice of such a hearing, then it is important that you attend. You must gather as much evidence as you can against the allegations the social workers are using and if you can, have the suggestion of a family member who may be able to take your child/ren as an alternative to foster care. It is also important that you put forward the case law as outlined above and in particular Munby J. As he then was in *X Council v B (Emergency Protection Orders)* [2004] EWHC 2015 (Fam); [2005] 1 FLR 341 and reiterated by Mr Justice McFarlane in Re X (Emergency Protection Orders) [2006] EWHC 510 (Fam) at paragraph 64:[xxx]

'64. In X Council v B (Emergency Protection Orders) [2004] EWHC 2015 (Fam); [2005] 1 FLR 341, Munby J undertook a review of the law and practice relating to EPO's. I gratefully adopt his masterful summary of both the domestic and European jurisprudence on the topic as a result of which (at paragraph 57) he drew the following conclusions:

"The matters I have just been considering are so important that it may be convenient if I here summarise the most important points:

(i) An EPO, summarily removing a child from his parents, is a 'draconian' and 'extremely harsh' measure, requiring 'exceptional justification' and 'extraordinarily compelling reasons'. Such an order should not be made unless the FPC is satisfied that it is both necessary and proportionate and that no other less radical form of order will achieve the essential end of promoting the welfare of the child. Separation is only to

be contemplated if immediate separation is essential to secure the child's safety: 'imminent danger' must be 'actually established'.

(ii) Both the local authority which seeks and the FPC which makes an EPO assume a heavy burden of responsibility. It is important that both the local authority and the FPC approach every application for an EPO with an anxious awareness of the extreme gravity of the relief being sought and a scrupulous regard for the European Convention rights of both the child and the parents.

(iii) Any order must provide for the least interventionist solution consistent with the preservation of the child's immediate safety.

(iv) If the real purpose of the local authority's application is to enable it to have the child assessed then consideration should be given to whether that objective cannot equally effectively, and more proportionately, be achieved by an application for, or by the making of, a CAO under s 43 of the Children Act 1989.

(v) No EPO should be made for any longer than is absolutely necessary to protect the child. Where the EPO is made on an

ex parte (without notice) application very careful consideration should be given to the need to ensure that the initial order is made for the shortest possible period commensurate with the preservation of the child's immediate safety.

(vi) The evidence in support of the application for an EPO must be full, detailed, precise and compelling. Unparticularised generalities will not suffice. The sources of hearsay evidence must be identified. Expressions of opinion must be supported by detailed evidence and properly articulated reasoning.

(vii) Save in wholly exceptional cases, parents must be given adequate prior notice of the date, time and place of any application by a local authority for an EPO. They must also be given proper notice of the evidence the local authority is relying upon.

(viii) Where the application for an EPO is made ex parte the local authority must make out a compelling case for applying without first giving the parents notice. An ex parte application will normally be appropriate only if the case is genuinely one of emergency or other great urgency – and even then it should

normally be possible to give some kind of albeit informal notice to the parents – or if there are compelling reasons to believe that the child's welfare will be compromised if the parents are alerted in advance to what is going on.

(ix) The evidential burden on the local authority is even heavier if the application is made ex parte. Those who seek relief ex parte are under a duty to make the fullest and most candid and frank disclosure of all the relevant circumstances known to them. This duty is not confined to the material facts: it extends to all relevant matters, whether of fact or of law.

(x) Section 45(7)(b) of the Children Act 1989 permits the FPC to hear oral evidence. But it is important that those who are not present should nonetheless be able to know what oral evidence and other materials have been put before the FPC. It is, therefore, particularly important that the FPC complies meticulously with the mandatory requirements of rr 20, 21(5) and 21(6) of the Family Proceedings Courts (Children Act 1989) Rules 1991. The FPC must 'keep a note of the substance of the oral evidence' and must also record in writing not merely its reasons but also any findings of fact.

(xi) The mere fact that the FPC is under the obligations

imposed by rr 21(5), 21(6) and 21(8), is no reason why the local authority should not immediately, on request, inform the parents of exactly what has gone on in their absence. Parents against whom an EPO is made ex parte are entitled to be given, if they ask, proper information as to what happened at the hearing and to be told, if they ask: (i) exactly what documents, bundles or other evidential materials were lodged with the FPC either before or during the course of the hearing; and (ii) what legal authorities were cited to the FPC. The local authority's legal representatives should respond forthwith to any reasonable request from the parents or their legal representatives either for copies of the materials read by the FPC or for information about what took place at the hearing. It will, therefore, be prudent for those acting for the local authority in such a case to keep a proper note of the proceedings, lest they otherwise find themselves embarrassed by a proper request for information which they are unable to provide.

(xii) Section 44(5)(b) of the Children Act 1989 provides that the local authority may exercise its parental responsibility only in such manner 'as is reasonably required to safeguard or promote the welfare of the child'. Section 44(5)(a) provides

that the local authority shall exercise its power of removal under s 44(4)(b)(i) 'only ... in order to safeguard the welfare of the child'. The local authority must apply its mind very carefully to whether removal is essential in order to secure the child's immediate safety. _The mere fact that the local authority has obtained an EPO is not of itself enough. The FPC decides whether to make an EPO. But the local authority decides whether to remove. The local authority, even after it has obtained an EPO, is under an obligation to consider less drastic alternatives to emergency removal. Section 44(5) requires a process within the local authority whereby there is a further consideration of the action to be taken after the EPO has been obtained. Though no procedure is specified, it will obviously be prudent for local authorities to have in place procedures to ensure both that the required decision-making actually takes place and that it is appropriately documented._

(xiii) Consistently with the local authority's positive obligation under Art 8 to take appropriate action to reunite parent and child, s 44(10)(a) and s 44(11)(a) impose on the local authority a mandatory obligation to return a child who it has removed under s 44(4)(b)(i) to the parent from whom the child was removed if 'it appears to [the local authority] that it is safe for the child to be returned'. This imposes on the local authority a continuing duty to keep the case under review day by day so as to ensure that parent and child are separated for no longer than is necessary to secure the child's safety. In this, as in other respects, the local authority is under a duty to exercise exceptional diligence.

(xiv) Section 44(13) of the Children Act 1989 requires the local authority, subject only to any direction given by the FPC under s 44(6), to allow a child who is subject to an EPO 'reasonable contact' with his parents. Arrangements for contact must be driven by the needs of the family, not stunted by lack of resources.'

As can be seen even if an EPO is granted it does not mean that removal should automatically follow, hence be ready to offer alternative approaches and ideas yourself.

Section 20 of the Children's Act 1989 is perhaps best described as 'voluntary placement of your child into local authority care' but more accurately should be described as 'compulsion in disguise.' That is certainly how the courts identified this section and its misuse by local authorities. The basis behind section 20 is: that there may be children who need accommodation because there is no one who has parental responsibility for them, because they have been abandoned or because the person who has been caring for them is unable to provide suitable accommodation or care. It is actually important that you digest the full section of this aspect of the act so it is set out here in full:

'20 Provision of accommodation for children: general.

(1)Every local authority shall provide accommodation for any child in need within their area who appears to them to require accommodation as a result of—

(a)there being no person who has parental responsibility for him;

(b)his being lost or having been abandoned; or

(c)the person who has been caring for him being prevented (whether or not permanently, and for whatever reason) from providing him with suitable accommodation or care.

(2)Where a local authority provide accommodation under subsection (1) for a child who is ordinarily resident in the area of another local authority, that other local authority may take over the provision of accommodation for the child within—

(a)three months of being notified in writing that the child is being provided with accommodation; or

(b)such other longer period as may be prescribed [F1in regulations made by the Secretary of State].

[F2(2A) Where a local authority in Wales provide accommodation under section 76(1) of the Social Services and Well-being (Wales) Act 2014 (accommodation for children without parents or who are lost or abandoned etc.) for a child who is ordinarily resident in the area of a local authority in England, that local authority in England may take over the provision of accommodation for the child within—

(a)three months of being notified in writing that the child is being provided with accommodation; or

(b)such other longer period as may be prescribed in regulations made by the Secretary of State.]

(3)Every local authority shall provide accommodation for any child in need within their area who has reached the age of sixteen and whose welfare the authority consider is likely to be seriously prejudiced if they do not provide him with accommodation.

(4)A local authority may provide accommodation for any child within their area (even though a person who has parental responsibility for him is able to provide him with accommodation) if they consider that to do so would safeguard or promote the child's welfare.

(5)A local authority may provide accommodation for any person who has reached the age of sixteen but is under twenty-one in any community home which takes children who have reached the age of sixteen if they consider that to do so would safeguard or promote his welfare.

(6)Before providing accommodation under this section, a local authority shall, so far as is reasonably practicable and consistent with the child's welfare—

(a)ascertain the child's wishes [F3and feelings] regarding the provision of accommodation; and

(b)give due consideration (having regard to his age and understanding) to such wishes [F3and feelings] of the child as they have been able to ascertain.

(7)A local authority <u>may not provide accommodation</u> under this section for any child if any person who—

(a)has parental responsibility for him; and

(b)is willing and able to—

(i)provide accommodation for him; or

(ii)arrange for accommodation to be provided for him,

objects.

(8)Any person who has parental responsibility for a child may at any time remove the child from accommodation provided by or on behalf of the local authority under this section.

(9)Subsections (7) and (8) do not apply while any person—

[F4(a)who is named in a child arrangements order as a person with whom the child is to live;]

[F5(aa)who is a special guardian of the child; or]

(b)who has care of the child by virtue of an order made in the exercise of the High Court's inherent jurisdiction with respect to children,

agrees to the child being looked after in accommodation provided by or on behalf of the local authority.

(10)Where there is more than one such person as is mentioned in subsection (9), all of them must agree.

(11)Subsections (7) and (8) do not apply where a child who has reached the age of sixteen agrees to being provided with accommodation under this section.'

The use of section 20 has been mired in controversy, simply because the local authorities' have been using this as a method for taking children into care and circumventing the need to obtain EPO's. Or it has been used as a tool of coercion, usually along with the presence of police officers. Effectively parents have been coerced into signing their children into voluntary care by social workers, who have said that if the parents did not do this, they would go to court or get the police to effect their protection powers. This has been done time and again when no court would have granted any such order. This is nothing short of a scandal of the highest order and although the courts have addressed it, the court of public opinion has largely been passed by and social workers received a rap on the knuckles rather than any thorough investigation of their methodology and ethics. Children have languished in local authority care unseen by the scrutiny of the courts for long periods of time and as a result HH Judge Bellamy issued practice guidance about section 20. This guidance can be found at Appendix C and it is worthy of your time.

The key point is that you are not obliged to give your children into voluntary care. If this is even suggested to you, then the social worker must obtain your *informed consent* i.e. you must fully understand and appreciate what you are about to agree to. You do not have to agree to this and if the social worker threatens court, then it is better to challenge them to make their application to the court. If they believed they had enough evidence to remove your child/ren, then they would apply to court or even get the police to utilise their police powers and then apply to court. If they are 'persuading' you to sign a section 20, you can pretty much guarantee they do not yet have the ability to apply for an order to remove your child/ren.

If you consent, then you are effectively agreeing that they have a basis to remove your child/ren and that could play against you in any further hearings. As HH Judge Bellamy pointed out in his guidance notes at footnote 3:

'Particular regard should be had to the decision of the Court of Appeal in Re N (Children)(Adoption: Jurisdiction) [2015] EWCA Civ 1112 and in particular the review of the use of

279

section 20 set out in the judgment of Sir James Munby P at paras 157 to–171. It is particularly appropriate to highlight the warning given at para 171 that: 'The misuse and abuse of section 20 in this context is not just a matter of bad practice. It is wrong; it is a denial of the fundamental rights of both the parent and the child; it will no longer be tolerated; and it must stop. Judges will and must be alert to the problem and pro-active in putting an end to it. From now on, local authorities which use section 20 as a prelude to care proceedings for lengthy periods or which fail to follow the good practice I have identified, can expect to be subjected to probing questioning by the court. If the answers are not satisfactory, the local authority can expect stringent criticism and possible exposure to successful claims for damages.[xxxi]*'

Hopefully parents will no longer be faced with this scenario, but it is still a strong possibility. Simply do not agree, tell the social worker to apply for their order and if that actually occurs ensure that you make this coercion known to the judge. Reiterate the guidance and above all ensure you have recorded the whole conversation as evidence. A child looked after under section 20 is purely a cooperative agreement, between the local authority and the parents (or the young person if they are aged over 16). Most importantly, you as parents retain full parental responsibility and have the right to remove your child at any moment and although it is best to provide notice of this intention to the Local Authority, your right is absolute. If you do, they are likely to make a court application, but if that occurs all the above still applies.

Alongside the attempted misuse of Section 20, social workers may also utilise a 'written agreement.' This will lay out all the 'do's and do nots' and 'can and cannot' that a social worker wishes to impose on you. It may be that you cannot have contact with your partner, or that one of you must leave the home and not return. It may be that they wish to place your children with another family member, but you must not see the children. It can be a host of many things.

The agreement may be prepared and written up, or it may be hastily written by the social worker in front of you, on a piece of paper torn from a note pad. The most onerous aspect, is that it will be a tool of coercion. Basically sign the agreement or the social worker will remove your children. The truth is this is not an agreement at all. An agreement is:

'accordance in opinion or feeling,

consistency

a negotiated and typically legally binding arrangement[xxxii].'

according to the Oxford English Dictionary.

This 'agreement' is none of the above. It is not negotiated, it is only the directions of a social worker. It is certainly not legally binding upon you in any way. Often it is presented to you in a pressured environment: that may be a social worker in your home, usually accompanied by a police officer or two. The option presented is usually sign or your child will be removed. That is pure coercion and a misuse of authority. It certainly violates Article 8 of the ECHR. As we have said before, do not sign anything. Ask to take legal advice about the agreement before you sign. This is where the real pressure will begin, you will probably be told that there is no time, that it needs to be signed there and then. In these circumstances, if it appears that they may effect the use of police, which may mean your child going into foster care rather than with a family member it will be very tempting to sign.

Do not let this pressure overwhelm you. Agree that your child can go to a family member and confirm that you will abide by the agreement for 24–48 hours, or a reasonable time frame, in order for you to obtain legal advice. But do not sign. Inform the social worker that you will obtain legal advice and then revert to them on the decision of whether you will sign the agreement in the longer term.

Reinforce to the social worker that by being forced to sign, without legal advice would prejudice your rights. Remind the social worker that what they are asking you to do is coercive and that you must provide informed consent. Without recourse to legal advice, your consent cannot be said to be informed.

Written agreements have no place in the role of child protection. It can effect the removal of a child from their family with no oversight from the courts, legal professionals or other child professional who are supposedly involved in today's multi-agency approach to child protection.

Section 31 of the Children Act 1989. The local authority can apply to the court for a child or young person to become the subject of a care order. A care order gives the local authority parental responsibility in addition to the parents, a responsibility that is actually weighted in their favour, i.e. they take control over your child's life (through a care plan and foster placement or even adoption). The local authority effectively becomes a corporate parent to your child. Children under Section 20 and those under Section 31 are deemed 'Looked After Children' (LAC). The relevant paragraphs of the section of the act stipulates that:

'1) On the application of any local authority or authorised person, the court may make an order—

(a) placing the child with respect to whom the application is made in the care of a designated local authority; or

(b)putting him under the supervision of a designated local authority

2) A court may only make a care order or supervision order if it is satisfied—

(a)that the child concerned is suffering, or is likely to suffer, significant harm; and

(b) that the harm, or likelihood of harm, is attributable to—

(i) the care given to the child, or likely to be given to him if the order were not made, not being what it would be reasonable to expect a parent to give to him; or

(ii) the child's being beyond parental control.

(3) No care order or supervision order may be made with respect to a child who has reached the age of seventeen (or sixteen, in the case of a child who is married).

[F2(3A)A court deciding whether to make a care order—

(a) is required to consider the permanence provisions of the section 31A plan for the child concerned, but

(b) is not required to consider the remainder of the section 31A plan, subject to section 34(11).

(3B) For the purposes of subsection (3A), the permanence provisions of a section 31A plan are such of the plan's provisions setting out the long-term plan for the upbringing of the child concerned as provide for any of the following—

(a) the child to live with any parent of the child's or with any other member of, or any friend of, the child's family;

(b) adoption;

(c) long-term care not within paragraph (a) or (b).....

...(5) The court may—

285

(a) on an application for a care order, make a supervision order;

(b) on an application for a supervision order, make a care order....'

It is applications under this section that the court must decide if your child goes into care and may be placed for adoption. Whenever a local authority issues proceedings for court, whether that starts as an EPO, Interim Care Order or even Supervision Order the vast majority of cases will come before the court under this provision of the act. Simply they wish to remove your child/ren permanently from you.

These are lengthy proceedings, but there is a cut-off of 26 weeks, i.e. a timetable is set, supposedly in the best interests of the child to resolve the issues within 6 months. Slippage of this timetable is only allowed if it is warranted in the terms of ensuring justice. This is where you will face a final hearing to determine your children's future. We shall deal with this in the chapter on the courts.

The final area of vital importance is Section 3 on parental responsibility. This is defined by the act as 'the rights, duties, powers and responsibilities which by law a parent of a child has in relation to the child and his property.' It is these rights which are effectively curtailed by the granting of a care order or dispensed with completely with an adoption order. There are other sections of the act that are important such as Section 50 Recovery Orders but these are dealt with in their context elsewhere in the text. It should be noted that other laws such as the Children's Act 2004 and the Adoption and Children Act 2002 and their equivalents in other jurisdictions are also of relevance for parents, but again where they are relevant they are dealt with at that juncture.

The guidelines

Although as we have seen there are differently named sets of guidelines for: England, Wales, Scotland, Northern Ireland and the Republic of Ireland, the underlying precepts have a commonality that is shared between them all. These are statutory guidance which means that they are not optional, the details in them are based upon legislation and social workers must follow these guidelines. We shall focus on two 'Working Together to Safeguard Children' (England), and 'Children First' (Republic of Ireland).

It is worth your time familiarising yourself with the document relevant in your jurisdiction as you can identify where social workers have not undertaken what they should have or have actually done something they should not have.

Working Together to Safeguard Children[xxxiii]

Whilst we cannot dissect every aspect of the Working Together guidelines, I intend to highlight some important areas that you need to be aware of.

Under the section 'The principles and parameters of a good assessment[xxxiv]' it highlights the key features of what are deemed 'high quality assessments':

- *child centred. Where there is a conflict of interest, decisions should be made in the child's best interests*

- *are rooted in child development and informed by evidence;*

- *are focused on action and outcomes for children;*

- *are holistic in approach, addressing the child's needs within their family and wider community;*

- *ensure equality of opportunity;*

- *involve children and families;*

- *build on strengths as well as identifying difficulties;*

- *are integrated in approach;*

- *are a continuing process not an event;*

- *lead to action, including the provision of services;*

- *review services provided on an ongoing basis; and*

- *are transparent and open to challenge.*

The points underlined, are of utmost importance when you are presented with a social worker's assessment of your family. Frequently such assessments lack evidence of any kind. The report is filled with supposition, opinion and conjecture. In other words they often lack the crucial evidence. 'It is believed' an oft coined phrase can precede all sorts of untruths and misrepresentations and many times, even that phrase is absent and it is a simple statement alleging something completely untrue and unevidenced. As we saw with health visitors, keep repeating the lie and it becomes accepted, even without a shred of evidence. Hence these statements must be challenged, not only as to their veracity but to their place in the assessment/report. Quote the section of the 'Working Together' and ask the social worker to produce the evidence for their allegation. If you have contrary evidence, produce it. If this is a report being discussed in a child protection conference, ask the chair to have the unevidenced section removed from the report and minuted as such. Again we are aiming to undermine the confidence in the social worker and their reports.

Many assessments are produced without a social worker actually spending any quality time talking with the members of the family. Where a report is produced, and you weren't involved, make this known and again refer to the guidance that the best quality assessments come from your full involvement, absent this the report/assessment is nothing but a biased document that should be withdrawn as it fails to meet the guidelines. It is in effect, poor social work practice and should not be allowed to stand.

Most importantly is the final point that assessments must be transparent and open to challenge. This is a bit of an ace up your sleeve, where either of the two points above are raised and any refusal to consider your challenges, for example by a chair of a child protection conference, then you can direct them to the guidelines. Where there is a failure to carry out their statutory duties correctly, then it is a matter that can be challenged by a judicial review. It is worth pointing this out 'informally' to them. Demonstrating you know the requirements that they must fulfil, and challenging them on all such failures, will help strengthen your position in undermining their case against you. Although it may actually seem minor, it is part of the overall strategy of weakening their case.

This is particularly important because paragraph 44[xxxv] goes on to say *'A high quality assessment is one in which evidence is built and revised throughout the process. A social worker may arrive at a judgement early in the case but this may need to be revised as the case progresses and further information comes to light. It is a characteristic of skilled practice that social workers revisit their assumptions in the light of new evidence and take action to revise their decisions in the best interests of the individual child.'*

Therefore where you can successfully challenge the assessments/reports of the social worker, they have a duty to reassess their judgments and assumptions. If they do not, you have an opportunity to challenge the whole basis of their intervention, through the courts if necessary. Further, if they fail to take into account your evidence/challenges, then you can make a formal complaint to the HCPC as they would be failing to meet the necessary standards and ethics of the HCPC.

The guidelines go on and describe the protocols: such as strategy meetings, section 47 enquiries, removal and child protection conferences, which we covered earlier. It also covers how and what the multiple agencies involved must do and also covers the role of the Local Safeguarding Children's Boards, serious case reviews and child death reviews. Hopefully the latter two will never be part of your involvement with social services, but it is worrying just how many children die in local authority care. What is remarkable about the latest edition of the Working Together protocol is the complete disappearance of references to Human Rights and only a nod to data protection. I'll let you draw your own conclusions about the relevance of that!

Children First: National Guidance 2011 [xxxvi]. (Ireland)

This is promoted as *'the comprehensive reference document, and a practical handbook to key actions for front-line practitioners [that] will deliver a sound footing for national consistency*

in our approach to child protection.'

Overall the guidance follows the same principles as the Working Together document and similarly intends to *'promote the safety and well-being of children. Parents and guardians have the primary responsibility for the care and protection of children. Many parents from time to time require support and help from the State in carrying out their parental role.'*

As noted with Working Together the key principles include the fact that *'Parents/carers have a right to respect and should be consulted and involved in matters that concern their family'* and perhaps of greater importance, a recognition of the law both domestically and in the European dimension that *'Children should only be separated from parents/carers when alternative means of protecting them have been exhausted. Re-union should be considered in the context of planning for the child's future.'* Sadly the high ideals do not appear so evident in social work practice, so this must be pointed out to the social workers and they must be directly challenged as to exactly what actions they are taking to fulfil this. Their response must be based on realistic and actionable points, not just lip service. This fact alone gives parents in Ireland a strong basis to challenge social work interventions. The District Court may well ignore this and have a more knee-jerk reaction to separation of children from their parents, thankfully the High Court has been much more responsive. It is a tool that can be utilised as described above.

What is significantly different about the Children First document is that it actually provides definitions of child abuse. See pages 8-12 of the document. This is very valuable as it provides a basis to challenge social workers upon the choice of 'harm' they record and to get them to define with evidence, the harm they allege. If they cannot, how can they allege such? This again is a useful tool in undermining their case against you. It is worth taking a little more detailed look at the most egregious of allegations of harm and that is emotional abuse.

'Definition of 'emotional abuse[xxxvii] *'*

2.3.1 Emotional abuse is normally to be found in the relationship between a parent/carer and a child rather

than in a specific event or pattern of events. It occurs when a child's developmental need for affection,

approval, consistency and security are not met. Unless other forms of abuse are present, it is rarely

manifested in terms of physical signs or symptoms. Examples may include:

(i)the imposition of negative attributes on a child, expressed by persistent criticism, sarcasm, hostility

or blaming;

(ii) conditional parenting in which the level of care shown to a child is made contingent on his or her

behaviours or actions;

(iii) emotional unavailability of the child's parent/carer;

(iv) unresponsiveness of the parent/carer and/or inconsistent or inappropriate expectations of the child;

(v) premature imposition of responsibility on the child;

(vi) unrealistic or inappropriate expectations of the child's capacity to understand something or to

behave and control himself or herself in a certain way;

(vii) under- or over-protection of the child;

(viii) failure to show interest in, or provide age-appropriate opportunities for, the child's cognitive and

emotional development;

(ix) use of unreasonable or over-harsh disciplinary measures;

(x) exposure to domestic violence;

(xi) exposure to inappropriate or abusive material through new technology.

2.3.2

Emotional abuse can be manifested in terms of the child's behavioural, cognitive, affective or physical

functioning. Examples of these include insecure attachment, unhappiness, low self-esteem, educational

and developmental underachievement, and oppositional behaviour. The threshold of significant harm

is reached when abusive interactions dominate and become

typical of the relationship between the child

and the parent/carer.'

What is interesting is that most of the examples are exceptionally difficult to prove or disprove, much will rely upon a subjective opinion. What it actually does do is fly in the face of a number of court rulings where parenting styles have been defended on the basis that social workers have sought to carry out 'social engineering'. A considered look at the list clearly shows that if your parenting style is not quite what a social worker believes it should be, then you are open to the allegation of emotional abuse.

It is exceptionally worrying that 'unhappiness' and 'educational and development underachievement' are listed as manifestations. A child may be unhappy for a number of reasons, they didn't get their own way, you refused to buy them something or did not allow them to go out, or even they just didn't get enough sleep the night before. Those are suddenly transformed into emotional abuse. With educational or development delays, there may be undiagnosed underlying reasons, everything from being on the autistic spectrum to just being a slower learner, yet it can be blamed on a parent as emotional abuse. Some individuals have not been diagnosed with autistic traits until well into adulthood, thus it can easily be missed or misdiagnosed (after all doctors only practice, practice at diagnosis, in other words it is an opinion...and that's why we ask for 'second opinions'), yet these days social workers can allege it is emotional abuse.

Whilst there is no doubt that some children do suffer from some forms of emotional abuse at the hands of adults, we have to ask if it is as widespread as social work figures indicate. There were six times as many children on child protection plans for emotional abuse compared to sexual abuse, and three times as many compared to physical abuse when one examines the statistics between 2009-2013 (NSPCC statistics) and the figures continue to rise. After examining many social workers reports for parents, there is a trend to allege emotional abuse as what appears to be a 'boost' to their case. This is especially true where the actual concerns from the initial referral and investigation are actually minor and would not in times past have warranted any intervention, or would have resulted in some tangible support to ensure the family's circumstances could be 'improved'. It is difficult to prove many of the emotional abuses, even where a child may have been in a household with domestic violence it is difficult to provide evidence of emotional harm. It is even more difficult to defend against it, especially where you are facing a psychologist's report that merely pays lip service to the social worker's opinions.

Perhaps the most destructive and deceptive manifestation that allegations of emotional harm take is in the form of possible 'future emotional harm.' Your child is removed on the basis of something that hasn't happened, but may. Critics call it social workers looking into their crystal balls. It is the equivalent of a thought crime. All this relies on, is the opinions of the so called 'professionals' and if you are unlucky, an example of something in your past used as an indicator to the future. Of course in all circumstances it is just as unlikely as likely because as yet there is no tangible proof of the clairvoyance of anyone, let alone social workers.

So how do you fight this effectively? We again start with our first principles, we challenge the evidence. Does your child have good school reports, not academically but are they settled, do they present as happy? Use such reports. Go back to the guidelines, is the allegation of emotional harm evidenced in behaviour of the child that has no other basis or possible explanation (i.e. have you been seeking a diagnosis for months for autism, or something similar? Provide the proof of those GP appointments, referrals to specialists and hospital letters. If it is in a social workers report as a standalone comment as highlighted previously–a booster- then challenge the social worker to provide the evidence. Challenge any allegation of your behaviour that may be being used to allege emotional harm with the same methods. It is preferable to challenge and 'nip-in -the bud' such allegations as early as possible because the courts will accept and find against you on such subjective allegations.

Chapter 5: How to Fight Back

(4) Rights

When you are faced with intervention by the State in the form of child protection, then your Human Rights are engaged, they cannot be ignored by the social workers. Whether it is under the auspice of The Universal Declaration of Human Rights, The European Convention of Human Rights or the respective Human Rights Acts of the various jurisdictions, they all provide you with inherent protection.

We shall look at your rights under the auspice of the European Convention of Human Rights[xxxviii].

The three rights we shall look at in closer detail are Article 6 Right to a fair trial, Article 8 Right to respect for private and family life and Article 13 Right to an effective remedy[xxxix]. That is not to say that the other articles may not come into play in your particular case, but these are most likely to be the universally applied ones in cases of social services interventions.

Article 6 Right to a fair trial.

1. In the determination of his civil rights and obligations or of any criminal charge against him, everyone is entitled to a fair and public hearing within a reasonable time by an independent and impartial tribunal established by law. Judgment shall be pronounced publicly but the press and public may be excluded

from all or part of the trial in the interests of morals, public order or national security in a democratic society, where the interests of juveniles or the protection of the private life of the parties so require, or to the extent strictly necessary in the opinion of the court in special circumstances where publicity would prejudice the interests of justice.

2. Everyone charged with a criminal offence shall be presumed innocent until proved guilty according to law.

3. Everyone charged with a criminal offence has the following minimum rights:

(a) to be informed promptly, in a language which he understands and in detail, of the nature and cause of the accusation against him;

(b) to have adequate time and facilities for the preparation of his defence;

(c) to defend himself in person or through legal assistance of his own choosing or, if he has not sufficient means to pay for legal assistance, to be given it free when the interests of justice so require;

(d) to examine or have examined witnesses against him and to obtain the attendance and examination of witnesses on his behalf under the same conditions as witnesses against him;

(e) to have the free assistance of an interpreter if he cannot understand or speak the language used in court.

The first point to note is that Article 6 applies to civil hearings as well as criminal, thus it encompasses all child care and private family law proceedings. You must be furnished with all the paperwork that the Local Authority seeks to rely on. You should be given this with adequate time to assess it and prepare your case against it, it is neither acceptable nor compliant with the Article to be given paperwork only a few days (or in some instances a couple of hours, as was done with one case of an application for an interim care order by one Local Authority) before an actual hearing. You are entitled to call witnesses, sadly many a case has seen a judge refuse such and now it is extremely difficult to call more than one 'expert' to testify. Joint instructions of one expert to report to the court is the norm.

The hearing must be fair and independent. That is, the judge must not demonstrate bias to one side over the other. It does sometimes happen where a judge prevents you or your counsel from speaking or raising a particular argument or evidence and there are examples of judges throwing their judicial weight around. Where any of the particulars of Article 6 are absent, then a course of appeal is open to you.

Article 8 Right to respect for private and family life.

1. Everyone has the right to respect for his private and family life, his home and his correspondence.

2. There shall be no interference by a public authority with the exercise of this right except such as is in accordance with the law and is necessary in a democratic society in the interests of national security, public safety or the economic well-being of the country, for the prevention of disorder or crime, for the protection of health or morals, or for the protection of the rights and freedoms of others.

This is perhaps the most important of all the articles when it comes to social services intervention and we need to look at proportionality in conjunction because the rights described are not absolute in their terms because as you can see they can be over-ruled. The exceptions allow for lawful breaches (i.e. under Statute law) or it is necessary to do so to protect health, morals or the rights of others. Can you see the simple get out clause there–the rights of others will refer to your children, to their rights and morals. So for any court it is a balancing exercise of the rights, in the circumstances.

Proportionality means that any violation must meet the 'necessary' test, that is, what is done or proposed cannot be in excess of what is needed to prevent harm. For example in Re K (Children) [2014] EWCA Civ 1195[xl]. This was a private law proceeding relating to long term contact issues. The boys had resided with the mother, but contact frequently broke down with the father. At one of the hearings a conditional order allowing the change of residence to the father for the summer should contact fail again was put in place. Consequently the contact failed again, and a judge invoked the conditional order. The boys absconded, and the upshot was an interim care order that separated the boys. On appeal it was found amongst other points that *'The proportionality of the removal of A on the grounds of 'safety' from the care of either or both of his parents was not justified; and the separation of the boys from each other was neither considered nor justified.'*

In Re B (A Child) [2013] UKSC 33[xli] the Supreme Court held that:

'115...Significantly different considerations are in play when the proportionality of the decision is in issue. A decision as to whether a particular outcome is proportionate involves asking oneself, is it really necessary. That question cannot be answered by saying that someone else with whose judgment I am reluctant to interfere, or whose judgment can be defended, has decided that it is necessary. It requires the decision-maker, at whatever level the decision is made, to starkly confront the question, "is this necessary". If an appellate court decides that it would not have concluded that it was necessary, even though it can understand the reasons that the first instance court believed it to be so, or if it considered that the decision of the lower court was perfectly tenable, it cannot say that the decision was proportionate.'

It is clear then that when the State interferes in a family's life it must be proportionate as to what is only necessary. For example it would not be necessary to remove a child just because a child's home was untidy and disorganised, but it would be proportionate to expect that the house was tidied and cleaned. There is a positive obligation in the Article that the state must respect private life and that means that social workers must approach all their cases with a fair balance and respect for your rights. If their approach and demands are arbitrary in their nature, not based on proper assessments or evidence then you can challenge the interference on the grounds of Article 8.

In order to respect your rights you must be involved in the decision making process. In _W v. United Kingdom_ (1988) 10 EHRR 29, para. 64, the European Court of Human Rights indicated that the key question arising is whether '_the parents have been involved in the decision-making process, seen as a whole, to a degree sufficient to provide them with the requisite protection of their interests_'. If you are not, then your rights have been violated and you have a claim. In _Soares de Melo v. Portugal 2016. Judge Sajo declared that the_ **_rights of parents must be considered by the courts, not solely the 'best interests' of children caught up in each case:_**

'_The best interests of the child comes into play when the_

obligations inherent in parental rights are not observed by the parent *or that [the parent] uses [his or her] rights abusively. The requirements of the [European] Convention [on Human Rights] are not fulfilled* <u>*if one ignores the importance of the need for parents and their children to "be together"...it is of utmost importance that the child welfare services fully respect the human rights of all, including parents, even when caring people are convinced that they only serve the best interests of children.*</u> *'*

You are not just a passenger on the journey, your rights are engaged and you must stand on them.

Article 13 Right to an effective remedy.

'Everyone whose rights and freedoms as set forth in this Convention are violated shall have an effective remedy before a national authority notwithstanding that the violation has been committed by persons acting in an official capacity.'

This simply means that if you believe and if it is found that your rights have been violated that you have the right to an effective remedy under the law. It specifically makes clear that it does not matter that the breaches have been by a person acting in an 'official capacity' i.e. a social worker, you are still entitled to seek redress for those breaches. This is your right to take action for the violations you may have experienced.

As we said there may be other rights that have been violated in your case, such as Article 14 Prohibition of discrimination, or Article 3 Prohibition of torture, which includes degrading treatment by the state, but before you allege such breaches ensure you do your homework. Read the Convention, look up relevant case law which can be found at the website of the European Court of Human Rights (HUDOC)[xlii] and that what you allege, fits the criteria for a violation. The ECHR can be used to challenge social services interventions prior to any court proceedings as well as within them.

Children's rights have also come directly into focus over the past few decades, particularly with the development of the *United Nations Convention on Rights of the Child.* It is to that we now turn.

The United Nations Convention on Rights of the Child was adopted and opened for signature, ratification and accession by General Assembly of the UN under resolution 44/25 of 20 November 1989 and its entry into force began on 2 September 1990, in accordance with article 49[xliii]. This is one of the most widely ratified conventions of the UN and has been ratified by the UK and Ireland. This means those countries have entered a binding agreement to meet the obligations and provisions in the convention and to promote, protect and fulfil the rights of children. Ireland though has not yet incorporated the Convention into its domestic law, which means it cannot be relied upon directly in the Irish Courts, though it does have weight as an important guiding principle.

Interestingly it is not just a child's rights that are covered, parental rights also feature, as its overarching basis starts with the fact that the Convention acknowledges the <u>primary role of parents and the family</u> in the care and protection of children, as well as the obligation of the State to help them carry out these duties. Note the obligation of the state and the use of the word help. That in and of itself follows what we have seen as to the original role of social workers, the over-riding legal duties of social workers under the legislation and the recognition of parents role in decision making under the ECHR. Unfortunately we don't find many families talking about the 'help' they received from social workers.

The Convention has four general principles:

'• that all the rights guaranteed by the Convention must be available to all children without discrimination of any kind (Article 2);

• that the best interests of the child must be a primary consideration in all actions concerning children (Article 3);

• that every child has the right to life, survival and development (Article 6);

and

• that the child's views must be considered and taken into account in all matters affecting him or her (Article 12).'

The Convention runs to 54 Articles although 1 through 41 are the direct rights of children, the rest are about the ratifications and processes. Although it is far from pragmatic to cover every Article we shall once again consider highly relevant ones to the intervention of social services in a family's life. For ease and a general overview the full list of Articles appears at Appendix D.

Article 3 (2) confirms the place of parents in consideration of child protection measures by the state. 'States Parties undertake to ensure the child such protection and care as is *necessary for his or her well-being, taking into account the rights and duties of his or her parents, legal guardians, or other individuals legally responsible for him or her, and, to this end, shall take all appropriate legislative and administrative measures.'* This can be argued as placing parents central to the policy making of the state with regard to children and families and again flows into the rights already seen above regarding being part of the decision making processes.

Article 5 refers to parental guidance of children: *'States Parties shall respect the responsibilities, rights and duties of parents or, where applicable, the members of the extended family or community*

as provided for by local custom, legal guardians or other persons legally responsible for the child, to provide, in a manner consistent with the evolving capacities of the child, appropriate direction and guidance in the exercise by the child of the rights recognized in the present Convention.' There is little argument with the clear message of Article 5 that parental rights in raising their child must be respected, which includes ensuring there is no discrimination based on a number of areas as detailed in Article 2 *'...irrespective of the child's or his or her parent's or legal guardian's race, colour, sex, language, religion, political or other opinion, national, ethnic or social origin, property, disability, birth or other status.'* This is important because there have been a number of cases where children have been removed based on a parent's beliefs or disability. Some parents have very different ideas of 'parenting' which may not be seen as the 'norm' (whatever that is–usually a social worker's opinion), but it is clear that children must not be discriminated against because their parents may have a different 'take' on something. Removing a child because a social worker does not like an alternative view, be that political or any other type propounded by a parent could be seen as a discriminatory action. Indeed this goes to the heart of social engineering, something the courts have warned about, as in North East Lincolnshire Council v G & L [2014] EWFC B192, Judge Jack noted:

'...the courts are not in the business of social engineering. The courts are not in the business of providing children with perfect homes. If we took into care and placed for adoption every child whose parents had had a domestic spat and every child whose parents on occasion had drunk too much then the care system

would be overwhelmed and there would not be enough adoptive parents. So we have to have a degree of realism about prospective carers who come before the courts.'

Article 9 goes to the heart of the child protection role of the state:

'1. States Parties shall ensure that a child shall not be separated from his or her parents against their will, except when competent authorities subject to judicial review determine, in accordance with applicable law and procedures, that such separation is necessary for the best interests of the child. Such determination may be necessary in a particular case

such as one involving abuse or neglect of the child by the parents, or one where the parents are living separately and a decision must be made as to the child's place of residence.

2. In any proceedings pursuant to paragraph 1 of the present article, all interested parties shall be given an opportunity to participate in the proceedings and make their views known.

3. States Parties shall respect the right of the child who is separated from one or both parents to maintain personal relations and direct contact with both parents on a regular basis, except if it is contrary to the child's best interests.

4. Where such separation results from any action initiated by a State Party, such as the detention, imprisonment, exile, deportation or death (including death arising from any cause while the person is in the custody of the State) of one or both parents or of the child, that State Party shall, upon request, provide the parents, the child or, if appropriate, another member of the family with the essential information concerning the whereabouts of the absent member(s) of the family unless the provision of the information would be detrimental to the well-being of the child. States Parties shall further ensure that the submission of such a request shall of itself entail no adverse consequences for the person(s) concerned.'

but within this we find a number of notable points that can be used to add weight to any challenge that parents bring against the State. Firstly it sets up the position that any removal of a child must be lawful and necessary, but most importantly it confirms a number of rights. The maintenance of personal relations and direct contact on a regular basis and the knowledge of where your child is located. Although there are caveats placed on these rights such as 'except if it is contrary to the child's best interests'. Any challenge brought to uphold these rights will place the burden of proof on the local authority to demonstrate that it would be contrary to the child's best interests.

Of course these are a child's rights too so with a mature enough child they could express their rights-of course you need to be able to let the child know what their rights are. This could be done at a contact session or at a LAC review, I am sure parents are imaginative enough to ensure that the message gets across. One right here that is often overlooked is the final sentence in point 4 of Article 9. Quite often local authorities will reduce contact to as little as possible if the parents start making court applications for more contact, or to discharge care orders. Social workers will often cite the need to stabilise a placement by reducing contact in such circumstances. It appears almost like an act of retribution for the parent having the audacity to try to see their child more often. Clearly any local authority who asks the court to reduce your contact because you have actually made an application to increase contact or discharge a care order would be in breach of this and thus it can be argued that such a request to reduce contact by the LA would be a violation of the rights under the convention. I cannot reiterate this enough, but you are seeking to have as broad a challenge to the social services as possible and as a famous supermarket says 'every little helps'.

Article 10 builds on this position of no adverse consequences if a parent makes an application to discharge a care order:

'1. In accordance with the obligation of States Parties under article 9, paragraph 1, applications by a child or his or her parents to enter or leave a State Party for the purpose of family reunification shall be dealt with by States Parties in a positive, humane and expeditious manner. States Parties shall further ensure that the <u>submission of such a request</u>

<u>shall entail no adverse consequences for the applicants and for the members of their family.</u>

2. A child whose parents reside in different States shall have the right to maintain on a regular basis, save in exceptional circumstances personal relations and direct contacts with both parents. Towards that end and in accordance with the obligation of States Parties under article 9,

paragraph 1, States Parties shall respect the right of the child and his or her parents to leave any country, including their own, and to enter their own country. The right to leave any country shall be subject only to such restrictions as are prescribed by law and which are necessary to protect the national security, public order (ordre public), public health or morals or the rights and freedoms of others and are consistent with the other rights recognized in the present Convention.'

Under Article 12 the rights of a child to be heard are reinforced:

'1. States Parties shall assure to the child who is capable of forming his or her own views the right to express those views freely in all matters affecting the child, the views of the child being given due weight in accordance with the age and maturity of the child.

2. For this purpose, the child shall in particular be provided the opportunity to be heard in any judicial and administrative proceedings affecting the child, either directly, or through a representative or an appropriate body, in a manner consistent with the procedural rules of national law.'

Perhaps this is one of the most salient points, yet it one of the most abused. Frequently children's views go unheard or are given little weight by professionals and judges. The provision of a Guardian ad Litem to provide that voice are nothing less than inadequate. The assessment role that the guardian plays within proceedings creates a conflict of interest. Equally obtaining such wishes, feelings and voices falls short if the third party is a psychologist. Third party advocates are sometimes employed, but all the above are 'professionals' within the child protection agenda and with that comes a bias, conscious or unconscious, but it is certainly there. In all reality children should be allowed to address the judge directly. We all know that this does not have to be in a court room, the judge's chambers are available and as to the age/maturity of a child, the youngest reported trial witness was three years old![xliv]

Your child has a right to have their voice heard, during child protection procedures and in any child care proceedings, if it is absent make it an issue for the LA and if it is absent in court, make it a basis of appeal. The rights are clear. In W (Children) [2010] UKSC 12 the Supreme Court said :

'22....The existing law erects a presumption against a child giving evidence which requires to be rebutted by anyone seeking to put questions to the child. That cannot be reconciled with the approach of the European Court of Human Rights, which always aims to strike a fair balance between competing Convention rights. Article 6 requires that the proceedings overall be fair and this normally entails an opportunity to challenge the evidence presented by the other side. But even in criminal proceedings account must be taken of the article 8 rights of the perceived victim: see SN v Sweden, App no 34209/96, 2 July 2002. Striking that balance in care proceedings may well mean that the child should not be called to give evidence in the great majority of cases, but that is a result and not a presumption or even a starting point.

23. The object of the proceedings is to achieve a fair trial in the determination of the rights of all the people involved. Children are harmed if they are taken away from their families for no good reason. Children are harmed if they are left in abusive families. This means that the court must admit all the evidence which bears upon the relevant questions: whether the threshold criteria justifying state intervention have been proved; if they have, what action if any will be in the best interests of the child? The court cannot ignore relevant evidence just because other evidence might have been better. It will have to do the best it can on what it has.

24. When the court is considering whether a particular child should be called as a witness, the court will have to weigh two considerations: the advantages that that will bring to the determination of the truth and the damage it may do to the welfare of this or any other child. A fair trial is a trial which is fair in the light of the issues which have to be decided. Mr Geekie accepts that the welfare of the child is also a relevant consideration, albeit not the paramount consideration in this respect. He is right to do so, because the object of the proceedings is to promote the welfare of this and other children. The hearing cannot be fair to them unless their interests are given great weight.

25. In weighing the advantages that calling the child to give evidence may bring to the fair and accurate determination of the case, the court will have to look at several factors. One will be the issues it has to decide in order properly to determine the case. Sometimes it may be possible to decide the case without making findings on particular allegations. Another will be the quality of the evidence it already has. Sometimes there may be enough evidence to make the findings needed whether or not the child is cross-examined. Sometimes there will be nothing useful to be gained from the child's oral evidence. The case is built upon a web of behaviour, drawings, stray remarks, injuries and the like, and not upon concrete allegations voiced by the child. The quality of any ABE interview will also be an important factor, as will be the nature of any challenge which the party may wish to make. The court is unlikely to be helped by generalised accusations of lying, or by a fishing expedition in which the child is taken slowly through the story yet again in the hope that something will turn up, or by a cross examination which is designed to intimidate the child and pave the way for accusations of inconsistency in a future criminal trial. On the other hand, focussed questions which put forward a different explanation for certain events may help the court to do justice between the parties. Also relevant will be the age and maturity of the child and the length of time since the events in question, for these will have a bearing on whether an account now can be as reliable as a near-contemporaneous account, especially if given in a well-conducted ABE interview.

26. The age and maturity of the child, along with the length of time since the events in question, will also be relevant to the second part of the inquiry, which is the risk of harm to the child. Further specific factors may be the support which the child has from family or other sources, or the lack of it, the child's own wishes and feelings about giving evidence, and the views of the child's guardian and, where appropriate, those with parental responsibility. We endorse the view that an unwilling child should rarely, if ever, be obliged to give evidence. The risk of further delay to the proceedings is also a factor: there is a general principle that delay in determining any question about a child's upbringing is likely to prejudice his welfare: see Children Act 1989, s 1(2). There may also be specific risks of harm to this particular child. Where there are parallel criminal proceedings, the likelihood of the child having to give evidence twice may increase the risk of harm. The parent may be seeking to put his child through this ordeal in order to strengthen his hand in the criminal proceedings rather than to enable the family court to get at the truth. On

*the other hand, as the family court has to give less weight to
the evidence of a child because she has not been called, then
that may be damaging too. However, the court is entitled to
have regard to the general evidence of the harm which giving
evidence may do to children, as well as to any features which
are particular to this child and this case. That risk of harm is
an ever-present feature to which, on the present evidence, the
court must give great weight. The risk, and therefore the
weight, may vary from case to case, but the court must always
take it into account and does not need expert evidence in order
to do so.*

*27. But on both sides of the equation, the court must factor in
what steps can be taken to improve the quality of the child's
evidence and at the same time to decrease the risk of harm to
the child. These two aims are not in opposition to one another.
The whole premise of Achieving Best Evidence and the special
measures in criminal cases is that this will improve rather
than diminish the quality of the evidence to the court. It does
not assume that the most reliable account of any incident is
one made from recollection months or years later in the
stressful conditions of a courtroom. Nor does it assume that an
"Old Bailey style" cross examination is the best way of testing*

that evidence. It may be the best way of casting doubt upon it in the eyes of a jury but that is another matter. A family court would have to be astute both to protect the child from the harmful and destructive effects of questioning and also to evaluate the answers in the light of the child's stage of development.

28. The family court will have to be realistic in evaluating how effective it can be in maximising the advantage while minimising the harm. There are things that the court can do but they are not things that it is used to doing at present. It is not limited by the usual courtroom procedures or to applying the special measures by analogy. The important thing is that the questions which challenge the child's account are fairly put to the child so that she can answer them, not that counsel should be able to question her directly. One possibility is an early video'd cross examination as proposed by Pigot. Another is cross-examination via video link. But another is putting the required questions to her through an intermediary. This could be the court itself, as would be common in continental Europe and used to be much more common than it is now in the courts of this country.

29. In principle, the approach in private family proceedings between parents should be the same as the approach in care proceedings. However, there are specific risks to which the court must be alive. Allegations of abuse are not being made by a neutral and expert local authority which has nothing to gain by making them, but by a parent who is seeking to gain an advantage in the battle against the other parent. This does not mean that they are false but it does increase the risk of misinterpretation, exaggeration or downright fabrication. On the other hand, the child will not routinely have the protection and support of a Cafcass guardian. There are also many more litigants in person in private proceedings. So if the court does reach the conclusion that justice cannot be done unless the child gives evidence, it will have to take very careful precautions to ensure that the child is not harmed by this.

30. It will be seen that these considerations are simply an amplification of those outlined by Smith LJ in the Medway case, at para 45, but without the starting point, at para 44. The essential test is whether justice can be done to all the parties without further questioning of the child. Our prediction is that, if the court is called upon to do it, the consequence of the balancing exercise will usually be that the additional benefits to the court's task in calling the child do not outweigh the additional harm that it will do to the child. A wise parent with his child's interests truly at heart will understand that too. But rarity should be a consequence of the exercise rather than a threshold test (as in Huang v Secretary of State for the Home Department [2007] UKHL 11, [2007] 2 AC 167, para 20). [xlv]

Article 16 provides for rights that are a reflection of the ECHR article 8:

'1. No child shall be subjected to arbitrary or unlawful interference with his or her privacy, family, or correspondence, nor to unlawful attacks on his or her honour and reputation.

2. The child has the right to the protection of the law against such interference or attacks.'

This of particular interest where children have been placed into care either on a temporary basis or as the result of a full care order. The removal or denial of mobile phones, laptops and the like is a flagrant breach of a child's rights to correspondence. I don't believe it has been tested in a court, but it is an interesting challenge to throw at social work departments.

Article 18 deals directly with parental responsibilities:

'1. States Parties shall use their best efforts to ensure recognition of the principle that both parents have common responsibilities for the upbringing and development of the child. Parents or, as the case may be, legal guardians, have the primary responsibility for the upbringing and development of the child. The best interests of the child will be their basic concern.

2. For the purpose of guaranteeing and promoting the rights set forth in the present Convention, States Parties shall render appropriate assistance to parents and legal guardians in the performance of their child-rearing responsibilities and shall ensure the development of institutions, facilities and services for the care of children.

3. States Parties shall take all appropriate measures to ensure that children of working parents have the right to benefit from child-care services and facilities for which they are eligible.'

So there it is in black and white, the responsibility for bringing up a child is the parents, not the State and the State should render appropriate assistance to allow parents to so do. Stand on this right, the social worker's charge should not be down the track of threats to remove, but what assistance can be offered. Of course if they do offer assistance it must be realistic and measurable by outcome. Ask the social workers, the chair of protection conferences, the Director of Children's Services, just how are they meeting **all** of their responsibilities to you.

Once again there are articles on disability and health services that may be relevant to your case. You need to make yourself aware of the rights available to you and your children and make effective challenges based upon them. If you don't stand on your rights, then social workers will simply walk all over them.

There is another convention that appears to get little recognition, indeed it has yet to be even ratified in some countries such as Ireland but it is just as important to fighting a case against social services for some families as what is listed above. That convention is the United Nations Convention on the Rights of Persons with Disabilities.

'The purpose of the present Convention is to promote, protect

and ensure the full and equal enjoyment of all human rights and fundamental freedoms by all persons with disabilities, and to promote respect for their inherent dignity. Persons with disabilities include those who have long-term physical, mental, intellectual or sensory impairments which in interaction with various barriers may hinder their full and effective participation in society on an equal basis with others.[xlvi] '

The key articles of the convention follow:

'*Article 3 - General principles*

Respect for the evolving capacities of children with disabilities and respect for the right of children with disabilities to preserve their identities.

Article 7 - Children with disabilities

1. States Parties shall take all necessary measures to ensure the full enjoyment by children with disabilities of all human rights and fundamental freedoms on an equal basis with other children.

2. In all actions concerning children with disabilities, the best interests of the child shall be a primary consideration.

3. States Parties shall ensure that children with disabilities have the right to express their views freely on all matters affecting them, their views being given due weight in accordance with their age and maturity, on an equal basis with other children, and to be provided with disability and age-appropriate assistance to realize that right.

Article 14 - Liberty and security of the person

1. States Parties shall ensure that persons with disabilities, on an equal basis with others:

- *Enjoy the right to liberty and security of person;*
- *Are not deprived of their liberty unlawfully or arbitrarily, and that any deprivation of liberty is in conformity with the law, and that the existence of a disability shall in no case justify a deprivation of liberty.*

2. States Parties shall ensure that if persons with disabilities are deprived of their liberty through any process, they are, on an equal basis with others, entitled to guarantees in accordance with international human rights law and shall be treated in compliance with the objectives and principles of this Convention, including by provision of reasonable accommodation.

Article 18 - Liberty of movement and nationality

2. Children with disabilities shall be registered immediately after birth and shall have the right from birth to a name, the right to acquire a nationality and, as far as possible, the right to know and be cared for by their parents.

Article 22 - Respect for privacy

1. No person with disabilities, regardless of place of residence or living arrangements, shall be subjected to arbitrary or unlawful interference with his or her privacy, family, home or correspondence or other types of communication or to unlawful attacks on his or her honour and reputation. Persons with disabilities have the right to the protection of the law against such interference or attacks.

2. States Parties shall protect the privacy of personal, health and rehabilitation information of persons with disabilities on an equal basis with others.

Article 23 - Respect for home and the family

2. States Parties shall ensure the rights and responsibilities of persons with disabilities, with regard to guardianship, wardship, trusteeship, adoption of children or similar institutions, where these concepts exist in national legislation; in all cases the best interests of the child shall be paramount. States Parties shall render appropriate assistance to persons with disabilities in the performance of their child-rearing responsibilities.

3. States Parties shall ensure that children with disabilities have equal rights with respect to family life. With a view to realizing these rights, and to prevent concealment, abandonment, neglect and segregation of children with disabilities, States Parties shall undertake to provide early and comprehensive information, services and support to children with disabilities and their families.

*4. **States Parties shall ensure that a child shall not be separated from his or her parents against their will, except when competent authorities subject to judicial review determine, in accordance with applicable law and procedures, that such separation is necessary for the best interests of the child. In no case shall a child be separated*** *from parents on the basis of a disability of either the child or one or both of the parents.*

5. States Parties shall, where the immediate family is unable to care for a child with disabilities, undertake every effort to provide alternative care within the wider family, and failing that, within the community in a family setting.

There are some very significant points here for families where either the parents or a child are classed as having a disability. Discrimination on the basis of disability means according to the UN convention *'any distinction, exclusion or restriction on the basis of disability which has the purpose or effect of impairing or nullifying the recognition, enjoyment or exercise, on an equal basis with others, of all human rights and fundamental freedoms in the political, economic, social, cultural, civil or any other field. It includes all forms of discrimination...'*

A regular feature of reasoning for removal of a child can boil down to the existence, real or alleged by social workers, of some sort of disability, either of the child or its parents. We have seen the frequent use of 'traits' to ascribe some sort of mental illness/instability on the part

334

of parents. There are cases of where a parent may be suffering a debilitating illness, such as requiring dialysis, or even hospitalisation for an accident which has led to the removal of a child from their care. Yet it is clear in Article 23 at point 4 that in no case shall a child be separated from parents on the basis of a disability of either. In such circumstances it is a fair point that child protection was the incorrect path to follow and that a child in need plan may have been more apposite. This argument and challenge can be made right at the beginning of any intervention and raised as an issue of discrimination contrary to the UN Convention.

We also see the importance of the child's voice once again in Article 7. There is a clear theme in all the rights outlined that children must be seen and heard. Unless your child is a baby or very young toddler there seems no reason why an appropriate method of giving the child a voice should be ignored.

We have already considered the codes of standards and ethics of social workers (and the codes are in Appendices A & B) in the context of complaints to their professional bodies. There is nothing preventing you raising those codes directly with the social worker and their managers, at child protection conferences and other such meetings. Identify their behaviour and match it to where it fails to meet the code. Ask (verbally or in formal communication) why they feel that they can act outside of the codes? If in a meeting ask the other's around the table if they think it is acceptable to act outside of professional standards–okay-you are likely to find they all have a sudden interest in the veneer on the table, but you are making them aware that just simply agreeing with a social worker may not be in their best interests, because after all they are all vicariously liable for the decisions taken. More on vicarious liability later.

The other point is that all the professionals reigned against you in child protection are public servants-a public officer is a person who carries out a public duty or has an office of trust. Although some may argue that they are not public officers, in all reality it boils down to the nature of the duties and the level of public trust involved that are relevant rather than the manner or nature of appointment. There are various public standards that must be adhered to but the overriding factor is the trust placed in the individual. At this stage we need say no more other than the highest standards of integrity should be evident, however we shall return to this particular aspect under the offence of Misconduct in Public Office.

In this chapter you will hopefully seen a range of challenges to the social worker's interventions. They are not a piece-meal approach but as highlighted form part of a wider strategy of challenging various aspects and professional roles to undermine the case being established against you. The aim is to ensure that all the assumptions and presumptions made about your family are challenged at the earliest opportunity. Do not let the tiniest issues slip by. Wherever possible make all your challenges formal and in writing, insist on responses being in writing, do not accept the telephone call, you need to establish the paper trial. Remember to record all interactions. When you receive a report, go through it with a fine tooth comb, highlight all the inaccuracies, misrepresentations and lies and write a response listing all of these with the evidence you have to the contrary.

Do this as soon as possible and copy it in to the list on page 221-2. Of course do point out your concerns about the poor practice and inaccurate information. Even with all the above reigned against them, the social workers may not give up or actually correct anything to your satisfaction, in that case it is time to step up the challenge and as we shall see in the next chapter utilise the law for your protection.

Chapter 6 Legal Remedies

The Local Authority may be acting under its statutory obligations and utilising the law on child protection against you, but the law can also work for you. There are a range of legal challenges that you can launch against the intervention and the beauty of this is that it may bring an end to their involvement or a change in attitude in your favour without you actually having to go all the way to court proceedings.

It is noteworthy that this approach has been successfully used by families in the UK and Ireland with a number of cases in Ireland going all the way through the courts and seeing children either not removed or returned to their loving homes. Once again this course of action offers no guarantees, but it is another front in the battle against social service interventions.

We are going to first turn to the use of Judicial Reviews. We shall cover this aspect in detail both for the UK and for the Republic of Ireland because the process differs somewhat between the two.

Judicial Review

A Judicial Review is a court proceeding whereby a judge reviews the lawfulness of a decision or an action that a public body has made. It is also a method to challenge the lawfulness of decisions made in the lower courts, tribunals and a range of administrative bodies. Judicial reviews look at the way a decision has been made and not necessarily at the outcome of the decision. That means the judge is not looking at the merits of a decision but how the decision was taken. The decision maker must not go beyond the limits of their authority.

In any decision making process you are entitled to fair procedures in how the decision is reached. This means that the decision-maker must not act with bias and must give you a fair hearing. You must be given an adequate opportunity to present your case. You must be informed of the matter and you must be given a chance to comment on the material put forward by the other side. The decision maker must comply with all legal requirements governing the decision. The relevance of this becomes clear when one recalls the two important ECHR judgments - _W v. United Kingdom_ (1988) 10 EHRR 29, para. 64, & Soares de Melo v. Portugal 2016, both of which confirmed the importance of the involvement of parents in the decision making process. It also goes to the heart of ensuring that your challenges to inaccurate information, misrepresentations and failure to follow correct procedures, ethics and standards has a legal route of review.

To bring a judicial review, you must have 'sufficient interest', that is you have been affected by the decision and demonstrate that you have grounds and an arguable case. If you bring a case, the High Court will examine the decision and how it was reached and will decide if it was illegally made or not. The court on finding an illegal decision can cancel or quash (reject as invalid) the decision. This is usually done by an order of *certorai*. If a decision maker hasn't undertaken to make a decision, or refused to do so when obliged to then the court can order the decision maker to make the decision. This is called an order of *mandamus*. It is also possible to obtain orders of an injunctive nature, make a declaration and to award damagesxlvii. The potential advantages of a judicial review cannot be overlooked.

With regard to grounds for judicial review you must demonstrate at least one or more of the following that a decision is:

- illegal-arises when a decision-maker misdirects itself in law, exercises a power wrongly, or improperly purports to exercise a power that it does not have, which is known as acting 'ultra vires';

- irrational-a decision may be challenged as unreasonable if it "is so unreasonable that no reasonable authority could ever have come to it";

- procedurally improper–a failure to observe statutory procedures or natural justice; or

- in breach of legitimate expectation, (either procedural or substantive)–when a public body is, by its own statements or acts, required to respond in a particular way but fails to do so. There cannot, however, be any expectation that the body will act unfairly or beyond its powers and the need to observe expectations must not fetter the public authority.

Social services as an arm of local government can be challenged as to the lawfulness of their decisions. Usually where there is a legal problem with the decision, then it often follows that there are substantive issues too. This means that not only the decision is unlawful but usually there has been some infringement of rights. This may mean that the decision cannot be taken again and produce the same results. So we now have a mechanism to challenge the social services intervention in your family utilising the law.

Before we look in a little more detail about the process of undertaking a judicial review there are a few aspects, common to both the UK and the Republic of Ireland that it is important to note.

(i) A judicial review requires the permission of the court. That means you must ask (apply) for leave to bring the proceedings.

(ii) There is a tight time limit of three months from the decision/issue you wish to challenge. These time limits are generally strictly applied, so it is essential that you act promptly.

(iii) You must be directly affected by the decision–as we said sufficient interest.

(iv) You must have an arguable case with grounds for the action.

(v) Remember generally the loser pays the winner's costs.

Let us turn now to the process in England and Wales (though

you find the process is very similar in Scotland and Northern Ireland). The first step is to issue a Letter before Claim to the Director of Children's Services at your local authority. This is a requirement under the Civil Procedure Rules part 54[xlviii] and the court will not take kindly to you missing this step. In this letter you must set out your proposed claim. A template appears below:

---

[i] SFR 41/2016, 29 September 2016 – www.gov.uk

[ii] https://www.theguardian.com/society/2009/apr/20/care-system-failures

https://www.nao.org.uk/wp-content/uploads/2015/07/Care-leavers-transition-to-adulthood-summary.pdf

[iii] https://www.bbc.co.uk/news/amp/education-41581805

[iv] http://www.familylawweek.co.uk/site.aspx?i=ed117048

[v] From http://ukfostering.org.uk/ "Our foster carers are paid a weekly allowance, per child, ranging from £354 per week or significantly higher for a child remanded into care or a child with special needs. This is significantly above the government's minimum fostering allowances which are currently in place.

What does the fostering allowance cover?
The Fostering Allowance is in effect a foster carer payment, and includes payment for each carer's skills and commitment as well as an allowance for the maintenance side of fostering.

The maintenance element of this allowance includes:

• expenses for clothes
• pocket money and savings
• food
• leisure activities
• most school transport

At UK Fostering we also add an additional payment to the allowance for children's birthdays, religious or cultural festivals (Festival allowance) and a respite allowance.

Fostering allowance payments
Our foster carers receive payment promptly and at an agreed day, on a fortnightly basis. We issue a monthly statement of the payments to each carer and ensure that our carers have access to an accountant who can advise them on any finance or tax related questions.

It is also worth noting that several years ago, the government introduced favourable tax benefits for foster carers, and according to the Inland Revenue, all foster carers are deemed to be self employed."

vi   £15,000 to £57,000 for councils' own foster care provision; and £18,000 to £73,000 for other providers' foster care. National Audit Office 2014 -https://www.nao.org.uk/wp-content/uploads/2014/11/Children-in-care1.pdf

http://www.dailymail.co.uk/news/article-2309362/Social-services-search-mother-Kiya-Pasks-home-Boots-pharmacist-reported-her.html

viiihttp://www.marilynstowe.co.uk/2017/06/06/social-worker-struck-off-after-lying-to-colleagues/

https://www.4socialwork.com/blog/2016/08/social-worker-struck-off-for-falsifying-assessments-claimed-he-was-bullied

[ix]   See Chapter 11on the *Persecution strategies in a child care order investigation*- Linda Ärlig Department of Social Science, the Psychology Section, University of Örebro, Sweden

[x]

https://www.gov.uk/government/uploads/system/uploads/attachment_data/file/271429/directors_of_child_services_-_stat_guidance.pdf

[xi]   Ibid pp-3-4.

[xii]   Ibid p.5

[xiii]   AIMS Journal, 2004, Vol. 16 No 3

[xiv]   Ibid.

[xv]   Example taken from Newcastle Safeguarding Children Board https://www.nscb.org.uk/staff-and-volunteers/procedures/role-chair-child-protection-conference

[xvi]   https://ico.org.uk/for-the-public/raising-concerns/

[xvii]   Ibid. & https://ico.org.uk/concerns/

xviii http://www.familylawweek.co.uk/site.aspx?i=ed127643

xix http://www.thecanterburyclinic.com/dr-celest-van-rooyen.html

xx http://www.bailii.org/ew/cases/EWHC/Fam/2014/270.ht ml

xxi https://arachnoid.com/trouble_with_psychology/ Paul Lutus.

xxii http://www.legislation.gov.uk/ukpga/1989/41/section/26

xxiii www.somerset.gov.uk/EasySiteWeb/GatewayLink.aspx?al Id=56738

xxiv http://www.hcpcuk.org/assets/documents/10004EDFStan dardsofconduct,performanceandethics.pdf http://coru.ie/uploads/documents/typeset_Social_Worker_Cod e_Feb_2010.pdf

xxv http://www.legislation.gov.uk/uksi/2009/309/contents/ma de

xxvi https://www.ombudsman.org.uk/making-complaint

xxvii National Archives Home Office circular 017 / 2008

xxviii https://police.community/topic/1784-r-v-syed-power-of-entry-to-save-life-limb/

xxix

http://www.irishstatutebook.ie/eli/1991/act/17/enacted/en/html

xxx   http://www.familylawweek.co.uk/site.aspx?i=ed1899

xxxi   Appendix C p.623

xxxii Oxford English Dictionary

xxxiii https://www.gov.uk/government/publications/working-together-to-safeguard-children--2

xxxiv Ibid p 21

xxxv   Ibid p 21

xxxvi

https://www.dcya.gov.ie/documents/Publications/ChildrenFirst.pdf

xxxvii Ibid p 8.

xxxviii

http://www.echr.coe.int/Documents/Convention_ENG.pdf

xxxix Appendix I outlines the first 14 Articles of the ECHR.

xl   http://www.familylawweek.co.uk/site.aspx?i=ed132053

xli   http://www.familylawweek.co.uk/site.aspx?i=ed114409

xlii   https://hudoc.echr.coe.int/eng

xliiihttp://www.ohchr.org/EN/ProfessionalInterest/Pages/CRC.a
spx

Jonathan Brown, The Independent, Saturday 12 November
2011.

xlv   http://www.familylawweek.co.uk/site.aspx?i=ed54115

xlvi

       https://www.un.org/development/desa/disabilities/conven
tion-on-the-rights-of-persons-with-disabilities/convention-on-
the-rights-of-persons-with-disabilities-2.html

xlvii   Remedies -The question of remedies is often critical in judicial
review proceedings, as it may determine not only whether it is
worthwhile bringing a claim, but also whether permission will be
granted to bring the claim.

One or more of six forms of final relief are available, and all are
discretionary. These are:

- an order quashing the decision in question (quashing
  order);
- an order restraining the body under review from acting
  beyond its powers (prohibitory order) – this is rare as an
  injunction will usually suffice;
- an order requiring the body under review to carry out its
  legal duties (mandatory order);
- a declaration;

- a stay or injunction;
- damages.

[xlviii] https://www.justice.gov.uk/courts/procedure-rules/civil/rules/part54

LETTER BEFORE CLAIM

Proposed claim for judicial review

The Defendant:

The claimants:

Reference details

Case Refs:

The details of the matter being challenged

The issue

The details of the legal advisers, if any, dealing with this claim

The details of any interested parties

Copies of this pre-action letter will be forwarded to the following:

The details of any information sought

The details of any documents that are considered relevant and necessary

The address for reply and service of court documents

Proposed reply date

The date of service of this document is…... , the date by which responses are expected is…. (14 days)

It is important that you clearly establish what decisions and actions that the local authority have taken that you are challenging, establishing how and why you believe it is unlawful in the issues. That may include case law that backs your position, legislation, statutory guidance and human rights violations. The respondent has 14 days to reply to your issues. Look at the example below–it is a fictional example to demonstrate a number of issues.

LETTER BEFORE CLAIM

Proposed claim for judicial review

under the pre-action protocol for Judicial Review

The Defendant:

_____

Director   of   Children's   services

_____

_____

Sad Town

The Claimant:

Mr & Mrs_____

_____

_____

Sad Town

The details of the matter being challenged

- The decision of Social Worker XXXX to initiate a

Public Law Outline procedure in order to obtain a Care Order with regard to my unborn child without due regard to process and protocol as laid down in the Working Together document and statutory requirements under the Children's Act 1989-in particular a full multi-agency pre-birth assessment.

- For the above named Social Worker to threaten and intimidate the claimant with her decision to remove my unborn child at birth based solely on her knowledge of previous social care interventions that were not only inaccurate, but took no account of changed circumstances since those events.

- The failure to follow correct statutory and working guidelines by not convening a multi-agency pre-birth conference. That such a conference could not have been informed by an up-to-date pre-birth assessment as no such assessment has been carried out.

- The issuance of a false instrument contrary to sec 8 of the 1981 Forgery and Counterfeiting Act. For clarity:

'Meaning of "instrument". (1)Subject to subsection (2)

below, in this Part of this Act "instrument" means—(a)any document, whether of a formal or informal character;'

Whereby the 'Letter of Intention to Commence Legal Proceedings' fails to follow correct procedure, does not offer a legal meeting whereby I, along with a legal representative can discuss how the 'things the LA are worried about' can be examined and a plan put in place to alleviate these worries. There is no statement as to what is required of the claimant to address these worries, nor is there evidenced concerns only opinion. The section on 'What Social Services have done to help' actually fails to record any such help. The entire section does not list any one categorical statement of explicit help, only a continuation of unfounded criticisms of the Claimant.

- The document as a whole fails to fulfill the criteria for a properly executed legal document under the PLO process. See *The Children Act 1989, Guidance and Regulations, Volume 1, Court Orders.* Examples of the correct protocols follow:

'The PLO Pre Proceedings puts a lot of emphasis on streamlining the Care Proceedings process. It also anticipates that Local Authorities will have undertaken appropriate

355

assessments prior to issuing proceedings and that the child/young person and parents are fully aware early on of what the issues are, what needs to change and that proceedings are being considered.'

*'The decision to initiate the PLO Pre Proceedings process must be based on an up-to-date Core Assessment. It is also to be expected that if consideration was being given to start the PLO Pre Proceedings process that the risk to the child/young person was such **that a Section 47 investigation had been undertaken and a Child Protection Case Conference held.'***
Neither of these basic protocols have been followed.

- Both the Sections: *'things the LA are worried about'* & *'What Social Services have done to help'* are full of factual inaccuracies, misrepresentations and a number of defamations. This demonstrates an unprofessional lack of due diligence and calls into question the integrity and honesty of the Social Worker XXXXXX.

- The on-going decision to be in breach of the Human Rights Act, Article 8 the right to respect for private life and unnecessary and disproportionate interference by a public body.

- A clear indication that XXX Borough Council are prepared to be in breach of the United Nations Convention on Rights of the Child namely Articles 3, 4 and 5 upon its birth.

- The on-going decision to fail to act with due diligence, follow protocol or procedure in line with the Children Act 1989 & 'Working Together' Document 2015

- The on-going decision to be in breach of the Human Rights Act, Article 8 'the right to respect for private life without interference by a public body' & Article 7 'no punishment without crime' The Defendant is a public authority and that as such it is unlawful for it to act in a way which is incompatible with a Convention right under s 6(1) HRA, those rights including the right to respect for the Claimant's private and family life under Article 8 of the European Convention on Human Rights (ECHR): The rights that the Claimant have to be weighed and in particular balanced in the favour of any (vulnerable) child of which English statute requires the child's rights to be paramount. If the defendant claims it is asserting that provisions of an English statute take priority over the Claimant's rights under Article 8 it is an incorrect statement of the law. On the contrary, s 3 HRA requires primary and subordinate legislation to be read and given effect in a way which is compatible with the Convention rights, so far as it is possible to do so.

11. Under *'things the LA are worried about'* number 7 and *'What Social Services have done to help'* number 4 reference is made to *'flee the country'* and *'intending to leave the country to have her baby'* has no relevance to the LA. Are the LA threatening to violate the Claimant's right to leave the UK? This is a **Fundamental** right as given to all European Citizens under the *Charter of Fundamental European Rights of the European Union*–Article 45 states:

1. Every citizen of the Union has the right to move and reside freely within the territory of the Member States.

2. Freedom of movement and residence may be granted, in accordance with the Treaty establishing the European

Community, to nationals of third countries legally   resident in the territory of a Member State.

As France Frattini, the then EU Commissioner for Justice, Freedom and Security stated:

'The right of freedom of movement for individuals...is a basic right that must be guaranteed....'

The defendant has previously referred to the Children's Act 1989 (which provides that the child's welfare shall be the court's paramount consideration when it determines any question with respect to the upbringing of a child) together with the Defendant's duty under s 47 Children Act 1989 to investigate where it has reasonable cause to suspect that a child who lives, or is found, in an area is suffering, or is likely to suffer, significant harm.

Whatever provision(s) of English statutory law- the obligation under s 3 HRA requires those provisions to be interpreted in accordance with Strasburg jurisprudence unless it is not possible to do so. The limits of statutory interpretation under s 3 HRA are wide and can involve giving words a strained meaning which are not their natural and ordinary one: see R v

A (No 2) [2002] 1 AC 45, [44] - [45]. In the rare circumstances that a provision of English law cannot be read and given effect in a way that is compatible with a Convention right the court may consider making a declaration of incompatibility under s 4 HRA but not until it has given that Crown notice entitling a Minister to be joined as a party: s 5 HRA. In such rare circumstances a public authority is relieved of its obligation to act compatibly with the Convention right: s 6(2) HRA.

Despite the reference to the apparent superiority of English statute, therefore, it cannot in the Claimant's view be taken to be asserting that (unspecified) provisions of the Children Act 1989 are incompatible with Article 8. This is manifestly untrue for the reasons that follow.

(i) The mutual enjoyment by parent and child of each other's company constitutes a fundamental element of family life, even if the relationship between the parents has broken down, and domestic measures hindering such enjoyment amount to an interference with the right protected by Article 8:

Mc Michael v UK 20 EHRR 205 [86]; Venema v The Netherlands Judgment of 17 December 2002 [7]]: Elsholz v

Germany Judgment of 13 July 2000 [43J.]

(ii) Article 8 requires that the domestic authorities should strike a fair balance between the interests of the child and those of the parents. Gorgulu v Germany Judgment of 26 February 2004 [43]; Elsholz [50]; Summerfield v Germany Judgment of 8 July 2003 [64].

(iii) Whilst Article 8 contains no explicit procedural requirements, the decision-making process involved in measures of interference must be fair and such as to ensure due respect of the interests safeguarded by Article 8. What has to be determined is whether, having regard to the particular circumstances of the case and notably the serious nature of the decisions to be taken, **the parents have been involved in the decision-making process, seen as a whole, to a degree sufficient to provide them with the requisite protection of their interests:** Mc Michael [87]; Gorgulu [52]; Venema [91].

(iv) It is essential that a parent be placed in a position where he or she may obtain access to information which is relied on by the authorities in taking measures of protective care or in taking decisions relevant to the care or custody of a child.

Otherwise, the parent will be unable to participate effectively in the decision-making process or put forward in a fair and adequate manner those matters militating in favour of his or her ability to provide the child with proper care and protection: Venema [92].

(v) Both the storing by a public authority of information relating to an individual's private life and the use of it and the refusal to allow an opportunity for it to be refuted amount to interference with the right to respect for private life secured in Article 8: Rotaru v Romania Judgment of 4 May 2000 [46].

(vi) Public information can fall within the scope of private life where it is systematically collected and stored in files held by the authorities, especially where such information concerns a person's distant past, or where the information has been declared false and is likely to injure the person's reputation: Rotaru [43]–[44]

In breach of several of these principles the Defendant:

(i) kept and relied on inaccurate, out of date and incomplete information relating to the Claimant's private life.

(ii) Deprived the applicant of the opportunity to participate effectively in the decision-making process or put forward in a fair and adequate manner those matters militating in the Claimant's favour.

As far as the substantive aspects are concerned, the Defendant has no real prospect of establishing that its interference with the Claimant's right to respect for private and family life was/is necessary, in the sense that it was proportionate to a pressing social need, in pursuit of one of the legitimate aims under Article 8(2). Indeed, the decision to interfere with the Fundamental Rights afforded under the Charter of the European Union namely Article 45–the freedom to travel and settle anywhere within the EU borders by inference in the PLO letter by making this a 'threshold' type statement is a serious violation.

The Defendant's belief at the time (whether reasonable or not) as to whether it was acting in the best interests of the child is not the relevant criterion under the ECHR. The test is whether the actions taken were a proportionate response to the threat actually posed to the welfare of the child. That requires a proper assessment of the risk posed by the Claimant before any decisions are taken which may prove difficult to reverse.

The onus is not on the Claimant to try to take action after the event. Thus, to ensure arbitrary decisions are not made procedural safeguards must be in place to permit the parent to be involved in the process. These were not in place in the claimant's case. The absence of sufficient procedural safeguards to protect the claimant's interests meant that the Claimant has now been presented with a fait accomplis.

The Defendant relies on rumour, speculation, hearsay and unsubstantiated allegations.

The Defendant's stance is also causing further distress to the Claimant which will be relied on in aggravation of damages. The Claimant would draw the Defendant's attention to Lillie & Reed v Newcastle City Council and others [2002] EWHC 1600 in which the authors of a report into alleged child abuse at a local authority nursery who ignored evidence tending to exculpate the Claimants and failed, amongst other things, to reflect accurately the Claimants' side of the story were found to have acted maliciously, despite their honest belief that the children had been abused. The court was particularly unimpressed with the Defendant's misrepresentation of the reasons why the allegations had not previously been able to be substantiated. In that case. the Claimants were alleged to have physically and sexually abused approximately 30 children in their care for more than a year. The case against them was based on extensive verbal and behavioural disclosures by the children themselves. After a 6 month trial Eady J was satisfied that the Claimants were entirely innocent and had been the victims of a witch-hunt. The court awarded damages of £200,000 to each claimant.

The above issues & decisions are exacerbated by the following:

Repeated instances of Misconduct & Malfeasance in Public Office by the Defendant & staff/agents

Issuance of False Instruments contrary to section 8 of the 1981 Forgery and Counterfeiting Act

Breach of Data Protection Act 1998

Repeated lack of transparency-HCPC Code of Ethics, Working Together 'public scrutiny'

Continued processing of inaccurate data contrary to the Data Protection Act and sharing of said information.

The issue

In January 2016 the Defendant issued a Public Law Outline letter that failed to adhere to correct legal procedure, guidelines and precedent.

The Defendant failed to carry out transparent, unbiased and up-to-date to date assessments constitutes a violation of our Human Rights, and those of the whole family as a result, namely Article 8. In addition, note violation of Articles 3, 5, 6, 7, 12, 28 & 30 of the Universal Declaration of Human Rights.

The Defendant has personally corresponded in an intimidatory and defamatory manner,

In summary, the Claimant believes that the process followed in this case is so fundamentally flawed and lacking in the essential minimum requirements that it was and is unlawful.

Please note that many allegations of wrong-doing perpetrated by your officers/agents/employees have been either voice recorded and /or videoed and transcripts are being prepared.

The details of the action that the Defendant is expected to take:

- All actions and interventions to cease forthwith.

- No Further Action as the only recorded outcome.

- That all inaccurate records are expunged forthwith.

- That financial compensation commensurate with harassment, intimidation, *ultra vires* actions and defamations of our family is offered for our consideration within 14 days.

- That the employees/officers/agents for whom we can provide evidence of the wrong-doing and illegal actions are subject to full disciplinary hearings and reported to the HCPC within one month. Where there is a basis for a criminal charge of Misconduct or Malfeasance in Public Office that those perpetrators are reported to the Police.

- Written clarification and apology.

The details of any interested parties

Lord Justice Munby

Royal Courts of Justice

Strand

London WC2A 2LL

Christopher Booker (Journalist)

Sunday Telegraph

111 Buckingham Palace Road

London

SW1W 0BT

Tatjana   **Zdanoka**

ASP08H140

European   Parliament

rue   Wiertz   60

1047   Brussels

Belgium

The details of any information sought

Full un-redacted disclosure of all:

Social Care reports,

outcomes,

meeting notes & minutes,

email correspondence within and without the LA regarding the Claimant.

The details of any documents that are considered relevant and necessary

Complete, up to current date records required in line with the following:

- Section 7(1) of the Data Protection Act 1998 – and as per the statutory entitlement to access personal data

- Freedom of Information Act 2000 where applicable with regard to the information held by XXX Borough Council

- Section 35(2) of the Data Protection Act - provides for material to be disclosed if it is necessary for the purposes of establishing, exercising or defending legal rights and for the purpose of or in connection with, any legal proceedings (including prospective legal proceedings), which in this instance is the case.

The address for reply and service of court documents

Mr & Mrs_____

1_____

_____

Sad Town

Proposed reply date

The date of service of this document is xx[th] of Month 20XX, the date by which responses are expected is XXth of Month 20XX.

Quite often the issuance of this letter can have a major effect. There may be a change of personnel dealing with you, there may be a request to have a meeting to discuss how to resolve things, I have even known it to elicit the question 'what can we do?' Of course you just want them to go away so tell them in no uncertain terms. You want the inaccuracies in the records correcting and you want the case closed, moved to a child in need with the requested supports, or whatever suits your case. The point is, if it is done properly and you have a genuine case it is unlikely that the LA will want to defend the case and be exposed not only to the judgment, costs and possible damages but also to the negative publicity. Of course there are those who will point to a ruling by Judge Munby, President of the Family Division where he found in a Judicial Review that the issues should have been dealt with not by Judicial Review but within the family court proceedings. The difference here is that the family were already in child care proceedings when the judicial review was brought, we are of course talking about challenging the local authority *prior* to the issuance or any public law outline (or a direct challenge to it) or court proceedings. There is nothing to stop you issuing such a letter before claim under the pre-action protocol whilst at the early stages of intervention or during child protection procedures.

The great advantage you have is that you can issue the pre-action letter without having any of the worries or costs of actually going to court and it may have the positive affect you are seeking. I know that seems like giving the game away to any child protectionist who reads or is told of this, however, the real point is that even if they have read it they cannot know for sure if you will proceed to court or not if the pre-action letter does not receive a positive response. Plus an added advantage is that you can still make the formal application for permission and if granted you will have to serve on the LA anyway and once again they may choose not to defend but to try to reach an agreement. You can still withdraw your application with minimal cost. Hopefully the advantages of this process are clear. After your complaints, challenges and criticisms of social workers and other professionals failings, the fact that you are aware of your rights and knowledge of the system should make any LA take seriously the threat of a judicial review.

Of course if their response is unsatisfactory you can lodge the claim in the Administrative division of the High Court. The test as we said to obtain permission is an arguable case and 'standing': that is a genuine interest in bringing the case. If the pre-action letter and application to court are firmly grounded, then permission should not be an issue.

A quick note here about the relationship between complaints and judicial review. Generally, a court will expect you to exhaust the complaints procedure before you issue a judicial review. However, as we know LA's can drag their feet, ignore the demand to instigate the next level of complaint and effectively close a complaint down by simply failing to respond. Any such actions are acceptable enough reasons to move to judicial review because you believe that justice and fairness will not be upheld by the LA through their complaint process. In other words, you again take advantage of their failings, or if we are being cynical their attempts to ignore the complaint long enough to institute their own care proceedings, whereby your complaint is put on hold until the outcome of the said proceedings.

If you end up applying and gaining permission for judicial review, then the case proceeds in the court. The defendant will submit their evidence, probably trying to show how carefully the decision was taken. This should hold no sway with the judge, a decision made unlawfully is unlawful full stop. However, you need to be prepared for this approach of the defence and ready to argue such issues as procedural failures, lack of evidence to support their decisions and the legal basis based on established case law at a domestic and European level. I know this sounds a tall order, but with this book in your hand and access to the internet it is more than possible–simply because judicial reviews are largely 'heard' on paper.

Urgent or straightforward cases do not take long to argue and sometimes the permission stage and substantive hearings are 'rolled up' and heard at the same time. This obviously keeps costs down. The full second or substantive stage of hearing usually takes place within a few months (though some do drag on) and both sides have to file skeleton arguments- i.e. summaries of the case/legal arguments. (Skeleton arguments are dealt with in Chapter 8) Hopefully, the impact of the pre-action protocol letter will be enough to effect the outcomes desired without resort to court proceedings.

Turning to the Republic of Ireland all the descriptions above with regard as to what a judicial review is, what it can do, the remedies and requirements all still apply, however the process is slightly different. The biggest difference is that there is currently no necessity to issue a letter before claim under any pre-action protocol.

That said, although there is no necessity it does not mean that you cannot issue a style of a letter before claim. Some families in Ireland have actually issued a modified letter, it does not need to include all the detail as above but an outline of the issues and a demand for what the family wanted social services to do. It has proved effective in a number of cases. Although it is best not to rehearse your arguments to them (as this would give them too much of a 'heads up' of what would be in any judicial review) it can act as a 'warning shot across the bows' and possibly have the effect of changing their approach. An example of such a letter sent to the local SS by a pregnant mum who had fled to Ireland is below. It should be noted that this letter prevented any application for a care order on the new born and saw a support plan put in place instead of removal.

Your name

Address

Ireland

Social Worker name

Child and Family Agency,

_____,

_____

Date

NOTICE OF INTENTION TO SUE FOR JUDICIAL REVIEW

Dear XXXX,

By way of courtesy, please take this as a formal notice of intention to sue [local office] Social Services and by default TUSLA–the Child and Family Agency, under the process of Judicial Review for their misfeasance, malfeasance and nonfeasance according to statute, best practice and European Convention and Human Rights.

Although it is our prerogative to not animate our case prior to proceedings we wish to draw your attention to the failure to adhere to the 'Children First' practice guidance, the statutes of the Child Care Act 1991, the Irish Constitution as well as the Charter of Fundamental Rights of the European Union and the Convention of Human Rights.

Further my position is backed by Article 7 of the United Nations Convention on the Rights of the Child of 20 November 1989 that a child has, as far as possible, the right to be cared for by his or her parents. It is, moreover, appropriate to recall that the mutual enjoyment by parent and child of each other's company constitutes a fundamental element of family life even when the relationship between the parents has broken down (see, inter alia, the Eriksson v. Sweden judgment of 22 June 1989, Series A no. 156, p. 24, para. 58).

As outlined to you, there are Appeals and Judicial Reviews pending in the UK, along with possible private prosecutions of individuals who have lied and perjured themselves to remove my first born child. Further legal action is pending and there will be an instigation of further actions in the Republic of Ireland against individuals should it be necessary.

I moved freely to the Republic of Ireland as a European Citizen as is my right under Article 45 of the Charter of Fundamental Rights of the European Union. At the time of my move there were no proceedings, or active involvement of social services in the UK. There was no pre-birth assessment undertaken by the UK, there was no child protection plan or any other plan in process at the time of my move. Therefore the onus lies upon the Irish authorities to undertake their own assessments and consideration of any concerns raised–although as you yourself have confirmed on two occasions the Child and Family Agency have no concerns regarding myself or my unborn child.

Therefore your deprecation to the demands of the UK when they have no jurisdiction over myself, or my unborn child leaves you open to legal action for your failure to adhere to international law and your own requirements.

I am and do reside legally in the Republic of Ireland as is my right. I am supported financially by a private income and by a supportive network of friends and professionals including mid-wives, doulas and good Samaritans, as well, of course, by my family who are in the process of retiring to the Republic.

I hereby give you notice to undertake both your moral and legal duties towards my self as a resident in Ireland or I shall have no hesitation in bringing proceedings against the agency and individuals in the High Court.

Yours sincerely

XXXXXXXXX

Cc Area Manager Local SS

This is of course unnecessary, but it may save the work of

preparing the actual judicial review and attending court. However, your circumstances may require you to issue the judicial review so we will look at that process now.

Judicial reviews in Ireland are started by making an application direct to the High Court. Although emergency applications may be made anytime, it is generally expected that the application for a judicial review is made on a Monday whilst the judicial review judge is sitting. You will need two forms: a number 13 High Court Form of 'A statement to ground application for Judicial Review', a number 14 High Court Form of 'Affidavit verifying statement grounding an application for leave to apply for judicial review', along with an ex parte docketxlix.

The affidavit must be notarised that is it must be signed and stamped by either a practicing solicitor or a notary public. Fortunately just by the Four Courts in Dublin is Orca Printl where you can not only get your documents notarised but copies made and even pay stamp duty (Court fees) if required. You must also include any evidential documents that you seek to rely onli, they must also be stamped. It is worth getting a handful of copies of the stamped forms made whilst at Orca as you will need the original for the court office, one for the court, one for you and if successful copies for the defendant(s).

Once you have your affidavit and any other material stamped, you then need to attend at the Central Office of the High Court to have your application accepted by the court. Once the court stamp is obtained and any necessary fees are paid (there is no need for any fee where you issue a judicial review that includes an order for *certorai*) then you need to ascertain which court room the judicial review judge is in and attend at that court as soon as possible.

On arrival at the court room walk in, be aware that a hearing may be taking place as you do, so enter quietly and respectfully. You will next need to identify the clerk of the court (usually sitting to the side and slightly below the presiding judge) and quietly attract their attention so that you may approach the bench and hand over a copy of your forms and ex parte docket. They may hand you a form to fill in and return to them as well. This puts your application before the judge. You will then wait in court for your case to be called. When called you may be asked questions by the judge whilst they consider your application. The judge may refuse, grant some or all of your application or in some instances effectively put you on hold. That is they will refuse your application at that point, but advise you to reapply, if for example, an upcoming District Court hearing does not go in your favour.

If permission is granted you will be given a date for return and have to serve on the defendants (usually the CFA, Garda or both). This will then require you to serve the paperwork on the defendants and issue them with a notice of motion for the date that the court has set. You will also have to confirm to the court via an affidavit that the defendants have been served with your application and notice of motion. This then allows the defendants to attend court and to issue their defence. The notice of motion to be in a form as below:

2017 No. xxx JR

THE HIGH COURT

JUDICIAL REVIEW BETWEEN

your name(s)

                    [APPLICANT]

AND

XXX DISTRICT COURT & TUSLA - CHILD AND FAMILY AGENCY

                    [RESPONDENTS]

NOTICE   OF   MOTION

TAKE NOTICE THAT on the [date for return provided by the judge] in the forenoon, or at the first available opportunity thereafter the Applicant hereby applies to this Honourable Court sitting at the Four Courts, Dublin for the following reliefs:

list the reliefs granted at the ex parte hearing

and being granted the order that the Applicants do have leave to apply by way of application for judicial review for the reliefs set forth at paragraph **D** excluding any reliefs [the judge   set   forth]

WHICH SAID APPLICATION shall be grounded upon the Pleadings and Proceedings already had herein, this Notice of Motion, the Affidavit and grounds of the Applicant sworn on the xx day of month 20xx, and the perfected Order of this Justice xxx dated the xxth of month, 20xx.

Dated: xxth day of month 20xx

_____

your name

Applicant

To : The Chief Registrar

   The High Court

   Inns Quay

   Dublin 7

To: CEO Child and Family Agency (Tusla)

   The Brunel Building,
   Heuston South Quarter,
   Saint John's Road West,
   Dublin 8.

D08 X01F

To: Tusla Child and Family Agency

Local Social work Offices

To: District Court *[that may have been involved in your case]

Address

[* do not name judges in your applications – just name the District Court involved.]

If your application has been successful, the clerk of the court may ask you to email them a copy of the application in word format and you will receive a copy of the judges order with the reliefs listed which you need to serve on the defendants.

The proceedings will then follow with exchanges of evidence/affidavits and it will move to the substantive hearing.

Although this is an extremely powerful tool of the law you must approach it with considered application. Do not skimp on your research, or effort in drawing up your paperwork. To help you examples are provided in Appendix E, they are not simply copy and paste examples as you must make everything relevant to your case, but they offer the opportunity to see what is required to achieve permission (the example provided obtained permission for judicial review).

Judicial reviews can be quite lengthy at times so do not expect overnight miracles, however because children are involved they are usually dealt with expeditiously. It is worth making sure you take someone along to the hearing to take notes because it can be an overwhelming experience.

Of course neither in the UK or Ireland descriptions of a judicial review process is there room to cover every tiny detail, so it is worth acquainting yourself with the practice directions and rules of the court. This is not a case of leaving you 'high and dry', but if you pursue this course, then it is in your own interests to become as knowledgeable as possible about the process and rules.

Defamation

We have already considered the fact that social workers are prepared to embellish, misrepresent and in short, at times lie on reports and what they have to say about you, frequently in front of your face. These reports and words are often uttered at child protection meetings and reports circulated widely to the multi-agency partners. Many of the agencies supply their own reports, largely based on the allegations of in the social worker's report. Although they all have a statutory duty and believe they can hide behind qualified privilege if they disseminate lies about you and you have the evidence to counter those lies then you could issue defamation proceedings against the individual.

Although this may appear a tall order it has been used successfully by families to have inaccurate reports withdrawn and to remove individuals from the process. Once again in the UK it can be done as the 'warning shot across the bows' as the action is initiated, like the judicial review under a pre-action protocol and a letter before claim. In snooker they call this a shot to nothing, take the shot and your cue ball will remain safe, though you just might make the pot and win the game. Again we are employing a strategy, one that hopefully undermines the case against you and may make their actions change for the better.

In the UK defamation is covered by statute (Defamation Act 2013) and common law. It is a Tort. That is a wrongful act or infringement of rights that leads to a legal liability. Libel (written) and slander (spoken) are the two versions of defamation. Slander is the publication of words or actions in a temporary form, whilst libel is the permanent form.

Defamation is when there is a publication to a third party of information that contains untrue aspersions that degrade the reputation and character of individuals, (or companies) in the 'eyes of right thinking members of society'. The meaning of the words or actions used are used in establishing slander or libel. The words are not interpreted in a legal context but in their given ordinary and standard meaning.

In order to have a meritable case there are some basic requirements. Under a claim for slander:

- There must be an accusation

- There must be proof of special damage; though there are exceptions

- The claim must be against an identifiable individual(s)

- the statement must make someone think less of the individual(s) to whom it refers.

Under libel:

- it is not limited to the written word

- The claim must be against an identifiable individual(s)

- the statement must make someone think less of the individual(s) to whom it refers.

Under the 2013 act a requirement of serious harm was introduced[lii] at section 1 that a publication has caused or is likely to cause serious harm to the reputation of an individual. Unless this is present then there can be no defamation. There is also a statutory limitation of twelve months to bring the claim from the original publication of the words or actions. There may be instances where a claim may be brought outside of this time frame, but only if the court believes it would be equitable to do so. As with judicial review it is better to act sooner rather than later.

There are established defences to any claim of defamation and you must examine your alleged case to establish what the defendant may seek to use in their defence and find points that undermine such a defence.

The defences are:

1. The Truth. This is a complete defence. The defendant must

show that the statement complained of is substantially true–the burden of proof falls to the defendant.

2. Honest Opinion. This is a new defence under the 2013 Act and replaces the defence of fair comment that was available under common law. However, to establish this defence the defendant will have to establish three things:

(a) The statement complained of must be an expression of opinion;

(b) The statement complained of must indicate the basis of the opinion;

(c) The opinion must be one that an honest person could have held on the basis of a fact which existed at the time the statement was published or a privileged statement published before the statement complained of.

3. Privilege. This is divided into two standards–absolute and qualified. Those you may find involved in child protection are likely to rely on the qualified privilege defence. Absolute privilege means that there is no recourse to defamation, and it applies to judicial proceedings, or MP's speaking in parliament. Qualified privilege provides lesser protection and

applies where '"*the person who makes a communication has an interest or a duty, legal, social or moral to make it to the person to whom it is made" Adam v Ward [1917] AC 309.*' Qualified privilege does not justify statements known to be false that are made with actual malice. Of course proving malice is exceptionally difficult, but frequently there is wider evidence that supports the claim of malicious intent. This is particularly useful where you have provided *bona fide* evidence to refute the claim of an allegation to a social worker, yet they continue to write reports/speak about it. The general test is the duty and interest test.

4. Innocent dissemination can be pleaded if the person can demonstrate that they were not the author or publisher of the statement and had no reason to believe that their 'publication' was defamatory. It would of course be stretching the defence for social workers and the rest of the child protection individuals to claim they were not aware that a statement was untrue, particularly if you have challenged and provided contrary evidence to them as per number three above.

5. Consent, if you consent to the publication there is no case. Equally if you accept an apology, then you cannot bring a claim for defamation. Quite often, even where you may get an

apology from the local authority for their untrue allegations, the damage is already done to your reputation and is likely to have a bearing on the overall run of the case against you, therefore think carefully before accepting such an apology.

There are other defences but they mainly deal with where the media are involved or material published to a website, these are not likely to be relevant to any action you consider.

What can the outcome be of a successful claim? Damages can be ordered to compensate the claimant for harm caused by the defamatory material and to vindicate their reputation. There are three types of damages: general, aggravated and exemplary[liii]. An injunction can be sought by a claimant to prevent further publication of the defamatory material. The claimant must prove that the defendant was acting in bad faith. Injunctions can be granted on an interim basis.

Again the advantage is that you must issue a letter before claim under the pre-action protocol of the civil procedure rules[liv]. The rules specify what must be contained in the letter before claim:

'3.1 The Claimant should notify the Defendant of his/her claim in writing at the earliest reasonable opportunity.

3.2 The Letter of Claim should include the following information:-

- *name of Claimant;*
- *sufficient details to identify the publication or broadcast which contained the words complained of;*
- *the words complained of and, if known, the date of publication; where possible, a copy or transcript of the words complained of should be enclosed;*
- *factual inaccuracies or unsupportable comment within the words complained of; the Claimant should give a sufficient explanation to enable the Defendant to appreciate why the words are inaccurate or unsupportable;*
- *the nature of the remedies sought by the Claimant.*
- *Where relevant, the Letter of Claim should also include:-*
- *any facts or matters which make the Claimant identifiable from the words complained of;*
- *details of any special facts relevant to the interpretation of the words complained of and/or any*

particular damage caused by the words complained of.

3.3 It is desirable for the Claimant to identify in the Letter of Claim the meaning(s) he/she attributes to the words complained of[iv].'

An outline example template letter can be found at Appendix F.

You can issue such letters against any of the professionals involved in your case where they have made defamatory statements against you. As highlighted above, this can have the effect of having reports or sections of them withdrawn, personnel changed and hopefully provide an opportunity to ensure the record is set firmly in your favour. Many LA's can be belligerent in their approach to parents and fail to respond or (most likely) attempt to rely on the claim of qualified privilege. You can write again, with the threat of issuing proceedings or responding to the fact that you do not believe that there is a basis to rely on qualified privilege and supply the evidence/arguments to demonstrate this. It may change their response or elicit no reply.

It is then down to you to decide whether to issue the actual court application. Costs can be substantial in defamation cases and you need to consider whether you will self litigate or employ a legal representative. If you issue proceedings and lose, then you could end up with a very high bill. However, just the action of issuing proceedings may bring the LA or other agency to the negotiating table. You can withdraw your application if required.

To begin a claim you will need a part 7 form[lvi]. You can apply for a fee remission for court fees[lvii] and can apply on an EX160. Take or send the form to the court:

Room E07
QB Issues and Enquiries
Central Office
Royal Courts of Justice
Strand
London
WC2A 2LL

You'll need to have a copy for you, a copy for the court and one copy for each of the defendants in the case. The court will stamp the documents which you must then serve on the defendant(s). You need to serve on the defendants your application form, an acknowledgement of service form (n9c)[lviii], an admission form[lix] and a defence and counterclaim form

(n9d)[lx], as well as your particulars of claim. This must include according to the civil procedure rules:

'1) (a) a concise statement of the facts on which the claimant relies;

(b) if the claimant is seeking interest, a statement to that effect and the details set out in paragraph (2);(c) if the claimant is seeking aggravated damages or exemplary damages, a statement to that effect and his grounds for claiming them;

(d) if the claimant is seeking provisional damages, a statement to that effect and his grounds for claiming them; and

(e) such other matters as may be set out in a practice direction.

2) If the claimant is seeking interest he must –

(a) state whether he is doing so –

(i) under the terms of a contract;

(ii) under an enactment and if so which; or

(iii) on some other basis and if so what that basis is; and

(b) if the claim is for a specified amount of money, state –

(i) the percentage rate at which interest is claimed;

(ii) the date from which it is claimed;

(iii) the date to which it is calculated, which must not be later than the date on which the claim form is issued;

(iv) the total amount of interest claimed to the date of calculation; and

(v) the daily rate at which interest accrues after that date.

(Part 22 requires particulars of claim to be verified by a statement of truth)'

The interest is not likely to be relevant to your claim as you will applying for damages of an unspecified amount. The particulars document should include the arguments and facts in support of your case. You can provide the particulars when you serve the forms or within the next 14 days (send a copy to the court too).

Once you have served these on the defendant(s) you need to fill out a N215 form: Certificate of Service[lxi] and return it to the court. The defendant has 14 days to acknowledge the claim. If they do this, they can ask for more time to respond. They have 28 days to respond to the claim once you've given them both the claim form and the particulars and if they don't respond you may be able to ask the court to make a judgment in your favour, using form N227 Request for Judgment[lxii].

If they defend the case, then there will usually be a case management hearing to decide the timetable, evidence sharing and any other aspects that are required.

You can prior to trial make an application for orders such as injunctions, such applications are made on the relevant Queen's Bench forms[lxiii]. These interim applications are usually heard by Masters of the High Court. Cases are usually heard by a High Court Judge in the Royal Courts of Justice or a Circuit Judge outside London. The courtroom will usually be open to the public. There may also be a jury. Both sides will have the chance to:

- make opening and closing statements
- call expert witnesses (if you've received prior

permission from the court)

- present expert reports
- question the witnesses

In most cases there is no decision on the final day of the hearing, the judgment will be communicated to you shortly after.

By and large the legal premise of defamation in Ireland is the same. The 2009 Defamation Act updated the law in this area, reducing the time limit to a year to bring claims and laying out defences and remedies similar to all intents and purposes to the UK situation. There is no requirement to add to the above regarding the general principles.

As above, it is usual to serve a warning letter on the defendant. This is effectively a letter before claim and it sets out your claim. You are effectively asking the defendant to accept liability, and request to be compensated within a set period, for example 14 days. If this does not have the required effect, then an application can be instigated in the High Court upon a Plenary Summons. The Template is below:

No. 1.

O. 1, r. 2

PLENARY SUMMONS.

———

THE HIGH COURT.

19

No.

Between A. B.,

Plaintiff,

and C.D.,

Defendant.

To the defendant

of .... in the County of ....

This plenary summons is to require that within eight days after the service thereof upon you (exclusive of the day of such service) you in person or by solicitor do enter an appearance in the Central Office, Four Courts, Dublin, in the above action; and TAKE NOTICE that, in default of your so doing, the plaintiff may proceed therein, and judgment may be given in your absence.

BY ORDER,

Chief Justice of Ireland,

the ... day of ..... one thousand nine hundred and .....

N.B.—This summons is to be served within twelve calendar months from the date hereof, and, if renewed within six calendar months from the date of the last renewal, including the day of such date, and not afterwards.

The defendant may appear hereto by entering an appearance either personally or by solicitor at the Central Office, Four Courts, Dublin.

GENERAL   INDORSEMENT   OF   CLAIM.
The plaintiff's claim is .....

(Signed)

This summons was issued by the plaintiff ..... who resides at .... (*state address accurately*) and is ....., and whose address for service is .... *or*, ...

This summons was issued by ...., whose registered place of business is ...., solicitor for the plaintiff, who resides at ...... and is ....

This summons was served by me at .... on the defendant
.... on ..... day the ... day of ..... 19...

Indorsed the ... day of ..... 19...

(Signed)

(Address)

This summons is issued by the plaintiff in person who resides
at [insert plaintiff's address

and is [insert plaintiff's occupation]'

'this summons was served by me on the defendant at

[insert place of service] on the (insert date) day of (insert
month and year)

Signed: (person who served the summons signs here)

Address (insert address of the person who served the
summons)'

If the plaintiff is male and has no occupation the word
'gentleman' should be used. If the plaintiff is female and has no
occupation the word 'housewife' can be used. When a
summons is served on a defendant a record of that service
must be made on the actual summons. This is done within 3

days of service of the summons by the person serving the summons.

An appearance[lxiv] must be entered by the defendant in Central Office of the High Court within 8 days of service of a plenary or summary summons. If no appearance is entered within 8 days, the Plaintiff is entitled to apply to Court for judgment in default of appearance. However, a Defendant can enter an appearance after 8 days has expired, and can enter a late appearance any time up the granting of a judgment.

After an Appearance, you are then required to deliver your statement of claim. This is a formal statement setting out the facts of the claim to allow the defendant to see the case against him, and to show the basis of the claim for damages. Again, all the required detail of the statements/actions complained of must be set out. If it does not appear in the statement of claim, it cannot be introduced at trial. You must serve the statement of claim within 21 days.

When the defendant has received the Statement of Claim, he will serve a Notice for Particulars of the Plaintiff's claim. Usually there is no issuance of a defence until the Notice of Particulars has been replied to by you. The Notice for Particulars need to be accurate and you are responsible for the factual accuracy of your replies, check it carefully. The defendant has 28 days from the date of delivery of the Statement of Claim to respond with the defence. Usually this takes longer. Any denials of your claim by the defendant has to be full and comprehensive. Any facts not denied will be taken as an admittance. You are entitled to deliver a reply to the defendant's defence., it is not necessary, though. If you do not, then pleadings are deemed closed and the case can be set down for a hearing.

Once the pleadings are closed, the action can be set down for trial after service of a notice for trial. The action must then be set down for hearing within 14 days of service of the notice for trial. This is done by filling in a notice for trial in the format below:

NOTICE OF TRIAL (ORDINARY FORM).

[Title of action].

Take notice of trial of [*this action or the issues in this action ordered to be tried or as the case may be] for such day, not being less than **twenty-one days from the date of service of this notice, as shall be fixed by the Court.

Dated

(Signed)

To

*Insert as appropriate

**where short notice of trial has been given in accordance with Order 36 rule 16, insert lesser amount of notice to be given.

You should state a jury (as in a chancery or non jury matter) or before a jury (as in a jury matter). The Notice of Trial is served on the solicitors acting for the other party or the individual if they represent themselves. This is done before lodging the documents in the Central Office. The notice of trial and setting down docket must be issued within 14 days from date the notice of trial was served-if outside the time the notice of trial must be reserved. Pleadings for the trial Judge are lodged on the trial date. Once Notice of Trial is served a personal endorsement of service (example below) is written on the back of the document by the person serving the document. If service has been effected by post, proof of postage (registered post slip) should be attached to the Notice of Trial.

' I (Server) served a true copy of the within notice of trial on the_____day of ____ by hand/registered post on (insert name of solicitors for the other side) at (insert address where service was effected).'

Dated: Signed:

A setting down docket is then required. This document is not served on the party but filed in the central office and requires €250 stamp duty. Details of the date and venue for the hearing are given on the front of the docket. The back of the docket should clearly set out the following information:

- Date and venue for the hearing

- Full title of the case

- Record Number of the case

- Date the Notice of Trial was served

- Cause of Action

- Plaintiff's Solicitors Name & Address

- Defendant's Solicitors Name & Address

The Book of Pleadings is for the Judge and is not required until the trial date. An example docket is below:

THE HIGH COURT

SETTING DOWN FOR TRIAL

RECORD NO.

BETWEEN:

PLAINTIFF

and

DEFENDANT

Sir, I request you will enter this Action for Trial on

In the County of   .

Signed:

Solicitor for the Plaintiff

To: Chief Registrar

Central Office

High Court

Four Courts

Dublin 7

  For Trial on

 Before a

In the County of

             and

 Record Number:

Date when Notice of Trial was served:

Cause of Action:

Plaintiffs Solicitors:

Defendants Solicitors:

Your case will then be heard in a similar process as described above.

Preferably in the instance of judicial review and /or defamation proceedings we are hoping to effect the challenge and change at the letter before claim stage. It is part of the strategy of undermining the case that social services have against you, it can be used against individual professionals and it can demonstrate that you are aware of and able to use your rights effectively. Wherever their allegations are increasingly put into doubt it becomes more difficult for them to proceed to care proceedings.

False Instruments & Private Prosecutions

It is not unknown for social workers or their child protection counterparts to act contrary to the criminal law. It may not even be done intentionally, however ignorance of the law is no defence. We have looked in considerable depth at challenging incorrect and misrepresented opinions, comments and representation of parents in the social worker's and other professionals reports. One of the key points we made was to challenge every aspect, every detail and where you have evidence to the contrary to use it. Once you have provided that correct information then the records should reflect it, but they frequently do not and the same untruths continue to trotted out. As we pointedly said the continued repetition of the lie becomes the truth as far as they are concerned.

Few know or appreciate the fact that this action actually can constitute a criminal offence. One with which you could effectively prosecute the social worker/professional. That law is the 1981 Forgery and Counterfeiting Act.[lxv] If someone issues a document with the intention that you or another should believe the contents of that document, knowing that it is untrue they are guilty of issuing a False Instrument contrary to section eight of the act. If you can prove the information on the document is false or has been altered to make it factually untrue, you should make a formal allegation of the crime under the above act to the police.

Section three of the act states:

'It is an offence for a person to use an instrument which is, and which he knows or believes to be, false, with the intention of inducing somebody to accept it as genuine, and by reason of so accepting it to do or not to do some act to his own or any other person's prejudice.'

Section eight states:

Meaning of "instrument"

'(1)Subject to subsection (2) below, in this Part of this Act "instrument" means—

(a)any document, whether of a formal or informal character;

(b)any stamp issued or sold by [F15a postal operator];

(c)any Inland Revenue stamp; and

(d)any disc, tape, sound track or other device on or in which information is recorded or stored by mechanical, electronic or

413

other means.

(2)A currency note within the meaning of Part II of this Act is not an instrument for the purposes of this Part of this Act.

(3)A mark denoting payment of postage which the [F16a postal operator authorises] to be used instead of an adhesive stamp is to be treated for the purposes of this Part of this Act as if it were a stamp issued by [F17the postal operator concerned]

[F18(3A)In this section "postal operator" has [F19the meaning given by section 27 of the Postal Services Act 2011].]

(4)In this Part of this Act "Inland Revenue stamp" means a stamp as defined in section 27 of the M1Stamp Duties Management Act 1891.'

Clearly 1(a) provides the basis for our action.

Whilst Section nine states:

(1)An instrument is false for the purposes of this Part of this Act—

(a)if it purports to have been made in the form in which it is made by a person who did not in fact make it in that form; or

(b)if it purports to have been made in the form in which it is made on the authority of a person who did not in fact authorise its making in that form; or

(c)if it purports to have been made in the terms in which it is made by a person who did not in fact make it in those terms; or

(d)if it purports to have been made in the terms in which it is made on the authority of a person who did not in fact authorise its making in those terms; or

(e)if it purports to have been altered in any respect by a person who did not in fact alter it in that respect; or

(f)if it purports to have been altered in any respect on the authority of a person who did not in fact authorise the alteration in that respect; or

(g)if it purports to have been made or altered on a date on which, or at a place at which, or otherwise in circumstances in which, it was not in fact made or altered; or

(h)if it purports to have been made or altered by an existing person but he did not in fact exist.

(2)A person is to be treated for the purposes of this Part of this Act as making a false instrument if he alters an instrument so as to make it false in any respect (whether or not it is false in some other respect apart from that alteration).

It does not necessarily require you to pursue this down the criminal route, you could make reference to the issuance of false instruments and point out where these appear in the paperwork in your complaints, in judicial review and defamation letters before claim. As you probably rightly suspect, the police will not pursue this once you mention the involvement of social services if you attempt to report the crime. This is where private prosecutions enter the frame.

In Ireland it is the <u>Criminal Justice (Theft and Fraud) Offences Act 2001</u> [lxvi] that provides the same basis for making a claim of the criminal action of issuance of a false instrument. Section 26 states:

'(1) A person who uses an instrument which is, and which he or she knows or believes to be, a false instrument, with the intention of inducing another person to accept it as genuine and, by reason of so accepting it, to do some act, or to make some omission, or to provide some service, to the prejudice of that person or any other person is guilty of an offence.

(2) A person guilty of an offence under this section is liable on conviction on indictment to a fine or imprisonment for a term not exceeding 10 years or both.'

Both in the UK and Ireland you have the right to bring an application to begin a private prosecution. A member of the public can bring a private prosecution for any offence unless the offence is one for which the consent of the Attorney General or the Director of Public Prosecutions (DPP) is required before a prosecution can take place. S.6(1) of the Prosecution of Offences Act 1985[lxvii].

It is relatively simple (and free) to instigate a private prosecution. It simply requires you to lay your information for prosecution at the Magistrates court either to a Magistrate, Magistrate's Clerk or a District Court judge. There is no official form, so long as the material is presented in a written format it is acceptable.

There are some guidelines as to what you should include The written information must contain a statement of the offence that:

a. Describes the offence in ordinary language.

b. Identifies any legislation that creates it.

c. Contains such particulars of the conduct constituting the commission of the offence as to make clear what the prosecutor alleges against the defendant.

More than one incident of the commission of the offence may be included in the allegation if those incidents taken together amount to a course of conduct having regard to the time, place or purpose of commission.

In deciding whether to issue a warrant, the magistrate or clerk should ensure that:

a. an offence known to law is alleged;

b. it is not out of time;

c. the court has jurisdiction;

d. the informant has the necessary authority to prosecute (R. v. Gateshead Justices ex p Tesco Stores Ltd. [1981] QB 470 at 478).

There is no obligation upon a magistrate or clerk to make any inquiries before issuing a warrant. A warrant may be issued without giving the parties an opportunity to make representations and without a hearing. You may be called to be questioned by the magistrate or judge if they seek clarification. A warrant may be for the arrest of the individual or to compel them to attend the court.

In respect of anyone appearing before the magistrate's court on an indictable only offence, the magistrate's court must immediately transfer the case to the Crown Court. (S.51(1) Crime and Disorder Act 1998.)

One major disadvantage is that the Crown Prosecution Service is always entitled to take over the conduct of the private prosecution at any stage of the proceedings and may discontinue them if it thinks it would be appropriate to do so. Upon a review of the case papers, the CPS may take over and continue with a private prosecution if it is demonstrated that:

a. the evidential sufficiency stage of the Full Code Test is met (i.e. can the evidence be used in court, is it reliable and is it sufficient to provide a realistic prospect of conviction);

and

b. the public interest stage of the Full Code Test is met;

and

c. there is a particular need for the CPS to take over the prosecution.

Where it is assessed that the above criteria is not met then the CPS may stop the prosecution. Even so, it is easy to appreciate the power of this legal tool. A social worker faced with such a prosecution would have to report it to their employer and the HCPC, it could lead to their immediate suspension whilst the prosecution is outstanding. It also gives a very strong signal to the other professionals involved in your case. Ultimately in all of these legal approaches you are redressing the balance of power. It is terrible to say it, but there are far easier cases to deal with than yours, if you are utilising the full range of strategic challenges and hopefully they will look for a way out, in other words closing your case.

In Ireland the procedure is very similar. Under the Petty Sessions (Ireland) Act 1851, you are entitled to appear before a District Court Judge and make a complaint either orally or in writing, either on oath or without. The judge decides which way to approach the complaint.

You should brief particulars of:

- Name and address of the alleged offender
- Name and address of the complainant
- The basic facts of the alleged offence, including when it is alleged to have been committed
- and the piece of legislation which applies to the offence

When the information has been put before the judge, he/she must decide whether it justifies a summons. If the judge issues a summons it will require the alleged offender to appear at a sitting of the court. Indictable offences do not have time limits imposed and can be prosecuted at any time after the alleged offence, however if the offence is a minor or summary offence, the complaint must be made to the District Court clerk within 6 months of the alleged offence.

It is best to see these possible actions as methods to advance your case against the social workers and their professional colleagues. There have certainly been successes in the field of private prosecutions, including that of social workers, but you need to be sure of your grounds, your evidence and that there is a statute that creates the offence. The public interest test seems to be met by the fact that statutory powers vested in social workers means that anyone could be affected by their criminal behaviour. It is certainly not to be underestimated as a tool for a parent facing a social services intervention where the rights of the family are being abused.

Misconduct in Public Office

We have touched upon the role and expectations of those holding public office, and the offence of Misconduct in Public Office is a serious one, carrying a maximum sentence of life imprisonment. The Law society wants to see the law updated, and the penalties adjusted, but at this juncture those changes remain glints in the eye of the law society. It would prove very difficult though to make much headway with a private prosecution of this offence. I grant you it's not impossible but I suspect the CPS would be keen to take over and abandon the prosecution. That does not mean that it cannot be helpful to us. Below is a quote I would suggest that you add to the bottom of every piece of correspondence you have with the LA and its child protection partners:

'It is your legal duty as a public officer to help to stamp out malpractice and corruption within public services. It is a criminal offence to take action or knowingly disregard information available to you in circumstances where you have reasonable grounds to believe that physical, psychological or

financial harm may be caused. Your wider legal duty of care overrides any statutory process within your organisation and any instruction from your employer.

A public officer who wilfully neglects to perform his/her duty and/or wilfully misconducts him/herself to such a degree as to amount to an abuse of the public's trust in the office holder, risks prosecution for 'Misconduct in Public Office'. This includes ignoring malpractice.

The offence carries a maximum sentence of life imprisonment.

*You must report **as soon as possible** any concerns that you may have to a body independent of your employer. You may contact whistleblower@citileaks.org.uk with details of your concerns which will be added to a time/date stamped log that can be referenced by you in any future dispute. An anonymised copy of the log will be sent to ministers. The involved agencies will be held to account.'*

This however, can prove to be exceptionally useful where you have provided evidence to the social workers that contradicts their reports and position but they continue to utilise the inaccurate information in reports and to child protection conferences and the like. Firstly gather your evidence together. Identify each allegation/opinion that you can refute and match your evidence to it. Put together a file of such. Then ask for a meeting with your child's Head-teacher/teacher (whoever attends the conferences) or your health visitor/ GP or some other such professional involved with your family, such as a family worker. Take them through the allegations and show them the evidence that refutes the LA's claims. At the end of the meeting hand them a letter in the format below:

Name

Address 1

Address 2

Address 3

Name of the person meeting with

Address 1

Address 2

Address 3

[Date]

Dear XXXX,

Having presented you today with substantial evidence which clearly refutes the assertions, assumptions, presumptions, lies and defamation perpetuated by XXX County Council's Children's Social Care, we wish you to consider the following information:

It is your legal duty as a public officer to help to stamp out malpractice and corruption within public services. It is a criminal offence to take action or knowingly disregard information available to you in circumstances where you have reasonable grounds to believe that physical, psychological or financial harm may be caused. Your wider legal duty of care overrides any statutory process within your organisation and any instruction from your employer.

A public officer who wilfully neglects to perform his/her duty and/or wilfully misconducts him/herself to such a degree as to amount to an abuse of the public's trust in the office holder, risks prosecution for 'Misconduct in Public Office'. This includes ignoring malpractice.

The offence carries a maximum sentence of life imprisonment.

*You must report **as soon as possible** any concerns that you may have to a body independent of your employer. You may contact <u>whistleblower@citileaks.org.uk</u> with details of your concerns which will be added to a time/date stamped log that can be referenced by you in any future dispute. An anonymised copy of the log will be sent to ministers. The involved agencies will be held to account.*

We trust that you appreciate and fully understand the implications of your vicarious liability by virtue of your continued involvement with this case and that you will uphold your duty in ensuring that the information you have been shown today will be acknowledged and acted upon as per the above statements. Failure to act upon this information may result in legal proceedings.

Yours Sincerely

You have now just launched the proverbial cat amongst the pigeons. It is beholden on the recipient to make it know to the local authority that they are aware that evidence to the contrary of the assertions they have made exists and should be corrected. You can raise this at any conference or meeting and ask the person you met with directly about what they have seen. Have copies ready of the contrary evidence ready to pass around. It leaves no place for the social workers and the LA to continue spreading their inaccuracies. You may utilise this strategy with any number of the professionals, in fact the more the better. It is very difficult for a social worker to keep peddling the same lies when the attendees sat around the child protection conference table have seen the evidence that disputes what the social worker alleges.

If you have instigated some or even all of these challenges against the LA, then your case should be receiving a lot of attention. Hopefully they will be seeking an exit strategy that allows them to save face, but most importantly remove their intervention from you. Clearly some of you will ask, 'but if the information is all laid out here, aren't the local authority likely to just ignore us because letters before claim may not go all the way to proceedings, or private prosecutions be taken over by the CPS and abandoned.... why should they take us seriously?'

The simple answer is that they just do not know if you will proceed to issue proceedings, or that that the CPS will take over the case and abandon it. In other words they cannot rely on it. If you have done what you have threatened, such as HCPC complaints, ICO complaints, written to the Director of Children's Services, copied in the CEO, Councillors, MP and all those listed. If you have raised issues around Human Rights, the rights of the child, disability conventions and other challenges, then they cannot be assured that you won't pursue things as far as possible. Is it a risk they are prepared to take? They must always be mindful of any negative findings and publicity that their illegal, immoral or just plain nasty actions will bring if exposed. At the end of the day, for any parent it is better to try than to acquiesce to their will.

Chapter 7 How to Fight in Court

Before we go any further I wish to address the usual criticism that is leveled against the family courts by parents: that they are inherently corrupt. I cannot accept that generalised position. Having supported families in courts ranging from the family court (UK) / District Court (Ireland) through to the High Court and Appeal Courts I cannot honestly say I have seen any evidence of corruption. Instead, I would suggest that there are a number of issues that weight the court in favour of the social services and against the parents. There are a number of belligerent judges who see only saintly social workers and pariahs of parents before them, but even then these are few and far between. What must be borne in mind is that judges make their decisions based on the information placed before them. That information largely emanates from social work reports and the 'experts' they employ to present a picture of the family to judges.

If you look ahead to Chapter eleven, you will see the strategies social workers use to paint parents as poorly as possible. If you look back, you will see the issues we have considered are necessary for you to challenge and the methods that can be employed. In short, it is the social workers who create a picture of you that is presented to the court. If you were to sit in family proceedings and hear the evidence they present, full of their lies, misrepresentations and half truths you would probably also think as many judges do, that a child is better placed and served outside of its biological family. Few legal aid solicitors and barristers fight your corner, many simply acquiesce to the LA's demands, regardless of your instructions. From my experience, it is not the court process per se that is corrupt, it is the 'evidence gathering' process run by social workers that is the problem. Hence my efforts in trying to equip you with a series of challenges to prevent the LA from even considering proceedings.

I have to believe that the courts are not inherently corrupt because I advocate and support families in launching their own legal challenges through the courts. We have had much success at High Court and if the courts were corrupt, I am certain that our applications would not be entertained, never mind given a serious hearing.

In terms of judges, I think the vast majority are inherently honest. Yes, we can all point out to the odd example where a judge has been found wanting in terms of honesty and integrity, but to paint them all as bad people simply adopts the same process as social workers take with parents. However, what I do believe, is that there is a definite judicial conservatism that makes judges quite risk averse. When faced with an application for an emergency removal, the over-riding factor may be their concern of 'getting it wrong' and being blamed for an ill that befalls a child, because they refused to grant an emergency order. Fear of their face on the front page of the press with a call for their scalp could, in some instances lead them to trust unquestioningly a social workers evidence to court, rather than apply a rigorous assessment of the law and the evidence. It is human nature and in the field of child protection driven by an agenda that is much larger than the judges. I am not saying that is right, just it can be understood and explained.

That is not to say that judges do not give perverse judgments. Look at this example articulated by Christopher Booker in his column in the Telegraph Newspaper:

'This involved the very intelligent and devoted mother who, a few months after her daughter was born, fell by accident backwards out of a first-floor window, leaving her temporarily paralysed...

So quickly did the social workers move to take her baby into

431

care that they had soon assembled a string of damning accusations against her: that she was a drug addict and alcoholic whose fall had been a suicide bid. All these claims were, I gather, shown by the evidence, including that of drug and alcohol tests, to be completely spurious... Instead of admitting their initial mistake, stuck to their guns, within weeks making the first moves needed to have her baby adopted.

Briefed by the local authority, which does not deny it, the local paper published a lurid story on the case, branding the mother as an alcoholic druggie who had tried to kill herself. The mother was allowed a last "goodbye session", as the social workers call it, with her now three-year-old daughter, who rushed into her mother's arms, according to a family friend who was present, unable to grasp that she would not see her mother again.

This month, in a last desperate bid to get her daughter back, the mother appealed to another judge to stop the adoption order, relying on the rule that such an application can be granted if the mother can show that her "circumstances have changed". When she yet again, I gather, produced medical evidence, going back several years, to show that she had never been a drug addict or an alcoholic, the new judge apparently accepted this as convincing. But, astonishingly, the judge went on to rule that, since the mother had never been either of these things, her circumstances could not be said to have "changed". The adoption must therefore still go ahead.[lxviii]'

That appears to be a pedantry of the highest order and it is understandable that parents believe the courts are corrupt when they see and hear of such judgments. I do not know what happened to the lady in question, I hope she appealed and won her case.

The court arena in terms of care proceedings and family law is a massive body of information. From family procedure rules, through to appeal court rules, multiple types of reports and submissions, the various hearings from case management through to issue resolution hearings and final hearings. It is in all honesty a wealth of information that takes up multiple volumes of legal publications. I do not propose and indeed, could not cover every eventuality that a parent may face when issued with family court proceedings. I hope to give enough insight to help guide parents on their way.

The Family Court is often referred to as a secret court because it is held under the *in camera* rules. This is supposedly to protect your child's privacy, however it can also lead it to become effectively unaccountable and there are endless streams of parents who have suffered injustices because of it. Slowly the process is becoming more transparent but parents are still being told that they cannot discuss their case.

If your solicitor or social worker tells you this they are either out of date or deliberately misleading you (or even worse they are displaying their ignorance of the very laws they are supposed to be working under). Under Section 62 (paragraph 251 explanatory notes) of the Children's Act 2004 you can show your paperwork and talk about your case with anyone you wish as long as you do not reveal to the press, the public or sections of the public at large any information that identifies your child. Further once your case has finished, you can discuss your case with anyone, even the press and even if it reveals you and your child. This is confirmed by the Appeal court judgment in Clayton -v- Clayton whereby the court ruled that '*Once the proceedings have concluded, the protection given by the Act comes to an end, the entitlement to anonymity* '

On the Prevent Intervention Now website is a set of basic guidelines regarding court and they are worth repeating here:

434

1. Never agree threshold or parts of it are met. This is effectively saying 'I am guilty' and no matter what you are told-agreeing some or all it will bring your children back- it won't.

2. Oppose every order applied for, if you consent then you closing off any route of appeal.

3. Ensure that what you want to say is said–often a solicitor or barrister will stop you saying what you wish, if you can, represent yourself.

4. If your solicitor is failing you, get rid of them, this can be easily done. Practice form N434 can be used or a simple letter addressed to the solicitor and the court/judge. In Ireland use form 42.04.

5. Case law is your greatest weapon and your solicitor should be using it, if they aren't ask them why. Become familiar with the key cases and use them.

6. If a care order has been made remember you can apply to discharge it every 6 months provided you can bring a change of circumstances.

7. If a care order is granted ensure that precise contact with your child is agreed in court and ask the judge to include it in the order.

8. You can appeal any order–though you may need to get permission for leave to appeal first.

9. Even when an adoption order is applied for you can oppose it and even if granted it can be appealed, again if you can prove a change of circumstances.

10. Remember there are other judicial avenues you can pursue outside of the family court to help your case.

11. Your child if of an age and maturity and especially if they are ten or over have a right to be heard, preferably directly by the judge. Do not simply accept that the child's voice is heard through the Cafcass guardian, this is just another social worker who no doubt will be in full support of the social services position.

12. Every order can be appealed as long as you have not consented to it, don't let your solicitor or barrister tell you that you cannot appeal–you can.[lxix]

When you are served with Public Law proceedings in England and Wales, you will receive a letter and in some instances a copy of the C100 application form that the LA has submitted to court. There may also be other paperwork in the bundle, including social workers statements, chronology of their intervention with you and a Threshold statement. Sometimes you will just receive a letter with the court date and time, despite that all the above should really be provided to you. If you have had a PLO meeting and instructed a solicitor for that, the bundle of papers may go directly to them.

The Local Authority could be applying for: an interim care order, a supervision order, or the lesser utilised Family Assistance Order. The application could be for interim care or supervision orders, or in some instances a Special Guardianship Order, or a Care and Placement order to release a child for adoption.

The process is similar in Scotland, Northern Ireland and in the Republic of Ireland, effectively a notification of a court date and associated paperwork. The forms may be slightly different, but the effect is the same.

You are entitled to legal aid for care proceedings, so you can obtain legal representation for free. The local authority may have already provided you with a list of local family law solicitors, or may include such a list in their paperwork. Your choice of a solicitor can make a huge difference to your case. It is best to avoid local solicitor firms as many of them also work for the local authority. So one day they may in court to represent you, the next day representing the local authority. These local authority contracts are very lucrative and much better paid then legal aid. It is unlikely that a solicitor will want to 'bite the hand that feeds', by fighting hard for you and upsetting the local authority. We all know that they should work in the best interest of their clients, irrespective, but in all reality and as many parents attest, their local solicitors have seriously let them down. They encourage parents to accept the local authority's position, to not contest their applications, to agree to threshold and generally make the local authority's job all the easier. Of course, not every solicitor is like this, but there is more than enough anecdotal evidence that this is what many parents find.

To try to avoid these potential pit-falls it is best to go outside your county to instruct a solicitor. You will also find that as a couple you will have to instruct separate solicitors. (In Ireland you can instruct just one solicitor). Of course you can self represent as a litigant in person. There are advantages and disadvantages to this. You can at least ensure you get to say exactly what you wish, but you will also need to do vast amounts of research to understand the court procedures and law.

Legal aid in Ireland is organised differently to the UK. Whilst in the UK you may choose your solicitor, and they will then apply for your legal aid funding, in Ireland you must apply to the Legal Aid Board and they then appoint you a solicitor. Clearly in these circumstances, you cannot obtain a solicitor of your choice that you believe will fight your case. In effect you are at the mercy of the system. There are good and bad solicitors, just as there are good and bad exponents of in all professions or trades, but when you are simply appointed a solicitor, you have no means of ensuring that that one has the skills, experience or passion to do your case justice.

The Children and Families Act of 2014 (UK) introduced a strict timetable for public law proceedings, there had been a great deal of concern about such cases drifting on for years, leaving children in effective limbo. The act introduced a time limit of 26 weeks (6 months) for such proceedings to be concluded, unless there are exceptional reasons to extend this timetable.

Children are entitled to a solicitor too, and these are appointed via the child's Guardian ad Litem, who will be from Cafcass.

We saw in the chapter on the villains the role of the Cafcass officer. Recommendations by Guardians in care proceedings are often accepted by judges and they will frequently make their orders based upon what the Guardian advises.

The court process will usually be made up of a number of different types of hearing, these are:

Case Management Hearing

This is usually held between twelve and eighteen days of the local authority's care application. It must be no later than twenty five days. At this hearing the judge will give directions to ensure all reports, assessments and statements are time-tabled and further hearing dates are set. Sometimes there are more than one case management hearing and these are referred to as 'further case management hearings'.

Contested Removal Hearing

If at the outset of proceedings, the local authority wish to remove a child from the parents into their care and the parents are opposed, then there will be a contested removal hearing. The court will hear evidence from the social workers, the guardian and the parents. Such hearings can take substantial time.

Issues Resolution Hearing

This is held towards the end of the court's timetable, once all the assessments and paperwork have been collated into a court bundle. The local authority should have their proposed care plans ready and the parents their own. The issues resolution hearing seeks to see if any of the issues can be agreed. For example it may be that the parents agree that a child can be placed in the care of a family member, possibly under a Special Guardianship Order. If there are agreements, then the court can make its orders at that point and dispense with the next hearing. If there cannot be agreements then the case will continue.

Fact Finding Hearing

If serious allegations have been, such as one party alleging sexual abuse of children by the other party, or who may be responsible for fractures found in a child, then a fact finding hearing may be ordered. This is to allow the court to hear the evidence regarding the allegations and to make a decision whether the incidents happened or not. This decision is done on the civil standard of the 'balance of probability'. So although an allegation may have been investigated by the police and a criminal court has delivered a 'not-guilty' verdict, the family court can examine this allegation and come to a conclusion. Even where parents are found not guilty in a criminal court, they can be found to have perpetrated the allegation in the family court. It effectively gives the local authority and the judiciary two bites of the cherry.

Final Hearing

Depending on the complexity of the case the final hearing can run for a number of days. Witnesses can be cross examined and all the evidence is heard and tested. At the completion of this the judge will make their decision and make any necessary orders.

If your child is made subject to a care order, and the plan is for adoption, then there will be a care and placement order, which will mean in the future there will also be an Adoption Hearing

One very important aspect in this timetable is that under the rules parents who wish to have new assessments of themselves or other family members or to obtain an expert evidence must formally apply to the court in time for the case management hearing. So it is vital that if you wish to do any of these things that your solicitor is instructed in the same without delay.

For most parents going to court may be the first time they have stepped foot in a court room. It can be a very intimidatory experience. Most courts sit from 10.00 or 10.30 AM. Ensure you arrive in plenty of time, especially if you are meeting your legal representative prior to the hearing. It is unlikely that you will be called at the outset of the day's business, so expect to be sat waiting whilst the court calls cases in the order they are ready to proceed.

On arrival make sure you identify the usher (usually in a black gown) to confirm your attendance. The family court is not open to the public and usually does not have the formality of wigs and gowns for judges and barristers. Although the press are entitled to be present they are not allowed to publish anything that identifies you or your children. Even though you may be upset and angry at the situation, try to remain calm and treat the court and its officers with respect. This will get you much more recognition than shouting and calling the courts corrupt or some such diatribe.

Threshold

No court can make a care order under the Children Act 1989 unless the threshold has been met.

Under section 31:

'(2) A court may only make a care order or supervision order if it is satisfied:

(a)that the child concerned is suffering, or is likely to suffer, significant harm; and

(b)that the harm, or likelihood of harm, is attributable to—

(i)the care given to the child, or likely to be given to him if the order were not made, not being what it would be reasonable to expect a parent to give to him; or

(ii)the child's being beyond parental control.'

The threshold is a two stage test. Part one of the test is as above and part two is the 'welfare stage.' The welfare stage says that even if the threshold is crossed, any order must only be made if it is in the child's best interests. (It is what is called the no order rule: in that an order should only be made if there is a need and not just simply because the court can make an order).

Effectively the local authority has to prove on the evidence that the child has or is, likely to suffer significant harm. If the threshold cannot be crossed, then there can be no orders and the proceedings must come to an end. Parents are now served with the threshold criteria that the local authority will rely on at the outset of proceedings. Therefore the first thing a parent must do is to challenge the threshold criteria, usually at a contested removal hearing, although I have known that once served with a response to a threshold document local authorities have chosen to withdraw applications for interim care orders and continue proceedings whilst the children remain at home.

The President of the Family Division, Sir James Munby, gave some clear guidance on what a threshold document should look like and contain. Although it was written as a direction to those legal representatives preparing such documents, it can give us a few pointers in our challenge against the threshold[lxx]. For example the President states:

'The threshold statement can usually be little more than a page, if that. We need to remember what it is for. It is not necessary for the court to find a mass of specific facts in order to arrive at a proper threshold finding. Take a typical case of

chronic neglect. Does the central core of the statement of threshold need to be any more detailed than this?

"The parents have neglected the children. They have

• Not fed them properly

• Dressed them in torn and dirty clothes

• Not supervised them properly

• Not got them to school or to the doctor or hospital when needed

• Not played with them or talked to them enough

• Not listened to the advice of social workers, health visitors and others about how to make things better: and now will not let the social worker visit the children the home [the evidence to support the case being identified by reference to the relevant page numbers in the bundle]."

I think not. [lxxi]

If you are faced with a threshold statement such as this, you can take each point and provide the evidence to the contrary. You an identify where such 'evidence' presented in the bundle is second, third or even fourth hand hearsay, based on what is in the social work reports and not direct witness evidence. This gives you a starting point to pick apart the local authorities threshold statement.

Justice Munby gave further clarification regarding establishing threshold in. RE A (2015).

'The President provided guidance in three distinct areas:

i. Prove the Assertion!

The President first deals with a perceived failure of local authorities to establish properly the matters upon which they rely (emphasis added):

"The local authority, if its case is challenged on some factual point, must adduce proper evidence to establish what it seeks to prove. Much material to be found in local authority case records or social work chronologies is hearsay, often second- or third-hand hearsay. Hearsay evidence is, of course, admissible in family proceedings. But, and as the present case so vividly demonstrates, a local authority which is unwilling or unable to produce the witnesses who can speak of such matters first-hand, may find itself in great, or indeed

insuperable, difficulties if a parent not merely puts the matter in issue but goes into the witness-box to deny it.

It is a common feature of care cases that a local authority asserts that a parent does not admit, recognise or acknowledge something or does not recognise or acknowledge the local authority's concern about something. If the 'thing' is put in issue, the local authority must both prove the 'thing' and establish that it has the significance attributed to it by the local authority." (Para 9).

ii. Plead Threshold Properly!

The second matter the President takes issue with is the pleading of the threshold findings sought (emphasis added):

"…*The schedule of findings in the present case contains, as we shall see, allegations in relation to the father that "he appears to have" lied or colluded, that various people have "stated" or "reported" things, and that "there is an allegation". With all respect to counsel, this form of allegation, which one sees far too often in such documents, is wrong and should never be used.* **It confuses the crucial distinction, once upon a time, though no longer, spelt out in the rules of pleading and well understood, between an**

448

assertion of fact and the evidence needed to prove the assertion. What do the words "he appears to have lied" or "X reports that he did Y" mean? More important, where does it take one? The relevant allegation is not that "he appears to have lied" or "X reports"; the relevant allegation, if there is evidence to support it, is surely that "he lied" or "he did Y". *(Para 10)*

The second fundamentally important point is **the need to link the facts relied upon by the local authority with its case on threshold**, *the need to demonstrate why, as the local authority asserts, facts A + B + C justify the conclusion that the child has suffered, or is at risk of suffering, significant harm of types X, Y or Z...* **the linkage may be very much less obvious where the allegation is only that the child is at risk of suffering emotional harm or, as in the present case, at risk of suffering neglect.** *"* (Para 12).

iii. Are Local Authorities/Courts Setting the Bar Too High?

Lastly, the President restates and approves various authorities on the standard of care expected of parents. The President asserts that it is "vital always to bear in mind in these cases" and to recognise the "diverse standards of parenting" that must be tolerated by society. The President cites Baroness Hale in Re B at para 15 (emphasis added):

"*We are all frail human beings, with our fair share of unattractive character traits, which sometimes manifest themselves in bad behaviours which may be copied by our children.* **But the State does not and cannot take away the children of all the people who commit crimes, who abuse alcohol or drugs, who suffer from physical or mental illnesses or disabilities, or who espouse antisocial political or religious beliefs.**"

The President also agreed with the somewhat controversial remarks of His Honour Judge Jack in *North East Lincolnshire Council v G & L* [2014] EWCC B77 (Fam) (emphasis added):

"*…The reality is that in this country there must be tens of thousands of children who are cared for in homes where there is a degree of domestic violence (now very widely defined) and where parents on occasion drink more than they should, I am not condoning that for a moment, but the courts are not in the business of social engineering. The courts are not in the business of providing children with perfect homes.* **If we took into care and placed for adoption every child whose parents had had a domestic spat and every child whose**

450

parents on occasion had drunk too much then the care system would be overwhelmed and there would not be enough adoptive parents. *So we have to have a degree of realism about prospective carers who come before the courts*."'

As in the basic guidelines, do not agree that threshold is met. You must challenge it. If you agree, then the first test is passed and you have effectively confirmed that you are responsible for causing harm to your children. It is a tall order to come back from this. As we also said before, do not be taken in by solicitors or barristers encouraging you to agree on the basis that this will help you get your children home. It won't. Every application for an order must be challenged.

The Welfare stage requires the court to consider the following checklist in the context of the over-riding principle that the child's welfare must be the paramount consideration, with no undue delay (proceedings to be completed in twenty six weeks):

- the ascertainable wishes and feelings of the child concerned (considered in light of his age and understanding)

- the child's physical, emotional and educational needs
- the likely effect on the child of any change in his circumstances

  the child's age, sex, and background and any characteristics of the child which the court considers relevant
- any harm which the child has suffered or is at risk of suffering
- how capable each of the parents, and any other person in relation to whom the court considers the question to be relevant, is of meeting the child's needs
- the range of powers available to the court under this Act in the proceedings in question

The court should make a careful analysis of each of these welfare issues if it fails to do so then any order and judgment it makes could be open to an appeal.

Although the case itself was in regard to adoption, the principles that <u>Re B-S (Children) 2013</u>[lxxii] laid out in relation to such an analysis, applies to *any* order that the court makes in relation to children.

The key points from this judgment to note are: although the

child's interests are paramount, the court must not forget that the child has a right to be brought up by their family. There must be a properly evidenced analysis from the local authority and Guardian that considers all the options that are available, along with reasoned arguments for and against each option. The court *must* consider all the realistic options when coming to a decision. The court should be minded to take the least interventionist approach and should consider what supports are available for the parents in assessing their capacity. There should not be a linear approach to considering the evidence and options. The appeal court said of this:

We emphasise the words "global, holistic evaluation". This point is crucial. The judicial task is to evaluate all the options, undertaking a global, holistic and (see Re G para 51) multifaceted evaluation of the child's welfare which takes into account all the negatives and the positives, all the pros and cons, of each option. [lxxiii]

It was made plain that under Article 8 of the European Convention [of Human Rights] that there was a positive obligation on the State to try to keep families together.

As you may imagine Re-B-S (along with RE -B and other associated judgments referred to in RE B-S) has had a significant impact on the court's approach to not just adoption hearings but all child care proceedings.

As with most court cases the format is usually the applicants legal representative that speaks first, laying out what application has been made and why. You or your legal representative then speaks as to why you oppose the application. The judge then may ask a series of questions of both sides. In contested removal and final hearings witnesses or experts may be called and cross-examined.

To prepare for court, you need to:

(i) challenge the threshold statement including:

(ii) finding and presenting evidence that contradicts the local authorities evidence,

(iii) researching and presenting case law precedents

(iv) ensuring you understand the applicable laws and court rules and procedures,

(v) identifying any expert evidence or witnesses that you wish to call

and

(vi) identify your rights under ECHR, and the United Nations Conventions.

Hopefully, if you have followed the suggested challenges to local authority involvement in your family contained in this book, (i) and (ii) should be relatively easy to compile. We have covered ECHR and the UN Conventions, so you also have a head start on number (vi). Now we shall turn to researching and presenting case law precedents and take a look at the applicable laws and court rules and procedures.

The court rules are available on line, both for the UK[lxxiv] and Republic of Ireland[lxxv]. A lot of the details contained in these directions are only of concern to the local authority and the courts. They set out how the practical details of the hearings and paperwork are to be dealt with and really does not concern parents. However, it useful for parents to understand this background and it is worth reading the directions in full. What is useful is the glossary of terms at the end of the directions that provide explanations of some of the terms you may hear.

Specific points to note are:

'Parents' Response' means a document from either or both of the parents containing –

(a) in no more than two pages, the parents' response to the Threshold Statement, and

(b) the parents' placement proposals including the identity and whereabouts of all relatives and friends they propose be considered by the court;

(c) Information which may be relevant to a person's capacity to litigate including information about any referrals to mental health services and adult services;'

'Social Work Chronology' means a schedule containing –

(a) a succinct summary of the length of involvement of the local authority with the family and in particular with the child;

(b) a succinct summary of the significant dates and events in the child's life in chronological order- i.e. a running record up to the issue of the proceedings; providing such information under the following headings-

(i) serial number;

(ii) date;

(iii) event-detail;

(iv) witness or document reference (where applicable);

'Social Work Statement' means a statement prepared by the Local Authority limited to the following evidence –

Summary

(a) The order sought;

(b) Succinct summary of reasons with reference as appropriate to the Welfare Checklist;

Family

(c) Family members and relationships especially the primary carers and significant adults/other children;

(d) Genogram;

Threshold

(e) Precipitating events;

(f) Background circumstances –

(i) summary of children's services involvement cross-referenced to the chronology;

(ii) previous court orders and emergency steps;

(iii) previous assessments;

(g) Summary of significant harm and or likelihood of significant harm which the LA will seek to establish by evidence or concession;

'Parenting capability'

(h) Assessment of child's needs;

(i) Assessment of parental capability to meet needs;

(j) Analysis of why there is a gap between parental capability and the child's needs;

(k) Assessment of other significant adults who may be carers;

Child impact

(l) Wishes and feelings of the child(ren);

(m) Timetable for the Child;

(n) Delay and timetable for the proceedings;

Permanence and contact

(o) Parallel planning;

(p) <u>Realistic</u> placement options by reference to a welfare and proportionality analysis;

(q) Contact framework;

Case Management

(r) Evidence and assessments necessary and outstanding;

(s) Any information about any person's litigation capacity, mental health issues, disabilities or vulnerabilities that is relevant to their capability to participate in the proceedings;

This gives you an appreciation of the process that the local authority has undertaken. What the court is looking for and the rules you are expected to abide by, particularly if you are a litigant in person.

Of greater value to you will be an understanding of the law under which the application is brought. We have referred to many aspects of the Children Act 1989 already. When faced with care proceedings the relevant sections of the act are:

Section 1 Welfare of the child.

(1)When a court determines any question with respect to—

(a)the upbringing of a child; or

(b)the administration of a child's property or the application of any income arising from it,

the child's welfare shall be the court's paramount consideration.

(2)In any proceedings in which any question with respect to the upbringing of a child arises, the court shall have regard to the general principle that any delay in determining the question is likely to prejudice the welfare of the child.

This is particularly important because it is the over-riding basis of any court action under the Children Act 1989, particularly:

Section 14: Special Guardianship Orders,

Section 16: Family Assistance Orders,

Sections 31 – 42 Care and Supervision Orders.

It simply means that anything the court orders must have the welfare of the child as its guiding principle and this must be achieved with the minimal of delays.

In common law countries, such as the UK and the Republic of Ireland, case law is of particular importance because the doctrine of precedent applies. This means that previous decisions in court cases obliges all subsequent cases to follow the precedent set. The courts are hierarchical in structure so the decisions of higher courts bind the lower courts to following that decision. For example a High Court decision must be followed by a judge in a county (family) court. Many appeal court rulings are invaluable in setting the decision making in the lower courts. The principle is *'stare decisis'*, which means stand by what has been decided.

There are two types of judicial precedent a <u>binding</u> precedent where past decisions must be followed and a <u>persuasive</u> precedent where a decision will be considered, but it is not a requirement to follow it.

These precedents, particularly appeal court rulings in family cases, can help a parent argue and win their case. Not all past judgments are published, but there are a considerable amount available and the numbers are increasing all the time. Most can be found online at the British and Irish legal Information Institute or Bailii[lxxvi]. There are other sources too, such as Family Law Week[lxxvii] and some legal bloggers draw attention to important and interesting cases, such as Suesspiciousminds[lxxviii] and the Marilyn Stowe blog[lxxix].

Obviously there is not room here, to consider every piece of case law that could be relevant to a family facing care proceedings. I have provided a list of some pertinent cases in Appendix G. We shall now briefly examine how to use the precedents.

The first step, once you have identified a case precedent that you believe is relevant, is to compare your situation to the facts in the case. That way you can compare or distinguish similar issues and divergent issues. There is always an argument to be made that 'your case is different...' by your opposition counsel because there are always subtle nuances to the facts. To be more confident of your ground, it is a good idea to try to find a few cases that demonstrate the precedent. Often you will find cases that quote from the case you have found. Again, compare the facts, look for the similarities and use those to strengthen the argument that the precedent must apply to your case.

Often judgments interpret how the statute (legislation) e.g. a section of the Children Act, should be applied. It is helpful to extract the language used in these cases to ensure that in your case the applicable law is being used in its correct interpretation and application.

You can also identify trends in case law, there are some instances where a particular issue appears to get overt attention and commentary from the judiciary. Take, for example, the use of Section 20 voluntary accommodation under the Children Act. Recently there have been a spate of cases where the judiciary have reinforced how they interpret the law regarding Section 20. This led to some parents being granted damages for Human Rights violations and for HHJ Bellamy to issue a set of guidelines on the correct use and application of Section 20. Where you can identify a trend, then it is valuable to compare your case to it and where there are similar issues, to rely on the findings of the previous cases, and to demonstrate what may be misapplication or wrong-doing in your case.

What you also must be mindful of, is that you may come across cases that do not support your position. You cannot ignore these because there is no doubt that the LA barrister will use them. This time, you are applying the reverse of the above and looking for why these cases do not apply to your case. Again, it goes back to the facts. Look for how the circumstances in the case in question, is different from yours.

You must also be aware that some cases will have been superseded by other cases, particularly if a higher court has heard an appeal on the case. As we mentioned above, the courts have a hierarchy, so keep in mind that an Appeal court judgment can supersede a High court judgment, a Supreme court judgment can supersede the Appeal court. Also look out for what are termed dissenting judgments. This could be a different judgment looking at the same issues as a previous case, or a judge sitting in a three judge hearing (such as in the appeal courts) and one of the judges not agreeing with the other two on one or all of the points. Such dissenting judgments might be useful to you and may persuade a judge as to the merits of that dissent in your case. For a dissenting judgment see 'In the matter of B (A Child) [2013] UKSC 33'. Lady Hale dissented in this case. This was an appeal to the Supreme Court by parents concerning the application of the criteria for making a care order under section 31 of the Children Act 1989 when the risk is of future psychological or emotional harm, and the role of the appellate courts once the trial judge has made an order. The appeal was dismissed, however Lady Hale dissented and took the view *that this was a case based on the mere possibility that the child would suffer psychological harm in the future. There was no risk that these parents would neglect or abuse their child. Even if this were sufficient to cross the threshold laid down in section 31(2) of the Children Act 1989, it had not been demonstrated that a care order with a view to adoption was necessary to protect the child–that 'nothing else would do'–when nothing else had been tried. The care order was not, therefore, a proportionate response to the harm which was feared.'*

Finally, it is a good idea to quote the relevant sections of a judgment in your submissions, and to provide a full copy of all the precedents you refer to. This means the judge can then look at the relevant sections in the context of the whole case.

These guidelines apply equally in the Republic of Ireland, although the court process is slightly different, the means to challenge the case is the same.

Adoption

Although we have considered orders that can be made under the Children Act 1989, a care order may be granted alongside a Placement order under the Adoption and Children Act 2002[lxxx]. Under section 21 of the act:

'(1)A placement order is an order made by the court authorising a local authority to place a child for adoption with any prospective adopters who may be chosen by the authority.

(2)The court may not make a placement order in respect of a child unless—

(a)the child is subject to a care order,

(b)the court is satisfied that the conditions in section 31(2) of the 1989 Act (conditions for making a care order) are met, or

(c)the child has no parent or guardian.

(3)The court may only make a placement order if, in the case of each parent or guardian of the child, the court is satisfied—

(a)that the parent or guardian has consented to the child being placed for adoption with any prospective adopters who may be chosen by the local authority and has not withdrawn the consent, or

(b)that the parent's or guardian's consent should be dispensed with.

This subsection is subject to section 52 (parental etc. consent).

(4)A placement order continues in force until—

(a)it is revoked under section 24,

(b)an adoption order is made in respect of the child, or

(c)the child marries or attains the age of 18 years.'

A placement order allows the local authority to seek an adoptive family for the child. As can be seen it is a small step from the granting of a full care order to a care and placement order where the child is of an adoptable age. In reality this largely means babies and children under six or seven. Parental rights are shared between the local authority and the biological parents, but in for all practical purposes there is little exercise of those rights on behalf of the parents.

You may apply to the court to revoke (remove) a placement order. However unless you are the child or the local authority such an application requires leave (i.e. permission) from the court to bring the application. Such permission can only be granted where there has been a change of circumstances since the placement order was made. It should be noted that if a placement order is revoked and your child was subject to a care order that care order is revived and will probably require an application to discharge such. If the child is placed directly with potential adopters, then you cannot apply to revoke the placement order.

The court may order some contact through the placement order, however if the child is placed directly with the potential adopters then no contact will be granted. Further, in those circumstances, you will not be invited to review meetings with the Independent Reviewing Officer. Some potential adopters will be open to maintaining contact, some won't. The usual scenario for adopted children is that 'letter-box' contact is allowed. This means you may write a letter to your child once or twice (perhaps more) a year.

The form needed to apply for a revocation of a placement order is A52[lxxxi].

The child must be in place with the potential adoption family for ten weeks before they can apply for an adoption order. If an application is made, you can oppose this under section 47 of the Adoption and Children Act 2002[lxxxii]. However this again requires permission of the court and must be based on a change of circumstances. As before, the court must assess the welfare of the child before making an adoption order under a welfare test similar to the one used under the Children Act

1989 that we examined above.

This includes assessing: the child's wishes and feelings (considered in the light of the child's age and maturity), the effect on the child throughout its life, along with its needs and relevant background and characteristics. It must examine the harm suffered or likely to suffer as defined in the Children Act 1989 and wider family relationships and the value of those being continued or not. It must also consider the wishes and feelings of the child's relatives or any such person regarding the child. It is also an opportunity to assess the willingness and ability of the child's relatives to provide the child with a secure environment and to meet their needs.

This means that there is a small, but realistic opportunity to have the child placed with a family member, possibly under a Special Guardianship Order at the eleventh hour.

In 2014 a new act was introduced: The Children and Families Act 2014. This amended section 51 of the Adoption and children Act 2002 regarding post adoption contact:

'9 Contact: post-adoption

(1) After section 51 of the Adoption and Children Act 2002

insert—

"Post-adoption contact

51A Post-adoption contact

(1) This section applies where—

(a) an adoption agency has placed or was authorised to place a child for adoption, and

(b) the court is making or has made an adoption order in respect of

the child.

(2) When making the adoption order or at any time afterwards, the court may make an order under this section—

(a) requiring the person in whose favour the adoption order is or has been made to allow the child to visit or stay with the person named in the order under this section, or for the person named in that order and the child otherwise to have contact with each other, or

(b) prohibiting the person named in the order under this section from having contact with the child.

(3) The following people may be named in an order under this section—

(a)any person who (but for the child's adoption) would be related to the child by blood (including half-blood), marriage or civil partnership;

(b) any former guardian of the child;

(c) any person who had parental responsibility for the child immediately before the making of the adoption order;

(d) any person who was entitled to make an application for an order under section 26 in respect of the child (contact with children placed or to be placed for adoption) by virtue of subsection (3)(c), (d) or (e) of that section;

(e) any person with whom the child has lived for a period of at least one year.

(4) An application for an order under this section may be made by—

(a) a person who has applied for the adoption order or in whose favour the adoption order is or has been made,

(b) the child, or

(c) any person who has obtained the court's leave to make the application.

(5) In deciding whether to grant leave under subsection (4)(c), the court must consider—

Part 1 — Adoption and contact

(a) any risk there might be of the proposed application disrupting the child's life to such an extent that he or she would be harmed by it (within the meaning of the 1989 Act),

(b) the applicant's connection with the child, and

(c) any representations made to the court by—

(i) the child, or

(ii) a person who has applied for the adoption order or in whose favour the adoption order is or has been made.

(6) When making an adoption order, the court may on its own initiative make an order of the type mentioned in subsection (2)(b).

(7) The period of one year mentioned in subsection (3)(e) need

not be continuous but must not have begun more than five
years before the making of the application.

(8) Where this section applies, an order under section 8 of the
1989 Act may not make provision about contact between the
child and any person who may be named in an order under
this section. [lxxxiii] *'*

Thus, there is the possibility of biological parents having contact with their child once adopted. Clearly the bar for this is set high. Firstly it requires an application for leave to bring the application, then the court must decide on how disruptive and harmful granting such an order may be. The adoptive parents may oppose. At face value it looks like a potential opportunity for the birth parent to maintain a relationship with their child. However we must consider that adoptions, are granted upon the finding of harm or likely harm and that the best interests of the child are served by being permanently removed from their natural family.

On the basis of that it looks like a false hope being granted to parents. Nevertheless, it could be a useful tool. If you let the potential adopters know, via the local authority that you and members of your family intend to apply for this post adoption contact, it could mean that the adopters are going to be faced with on-going litigation, which could potentially cost them money. This may have no effect whatsoever, it may change a potential adopters mind, but when you are fighting for your child any small possible hurdle you place in the way is worth attempting.

Opposing placement or adoption orders requires you to demonstrate a change of circumstances.

In *Re P (Adoption: Leave Provisions)* [2007] EWCA Civ 616; [2007] 2 FLR 1069[lxxxiv]. The court set out what it felt was the basis of a change of circumstances:

"The change in circumstances since the placement order was made must ... be of a nature and degree sufficient, on the facts of the particular case, to open the door to the exercise of the judicial discretion to permit the parents to defend the adoption proceedings."

The court also gave further guidance, reiterating the Supreme Court's judgment in *re B (A Child) (Care Proceedings: Threshold Criteria)* [2013] UKSC 33, [2013] 1 WLR 1911[lxxxv], that adoption was only allowed when 'nothing else will do.' The result being that a judge must not attach undue weight to the short term consequences (such as a disruption in the short term to the child) if the leave to oppose if given. In particular the fact the child is placed or adopted is not determinative and as a result the court must weigh up all the pros and cons with the best interests of the child at the heart of the matter. Within this, there are also the rights of the child to know his natural parents. These are the issues you must focus on highlighting in any such application for leave.

The change of circumstances will be very much personal to the facts and findings in your particular case. It is important to highlight areas such as: therapy completed, courses undertaken, changes in housing, relationships, and employment for example, particularly if they featured in some manner in your original case. It is important to not just 'tell' the court, but demonstrate by way of evidence. Certificates of completion of courses, positive 'expert' reports, photographs of improved living conditions are all such examples.

It is also a good idea to provide the court with your own 'care plan' demonstrating how you will support the return of your child, both in the short, medium and long term. This should include examples of wider support, either family and friends, a new partner or professional services. This not only demonstrates your change of circumstances but also a change in your approach and thinking to caring for your child. Such a demonstration indicates personal change and may be a powerful indicator to the court that the granting of your application is warranted to be heard further.

Sometimes the local authority use an approach of 'twin-tracking' or 'foster-to-adopt', whereby the plan is to apply for adoption and thus placing a child with foster parents who are already approved adoption parents. The process is used to cut the delay in providing a permanent placement for the child.

Adoption in Ireland

Until very recently adoption in Ireland had become quite rare after the historical adoptions usually organised under the auspices of the Catholic Church. However a referendum voted to bring Ireland into line with the approach of the UK with regard to children in care and adoption. The one advantage is that a child will not be considered for adoption until three years have passed with the parents unable to care for the child. Hence as described previously, this gives a parent much more time to prevent an adoption and have a child returned to their care. The same advice as above applies.

The court process is not easy to navigate and can be very

difficult for parents acting as litigants in person (which many end up doing, especially when opposing placement and adoption orders and in bringing appeals, due to a lack of availability of legal aid funding). Educating yourself about the process can help you bring proper challenges, whether by instructing your solicitors and barrister in what you wish to be done on your behalf, or by doing it yourself.

Chapter 8: How to Fight in Court: Appeals

As stated in the general guidelines, any order can be appealed. That does not mean you will actually get an appeal hearing, but the application to appeal an order is always present. You can ask the judge at the time of their order, for permission to appeal and in some circumstances, the judge may actually tell you that you have permission to appeal without you actually requesting it. Generally though you will require permission to appeal.

You cannot appeal an order just because you are unhappy with the judgment. The judge must have either erred in law (i.e. got something legally incorrect) or in fact, or the procedure was flawed leading to an unfair hearing. Much of what is covered above, if absent from your case, or incorrectly, or not fully applied could give you grounds for an appeal. You must also be aware that making an appeal in care cases does not necessarily stay the order (i.e. stop the order from proceeding), and that even a successful appeal can lead to a remittance of the case for a rehearing in your local family court and not the simple handing back of your child. In other words, an appeal may just be another starting point and not the end point in itself. The appeal court does not conduct a retrial but only reviews the decision of the judge below.

To appeal to the Court of Appeal you are required to first apply for permission to appeal (if you do not have permission already granted). This requires the filling out of an appellants notice, providing grounds for appeal and a skeleton argument.

Appellants Notice

This is form N161 [lxxxvi] for the appeal court in England and Wales. There are also accompanying notes to help you navigate the form. The form is quite explanatory in its presentation, but here are a few salient pointers to aid you in filling out the form.

In section one you will fill out your details and the name of the respondents. A simple mistake people sometimes make is in describing the applicant and respondent in the first fields. This section refers to the original case and it will the local authority who are the likely applicants and you, the parents the respondent. You are making the application as the appellant, hence your name goes in the appellants name box and the local authority will be the respondents. In section two, you will need the case reference from the family court hearing to put on the form, along with the name of the judge who made the order you are appealing, and the judge's status (ie District judge, High Court judge and so forth).

Section five requires you to set out the order you wish to appeal, which simply means copy out the order that was granted. There is also a box to confirm if you have issued the application 'in time'. Generally, you have twenty one days to appeal an order unless the judge gave a specific limit in their judgment. You can make an application for appeal outside of the time-limit, but you you must have solid grounds for doing so. It is far better to ensure that your application is 'within time', than trying to obtain permission to appeal outside of time.

Section six is the grounds of appeal and these must be provided on a separate sheet, attached to the appellants notice. This is where you must lay out how the lower court judge failed to apply the law correctly, i.e. why you think they got it wrong. Why the procedure was wrong or that the facts upon which the judgment was based where wrong. An example taken from Re B-S (Children) 2013:

'Ground   *1*

93. The first ground of appeal is that Parker J erred in law by applying an additional test to that laid down in section 47(5), namely a 'prospect of success test'. There is, with respect to counsel, nothing in this point. Both principle and the authorities to which we have referred require a court operating a leave filter, including under section 47(5), to have regard to the applicant's ultimate prospects of success. If and insofar as complaint is made that Parker J wrongly conflated the second and third stages in the Re W analysis, we agree, for reasons we have already given, that she was wrong to do so. But we do not think that this error of law in fact vitiated her essential reasoning or her conclusion. We note McFarlane LJ's view (Re B-S (Children) [2013] EWCA Civ 813, para 17) that if this had been the only point he would have been reluctant to grant permission to appeal because, as he put it, and we agree, the judge's general approach to the determination of the issue before her seems to have been more generally in line with authority.

Ground   ***2***

94. The second ground of appeal is that Parker J fell into error in failing to provide a full analysis as to why the change in circumstances was not sufficient to permit the mother to oppose the making of adoption orders. There is, in our judgment, no merit in this ground of appeal. The judge identified and explained the reasons why, despite the admitted change in circumstances, leave to oppose ought not to be given, including, in particular, the children's memories, their at least partial understanding of the current situation, and the risk that giving leave would risk great upset and behavioural regression.

Ground *3*

95. The third ground of appeal is that Parker J failed to give sufficient weight to the losses that would accrue to the children if adoption orders were made. Again, we cannot accept this. The judge was very well aware of what the children would be losing if adoption orders were made but, within the framework of the task imposed on her by section 47(5), had to look at the full picture, balancing what the children would, or might, lose if leave to oppose was not granted against what they would, or might, lose if leave to oppose was granted. We have already identified the factors that weighed in particular with the judge. The judge was in our judgment entitled to give the various factors, pro and con, the weight that she chose to attribute to them.

Ground   4

96. The fourth ground of appeal is that Parker J acted unfairly and in breach of Articles 6 and 8 in reverting to the original 'harm' issues and placing great weight upon them. This is linked with a complaint that the judge failed to look in any depth at the extent and breadth of the changes since the placement orders were made that were relevant to the adoption application. We cannot agree. The original 'harm' issues, as counsel describes them, were plainly relevant, and given their continuing impact on the children as found by the judge it was clearly open to her to attach considerable weight to them. In relation to the other part of the complaint we repeat what we have already said in relation to ground 2.

Ground   5

97. The fifth ground of appeal is that Parker J failed to give the mother and her representatives time to consider new material produced at the hearing by the local authority, thereby denying her a fair trial. We reject this complaint. The fact is that the mother and her representatives did have time to consider this material. And, importantly, no application was made either for an adjournment or for cross-examination.

98. The sixth ground of appeal, linking in with what McFarlane LJ had said, is that the test in section 47(5) does not afford someone in the mother's position a 'real' remedy, since placement is itself a bar to any ability to persuade the court to allow opposition to the making of an adoption order.'

Section seven is where you provide what is known as your skeleton argument. This is where you lay out the legal arguments to 'prove' your grounds. There is a guide to writing skeleton arguments provided by the Honourable Society of Gray's Inn[lxxxvii] and this is a useful document to consider before you approach writing a skeleton argument. The key points to remember are:

- You are persuading the court that you have a case to be reviewed,

- Select the best case law to support your argument,

- Follow the recommended layout, if you can't make it as simple to follow as possible, numbering paragraphs clearly, use wide margins and 1.5 line spacing. Use headings if appropriate.

- Names are better used than appellant or respondent.

- Head your document *'Skeleton argument on behalf of......'*

- Add in the date.

- The body is broken down into: introduction–what are you appealing, the issues, the facts and then the law.

- Apply the law point by point to your facts.

- Keep it brief, to the point and avoid 'padding' it out.

- In conclusion say what you want–i.e. permission for appeal.

Section eight does not apply so tick no.

Under section nine you will generally be asking the court to set aside the order. Section ten will only apply if you are making other applications to the court, such as a stay of execution of the order. If you wish to prevent the order you are challenging being carried out whilst you appeal is heard you will need to provide reasons for this at section eleven. As noted previously, this is unlikely to be granted. It is also in section ten where if you are applying out of time, then you must provide your grounds at section eleven.

Finally you need to sign the statement of truth. There follows a checklist of what must be provided to the court, tick what you are able to include. It is likely that you may not yet have the judgment available to you and you will have to apply for the transcript of the hearing. Anything you are unable to provide must be listed on the form 'reasons why you have not supplied a document'. You should not delay in issuing your application whilst awaiting the judgment from your case.

You will need to send multiple copies of your application to the court, follow the checklist carefully. At the very bottom of the form there is another signature required.

To apply for a transcript of your court hearing you will need to fill out form ex107[lxxxviii] and if your personal financial circumstances qualify you, then you may apply for a remission of court fees on form ex160[lxxxix] and ex 105[xc] for the transcript at public expense (send your request for the transcript and the 'at public expense form' to the local court where your case was heard).

The appeal court application is sent to:

Civil Appeals Office
Room E307
Royal Courts of Justice
The Strand
London
WC2A 2LL

The court will acknowledge the applications and issue a letter of instructions to serve on the respondents, who then have an opportunity to oppose the permission to appeal. The case is 'heard' on paper and you will be informed in writing of the outcome of your application for permission to appeal. If you are refused, you may be prevented from seeking an oral application as well, if not you may ask the court for an oral hearing to put forward your case for appeal.

In Ireland if your case was commenced in the District Court, it can be appealed to the Circuit Court. A case commenced in the Circuit Court may be appealed to the High Court. A High Court case may be appealed to the Court of Appeal. The general rules of appeal and what the appeal court will consider are very similar to the above.

To apply to the Circuit Court you must issue and serve your appeal on all parties within 14 days on form 101.1[xci]. This must be accompanied by a statutory declaration as to service thereof, with the Clerk for the court area within which the case was heard.

To apply for an appeal from the Circuit court to the High Court:

'*An appeal from the Circuit Court is made under Order 61 of the Rules of the Superior Courts. A notice of appeal must be filed within 10 days of the Circuit Court order or judgment. The notice must be served and service is indorsed on the back of the notice before it is lodged/filed. A sample of an indorsement of service is set out below.*

Where to lodge a notice of appeal

This depends on whether there is oral evidence in the case.

- *If there is oral evidence the appeal is lodged in the Circuit Court Office and the appeal is then heard by a High Court judge on circuit*

- *If there is no oral evidence the appeal is lodged in the Central Office and the appeal is heard in Dublin*

- *If the Circuit Court case was originally heard in Dublin the appeal is always lodged with the Central*

Office

- *Order 61 Rule 3 allows 10 days for the appeal to be served and lodged in the Central Office, if serving by post the appeal must be sent on the 9th day[xcii].*

An example of a notice of appeal is found at Appendix H.

To apply for leave to the Court of appeal in Ireland:

'*6. (1) Where under statute leave to appeal to the Court of Appeal is required to be sought, application for such leave shall be brought by notice of application (in this rule called the "application for leave to appeal") in the Form No. 2, which shall include the grounds on which leave to appeal is sought and, where relevant, the reasons why it is alleged that the conditions for leave to appeal are satisfied, and to which shall be appended a draft of the proposed notice of appeal. A return date before the Court of Appeal shall be assigned to every application for leave to appeal issued under this rule.*

(2) Subject to any provision to the contrary in any enactment which applies to the particular category of appeal, where under any enactment leave to appeal to the Court of Appeal may be sought in the court below or in the Court of Appeal,

any application seeking leave to appeal may be made to the Court of Appeal only after the court below has refused to grant leave to appeal.

(3) Subject to any provision to the contrary in any enactment which applies to the particular category of appeal, and to the provisions of this Order, the application for leave to appeal and an attested copy of the order of the court below shall be lodged not later than 28 days from the perfecting of the order of the court below against which leave to appeal is sought.

(4) A copy of the application for leave to appeal (and appended draft notice of appeal) shall be served not later than 14 days before the return date of the application for leave to appeal, on all parties directly affected by the application.

(5) The moving party shall lodge an affidavit of service of the application for leave to appeal on each respondent served.

(6) It is not necessary to serve parties to the proceedings in the court below who are not directly affected by the application for leave to appeal, but the Court of Appeal may direct notice of the application for leave to appeal to be served on all or any of the parties to the proceedings in the court below, or on any other person.

(7) A person served with an application for leave to appeal who intends to oppose the application shall lodge in the Office and serve on the moving party and each other person served with the application for leave to appeal a statement of that person's grounds of objection to the application for leave to appeal in the Form No. 3, not later than seven days before the return date of the application for leave to appeal.

(8) On the return date of the application for leave to appeal, (or on any adjournment of such hearing), the Court of Appeal may give such directions and make such orders, including the fixing of time limits, for the conduct of the application as appear convenient for the determination of the application in a manner which is consistent with the requirements of Order 86, rule 2, which may include:

> *(a) directions as to the service of the application for leave to appeal on any other person including mode of service and the time allowed for such service (and may for that purpose adjourn the hearing (or further hearing) or determination of the motion to a date specified);*

> *(b) directions as to the filing and delivery of*

any affidavit by any party or parties;

(c) directions as to the filing and delivery of written submissions.

(9) An order granting leave to appeal:

(a) shall specify the grounds on which leave is given;

(b) shall fix a time within which the notice of appeal is to be issued and served, and

(c) shall fix a date for the directions hearing on the appeal.

(10) When the Court of Appeal has determined an application for leave to appeal, the Registrar shall notify the parties of the determination.[xciii],

An example of Form 2 is found in Appendix H.

There is also the option of an expedited appeal in the Appeal court. Which may be used to have a High Court decision heard rapidly, such as in orders issued under Brussels II. The application is made on Form 4, found at Appendix H. Most applications will require a grounding affidavit, similar to the examples provided for judicial review.

Frequently a judicial review of the District court's decision is a better option than appeal, particularly for UK families who may have fled to Ireland and have been discovered and their children removed under interim care orders. In all instances the information given above will guide your application.

Chapter 9: Fight or Flight

Fleeing from social services is the most extreme option that you can take in deciding how to deal with their intervention. It is a huge upheaval, you will not only be leaving behind your home, probably a lot of your possessions but also, most importantly family and friends. You may be removing your child from school, from grandparents, their friends, the clubs they attend and ultimately the safe environment they call home. You are giving up a lot, but as many parents who have successfully fled have maintained, the fear that an even greater loss, that of your children makes the sacrifice of material things and even extended family a price worth paying.

So, when faced with social services on your doorstep should you stay and fight them or is your best option to flee and remove yourself from their jurisdiction? There is no easy answer to the above question, everything depends upon your individual circumstances but there are a few basic ground rules that you need to consider before you make your decision.

1. You need to be completely honest with yourself. Do the social workers have a valid claim against you and are they actually justified in their enquiries. If you have been reported for taking drugs, passed out and your children left to care for

themselves whilst you were unconscious then perhaps the social services have a point. Fleeing is not going to protect you, as the local authority will pursue you, seeking recovery orders, alerting Interpol, getting the police to call on your family to find out where you are. With a serious and valid claim against you the authorities will assist in the recovery of your children. In those circumstances it may be better to ask for help and put the onus back on the social workers to do their job and assist you. However, if the validity of the claim is nonsense and you have evidence to rebut it, then you have a basis to fight their assumptions. Of course, you may still feel that fleeing is the best option at that point, if nothing more than to give you space to organise your fight.

2. You need to assess as best you can, what you think the social workers agenda may be. Are they threatening in their approach to you, are they making noises about epo's (emergency protection orders) or going to court in the earliest communications with you? What are they requesting you should do in their reports–a risk assessment, a mental health assessment, access to your medical records? Are you likely to comply with their requests, attend their meetings or are you more likely to refuse engagement with them because they have totally got the situation wrong? If you don't wish to engage,

they could become heavy handed, very quickly. If you are not prepared to let the social worker into your home and see your children then that does give them grounds for applying for an epo[xciv]. Unfortunately all the time it is a finely balanced exercise in judging the best approach to take. Simply allowing the social workers to see your children, in one room only of your home, with you present all the time removes the chance for an epo on the grounds of not seeing the children, but still leaves the opportunity open to plan for and to flee. Alternatively a recording/videoing device could be set up in a room where the Social Workers will talk with the children.

3. Your decision making has to be based upon if you have had any dealings with social services previously. Have you had other children removed? Have you been in care yourself? Are you pregnant and they are threatening to remove your baby at birth for risk of future emotional harm? All these are danger signs that it is likely that the ultimate aim will be to remove your child. If you already have had children removed have your circumstances changed considerably since that decision, can you show and prove it?

4. Can you, honestly and without a shadow of a doubt prove that their assumptions and presumptions are wrong. Are you

strong enough emotionally and prepared to engage in what may be a lengthy battle to prove them wrong? Have you got the support network to help you do this, family, friends, access to support and help?

5. Perhaps the most important question of all is: can you support yourself if you leave? Remember that you may not be able to claim benefits in the country you flee to. Ireland has a rule that you have to be resident there for at least two years. There are exceptions to that rule and there may be ways to challenge it, but do not think there is any guarantee that you can rely on UK benefits, you may be able to claim them for up to three months, but it has not been unknown for social services to report you have left and to get your benefits stopped. The question of supporting yourself is the most crucial if your move is to have any chance of long term success.

There are many more questions that you will no doubt ask of yourself, ultimately what will drive your decision is the worry and fear that you have over the safety of your children and your self belief in your ability to fight the system.

So if you choose to flee what are your options?

As highlighted previously the ectopia network operates in 6 countries: Ireland, Denmark, Belgium, France, Spain and Northern Cyprus. Each choice comes with its own difficulties. The initial starting point has to be whether you and your children have passports. Without them or the possibility of obtaining them quickly; i.e. applying in person for a same day passport, if you can obtain a speedy appointment–the UK government class an urgent need for a passport as within one month, so even on the same day passport application idea it may take up to a month to obtain an appointment and there are rules as to the types of passport that can be obtained in this manner, for example, it cannot be used for a first time adult passport application- so without passports 5 out of the 6 countries are a non starter. Hence Ireland is the destination of choice for many fleeing parents. Ireland requires no passport for travel or entry for British citizens (if you fly, Ryan Air require a passport but sometimes will waive it for a photographic driving licence if arranged in advance, Aer Lingus will accept other photo ID).

There are many other options with some parents fleeing to the far-east for example, but of course for many families the cost of this is prohibitive and is all too often far too removed from the language, culture and lifestyle of home. As this book is designed to help you successfully deal with your social services intervention we shall stick to the countries where help can be directly found, rather than cast parents into the great unknown completely, as a result Ireland shall form our case study. The information that follows comes from the most frequently asked questions by parents who wish to flee to Ireland.

Fleeing to Ireland

Ireland offers the advantages of the same language and a very similar lifestyle and culture. The laws are recognisable, the school system similar enough to be easy to navigate and above all else if your child is born there it obtains the right to become an Irish citizen, fully afforded the rights of the Irish Constitution. Since the 1st January 2005 a child born on the island of Ireland is entitled to Irish citizenship if they have a British parent or a parent who is entitled to live in Northern Ireland or the Irish State without restriction of their residency. However it must be noted that the British Nationality Act 1981 provides for a child born outside of the UK if its Mother or Father is a British Citizen otherwise than by descent to be automatically recognised as a British citizen. Thus Children born of natural British Mothers/Fathers automatically confer

British Citizenship upon their child.

This is a complicated area of law in regard to the status of a child born outside of the UK to British parents, especially with regard to international laws of the Hague Convention and Brussels II (bis) and we shall return to this aspect later in this chapter.

Ireland is also a far more family orientated country than the UK, however it must be noted that Ireland is moving along the same path as the UK with an ever increasing nanny state and an ever increasingly draconian approach to ' child protection', but for the moment at least forced adoptions are few and far between. Even with the legislating of 'forced adoption policies' after the Children's Referendum no child will be considered for such until a period of three years has passed– thus offering greater scope to have a child returned than the 26 weeks approach of the UK system.

Getting there-Travel.

Ireland can be easily accessed by the following popular ferry ports:

Fishguard to Rosslare–Stena Ferries

Holyhead to Dublin -Irish Ferries & Stena Line

Liverpool to Dublin (no foot passengers) P&0 Irish Sea

Pembroke to Rosslare–Irish Ferries

There are also crossings from Scotland to Northern Ireland and from Liverpool, but this means that you are still technically on British soil until you cross the border into the Irish State.

Ireland can be reached from most major UK airports with regular flights from key departure points such as London, Birmingham, Cardiff, Bristol, Exeter, Manchester, Nottingham & Newcastle.

Ireland has three international airports: Dublin, Cork and Shannon and six regional airports Donegal, Galway, Kerry, Knock, Sligo and Waterford.

Ireland is well served by intercity and regional trains run by Irish Rail as well as Bus Eireann who run intercity and regional coach and bus services across Ireland. (There are also a number of privately operated services connecting the major population centres of Ireland-for example Wexford Bus and Citylink.) Perhaps most importantly they also are part of the "Eurolines" express coach service that links directly with the

UK. Currently it is is possible to board a coach for Ireland from: Birmingham, Leeds, Liverpool, London, Manchester and Milton Keynes as well as Glasgow and Edinburgh. These services are very reasonably priced particularly utilising the economy fares option. It also adds the advantage of travelling within a group and the anonymity that that can add.

Ian Josephs will reimburse pregnant mothers fleeing the social services if they contact him and give him proof of their pregnancy, hostile social work involvement and when you arrive in Ireland (or France) that they phone Ian to prove they have arrived and provide a receipt for all travel payments made. He will in fact reimburse the entire cost of coach and boat travel to the borders of Ireland, France or nearby European countries and even on occasion Northern Cyprus for the individual, partner and children. What Ian cannot do is support you once you have arrived.

Ireland: the issues.

Once you arrive in Ireland (or any other country) your first priority is obviously accommodation. If you have planned ahead (see the checklist below) then hopefully you will have already sourced accommodation, at least a B&B or a hotel for a few nights. This isn't always possible as sometimes people have to leave on the spur of the moment, however it is still possible to contact the ectopia network / Ian Josephs once you are on your way or you have safely arrived. To be certain of being able to secure accommodation you will need around €500 + for a deposit and up to 4 weeks rent in advance of around €120 a week for the cheapest level of accommodation. Rental accommodation is becoming increasingly difficult to find and secure so a bit of home work on sites like www.daft.ie if there is the opportunity, will pay dividends in the longer term.

Money: unless you have the means to be self sufficient either through personal income or money sent from family or friends you will quickly find yourself struggling. If you are on benefits, then you may be able to keep receiving them from the UK for a short period. If your benefits require that you have to attend a Job Centre or the like on a frequent basis then you could find that your benefits dry up almost instantly. Again if your planning is good, you could attend the doctors and make a convincing case for stress and mental strain due to the intimidating attacks and harassment from social services. This could be then used to get access to the Employment Support Allowance, which could buy you extra time on benefits.

Benefits are usually paid into your bank account these days, so it is useful if you can get a trusted family member or friend to get access to your British bank account to withdraw your benefits and transfer them into an Irish bank account, which you obviously need to set up shortly after arriving and securing some accommodation. If you really want to keep a low profile, you could change yours and your children's names by deed-poll and set up your new bank account in that name. You can continue claiming other benefits such as child benefit, child tax credits as they do not tend to need regular confirmation. Of course all of this is theoretical because it could equally be claimed that as you have left the country that continuing to claim benefits would actually be benefit fraud. Whether the authorities would pursue you for such an allegation is a matter outside the remit of this book. However the more pertinent downside of continuing to claim UK benefits whilst outside the jurisdiction is that it would be very difficult to argue in front of any judge that you had/were intending to be habitually resident in order to try to prevent the execution of a recovery order if you were still claiming UK benefits.

Hence the benefits question and the ability to support yourself is key to your long term survival and also to keeping your children should the British social services decides to apply for a recovery order. What are the alternatives if you do not have family support or access to benefits? Work in Ireland is available. However, due to the very generous benefits system, the work available is often low-paid, menial work that is usually taken up by EU immigrants as the Irish will not work in these positions when they can sometimes receive the same amounts or better simply for signing on for benefits. Saying that, there is a growing economy with some big name companies such as Apple, Coca Cola, Google, Yahoo and Vodaphone that are based in Ireland. Unfortunately the simple upshot is that if you run out of money and end up on the street or in a refuge, your children will be taken from you by the Irish social services.

If you are proposing to try to seek work in Ireland, or even apply for some benefits you will require a PPS number. This is the Irish equivalent of the UK's National Insurance number. The PPS number stands for the Personal Public Service Number and one can be obtained by completing the Reg 1 form that is available from the PPS offices located in each county or can be filled in on line. Along with a completed form, a valid ID must be produced- originals, not copies. For a UK citizen, a passport or birth certificate, along with a photographic id such as a driving licence and proof of an address in Ireland is required. Once this has been processed then a number will be issued to you. However, you can only obtain a PPS number if you can show that you need one for a transaction with a specified body or have employment lined up.

The issue of whether you can claim benefits in Ireland is a grey area. The consensus is that you need to be resident in Ireland for two years. However, the Section 246 (4) of the Social Welfare Consolidation Act 2005, incorporates into Irish law 5 factors that have been set down in judgements given by the European Court of Justice (ECJ) as relevant to determining whether a person is habitually resident. The following are the five factors:

Factor 1-Length and continuity of residence in Ireland or in any other particular country

Factor 2-Length and purpose of any absence from Ireland

Factor 3-Nature and pattern of employment

Factor 4-Applicant's main centre of interest

Factor 5-Future intention of applicant concerned as they

appear from all the circumstances.

It should be noted, and as emphasised by the ECJ, these factors are not exhaustive and any other relevant information must also be considered. Therefore, the list should not be used as a means of scoring points for and against a person satisfying the condition.

Although no single factor is conclusive, the focus must be on 'determining the person's main centre of interest, having regard to all the relevant facts and circumstances of the individual.'

So technically the ECJ ruling allows, in some circumstances for UK nationals to claim habitual residency within a shorter time frame than the two years and hence access to Irish benefits. Common sense would determine that if you cut all ties back to the UK, seek a job or start a business, take a long term tenancy on a property, or if you have the means purchase one and get your children into schools along with obtaining your PPS number, you could have a good case for claiming habitual residency. It is as yet an untested area and the author certainly believes that under European law there may be a case if all the above are undertaken and a person is still denied access to Irish benefits.

Taking one of the above aspects further if you flee to Ireland then it is a good idea that if your children are of school age then you seek out a place for them as soon as possible. This not only goes some way to fulfilling the criteria listed above but also provides a good basis for an Irish judge not to grant leave on a recovery order as your children have settled. Further it means there is another set of professionals who can vouch for the fact that your children are happy, safe and secure.

The education structure in Ireland is broadly similar to the UK with primary schools, secondary and third level or Higher. The vast majority of schools are typically catholic in background–over 90%-but there are Church of Ireland Schools, non and inter denominational and a few other religions. Primary education is generally completed at a national school, a multi-denominational school, a gaelscoil or a preparatory school. National schools originated with the introduction of state primary education in 1831. Gaelscoilenna started in the mid 20th century and the Irish language is the working language in these schools and it is one of the fastest growing education sectors. Multi-denominational schools are a newer innovation. Often run by a non-profit company or organisation and welcomes all religious backgrounds. An example of such is the Educate Together network of Schools. Preparatory schools are generally the same as in the UK-independent and fee-paying.

In the secondary sector "Voluntary secondary schools", are usually just referred to as secondary schools and tend to be managed by a religious affiliation or private organisation, although the state tends to fund most of the costs with just over half the age cohort attending these schools. Vocational schools are managed by the Education and Training Boards, but again largely state funded as are the Comprehensive schools or community schools. These schools largely developed out of the combination of the previous two categories to create a very similar school to the UK's comprehensive secondary school. Gaelcholáistes are the Irish language schools secondary offering whilst what are known as Grind Schools are privately run schools independent and fee paying, who tend to focus on the students of school leaving/examination age. Although the names and structure may be slightly different within the three age sectors of primary secondary and tertiary, it is more than recognisable to the British citizen.

Ireland has its own social service–Tusla- the Child and Family

Agency, who increasingly are happy to act on the instructions of the British state. One of the dilemmas you must face is whether you contact Irish social services on arrival or attempt to stay well off their radar. There can be advantages to choosing to contact them. You can request that they carry out their own assessments and investigations into your family. Experience shows that without the added incentive of adoption, the Irish SS appear to be more balanced in their perspectives. It is not always the case, but it can sometimes bring a new pair of eyes and a new perspective. Generally, the rule is do not contact them, but in some circumstances it may be beneficial and work in your favour. If you are running from a domestic violence relationship and have moved to Ireland to protect yourself, you may find that the social workers are more inclined to support you, as you can clearly demonstrate that you are displaying protective behaviours. Even if the social services have been involved in the UK, by pre-empting them and talking with the local social workers you will create an impression of yourself with them before it can be sullied by UK reports. It is a fine balance, but could work in your favour, particularly if you need to attend an Irish court and ask a judge to deny the UK requests for orders/recovery.

You may find that some living expenses in Ireland may cost

you a little more for example, if you wish to bring and use a British registered vehicle for permanent use in Ireland you will be required to register it, possibly pay a vehicle registration tax and have a National Car Test (NCT) which is the equivalent to a MOT, regardless of whether your car has a current MOT or not. The equivalent of car tax is based on emissions and can range in price at the time of writing between a minimum of a couple of hundred Euros up to a couple of thousand Euros per year depending on age, CO_2 emissions or engine capacity. You also need to affix Irish plates within three days of the registration. If your car is less than six months old, then you will also be required to pay VAT when registering your car. All in all, it can be a very expensive move, once you calculate in house deposits, rent and your day-to-day living expenses.

If possible before you leave if you do not already have a European Heath Insurance card then obtaining one is essential (the old E111)[xcv]. This will allow you to receive services from a GP, hospital, dentist and obtain prescriptions for medicines, you just need to inform the service you are claiming under the EU regulations. Treatments will then be free of charge. According to the HSE "If your GP refers you for a public out-patient appointment, to a public hospital for an x-ray or blood test, or to an Emergency Department, you will not be charged for the hospital services. If you go directly to an Emergency Department without a GP referral, there is a charge for the service." Longer term you can apply for a GP Visit card or Medical card which will give you access to free treatment, however these cards are means tested and eligibility criteria do apply. Of course, you will have to carry out your own research and contact the local HSE offices to ensure you access everything you are entitled to claim as a permanent resident.

These days most of us have a mobile phone, but as you cross the Irish sea, you may find that your phone will not work. If you have a contract phone with EU data roaming, then you may still have access, but it can be incredibly expensive. Expense is not the only consideration if your phone is attached to the network then you are instantly traceable. You may not think that you would be tracked in such a way, after all you are not a hardened criminal or a murderer, but it has not been unknown for the police to access such records to trace a family. The way around this is to get your phone unlocked and purchase a pay as you go sim card from an Irish telecommunications provider. This way you will help stay off the radar and to be doubly sure any calls you make to family ensure you withhold your number. It is not fool-proof, but it does make it much more difficult to track you.

If your move is permanent, then you will also have to sort the home you have left behind. In fact if you are to demonstrate, if you have to, that your move is permanent and that the UK social services have no further jurisdiction then you need to cut all ties with your life in the UK. If you have a house that you own/mortgage you need to sell it. If you are renting, you must give notice of the termination of your lease. You may need to arrange to remove your possessions and have them brought to Ireland, or placed into storage or with family/friends. Make sure all your contracts are cancelled, gas, electricity, council tax. The more permanent you move appears the better the case you can present.

Many aspects of the above can be sorted with time and the list is not exhaustive as there is neither the space nor the option to cover every individual circumstance, but hopefully it goes far enough as a case study to give the reader an accurate idea of the range of issues that need to be considered, not just for moving to Ireland, but if you choose to flee to any other country. Each country will come with its own issues and it is worth undertaking a little background research for any country you are considering, hopefully the above will give you a guide as to the areas you may need to investigate.

What advantages are there to fleeing?

Again, the advantages can be very individual and depend upon your own circumstances, but there are universal advantages. The most important of which is security, at least for a while. By fleeing you are not within the immediate reach of the social services and police. There can be no knock at the door and removal of your children. It removes the dread of the clatter of the letter box and another round of paperwork that paints a picture of you that you cannot recognise. In short, it provides a breathing space and although in the back of your mind you are aware that the local social services and/or police may become involved due to the actions of the authorities in the UK, this is not necessarily inevitable. As above, in some circumstances it may actually work in your favour.

The local authorities in your chosen destination may operate very differently and take a view that is based on their own observations and assessments, not just what is provided by the UK social services. This has happened a number of times, including instances where judges have ruled that children cannot be taken from their jurisdiction because the local social services have a very different view to the UK ones. Indeed it can be useful to seek out a new assessment and to cooperate with the local social workers, particularly if you believe, or if in fact the UK local authority is seeking recovery orders.

The breathing space offered by fleeing is also crucial to being able to formulate your longer term strategy. It may offer the opportunity to meet with or at least converse with the lay advisors and McKenzie friends in the networks and develop your response. You can still fight your case from a long distance, you can utilise email communications with the local authority to make complaints, issue legal proceedings against them and simply put them "on the back foot".

Of course it also offers the opportunity of a fresh start and possibly a better quality of life. One thing is for sure, when you are faced with the prospect that you may lose your children, it quickly reminds you of what is truly important in life. You may have left behind many material things, but none of that compares to knowing you still have your precious children with you. Arriving in a foreign land with your life in suitcases is sobering, but it takes a family back to the very raw basis of what is important. Family and your children become central and focused once again. The basics of shelter, food and drink become the priority and the taking for granted of such things is put sharply into perspective. Fleeing does not have to be a negative, in the longer term it can bring a more balanced and centred outlook on life.

Sometimes the fact that you have disappeared can also just simply stop the social services intervention. It can be too expensive, too much effort and actually demonstrate the fact that the concerns raised were of little genuine basis that it is not worth the local authority's efforts. It has and does happen but it is not an expectation to rely on. Often local authorities will pursue a case as far as they possibly can–it comes from the completely misplaced idea that they are the ultimate authority on child protection, and of course the fact that you have fled is often used as an excuse that you must be abusing your children–otherwise why did you run? The fact that parents flee because they have seen the lies told about them and their children, do their research and quickly come to the conclusion that they cannot rely on the local authority, police or courts for justice is entirely lost on the child protectionists who work on the basis of guilty before proven innocent.

Parents who love their children run, because they wish to try to protect them from the system that would happily place them in care, a care system that is provably full of abuse, if a parent did not care about their children then they would not run, it would probably never even enter their mind. Yet this basic psychology of parental action is completely lost on the social workers. As noted in P.H.& Anor-v-Child and Family Agency 2016:

'In particular, the fact that the applicant came to Ireland, sought to lie doggo, attempted to avoid official attention through the use of false names, checked herself out of hospital, may have been in pyjamas when doing so, moved address within Ireland, and so forth, is not so much suggestive of a propensity towards abuse and neglect as it is of a well-founded fear of the results of official attention. Such conduct by the applicant or, more generally, others so situated, is more properly understood as reflective of a wish to be permitted to parent one's child rather than of an incapacity to do so.'

It is not just the distance, a breathing space or the possibility of fresh assessments that makes fleeing so appealing, it is also the freedom to be yourself again. Having social workers, police or other professionals on your doorstep can be a real social stigma. It can create for some families a real feeling that they need to become insular, to "lie low" and, worst of all to bottle up and hide away what is happening to them. This sometimes is actually made worse by social workers, who contrary to your actual legal rights tell you that you must not discuss the case with anyone else. Apart from this being wildly inaccurate, breaching your legal rights and isolating you, also creates a social strain upon you. Parents at the school gate, teachers of your children–what are they privy to, what have they been told? What are they thinking of me, of us, of our family? This is all an added strain, a stress that can be simply lifted by becoming a stranger in a strange land. By fleeing you and are your family become unknowns, you can hold your head high once again, as the people passing you by do not know the involvement you are facing. No longer do you feel like all eyes are on you. In reality those eyes probably aren't on you and the neighbour, parent at the school gate, or sometimes even the teacher probably knows little of what is happening to your family. However, simply the fact that you are conscious that once you flee, those around you know nothing of your circumstances can be a relief in itself. That relief can help build your confidence and belief in your ability to fight back.

The advantages to fleeing can be clearly seen, although it does not mean that your fight is over, that your children are not at any further risk from the social services agenda, or that other considerable stresses and strains will be heaped upon you as you try to survive in another country. It does though provide a real platform to safeguard your children.

<u>Preparing to flee–the check-list.</u>

Choosing the flight option is not easy. With time and planning it can be a relatively simple option, but for most parents it is a last minute, panicked bid for escape. Hence, if you are ever faced with having to take that decision a basic check-list to prepare is essential. In the light of the ever growing and pervasive development of child-protection every parent should follow this guide to ensure that if they are required to take this drastic step, it is easy to organise.

1. No matter if social services have never darkened your door, ensure that you and your children have up-to-date passports. Even if you do not intend going abroad for holidays, it is worth the small cost to know that you can leave the country, for anywhere in the world (bar obtaining necessary visas for some countries) at any time. There is a fast track system for obtaining passports, but as highlighted above it is not particularly fast if you are a first time adult applicant.

2. Keep all your passports, key paperwork, like birth certificates, driving licences etc. together in a large envelope or folder that can be simply picked up and taken with you.

Also ensure that you keep social services correspondence together and portable, your contacts whilst fleeing may need it to help you fight your case.

3. Ensure you have appropriate suitcases, bags, holdalls and the like to take enough clothing, toiletries, and small toys and necessary paraphernalia for all your family.

4. Obtain a pre-pay credit card so that it can be topped up by your wider family at home for you, as well as the option of topping up yourself. You may need a credit card for transport, hotels etc. Being prepaid means that whatever your credit status, it is obtainable and also largely anonymous, which may be important. Even if you already have a credit card, a pre-paid one makes it harder to trace your whereabouts.

5. Learn where your nearest departure points are. Find out the timetables for public transport, even if you own a vehicle, and how to book tickets. This may seem basic and can be done at the last minute, but if you are aware, it gives a confidence to the plans you are making.

6. Speaking of plans, if you have the necessary passports/visas, work out a choice of countries to flee to and even the connections between and within them. It may be that

you travel first to Ireland, but you do not want to end up in the middle of the country if you may then move on to France or Spain. Do you need to be near the key ports/airports?

7. Know how you may fund yourself. Even if you are on UK benefits, be aware of little snags like having to "sign on." For example is it realistically feasible to rely on your benefits or will you have to acquire employment as soon as possible on arrival. Often social workers will help ensure benefits stop once it is understood you have actually left the country. Be realistic about your options for funding. Will family/friends help?

8. Find out who the network contacts are or any support groups/parents that have already fled the UK. Facebook groups may be helpful in this though it is wise not to give any information away on social media platforms. Who can you turn to for help and support? Do your "homework" and find a range of contacts who may help you. If you have followed this book closely you will already have a range of names to make initial contact with.

9. Where possible arrange for a trusted family member or friend to have access to your home and mail to ensure you are up to date with the latest social work reports. This can be

crucial, particularly if the lay advisors need access to reports to help build a case against the social services.

10. Do not advertise to family/friends your intentions. The less anyone knows the better. Rely on e-mail/twitter/Facebook to maintain friendships and keep up to date with your wider world, but wherever possible do not advertise the fact that you will be leaving town.

The legal position regarding fleeing.

Although there can be many legal complexities raised in the course of fleeing- from the Hague Convention, Brussels II, jurisdiction, habitual residency etc.-there are some simple over-riding legal points that need to be noted.

You currently have the right to travel and settle in the European Union under Article 45 of the European Charter of Fundamental Rights[xcvi]. (Take note that this may well be affected by the Brexit position in 2019). No-one has the authority to prevent you moving and settling in another European country, even if Social Services are intervening in your life. However there are a number of legal caveats to be aware of. If the Local Authority have:

a) Issued a Public Law Outline letter to you,

b) You have been issued Court proceedings,

c) You are in proceedings,

d) Your children are on an Interim Care Order, a Supervision Order, a Special Guardianship order or

e) A full Care Order

then you cannot legally take your child/ren out of the UK. If you were to, then the likelihood is that the Local Authority would obtain 'seek and return/recovery orders' and would engage other agencies in the search, such as the Police, Interpol, Tipstaff (court officers), International Child Abduction and Contact Unit, the High Court. Your left behind family members may be brought to court to reveal your whereabouts under threat of contempt of court, have their homes searched, and be pressured to conform.

However, if none of these apply and it is at the stage of a Social Worker compiling assessments, holding Child in need or Child protection meetings then you are still free to leave. Again, the advice above about possibly contacting local Social Services in the new country may be a positive move. What is vitally important to understand is that for pregnant mothers to be, where there is social services intervention/pre-birth assessments or even a direct threat of obtaining a care order application once baby is born, you are still free to leave the jurisdiction as no court can place an order on an unborn child. So the sooner you leave the jurisdiction the better. Of course it would be wise not to broadcast the idea that you may leave the country to the Social Workers as they have been known to pull underhand tricks to try to prevent you leaving.

The Hague Convention on the Civil Aspects of International Child Abduction, the 1996 on Jurisdiction, Applicable Law, Recognition, Enforcement and Co-operation in Respect of Parental Responsibility and Measures for the Protection of Children and Brussels II (bis) COUNCIL REGULATION (EC) No 2201/2003 concerning jurisdiction and the recognition and enforcement of judgments in matrimonial matters and the matters of parental responsibility, repealing Regulation (EC) No 1347/2000.

Under the auspices of the above, both left behind parents and Local Authorities have the ability to seek summary orders for the return of a child. To consider all the aspects of these draconian pieces of legislation that provides comity[xcvii] between each individual countries judicial processes is way beyond the scope of this book and would in fact fill several volumes of its own. However the key principles that any parent needs to know are outlined below.

The first key point is that the above laws are mainly procedural in their nature and do not generally take into account the substantive issues within a case, but are merely summary in their nature. The over-riding principle that the Court that has responsibility to hear the substantive case is the court of the child's habitual residence. As we have seen, a child does not necessarily lose its habitual residence by simply moving to another country–the matter is a case of the facts[xcviii]; including how settled, integrated, and how strongly defined that centre of interest has been established[xcix]. Thus a child taken from the UK to Ireland can still retain its habitual residency in the UK, even months after moving. For example if the family concerned are effectively 'on the run', moving from place to place with no fixed abode, etc. Then it is very difficult to argue that the child's centre of interest and hence habitual residency has moved.

Further, the Court first *seised* of an issue retains the

jurisdiction. Thus a child subject to contact hearings for example is abducted to another country by a parent, then no matter which country they have moved to the law is clear that the original court retains the jurisdiction and generally the child will be returned to that country for the court to determine the matter. Add to this that where there is a court order in place, say, for example, a Supervision order in favour a Local Authority and the parents remove the child to another country, then the original court retains jurisdiction for three months, regardless. Thus it can be seen that there is a strong arsenal at the disposal of Social Services to effect a return of your child/ren to the jurisdiction.

Secondly parents need to be aware of Article 15 of Brussels II, which effectively allows the return of a child to the country they have been removed from on the basis of a 'court better placed to hear the case'. For example a family who have fled with their child or pregnant and in the past have had other children removed into foster care, it could be argued that the Social Services who had an involvement in the past have a fuller picture of the family than the new country's Social Services do and hence that the UK Courts are better placed to hear the case than the country the family have relocated to.

Thirdly there are very limited defences to a Hague/ Brussels II case. Such defences are clearly defined within the legislation and beyond establishing that habitual residence of the new country is now in effect and hence the courts thereof now hold responsibility then parents must rely upon what are effectively a set of 5 possible defences. What is important to point out here is that these defences may not apply if your case is against Social Services, however they will if it is against the child's other parent.

Defence 1.

Consent or acquiescence (Article 13 (1) (a)) i.e. the other parent agreed for you to remove the child to another country or made no attempt to offer any objection when informed of the plan. For example leaving the situation unaddressed for a number of years. This defence is unlikely to be relevant to any Social Services involvement.

Defence 2.

Parent not actually exercising custody rights (Article 13(1)(a)) i.e. the other parent has not had contact, sought to enforce contact, sought a court order for such, etc. It could also be that a court has ordered no contact for that parent.

Again, this defence is unlikely to be relevant to any Social Services involvement, however there have been instances where the Social Services have used an absent parent to help effect a 'back-door' application for a return despite them having had no relationship with the child hitherto.

Defence 3.

Grave risk of physical or psychological harm or place in an intolerable situation (Article

13(1)(b)) this could be argued as a defence against Social Services, utilising the outcomes for care leavers, or if the child is to be placed by Social Services with a particular individual-on the child's return-who may pose a risk (ie domestic violence perpetrators etc). However case law indicates that it is unlikely to be seen as an effective defence when the applicants are Child Protectionists.

Defence 4.

Child's Objections (Article 13(1)(b)) although the child's voice (depending upon their age and maturity) are of increasing importance in such cases, it is sadly the case that such a voice is not definitive. This may help in cases of older children, but it must be clear that the child has not been coerced or influenced in the development of their objections.

Defence 5.

Child settled in its new environment (Article 12) may be the strongest defence alongside the jurisdictional issues of habitual residency that can help a fleeing parent. If there have been no court proceedings seised in the UK prior to the family fleeing, then it could be argued that local Social Services are competent enough to deal with any concerns and that the settled nature of the child is best served by remaining in the new state and the local authorities there can oversee any protection issues.

This is a strong argument as the welfare of the child is paramount, the safe-guarding is effected as if the child was back in its original residency and that the courts of the new state are able to undertake any required action in ensuring the safety of the child.

No one should rely on being able to sway the Courts in any of the above arguments due to the summary nature of the legislation. However it must be said that not all Local Authorities in the UK pursue such actions, some have simply left the situation to the new state's authorities. However there are certain actions that can be undertaken that will hopefully result in a reluctance to undertake such applications by the authorities. We shall return to this later.

There is one other aspect that fleeing parents must be aware of and that is the power of the High Court to act under what is called its inherent jurisdiction and issue a Wardship order. Making a child a ward of court is a rarely used, but it is a powerful tool that is available to judges in proceedings where a family may have fled the jurisdiction.

Wardship basically means that the High Court has the final say on every aspect of a child's life and nothing may be done to or on behalf of the child without the High Court's permission. Although in reality day-to-day care may pass to a Local Authority, any major decisions must be agreed by the High Court. A Wardship can last until the child attains the age of majority, or may be ended by the Court at any juncture. Although as said it is not often used, I would argue that it can actually be abused as an option by a Local Authority to circumvent the procedures required under the Hague Convention and Brussels II.

Wardship has its origins in the feudal history of the realm and has existed for many centuries, but was brought directly into family law in the High Court under s1(2) and Schedule 1 to the Administration of Justice Act 1970. It is effectively a delegated performance of the duties of the Crown to protect its subjects. Of course families affected by a Wardship order may disagree on this aspect. Any child under the age of 18 who has British citizenship and is either physically present in England and Wales or has 'habitual residence' in England and Wales can be made a Ward of Court. However it is interesting to note that an unborn child cannot be a Ward of Court.

Any person 'with a genuine interest in or relation to the child', the child themselves or a Local Authority (with the Court's permission) can apply for Wardship. All applications for Wardship must be started in the High Court though proceedings may be transferred back to the Family Court. The child becomes a ward of the court immediately upon the making of the application Any respondent must file an acknowledgement of service in the usual way and must also file a notice stating their address and either the whereabouts of the child or denying that they are aware of the child's location. Applications for a hearing must be made within 21 days and at that hearing if the court does not confirm the Wardship then it will lapse[c].

The Children's Act 1989 has significantly restricted the use of wardship by providing a statutory scheme to deal with most circumstances in both public and private law. Practice Direction 12D of the FPR makes clear that 'such proceedings (i.e. wardship) should not be commenced unless it is clear that the issues concerning the child 'cannot be resolved under the Children Act 1989'. Recovery orders as well as seek and find orders are always available to the Local Authority and the Court and that the use of Wardship can be argued as not legally competent in matters relating to fleeing families.

Section 100 of the Children Act 1989 further restricts the use of the Wardship jurisdiction in care cases. Whereas previously section 7 of the Family Law Reform Act 1969 gave the High Court power to place a ward of the court in the care, or under the supervision, of a local authority, s 100(1) makes it clear that this ceases to be the case under the 1989 Act. Section 100(2) further stipulates that the High Court's inherent jurisdiction cannot be exercised:

a. so as to require a child to be placed in the care, or put under the supervision, of a local authority;
b. so as to require a child to be accommodated by or on behalf of a local authority;

c. so as to make a child who is the subject of a care order a ward of court; or

d. or the purpose of conferring on any local authority power to determine any question which has arisen, or which may arise, in connection with any aspect of parental responsibility for a child.

Further any application for wardship and such leave being granted should only be granted if the court is satisfied that the result *'could not be achieved through the making of any order' which could be made otherwise than in the exercise of the inherent jurisdiction of the court and which the local authority is entitled to apply for'* and there is *'reasonable cause to believe that if the court's inherent jurisdiction is not exercised with respect to the child, he is likely to suffer significant harm'.*

Thus it can be seen that the Statutory remedies available through the Children Act 1989 were envisioned to provide the mechanisms for Local Authorities to deal with cases such as the one we are discussing i.e. fleeing parents. Hence it is this author's view that a Local Authority that seeks to use Wardship to effect a return that will effectively curtail the hearing of a Brussels II case in the courts of a different jurisdiction is actually an abuse of process unless they can

prove that without Wardship the child is likely to suffer harm. What is of exceptional interest to note here is that generally in such cases the child/ren are already in the care of the 'other' state by means of Article 17 and 20 of Brussels II[ci]. Thus it would seem highly disingenuous of a Local authority to even put to the High Court, never mind argue that unless Wardship is granted then the child is 'likely to suffer significant harm.' Where such a scenario occurs, it is worth the parents making an appeal of the Wardship order utilising the above arguments. This has a two -fold effect in that an application for a stay of the order can be made and the appeal itself can be used against any summary order for a return in the High Court of the country that the parents have fled to. As always there are never any guarantees but every obstacle that could be utilised should be.

A note for those who are pregnant and considering fleeing:

<u>You have 9 months to Plan</u>

If you are pregnant and it is likely that social services will be taking an interest in your as yet unborn child you have the one advantage of time–time to plan and time to act. This time must be used wisely if you are to have any chance of preventing your baby being taken at birth.

If you have had a child previously removed, particularly recently then it almost certain that social services agenda will be to remove your newborn and have a plan for adoption, If you were in care yourself, or the victim of domestic violence, have learning difficulties or have been 'diagnosed' by a social work appointed 'expert' as having some mental health condition then you are likely to be a target too.

It is likely that after your first midwife appointment that social services will be informed and from then on the ball will begin rolling to the inevitable unless you **act!**

Plan A

Once SS are involved, there will be a pre-birth assessment and conference. Engage fully with this-this is your opportunity to evidence change. Show to SS and all their hangers-on that you have changed since the issues that lead to a previous child's removal.

Examine what and why your previous child was removed and show evidence of how things are now different. It may be that you have undergone some counselling, completed a parenting course, secured new accommodation, got a job, left a previous 'risky' (in SS eyes) partner–prove these things to the conference and social workers.

Don't just be satisfied with presenting this evidence to the conference but send a letter outlining all of these changes and the evidence of them to the Director of Children's Services (UK) / Senior Social Worker & Area Manager (Ireland) and demand that the service upholds its statutory duty under the Children's Act 1989 (UK) / Child Care Act 1991 (Ireland) to work to keep families together or re-unite them as soon as possible. (once you have effectively put them on notice of this, it can open up other judicial routes if they fail in their statutory duty).

For the conference gather as many family members together as possible in support of you, grandparents to the unborn baby, aunts, uncles, etc. This is to show the extended support you have and also a range of possible kinship carers that may apply for a Special Guardianship Order. Remember your aim is not just to try to keep your child but avoid the possibility of a forced adoption. No adoption will mean there is always the opportunity to bring your child home.

Any changes that you are aware that you will still need to effect, do them–don't rely on social workers to help you, make those changes yourself. Social workers do not want to work with you–despite all their protestations of such–their agenda will be focused and one track–removal and adoption. If your changes do not prevent social workers going to court remember to oppose every order, right from the first hearing. Do not consent to any order! Make them fight and prove their case.

If asked to sign a section 20 'voluntary care' refuse, even if they threaten application for an Emergency Protection Order / Emergency Care Order–make them do that and oppose it. The bar is high for an EPO and this is your first opportunity to test the social services evidence. Remember it must be an immediate threat to the child for such an order.

Agree to any further assessments but only if those assessments are carried out whilst you have your baby with you–you cannot be correctly assessed if you are parted from your child.

Remember there could be the opportunity to go to a mother and baby unit or a mother and baby foster placement. Ask the court to give you the opportunity to prove that the changes you have effected and have evidence of are taken fully into consideration for a holistic overview.

Reminder, never consent to an order (even if your solicitor

barrister tells you to–refuse and say no-fight the order), this is important as you cannot appeal an order you have consented to. You do not want to close any avenue of testing the social worker's evidence.

Plan B

Once you know you are pregnant and before you bring this to the attention of a midwife or social services, you have the opportunity to consider leaving the jurisdiction.

This is not an option to be taken lightly without serious planning (and remember you have time to plan and act). The over-riding consideration is of course, finances. How will you support yourself and your baby? There is no point going any further in this plan unless you can answer this question in the positive. You will need money for accommodation, utilities, and of course day to day living as well as the associated expenses of having a baby. You cannot rely on benefits in the country you may move to–there are no guarantees that you will receive any, though it is worth doing some homework on what you may be able to receive (i.e. Child benefit is payable in many European Countries). Don't rely on UK benefits, you are only supposed to be able to claim them for three months after you leave the country and if social services do find out that you are pregnant and left it is not unknown for them to get your benefits stopped.

Maybe you have a partner who can support you, parents/grandparents who will provide resources, savings, etc. You need to be sure that you can survive-as being homeless in a foreign country with a child is likely to see social services there remove and accommodate any homeless child.

Although you have time you still need to act quickly, the sooner you are in a new jurisdiction and settling the stronger your chances are of stopping any attempt to 'return' your newborn under ether the Hague Convention or Brussels II. As outlined above these are draconian international measures that provide for 'returning' a child to the previous habitual residence of its parents. Don't leave it until the last minute to leave, do it as soon as practically possible. The longer you are there the stronger your defences against such a 'return'.

The ectopia network have contacts in a number of countries that help facilitate your move and can offer advice but none of these good people can accommodate you or pay your way.

You have every right to leave the country and settle in any European State under the Charter of Fundamental Rights of the EU, outside of these, countries farther afield may require visas. Remember unless you have a passport then you are limited to travel in the Common Travel Area, which is why Ireland has become such a popular destination.

It is important to consider that the authorities in a new jurisdiction may also become involved in your case, however a slightly different and less draconian approach may be found and there is always the 'fresh pair of eyes' that could make all the difference.

Do not attempt to conceal your pregnancy that in itself will be used against you. Engage the help of a good Solicitor or Lay Advocate to steer you through the process. It is far better to challenge Social Services sooner rather than later, but always remember do not trust what your social worker says, expect the worst from them and plan and fight accordingly, do not become lulled into a false sense of security by encouraging words from your social worker.

Before we leave the fleeing arena, it is necessary to address the issue of Northern Cyprus. Although it is mentioned within the context of the ectopia network and the availability of contacts and Good Samaritan's there, as well as a number of people who advocate fleeing to the Mediterranean idyll the author must issue the strongest warning against this. Over the last two years a number of families have returned from Northern Cyprus and they have reported that it is virtually impossible to settle there.

Cyprus is divided into two nations, Northern Cyprus ruled by Turkey and the Southern part of the island that is Cypriot. It is not the place here to recount the political history of the island, but the important point is that Northern Cyprus is not recognised by the international community, it is not part of the EU (Southern Cyprus is) and most relevant is that it does not have adherence to the Hague Convention, Brussels II or extradition treaties. Thus it has been seen as a safe heaven for those wishing to flee the authorities and it must be said that a number of families have in the past successfully moved to Northern Cyprus and avoided the UK Social Services and Courts.

Recent reports from families who fled there and have since returned is that it is increasingly difficult to settle there. Firstly the key issue is money. It is almost impossible to obtain citizenship of the country unless you are bringing in substantial sums of money. Although officially the amount seems to range anywhere between £10,000 to £20,000 (depending on how corrupt the said official dealing with your application for residency is) even those who were able to prove they had these sums were declined residency. Without residency then you must rely on either a tourist visa (which lasts for three months) or a student visa (which entails correct registration on an approved course at an approved institution). When a tourist visa expires, then you must leave the state in order to be able to renew your visa. This was as straight forward as crossing into Southern Cyprus and returning, however a recent case demonstrates the dangers of this. A mother who had fled to Northern Cyprus crossed the border to the South and because the South is part of the EU, they had the information that an arrest warrant was pending because she was wanted in connection with 'abducting' her children. She was arrested and returned to the UK. She faces up to 7 years in prison. Her children were returned and placed into care.

It is also reported that British families with children are being visited by the North Cypriot police and they have interviewed the children about living there. This has been effected upon those British families living there who have never had any issue with Social Services as well as those who have actually fled there. Effectively the Northern Cypriot regime is seeking international recognition and trying to be seen as helpful as

542

possible to the international community. Further being found without the necessary residency or visa has resulted in immediate expulsion into the clutches of the Southern (EU) authorities. Unless you are exceptionally well off, it is best that you do not consider fleeing to Northern Cyprus, it has been proven to be a risk not worth taking.

We must conclude that fleeing is not an easy option that there are many pit-falls as well as opportunities. The simple key is planning, understanding your rights and being prepared for the possible actions that could be brought against you. Timing can be very much the key factor and the ectopia/PIN network has had the best success in supporting families who have fled before court proceedings were initiated, or ladies who have fled early in their pregnancy.

Chapter 10 Pseudo Law or the Freeman on the Land you must avoid.

There is a wealth of information that a family dealing with social services can call upon on the world side web. Everything from websites, to blogs, to Facebook groups and a huge range of other resources. There is good information, there is questionable information, there are falsehoods and spurious advice. Any parent is free to pick from any and all the above to fight their case, but where I would urge caution is in the pseudo legal sphere of Freeman on the Land (FMOTL) and the idea of sovereign citizens.

Simply put freemen believe they can opt out of the law of the land and being governed because the 'laws' are just contracts to which they have not consented. It ranges from special arrangements of words that are your 'get out of anything' card to a belief that you do not have to pay taxes, mortgages, debts and the like. They will reel off things like Magna Carta and declare themselves in 'lawful rebellion', that governments and social services are corporations and that there is an international legal conspiracy set up to profit the 'elites'.

They rely heavily on common law, refusing to believe that Statutes (Acts of Parliament) carry any weight of enforcement. The courts are corrupt, being administrative courts, that are unlawful as they are not based on juries but rely on Admiralty law, the 'law of the sea', 'maritime law', or the 'universal commercial code' which they claim only applies to corporations. They go to great lengths to illustrate this: referring to standing in the 'dock' in a court room, the law of owner*ship,* citizen*ship* and *berth* (birth) certificates. In their rallying cries against judges and magistrates, where they choose to leave the bench rather than continuing to listen to the pseudo babble, the freeman then claims the judge has abandoned ship and they claim they have taken ownership of the court.

They frequently try to claim common law jurisdiction by asking 'do you have a claim against me?' which supposedly removes their consent to be governed by admiralty law and turns the court into a common law court, forcing the court to proceed according to their version of common law. There is a complete refusal to operate within the rules of the court. Freemen will also attempt to 'put the judge on their oath' to force them to act in accordance with common law, which entails asking to see evidence of the oath. Such actions usually end up with the person being threatened with contempt of court. This usually leads to a comeback of 'is that 'civil or criminal contempt?' This is because the freeman believe that civil contempt falls within admiralty law and that as there is no consensual contract it cannot apply. Equally they will then probably assert that it cannot be criminal contempt as there is no victim (common law belief that violations of common law require a victim). Of course the upshot is that they probably end up in the court's cells until they purge their contempt or even more seriously end up being sent to prison.

Court documents and the words spoken in court are supposedly in 'legalese'. The freeman asserts that this is a deliberately deceptive 'technical jargon language' of the Law Society. They claim that although legalese looks like English and uses English words, it is not English. For example they claim that 'summons' means an invitation. That 'understand' does not mean 'do you understand this?', but means 'stand under' as in do you accept the terms of the contract. Ask a freeman where this lexicon derives from and a source is peculiarly absent, bar the assertion that it is a secret jargon of the Law Society. Now you or I am free to go and purchase a law dictionary, such as *Black's Law Dictionary*, or even look up, and in some instances download, a law dictionary online. Ask yourself, if the secret jargon argument is real why are such dictionary's freely available? Why do you see such texts in a judge's chambers and on the bench?

There is no secret jargon and all legal interpretations of words can be easily found.

Freeman also believe that they have two personas, a real physical one–'the man', 'a human being' and a legal personality or *strawman*. What they refer to as a 'legal fiction'. This is allegedly created when a child's birth is registered. The name is capitalised, and that creates the legal fiction. Thus a freeman will attempt to present the birth certificate in court when the person's name is called. Thus by splitting the 'human being' from the legal fiction they believe they can absolve themselves from having to follow statute laws, to which they say they have not consented. Often they will present themselves as 'John of the family Smith' instead of John Smith. They often refuse to use or be referred to as Mr or Mrs. With their belief that admiralty law is used against them they believe that their legal fiction is required to operate in commerce. Therefore they claim their legal fiction is a vessel floating in the seas of commerce.

Perhaps the most common freeman argument that parents will be exposed to is the birth certificate, along with *Cestui Que Vie Act* of 1666. In the pseudo legal world of the freeman; birth certificates have three hidden uses:

- The government uses them to create your strawman and legal *person* to which all your responsibilities, debts and liabilities belong.

- As a form of registration, they transfer ownership of an individual to the state. This is what allows the state to seize your children if you don't play by *their* rules.

- They are financial instruments or birth-tracking bonds (aka live birth bonds) that are sold by the government and then traded on the sea of international commerce, using you as security

Of course the second of these is one that parent's may latch onto. They refuse, or delay registering their babies in the belief that without a birth certificate that social services cannot remove their child. Sadly, this is blatantly untrue. There are more than enough examples of children taken direct from the labour ward. What the freeman fail to appreciate is that social services can register your child's birth, in fact so can a midwife/health professional. There is no value in not registering your child with regard to social services.

With the other two aspects Freemen claim the government secures the value of its fiat currency using its own citizens' birth certificate 'bonds.'

Apparently by entering the numbers from your birth certificate into various stock-tracking sites you are able to see the current value of your 'bond' on the market. Market bonds are identified by a 9 digit code, whilst birth certificate numbers for the US are 11 digits long, UK birth certificate serial numbers are 10 digits long. In Canada the number is 12 digits long. The value of the birth certificate 'bond' is also claimed to be a method to discharge to your debts through a process called 'accepted for value'. I am sure there will be many freemen who *claim* to have successfully used this process, however the UK treasury has clearly stated that such a financial concept is a myth.

The *Cestui Que Vie Act* of 1666 is often cited along with the birth certificate. The relevant part of the act reads:

'Whereas diverse Lords of Mannours and others have granted Estates by Lease for one or more life or lives, or else for yeares determinable upon one or more life or lives And it hath often happened that such person or persons for whose life or lives such Estates have beene granted have gone beyond the Seas or soe absented themselves for many yeares that the Lessors and Reversioners cannot finde out whether such person or persons be alive or dead by reason whereof such Lessors and Reversioners have beene held out of possession of their Tenements for many yeares after all the lives upon which such Estates depend are dead in regard that the Lessors and Reversioners when they have brought Actions for the recovery

of their Tenements have beene putt upon it to prove the death of their Tennants when it is almost impossible for them to discover the same, For remedy of which mischeife soe frequently happening to such Lessors or Reversioners. If such person or persons for whose life or lives such Estates have beene or shall be granted as aforesaid shall remaine beyond the Seas or elsewhere absent themselves in this Realme by the space of seaven yeares together and noe sufficient and evident proofe be made of the lives of such person or persons respectively in any Action commenced for recovery of such Tenements by the Lessors or Reversioners in every such case the person or persons upon whose life or lives such Estate depended shall be accounted as naturally dead, And in every Action brought for the recovery of the said Tenements by the Lessors or Reversioners their Heires or Assignes, the Judges before whom such Action shall be brought shall direct the Jury to give their Verdict as if the person soe remaining beyond the Seas or otherwise absenting himselfe were dead.'

Many freemen claim this act declared all English citizens dead and lost beyond the seas unless they objected within seven years of their birth after which they would be declared dead without reasonable doubt. The State would then claim all the property of its citizens in trust.

However, the title to the section makes clear that if a person remains 'beyond Sea for Seven Years together' and with 'no Proof of their Lives', a judge may direct that the person is dead (as can be done with missing persons in this day and age) and their lands revert to the freeholder, or other family members. The intent of this act is obvious and does not carry the obtuse significance that the freemen claim.

Hopefully such examples demonstrate the danger of following this pseudo legal nonsense. If you walk into a family court or attempt to claim that social services have no authority over you under statute law, not only will this have no effect and possibly lead to an emergency care order because they cannot access your children, but it is likely to get you labelled at best, a conspiracy theorist, at worst, suffering from some mental health impairment.

The family courts have dealt with a few cases where the freeman on the land arguments have been deployed such as Re J (Child) 2013[cii]. The Court of Appeal wasn't directly dealing with the freeman arguments, as the mother had quite rightly dropped them, in favour of a more conventional approach but it gives a flavour how easily the wheels could have come off her case:

3. The paperwork reflected that, as had also been the case in front of Judge Bromilow, M and IM considered that they were claiming to proceed under "Common Law Jurisdiction and Authority". They considered that this affected the proceedings in a number of ways. For example, in M's skeleton argument for the appeal she said, speaking of the proceedings at first instance, that:

"we established Common Law Jurisdiction prior to the hearing and Mr Bromilow confirmed he was on his Oath before the hearing began. Therefore, as a Court de Jure was in effect, no consent means Mr Bromilow had no authority."

Another feature was that M treated the name by which she would normally be known as her "legal fiction" and insisted that she be addressed by a rather differently formulated version of it. Furthermore, she and IM did not consider they were bound by orders to which they did not consent.

4. The local authority submitted to us that M's then adherence to this notion of Common Law Jurisdiction and Authority had contributed to the case being challenging to manage. I have no difficulty in accepting that submission. The judge described the

552

material sent to the court by M by way of evidence as "voluminous" (§19 of the judgment) and that description is corroborated by the bundles supplied to us, containing both the original material that formed part of the care proceedings and new material generated for the appeal.

5. *M freely acknowledged to us that she had been under IM's influence and had developed misguided beliefs. She put this down to her vulnerability following an accident she had had, about which I shall say something later. She accepted that her reference to "Common Law" was wholly inappropriate, and she said she could understand why objection had been taken to IM. She made a prepared oral submission in support of her appeal which was in a distinctly different tone from that adopted in her written submissions and in which her former beliefs played no part. She also abandoned some of her grounds of appeal. <u>This was sensible given that they could not have succeeded</u>. The effect of M's new constructive approach was to enable us to concentrate on the issues that required determination.*

There is clearly no doubt that had this mother not changed track that she may have lost her child to the care system permanently, thankfully she fought on utilising the law as it it is written and her child did come home.

Another more recent case comes from 2016: A Child, Re [2016] EWFC B50 (22 July 2016)[ciii]. There were clearly serious concerns, of potential significant harm to a new born in this case. It involved a parent being a proponent of MMS (Master Mineral Solution) which he sold and trained how to make the solution. It was and still is marketed as a cure all, for everything from autism to cancer. Effectively the analysis of the solution reveals it to be industrial strength bleach, and the father advocated putting 27 drops of it in babies' bottles. There is no evidence that he or the mother did this or advocated it for their own child, but as much as anyone dislikes social services, it has got to be accepted that there was a real element of unassessed risk here. However, it is not the headline grabbing MMS that we are concerned with here, but the pseudo legal route that the parents chose to take.

Firstly the parents chose to dispense with their legal team and instead employ the services of a David Wynn Millar. He describes himself as a 'Plenipotentiary-Judge', an ambassador, banker, postmaster, King of Hawaii, and a genius with an IQ of 200. First of all he is not a judge, by trade he is said to be a tool and die welder. His claim to legal fame is in what he calls his Mathematical Interface for Language or *Quantum-Math-Communications and Language*. Within this, he claims only nouns have legal authority.

According to Miller, the addition of hyphens and colons identifies a person as a matter of fact, existing in the "now-time-dimension". The names as written in this way are distinguished from the names listed at birth and in "all-caps" (as on a birth certificate), which identify the legal estate and not the living being in fact. In fact, signing up to get a "birth certificate" creates a taxable Person (Corporation). Think we have heard this before. However his mathematical interface is simply pseudo legal nonsense. Take for example:

'FOR THE FORMS OF OUR PUNCTUATIONS ARE WITH THE CLAIM OF THE USE: FULL-COLON=POSITION-LODIO-FACTS, HYPHEN=COMPOUND-FACTS =KNOWN, PERIOD=END-THOUGHT, COMMA-PAUSE, AND LOCATION-TILDES WITH THE MEANINGS AND USES OF THE COMMUNICATIONS WITH THE FULL-COLON OF THE POSITION-LODIAL-FACT-PHRASE

WITH THE FACT/KNOWN-TERM OF THE POSITIONAL-LODIO-FACT-PHRASE AND WITH THE VOID OF THE NOM-DE-GUERRE = DEAD-PERSON'

It is easy to understand why the court found the parents' submission *'...a bizarre document which makes quite frankly not a word of sense....'* Turning to the judgment itself the court's comments regarding this 'bizarre' approach help demonstrate why freeman and pseudo legal arguments can never win out.

'23 The application was listed for hearing before myself on the 14th March 2016. On that occasion the parents represented themselves having dispensed with the services of their legal representation. Sadly on that occasion neither parent would respect the authority of the Court. The Father shouted at myself and was ejected from the Court. The parents were removed from the Court on 2 occasions. After the first occasion they were informed that they could re-enter the Court provided they respected Court procedures but sadly despite assurances that they would, they did not do so and they were ejected again from the Court. It was quite frankly impossible to hold any form of a hearing with them being present as they refused to respect the authority of the Court or the Court's

procedures. I asked the Mother at one point whether they were going to register the birth of their child (those assurances having been given to the Court on the 19th February 2016 that they would do so without delay) but at that point the Mother commenced reading a prepared script when she questioned the authority of the Court. As a consequence of that she was removed from the Courtroom as she refused to stop reading her script, and clearly had no intention of answering my questions or respecting the courts authority.'

'28 From documents that the Court considered on that occasion it was apparent that the parents had dispensed with legal representation in this country and had consulted with a self-styled Chief Federal Judge, David-Wynn Miller.

29 Various documents have been served on parties and the Court and on that occasion the court considered a document headed "Educational–Correspondence–Claim. It is a bizarre document which makes quite frankly not a word of sense but is a clear claim by them that the Local Authority have kidnapped their child. This has been a theme which has run through the documentation which has been on Facebook and on YouTube and has persisted throughout despite the injunctions which were made by Mr Justice Baker on the 14th March 2016.'

'34.Despite the order made by Mr Justice Baker the parents continued their campaign on the Internet and through social media and an application was made by the Local Authority to commit the parents to prison for contempt of Court. The matter came before Mr Justice Baker on the 14th April 2016. On that occasion he decided to adjourn the application to commit. He gave a full judgment and ordered that a transcript of the judgment in both English and Portuguese should be served upon both parents and the Maternal Grandparents. His judgment is yet a further plea to the family to engage in the Court process. In paragraph 23 of his judgment he said the following:

35.According to the postings on the internet it seems that these parents believe that their baby has been stolen by the local authority, with the connivance and collusion of the medical authorities, lawyers of the Court, so that he could be put through what they call a "forced adoption". That is completely untrue. If the parents believe it, they are deluded. If anyone is encouraging them in that belief, they are acting in a way that is wholly contrary to the interest of this child and his parents.

36. And in paragraphs 24 and 25:

If the parents want to do the right thing by their child, they should return to this country at once and co-operate with the Local Authority and the Court to ensure that all necessary assessments are carried out. There will be a fair hearing to determine whether the threshold for making a care order under section 31 of the Children Act is crossed and, if so, what order should then be made.

I implore these parents to think again, to put their baby's interests first, and come back and co-operate, so that the Court can make the right decision about X. There is a very real danger that, by continuing with their current internet campaign, they will only achieve the very thing they profess to be trying to avoid – permanent separation from their son.'

'62. In the light of the parents' failure to engage in the Court process the Court is unable to assess positively the capacity of the parents to meet the child's needs now or in the future. The parents behaviour and the misguided campaign they have pursued is evidence of them having no understanding of their child's needs. Even meeting the most basic need of forming an attachment with their child has been failed by their parents as they have not seen him since the 4th March, and instead they left the country.'

The parents clearly made a number of mistakes, not least the use of a 'snake-oil' seller-self appointed-'Chief Federal Judge', something he is clearly not, nor ever has been. Upon adopting his pseudo-law approach and challenging the authority of the court, their case was undermined, to the extent that they were removed from proceedings.

There is also a salient lesson here, they went public on Facebook and featured in the Daily Mail. That did nothing for their cause. Many times a parent believe they have the most heinous of cases and that publicity will not only bring major changes to the system, but they will save their child. Sadly, their cases are not so uncommon and publicity in the media brings nothing of value to them.

I have tested out many of the theories of the freeman on the land and I can attest that there is absolutely no value in the pseudo legal arguments that its proponents would have you believe are some sort of panacea to all your legal ills. I appreciate that maybe somewhere in the quagmire of these theories there may be some possible basis–for example the Bill of Rights 1689 says that any threat of a fine or forfeiture voids the offence and Magna Carta states that no fine can be imposed unless found guilty of an offence, yet there are now a whole range of fixed penalty fines which cannot be appealed. However, the legality of these have been laid by statute and in many cases the courts have interpreted and upheld the statute as it is written. In order to have a chance of winning in the system you must abide by the system's rules. If you step outside the rules, then not only will you fail, but may find yourself in a far worse position than you could have imagined.

My advice is to avoid the pseudo law proponents and do your own research, particularly in case law, if you wish to give yourself the best opportunity to remove social workers and the courts   from   your   life.

---

xlix

    http://www.courts.ie/rules.nsf/2b513051ef3462c980256d b700399501/2d26beb42c0a19d680256f230065c8aa?OpenDoc ument for the forms 13 & 14http://www.courts.ie/courts.ie/library3.nsf/0/43A9D9A6AD 3F49558025812100410896 for the docket

l   https://orcaprint.ie/

li

    http://www.courts.ie/courts.ie/library3.nsf/0/A2E1E0B08 9F2986B8025811C0037CE78

lii   Section 1

(1)A statement is not defamatory unless its publication has caused or is likely to cause serious harm to the reputation of the claimant.

(2)For the purposes of this section, harm to the reputation of a body that trades for profit is not "serious harm" unless it has caused or is likely to cause the body serious financial loss.

liii   General damages do not have to be pleaded but flow from the action. Aggravated damages takes into account the manner in which a tort was committed. For example injuring the persons feelings etc. Exemplary damages are punitive in nature, for example where the court is shocked by the conduct displayed.

liv

https://www.justice.gov.uk/courts/procedurerules/civil/protocol/prot_def

lv   Ibid.

lvi

http://hmctsformfinder.justice.gov.uk/HMCTS/GetForm.do?court_forms_id=338

lvii   https://formfinder.hmctsformfinder.justice.gov.uk/ex50-eng.pdf

lviii   https://formfinder.hmctsformfinder.justice.gov.uk/n9-eng.pdf

lix   http://formfinder.hmctsformfinder.justice.gov.uk/n9c-eng.pdf

[lx] http://formfinder.hmctsformfinder.justice.gov.uk/n9d-eng.pdf

[lxi] https://formfinder.hmctsformfinder.justice.gov.uk/n215-eng.pdf

[lxii] http://formfinder.hmctsformfinder.justice.gov.uk/n227-eng.pdf

[lxiii]
http://hmctsformfinder.justice.gov.uk/HMCTS/GetForms.do?court_forms_category=Queen%27s%20Bench

[lxiv]
http://www.courts.ie/rules.nsf/0/87fa49fe11fa0cd180256f23006202d8?OpenDocument#IIForm1

[lxv] https://www.legislation.gov.uk/ukpga/1981/45

[lxvi]
http://www.irishstatutebook.ie/eli/2001/act/50/enacted/en

/print#sec26

[lxvii] Section 6: Prosecutions instituted and conducted otherwise than by the Service.

(1)Subject to subsection (2) below, nothing in this Part shall preclude any person from instituting any criminal proceedings or conducting any criminal proceedings to which the Director's duty to take over

563

the conduct of proceedings does not apply.

(2)Where criminal proceedings are instituted in circumstances in which the Director is not under a duty to take over their conduct, he may nevertheless do so at any stage.

[lxviii] Christopher Booker writing in the Telegraph Newspaper 2013.

[lxix] http://preventinterventionnow.org/court.html

[lxx] https://www.judiciary.gov.uk/wp-content/uploads/JCO/Documents/FJC/Publications/VIEW+FROM+THE+PRESIDENT.pdf

[lxxi] Ibid. Pp 4-5.

[lxxii] http://www.familylawweek.co.uk/site.aspx?i=ed117048

[lxxiii] Ibid. Paragraph 44.

[lxxiv] https://www.justice.gov.uk/courts/procedure-rules/family/practice_directions/pd_part_12a

[lxxv] http://www.courts.ie/rules.nsf/lookuppagelink/Superior%20Court%20Rules%20Index

[lxxvi] http://www.bailii.org/

[lxxvii] http://www.familylawweek.co.uk/site.aspx?i=ho0

[lxxviii] https://suesspiciousminds.com/

lxxix http://www.marilynstowe.co.uk/

lxxx http://www.legislation.gov.uk/ukpga/2002/38/contents

lxxxi

http://hmctsformfinder.justice.gov.uk/HMCTS/GetForm.
do?court_forms_id=1076

lxxxii http://www.legislation.gov.uk/ukpga/2002/38/section/47

lxxxiii

http://www.legislation.gov.uk/ukpga/2014/6/pdfs/ukpga_
20140006_en.pdf pp7-8.

lxxxiv

http://www.bailii.org/ew/cases/EWCA/Civ/2007/616.htm
l

lxxxv http://www.bailii.org/uk/cases/UKSC/2013/33.html

lxxxvi https://formfinder.hmctsformfinder.justice.gov.uk/n161-
eng.pdf

lxxxvii

https://www.biicl.org/files/2223_skeleton_arguments_gui
de.pdf

lxxxviii

https://hmctsformfinder.justice.gov.uk/HMCTS/GetForm.
do?court_forms_id=161

lxxxix https://formfinder.hmctsformfinder.justice.gov.uk/ex160-
eng.pdf

xc https://formfinder.hmctsformfinder.justice.gov.uk/ex105-eng.pdf

xci This form may be found at Appendix H.

xcii

http://www.courts.ie/Courts.ie/Library3.nsf/16c93c36d36 35d5180256e3f003a4580/4fa0e2be3fffe31d802580dd0059c29 0?

xciii

http://www.courts.ie/rules.nsf/0/6805F0ACD71DD40F80 256F900064BDEB

xciv Children's Act 1989 Section 44 – 1 (b) *in the case of an application made by a local authority—*

(i) enquiries are being made with respect to the child under section 47(1)(b); and

(ii) those enquiries are being frustrated by access to the child being unreasonably refused to a person authorised to seek access and that the applicant has reasonable cause to believe that access to the child is required as a matter of urgency; http://www.legislation.gov.uk/ukpga/1989/41/section/44

xcv

http://www.nhs.uk/nhsengland/healthcareabroad/ehic/pag es/about-the-ehic.aspx

xcvi Article 45 Freedom of movement and of residence

1.Every citizen of the Union has the right to move and reside freely within the territory of theMember States.

2.Freedom of movement and residence may be granted, in accordance with the Treaty establishingthe European Community, to nationals of third countries legally resident in the territory of a MemberState.
http://www.europarl.europa.eu/charter/pdf/text_en.pdf

xcvii The legal principle that political entities (such as states, nations, or courts from different jurisdictions) will mutually recognize each other's legislative, executive, and judicial acts. The underlying notion is that different jurisdictions will reciprocate each other's judgments out of deference, mutuality, and respect.

xcviii The concept of 'habitual residence' under article 8(1) of [Regulation B2R] must be interpreted as meaning that it corresponds to the place which reflects some degree of integration by the child in a social and family environment. To that end, in particular the duration, regularity, conditions and reasons for the stay on the territory of a member state and the family's move to that state, the child's nationality, the place and conditions of attendance at school, linguistic knowledge and the family and social relationships of the child in that state must be taken into consideration.

xcix Mercredi v Chaffe it was held that the child's habitual residence is the place that reflects some degree of integration by the child in a social and family environment. In applying this test the court should take account of all circumstances of fact specific to that individual case, i.e. duration, regularity, conditions and reasons for the stay in that state and

567

connections with it. If the test led to the conclusion that the habitual residence could not be established then jurisdiction would have to be determined on the basis of the child's physical presence, under Art 13.

c   http://www.familylawweek.co.uk/site.aspx?i=ed113856

ci **Article 17 Examination of its own motion as to jurisdiction**
Where a court of a Member State is seised of a case over which it has no jurisdiction under this Regulation and over which a court of another Member State has jurisdiction by virtue of this Regulation, it shall declare of its own motion that it has no jurisdiction.

Article 20 Provisional and protective measures
- **1.** In urgent cases, the provisions of this Regulation shall not prevent the courts of a Member State from taking such provisional, including protective, measures in respect of persons or assets in that State as may be available under the law of that Member State, even if, under this Regulation, the court of another Member State has jurisdiction as to the substance of the matter.
- **2.** The measures referred to in paragraph 1 shall cease to apply when the court of the Member State having jurisdiction under this Regulation as to the substance of the matter has taken the measures it considers appropriate.

cii

http://www.bailii.org/ew/cases/EWCA/Civ/2013/1685.ht

ml

ciii http://www.bailii.org/ew/cases/EWFC/OJ/2016/B50.html

Chapter 11 The Persecution Manual

In late 2013 an important piece of research: The Rhetoric Case. Persecution strategies in a child care order investigation was published by Linda Arlig of the Department of Social Science, the Psychology Section, University of Örebro, Sweden[civ]. The report runs to ninety-seven A4 pages. The title has arisen from a comprehensive study of the 'persecution strategies' employed by Social Services by a Swedish academic.

I will let Linda Arlig give us the introduction to this report:

'Every year children and adolescents are taken into custody, thereby being separated from their parents. This is done in accord with the law containing special regulations concerning the care of young persons (LVU–Care of Young Persons Act). According to this same law, society has special responsibility for children and adolescents.

The social welfare committee can offer parents and children support and help on a voluntary basis according to the Social Services Act (SoL). LVU, which applies to care without consent, acts as a supplement to SoL. Both placements according to SoL and LVU should, in the opinion of the

Swedish Board of Social Welfare (SoS), "as far as possible, be for limited periods of time and focused on treatment, with reunion as the objective." (SoS report 1990:24). Any decision concerning care according to LVU is a strong emotional experience for the child and the parents. It implies limitations of the parents' right of decision concerning the child. For this reason, it is extremely important that no mistakes are made on the part of the social welfare committee.

An investigation that forms the basis of an LVU decision must be objective, impartial and worked through in accordance with the true facts. This is founded on the Constitution Act, Chap. 1, Para. 9. Taking a child into care can affect the investigator emotionally. So as not to affect the investigator's personal involvement or disturb the work, it is necessary that the work should follow certain rules. Investigation work should proceed with a critical-objective method, in which a number of basic criteria must be met. Examples of such criteria are: clarity, posing questions, relevant information, account of sources, precision, avoidance of emotional language, ethical considerations for the protection of private persons etc. (cf. Edvardsson, 1996).

When these criteria are not observed, partial investigations

571

lacking in objectivity may arise, which are characterised by the fabrication of evidence with the intention of influencing and persuading the reader and supporting the investigator's own purposes. Defective investigations can lead to wrong or unsuitable decisions being reached that destroy the future of the family.

1.2   Purpose and definition

The purpose of this paper is to critically examine six official reports in an LVU case, to investigate any occurrence of persecution strategies in its handling and, if so, to define and investigate them, as well seeing whether the matter meets the requirements of objectivity and impartiality prescribed by the Constitution Act, Chap. 1, Para. 9.

I use the definition of the concept persecution strategies by Edvardsson (1996, p. 173): "patterns of thinking and behaviour directed against persons and groups, which on the basis of the fundamental values concerning democracy, legal security, objectivity, self-determination, humanity and not causing physical/mental injury, can be considered as unacceptable."

I also call attention to the definition of the concept of

persecution strategies further developed by Jäderquist et al. (1994, p.2): "that it can to a certain extent be a conscious way of behaviour when one has a motive, e.g. custody, control, power, reprisals or other motive. One does work that is steered by the objective, which is nourished on conflicts. <u>The lack of objectivity depends not only on ignorance, lapses, giving one's imagination free rein, good faith and so on, but there are one or more reasons for being partial.</u>"'

Just from the introduction it is obvious that there is already a body of research that indicates an agenda runs through child protection, partly it seems from the very nature of the methodology employed and partly by the fact that individuals develop their own motives. Place that in the context of the risk averse climate post baby P and there is a recipe for the destruction of families.

'Jansson and Rönnbäck (1995) found 42 persecution strategies when they critically examined an investigation that formed the basis of taking into care according to LVU. The following main features of the behavioural pattern stood out:

The authority knows best

Blackening the names of the parents

573

Making children and parents to appear in need of care

Pushing through and sticking to decisions that have been made

Disregarding laws and regulations

Destroying relations of importance to the family

Influencing the reader

Disregarding elementary aspects of objectivity

Throughout the material the client perspective was ignored, negative material was emphasised and positive material withheld.'

I believe that practically every parent who has had social services involvement can relate to all the above. Of course there is not room in this book to examine the full details of all the persecution strategies identified, but I shall provide the list and then examine a few as 'case studies' to demonstrate to you, the reader what it is you looking out for and can then challenge. No matter what lies herein, there is no substitute for reading the whole report for yourself. Although the report is based on research of the social services, laws and constitution of Sweden, the findings apply equally to the UK and Ireland.

Numbering refers to the chapter/sub sections contained in the report:

5.1 Rhetorical strategy

5.1.1 Insinuating strategy, 5.1.2 Positive-negative argumentation strategy, 5.1.3 Negative reinforcement strategy, 5.1.4 Negative synonym strategy, 5.1.5 Repetition strategy, 5.1.6 Hammer strategy, 5.1.7 Multi-minus strategy, 5.1.8 Contrast strategy, 5.1.9 Strategy of selective use of words indicating uncertainty, 5.1.10 Generalisation strategy, 5.1.11 Strategy of making trivial statements in a negative context.

5.2 Strategy of making the client seem pathological

5.2.1 Strategy of implying that the client's criticism stems from the client's pathological condition, 5.2.2 Therapy strategy, 5.2.3 Strategy of making the client seem peculiar, 5.2.4 Strategy of making the client's behaviour seem too intense, 5.2.5 Strategy of persecution by use of the fundamental attribution error, 5.2.6 Scapegoat strategy, 5.2.7 Strategy of calling attention to non-existent "facts".

5.3 Suppression strategy

575

5.3.1 Strategy of ignoring the client's perspective, 5.3.2 Strategy of vagueness, 5.3.3 Strategy of gradually suppressing details, 5.3.4 Strategy of using the impersonal form.

5.4 Exaggeration strategy

5.4.1 Quantitative strategy, 5.4.2 Fabulation strategy, 5.4.3 Strategy of gradual intensification

5.4.4 Lying strategy, 5.4.5 Strategy of presenting irrelevant information, 5.4.6 Implicit theory strategy, 5.4.7 Strategy of exploiting and exaggerating events, 5.4.8 Strategy of collecting negative historical events of little or no relevance, 5.4.9 Strategy of referring to unspecified others, 5.4.10 Presumptive strategy.

5.5 Control and power strategy

5.5.1 Provocative strategy, 5.5.2 Strategy of trying to accuse the client of lying, 5.5.3 Anti-democratic strategy, 5.5.4 Strategy of presenting insulting values and comments, 5.5.5 Strategy of restricting the credibility of others' opinions.

5.6 The social authorities know best

5.6.1 Strategy of emphasising social authorities' resources,

5.6.2 Strategy of overconfidence in oneself and others, 5.6.3 Strategy of exceeding the limits of your competence, 5.6.4 Moralising strategy, 5.6.5 Strategy of justifying yourself and your actions.

5.7 Strategy of stressing one's own experience

5.7.1 Strategy of making vague references to experiences, 5.7.2 Strategy of ascribing an experience to the client, 5.7.3 Strategy of ascribing a negative attitude to the client.

5.8 Interpretational strategy

5.8.1 Strategy of using strategic interpretation, 5.8.2 Strategy of using signs as evidence, 5.8.3 Strategy of interpreting everything negatively, 5.8.4 Negative prognosis strategy.

Just a glance over the list and there are bound to be glaring instances that, even without further description will be instantly recognised by parents across the western speaking world.

It was exceptionally difficult to extract a few of the persecution strategies to act as more detailed examples. This was simply due to the fact that everyone of them held such resonance and demonstrate so clearly what I have seen in practically every social worker's reports: that is the whole point of the assessment and reports are to persuade the reader that the parents are bad, mad or just simply unfit.

'*5.1.3 Negative reinforcement strategy*

Junttila et al. (1994, p.28) defines this strategy "as using words that in the context further strengthen the negative message."

Throughout the investigations it occurs that investigators report a negative selection of information concerning the client and her situation. Much of the information is strengthened with negative words. Examples of strengthening words are "very worried", "reacted very strongly", "never, "altogether too much", "obvious signs", "complete personality change", "lost all control" etc. (the examples are taken from the investigations).

Andersson and Furberg (1984, p.140) point out: "With a value-charged word, I convey to the addressee that, according to my opinion, there is reason to harbour a certain feeling or take over a certain position." Through repetition of strengthening words, they can be changed into truths for the receiver. Möijer (1989, p.50) states "Value-charged words, abstract and other vague expressions can be used for the purpose of influencing because they are understood so differently by different people." '

'5.1.4 Negative synonym strategy

The strategy implies that, for the purpose of convincing, one describes a situation with a number of synonyms, where the other synonyms do not convey any new information to the reader. The words have a similar meaning and strengthen the negative message. The strategy contains a repetition technique with features of parallelism. Melin and Lange (1995, p.154) explain "Parallelism is a kind of contentual repetition that implies that the same thought or idea is repeated and verbally varied two or more times in some different way."

Liljestrand (1993, p.85) believes that the meaning of the expressions is often synonymous for the repetitions that contain parallelism.

The negative synonym strategy also means redundancy, that if what follows in a text can be foreseen, the continuation is unnecessary. Liljestrand (1993) explains that a text with high redundancy contains many purposeless repetitions, things

579

made more precise and corrections that are unnecessary from an information viewpoint.'

Go through any assessments or reports and highlight these negative reinforcing words and their synonyms. Are they set in a context backed by some factual evidence? If not, if they are vague and simply 'value charged' then challenge every one. Re-read the report without them included, is a different impression conveyed? Make this point to the social workers and professionals. If necessary write the report out excluding those words and distribute at a meeting to make your point.

'5.1.5 Repetition strategy

Jansson & Rönnbäck (1995, p.65) define this strategy "as through a strategic repetition of certain words, one achieves a propaganda effect about that which is said. This can be compared with proposed announcers who through repeated advertising are able to make people experience that they have a need for exactly the announcers' goods."

Edvardsson (1989, p.7) says that "values and opinions are changed into truths in the mass media by repetition."

Liljestrand (1993, p.82) points out that if non-literary text contains repetitions, it is usually seen as incorrect. "It can generally be said of all repetition that they are redundant features that do not add to the text anything of contentual news."

In Ivemyrs and Lindvall's (1995) paper, it was found that repetition occurred to a large extent in the 20 LVU investigations that they examined. "Common for strengthening words, factual information and phrases is that all considerations are used in a negative context. Strengthening words are used in 629 negative contexts compared with 199 positive ones." The authors believe that repetition is used in investigations to strengthen and put the focus on information that supports taking custody of the child.

Liljestrand and Arwidson (1993, p.97) say that "Many times repetition is used because the text is incorrectly planned and poorly thought through. The reader can then have a difficult time knowing whether it is something new that is being conveyed–especially if in the second time it is formulated with somewhat different words." '

This strategy confirms what we have alluded to previously that if the lie is repeated often enough it become a truth. At times, particularly on assessment reports, large sections are merely repeats of previous information. To the extent that it can actually be identified as a blatant cut-and-paste process. Yet it is reinforcing the negative presentation of your family. Again these repetitions can be removed from the reports by you, to demonstrate that the 'case' against you is not as strong or extensive as the original report may appear.

'5.1.6 Hammer strategy

A variation of the repetitive strategy is the hammer strategy. The strategy means that the investigator in a stereotypical and comprehensive way is repeating his negative understanding of the client in order to be able to influence the reader's understanding of the client. The investigator has "favourite words" for describing the client. The investigator tries to "hammer" his opinion in the reader. The strategy gives an additive effect.

The difference between the repetitive strategy and the hammer strategy is that, from the hammer strategy, the investigator's special and personal understanding of the client comes forth through descriptive favourite words that the investigator has. Examples of words in the rhetoric case are "remarkably", "especially", "strongly negative", "psychic imbalance", "psychic problems", "extreme aggression" etc. The investigator can also have favourite phrases, such as "sudden aggressive attacks" and "sudden and strong aggressive attacks".

Möijer (1989, p.50) maintains that, in an argumentary language style, repetition is used "to strengthen (hammer in) opinions and values."'

As above, these 'hammer' words are likely to appear devoid of context and evidence. That is because they are opinions, opinions that the social worker wishes to impose on the other professionals. This is often coupled with the next strategy:

'5.2 Strategy of making the client seem pathological

Edvardsson (1993, p.20) defines this strategy as "Trying to get a person to seem psychically disturbed, as needing care, as someone who "feels bad", as strongly emotional, as irrational/stupid, as aggressive, as paranoid etc."

"By defining other people as 'sick' or 'aberrant', we no longer need to take them so seriously. We can easily avoid the unpleasantness that others' opinions wake within us by dismissing the person as "abnormal" or "sick". (Moxnes, 1987, p.115).

Edvardsson (1989, p.23) points out: "To have the possibility of being able to interpret everything as a sign of pathology, a certain behaviour, its opposite and everything in between, of course means that everyone who is exposed to the pathologising strategy can be shown to be "disturbed". The fact that it is also theoretically difficult to penetrate with an impressive terminology makes it an excellent means for persecution and exercising power."

Möijer (1989), p.30) points out that professional language is abused, consciously or unconsciously. "Some experts use professional terms to impress their audience or sometimes simply to mislead. Others use advanced professional language for reasons of convenience or inconsideration." It can be seen from the material analysed that the investigators sometimes use "professional language" to give greater strength to the pathologisation of the client without indicating a factual foundation.

It also comes forth that an investigator defends his decision to write that the client has a messy home by writing that it is of an extreme nature. Edvardsson (1991) states that there are different factors such as messiness at home, clothing, language that make the attention of the social bureau more keen and can lead to negative judgements about the client. The factor of messiness in the home often comes up as an argument in investigations.

Throughout the investigative material it comes out that the investigators make the client appear aggressive, strange, psychically ill and need of care in several different ways. From the investigators' approach can be seen the strategy of making the client seem pathological, which is an overall strategy with several different sub-strategies.'

How many parents have found themselves accused of some sort of mental health issue by a social worker? I would have little hesitation in guessing that it makes an appearance in the vast majority of cases. The social worker is not qualified to make such assertions, but the damage is done because the negative reinforcement of this opinion is spread to the other professionals. This is further reinforced by:

'5.2.2 Therapy strategy

This strategy means that one maintains that a person needs therapy without giving objective reasons for the statement or reporting professional competence for making such a statement. An uncritical reader is easily influenced by the fact

585

that a person uses "psychological therapy terms" and professional language and thus neglects to further investigate how the statement has come to be made.'

If the social worker has no qualification to assess or comment on your mental health, they certainly do not have the ability to recommend or even suggest that some therapy should be undertaken. Look for the 'professional' language used, Google them if needs be, and again remove these redundant sections from the report. With all the challenges you have instigated it is more than likely that the social worker will attempt to use this against you. If this happens, then you can make reference to:

'5.2.1 Strategy of implying that the client's criticism stems from the client's pathological condition

The strategy implies that the investigator sees the client's criticism against him and the social service as an expression of psychic disturbance, aggression, that the client is peculiar etc.

The strategy of pathologising criticism violates the Swedish Constitution (Regeringsformen 2 chap 1§), according to which all citizens have the liberty to express thoughts, opinions and feelings. Edvardsson (1991, p.181) explains that when the client behaves critically or aggressively toward the social worker, this often leads to greater attention and diverse negative thoughts and discussions among them. He further explains that it is often felt that the person who is critical and verbally aggressive is psychically disturbed and unsuitable to care for his or her own child. Edvardsson feels that there are no objective grounds for this reasoning.'

The fact this is a recognised persecution strategy allows you to contextualise the social worker's position and raise issues as to their understanding of the situation. We have already dealt with a number of rights that parents and children possess, standing on these does not make you mentally unwell or unstable, quite the opposite. It demonstrates that you understand the procedures being utilised against you and are capable of challenging them. That of itself displays an appreciation of the processes and can be used to challenge the often used allegation of 'the parents do not understand the concerns of the local authority'. In fact this can be turned around and you can assert that the social worker and professionals do not understand the concerns you have with the approach that is being adopted.

'5.2.7 Strategy of calling attention to non-existent "facts"

In this strategy, the investigator and others mention situations etc. that have not occurred. The argumentation gives an intimation that there have been grounds for suspecting the client. The strategy consists of two sub-strategies.

Non-weakness argumentation strategy

Means that the investigator mentions weaknesses that the client does not have. The argumentation gives an intimation that there have been grounds for suspecting the client of this. The investigator's view of the client has influenced the argumentation.

Non-behaviour argumentation strategy

The strategy implies that the investigator mentions different behaviour/actions that the client has not displayed or done.'

This is a frequent occurrence, with parents consistently telling the same story: that social workers made up facts, everything from domestic violence incidents that never occurred, to convictions that do not exist for crimes never committed. There are never ending permutations of this approach being seen in reports and often repeated in court rooms with no evidence to prove the allegation. As the strategy clearly points out, it is a means by which the social worker can influence the views of others by creating a suspicion about the parents. Remember he who asserts, has the burden of proof, but if you find these non existent facts, you must seek to acquire the evidence to disprove them. Just saying it isn't enough. Get your police record or criminal disclosure, get your medical records, make subject access requests and present the evidence to the LA. Present it in the context of the strategy of calling to attention to non-existent 'facts'.

The following three strategies I have highlighted are probably the most used and easily spotted by parents and these strategies basically revolve around the fact that social workers appear unable to tell the truth.

'5.4.2 Fabulation strategy

In this strategy, the investigator has an underlying purpose, consciously or unconsciously, that makes him or her present and correct material so that it achieves his or her purpose. The consequence is that the investigator presents information that does not have an objective basis.

The fabulation strategy can occur when the investigator

generalises, exaggerates or shifts from making intimations to presenting them as certain facts. In the material examined, the fabulation strategy occurs a number of times when the investigator changed a text as it was being cited. This is expressed through words being removed, added, changed or that sentences have been changed in other ways.

Edvardsson (1993, p.20) defines fabulation as "presenting incorrect or vague, generalising (and sometimes obviously unrealistic) information without giving objective grounds and often in an unobjective, biased context, often also without reporting the source."

5.4.3 Strategy of gradual intensification

This strategy implies a gradual intensification in the text by using a certain way of writing. This may mean that an event is first describe to then make a generalisation. A variation of fabulation is gradual intensification of certainty and information.

5.4.4 Lying strategy

In this strategy, a statement is consciously made although the author knows that it is a lie. Lying is a technique for convincing (cf. Scharnberg, 1996) in which one consciously misleads the listener by e.g. hiding and producing incorrect information.

A fabulated event can lead to lying: "Fabulated versions tend to become increasingly more extreme and comprehensive, as time goes by. The cause derives from the changed adaptation level." (Scharnberg, 1996, p.89)

Lies can be presented in different ways. Anderberg (1993, p.44) makes a point of this. "Of course, conscious lies also occur. <u>There is the clear lie, which consists of saying something when one knows that that is not the case. But being misleading by concealing the truth can be just as effective and appears to some people like a golden middle road between lies and unpleasant truths.</u> The result is often the same."

Deux, Dane and Wrightsman (1993, p.136) refer to Rosnow's conditions, under which it is easier to believe a lie. The first condition occurs when the listener is generally uncertain. Lies are believable when listeners can use them to lighten ambiguity and create predictability. The other condition occurs when the listener experiences personal worry and is affected by the rumour's result. The third occurs if the lies contain a kernel of truth, when they are more believable than

591

completed fabulated lies. Finally, it is more probable that rumours will be believed when the listeners' degree of involvement in the result of the rumour is low. This means that the less that listeners are directly involved in the result, the more probable it is that they will believe a misleading communication and spread it further to others.'

Lies do not just misrepresent you, they drive a social worker's agenda and create complete distrust of the professional. Not only is it unethical, possibly defamatory and unprofessional, above all lies destroy objectivity. The presence of lies confirms the fact that child protection is based upon removal of children and not in support of families. Lies are used to strengthen the case because the truth would not be sufficient. Social workers are believed because they are the professional, you are just a mere parent. As before the lies must be challenged and evidence to the contrary supplied.

At this juncture it is worth pointing out that there is an aversion from solicitors, and other professionals to use the word lie or a liar. It may be couched in other synonyms, but a lie is a lie. Alleging that a social worker is a liar should be clear and unambiguous, particularly where you have the evidence to disprove the lie. If you establish that an allegation is a lie then I would suggest that you use that to your advantage. Use the same strategies, keep repeating phrases in meetings such as '*but how can you place reliance on that opinion as the social worker has already been proved to be a liar.*' and '*… but we know she tells lies, surely her professionalism in in question here.*' Lying is unprofessional and if you have the evidence, then it is certainly worth making a fitness to practice complaint about the social worker to the HCPC.

'5.5 Control and power strategy

This strategy implies that the authority claims to control the client's whole existence and that the authority exploits its power against the client.

Edvardsson (1986, p.10) refers to Minuchin, who presents different criteria for control and exercising power in the family. Minuchin et al. found the following:

being caught up together, i.e. clear boundaries do not exist between family members. Nearness is too great and family members become involved in and take responsibility for things that do not have to do with them. Boundaries between individuals are overdrawn. The space that an individual has to live becomes too small. Closed doors and private spheres are not allowed to exist.

overprotection, which hinders the development of independence, of competence and of interests and activities outside the safety of the family.

rigidity, i.e. when change is necessary, work toward this is thwarted. Effort is made to maintain the status quo.

conflict avoidance, e.g. by denial or diverting manoeuvres, when agreement and harmony is threatened. I mention Edvardsson, who says that these criteria are applicable for larger organisations than the family, such as Swedish care and control bureaucracies. Minuchin et al.'s description is called "smiling fascism on the family level" by Edvardsson. He defines "smiling fascism" as "getting people to obey and not make a fuss by using kind methods. The pertinent motivation in the one who is controlling can vary from strongly meaning well to conscious cynicism."

When authorities use total control and power strategies against the client, the client is forced to what Edvardsson calls counterstrategies, "i.e. offensive actions to protect himself or win over the authorities." Examples of counterstrategies on

594

the part of the client in the rhetoric case are her appeal for discontinuance of LVU care.

The control and power strategy has different sub-strategies.'

This strategy is one of effectively attempting to direct how a family dynamic should work. I think it actually goes further and moves into the area of social engineering. Be observant of a social worker attempting to pervert the family dynamic in this way. If you let such accusations slide and begin to try to please the social worker by enforcing unnatural dynamics in your family you will help support their efforts to break your family up. One of the best ways to counter this is to utilise another of the identified strategies, to challenge the social worker in that your 'normal family life' is aligned with the great mass of society, that their allegations are being decontextualised to effect a negative picture, when in all reality that is how the vast majority of people in society function.

We shall finish our closer look at the persecution strategies with two more examples.

'5.6.3 Strategy of exceeding the limits of one's competence

Jansson and Rönnbäck (1995, p.46) define this strategy as "not keeping oneself to one's professional area but making statements in other professional areas in which one lacks competence." Edvardsson (1996, p.41) comments "Reliability is also influenced by competence. It happens occasionally that investigators without medical or clinical psychiatric/psychological competence make medical judgements and perhaps even pronounce people sick. An investigator shall be aware of signs of poor health but refer the judgement to professionals with suitable competence."

When an investigator uses a strategy of exceeding the limits of his competence, the strategy also includes the strategy of overconfidence in himself and others. The investigator overestimates his own competence, consciously or unconsciously.'

This is a recurring theme as we have considered this numerous times already. It largely goes to the fact that social care professionals have appeared to have developed a latent narcissistic attitude to parents and families. That is to say they lack any empathy for others but have an inflated belief in themselves. Hence their willingness to attribute illnesses or traits to parents that they have no professional competence to

596

so do. And as we have seen, the inclusion of such allegations in reports which are then furnished to actual 'experts' clouds their assessments and creates an agenda to fulfil the social worker's assessment. This must be challenged, ask for the social worker to prove their qualification to make such assertions. If they cannot or do not provide such proof, then demand that the assertions are removed from the reports. Use the persecution manual to demonstrate your point.

The problem with this issue is that the social services organisation itself is believes that:

'5.6 The social authority knows best

Below [see the research at 5.6^{cv}, I have not reproduced the five strategies for the sake of brevity] *are described five different strategies through which it appears that the authorities have an understanding about themselves that they are better than the client, that they know best.*

Edvardsson (1989, p.14) discovered in his analysis of a case that there was no confession from the authority at all that information was incorrect or that judgements had been incorrect or any comments about contradictions, in spite of the fact that incorrect and doubtful information with resulting

597

incorrect judgements existed in the social investigation. Edvardsson comments that there was no self-criticism from persons at the authority. The infallibility syndrome thus comes out very strongly. Confessing an error would undermine the myth about the wisdom of the authorities.'

Linda Arlig's work is a treasure chest of valuable interpretations and identification of methods employed by social services against families. By equipping yourself with this knowledge you can bring substantial challenges, to any and all, reports and assessments that social workers write about you. It can be used as a guide and a blue print for identifying a social worker's agenda. By forensically dissecting the reports and removing the identified persecution strategies you will be able to reduce their allegations down to the base level. It is highly likely that for the majority these bases will be low level concerns that probably do not warrant further interference or at the most, some limited form of support. Once you remove the rhetoric, you begin to move the balance of power back into your favour.

Linda Arlig's findings do not exist just in an academic vacuum, but have been demonstrated by other commentators, maybe not as directly as persecution strategies, but clearly visible as such. Protestations to MPs by and large fall on deaf ears, again mainly because the subject is so emotive. It is not as though politicians are not aware of the concerns regarding how social services operate. I would wager that practically everyone of them has been contacted by a number of families in their constituencies. Parliament has been addressed by various commentators, not least the award winning journalist Florence Bellone. She gave evidence to the Select Committee on education in 2011[cvi]. She submitted evidence that included: *'incoherent allegations, fake evidence and lies'*. She identified 6 areas of concern.

1, How social services get involved with a family:

a) Denunciations

b) Asking social services for help

c)domestic Violence

d) Accident or illnesses

e) Having being removed from your own parents, adopted or raised in care.

2. Babies removed at birth and pre-birth assessments.

3 Use of Psychiatry.

4. Forced adoption and gagging orders.

5, Family Courts.

6. Parental units and people involved in child protection.

She also considered the 'in the best interests' ideology and linked it to profits.

There is nothing new in this list, it is the checklist of modern social work as we have demonstrated above. The report is available to all sitting MPs as well as any member of the public. The reason for high lighting this report is two fold. Firstly, it adds credence to counter the concept that it is only affected parents that have concerns about the social work methods and agenda. Secondly, it yet another example that what is described in this book is not the ruminations of some 'conspiracy theorist.

The concerns are there for all to see if they are looked for. There is no excuse for an MP to believe they have no part to play in exposing this assault on the family and that it is a matter for local authorities. This is a national scandal that requires urgent reform.

Social workers often defend their actions by saying *'We don't remove children, that is a matter for the courts'*. This is just semantics, the local authorities decide to initiate proceedings. They write the reports and fabricate the evidence that influence the court's decisions. If the local authorities did not make the applications, then no child would be removed through a court order. It is entirely the social workers who are to blame for this process.

We have highlighted the propensity of social workers to lie, to fabricate, to misinterpret and allege without evidence. It is clearly a *'modus operandi';* not one off mistakes, or even just one bad apple, it is institutionally endemic. What follows is just one example of how far a local authority will take these misrepresentations and lies. Although we shall not name individuals in this example we shall name the local authority in question.

This account involves Somerset County Council.

False allegations in contact cases are not rare occurrences. Quite often fathers, being the non resident parent are subject to such false allegations. Sexual abuse allegations are the most damning. Where there is such an allegation social workers will probably want to carry out a 'risk assessment' of the individual concerned.

In Somerset there is one, only one, assessor for the whole of the county. He is the 'specialist'. When one family were faced with a risk assessment with this individual, they did some research on him. The letter of appointment confirmed that this individual was the only assessor of this risk in Somerset Children's services, and that because he only saw clients in 'clinical settings', it was important to confirm the appointment. So the family asked for the credentials of this individual. What was provided made clear that this individual possessed no qualifications that would require him to be in a clinical setting. Further, the information provided by the local authority demonstrated he was nothing more than a social worker with some safeguarding training and a few courses in risk assessments of sexual abuse.

The obvious question was where did this claim of a 'clinical setting' come from? The actual appointment was to have been held at County Hall. It seemed strange to the family that County Hall would have 'clinical settings', but possibly there could have been. Further the information said that he too had an 'assessor' that had 'clinical oversight' of this 'specialists' work. To most people that claim would conjure up some the idea of a medically qualified professional overseeing the work of the assessor.

So, the next question posed of the local authority was 'who is the person with 'clinical oversight?' and a request for the copy of this person's CV.

The local authority responded with a name and a CV. The individual with oversight had no clinical experience or qualifications. Again, they were just an ex-social worker. The next step was to make a Freedom of Information request to the local authority to establish if County Hall had rooms designated as 'clinical settings', and if so how many and their uses.

The Freedom of Information response confirmed that were no such settings at County Hall. Just to be doubly sure a follow up request was submitted. 'Did County Hall have first aid rooms and if so would members of the public ever have meetings with professionals in them?' Again the response was in the negative regarding meetings with the public.

Therefore the assessor had no clinical qualifications, the individual providing oversight had no clinical qualifications and the venue for the appointment had no rooms that could be described as a clinical setting. In other words the letter received by the family was a total misrepresentation of the truth. It presented a falsehood to the parents. If the starting point for an assessment is a fabrication of the 'authority' of the assessor, then what hope is there that the assessment itself will be reliable?

Further, why does the local authority feel the need to mislead parents about their staff and assessments? These are questions for the local authority to answer, but we can speculate based on our knowledge of the *Persecution Manual*. Clearly the institution itself has become blinded by its own agenda. That the process of child protection has become purely focused on creating pariahs of parents in order to justify the removal of children. If the evidence is absent, then the social workers will make it up. It is a sad indictment of the system.

Finally, to claim to have some sort of psychology, psychiatry or 'medical' qualification in order to undertake such assessments is not only misleading, but a serious offence at law. Section 49 of Medical Act 1983 makes such a claim an offence. The letter claiming such is also a false instrument under section 8 of the 1981 Forgery and Counterfeiting Act.

The Persecution Manual is real. I doubt very much that social

604

workers even realise that they are acting in a such underhand manner, so ingrained and set is the agenda of 'child-protection' no matter what the truth is.

Conclusion

There are those who will encourage you to work with the social workers. They will tell you that you can survive safeguarding and get your children returned. That is possible for some families I am sure. I think it can be especially pertinent when social workers do actually have a basis for their concerns. I am more interested in helping families that find themselves at the mercy of child protection, who at one time would have never had a social worker darken their door. The rise in the number of children on child protection plans and those taken into care is not, I would say based on an increasing level of child abuse, but an increasing ideological belief in that the state knows best. Lord Munby, President of the Family Division in England and Wales appears to agree. He stated in an emergency statement issued in September 2016 that:

"I do not believe that child abuse/neglect is rising by 14%, let alone 20% a year. So this cannot be the sole explanation. It follows that changes in local authority behaviour must be playing a significant role."[cvii]

What were once 'normal' parts of growing up have become demonized by the child protection industry. Bruises from

606

young children playing rough and tumble are suddenly looked on with a suspicion, disciplining your child is no longer acceptable, being late for school or late picking your child up is enough to generate a referral to social workers.

That cannot be right on any level. The system is destroying childhood and by that, destroying families. Risk aversion has become the watchword. No longer is the agenda about protecting children, it is about protecting social workers. The baby P case was the catalyst, it sparked a political reaction against social workers and since then the profession has exercised a defence by going on the attack: against families. I have said it before and I make no apology in reiterating it here; where there is no evidence to back a case against a parent, then the social worker will fabricate it. I may sound like a conspiracy theorist, except for the fact that we have seen that social workers do in fact have a *modus operandi*. The study into the persecution manual has demonstrated that it is not a figment of parents imagination, but all too real a practice. It takes a number of forms within it, but ultimately it leads to the removal of many children from loving, caring, law abiding parents.

The courts are in crisis according to Lord Munby, the

increasing number of applications for care proceedings is, on his evaluation, not sustainable. We have to believe that the system must also be struggling in the recruitment of enough foster carers, enough social workers or those other child protection professionals that are needed. The Government declared that social work training required a complete overhaul, and at one stage was considering criminal charges for misconduct by a social worker[cviii], but the actual bill as enacted[cix] has fallen short. Clearly the government was aware of the issues, but has since climbed down.

The legal profession has by and large let down many families. Finding a good solicitor and barrister to fight your corner is not easy, especially if you are legally aided. As we have said, that is not to say that genuine fighters for justice do not exist: they do, they are sadly the exception and not the rule. They are also exceptionally busy because they have a reputation that they challenge the system for parents. For a number of years the lay advocates had almost given up on trying to obtain legal representation for families as it was often a shortcut to care orders and poor representation. Thankfully we have found some true, dedicated professionals who will go over and above in fighting a family's case, especially in Ireland.

As seen, this increasing phenomenon of removal of children is not peculiar to the UK: Ireland, the USA and other Western and English speaking nations all seem to be following this trend. That of itself must raise serious questions. The European Union has been petitioned and the response while positive in the support of parents, has actually done little.

So what may we conclude?

No family is safe, the march of child protection idealism has not yet reached a point of radical evaluation, until it does every child is a potential statistic in the machine. As the profit side of child protection continues to grow, so will the demand for children. Like the US prison system, private investors and corporations took over the running of prisons, swiftly followed by many prisons entering corporate hands in the UK. For a corporation to run a prison profitably it needs prisoners and the system must provide them. For private companies, like G4S to enter the world of child protection by setting up children's homes, the system must provide the 'in-mates'. Local authorities are the system by which these homes are filled.

Despite the not so infrequent stories that grace the tabloid press, telling of the horrors of the so called care system, the public at large still seem to believe that children are not removed from parents unless there is a real case of abuse. They do not know of the persecution strategies, the profits that can be made from the 'care' system or even the hugely negative outcomes that being in care has for a child. Most of all they do not think that they will ever see the face of a social worker at their door because they are 'good' parents. They are yet to appreciate that they may be the next in line.

I have been dedicated, full time, to supporting families fight their case against social services in the UK and Ireland for the last few years, before that I did the same on an ad hoc, part time basis. Along that road everything you have read in this book has been tried and tested, refined and adapted. The approaches have not worked in every case, every time, but every challenge has been successful in its own right in one case or another.

I cannot promise you that what you have read here will achieve the results you want, but it does offer you a guide to challenging social workers and their child protection associates that you are unlikely to find from many solicitors. What I have provided is not legal advice, as I am not qualified to do so, and none of this should be construed as such. What it is-is advice from one parent to another, who has experienced the system, fought back and won. It provides strategies that parents can harness to fight their corner. It should give you the confidence to build your case against them, and if nothing else by following some or all of the suggestions herein, you should hopefully feel that at least you gave it your all in protecting your family from the 'child protectionists'.

Coming to a final full stop in this book has been exceptionally difficult. There is so much more to say and develop. I have tried hard to maintain the focus on the 'bigger' issues that parents face, but there is so many other aspects I could have included. If the need and demand is there, they may appear in a Volume II.

I wish you luck on your journey.

Appendix

Appendix A: HCPC Standards of Conduct Performance and Ethics – taken from the HCPC website

Registrants must:

–promote and protect the interests of service users and carers;

–communicate appropriately and effectively;

–work within the limits of their knowledge and skills;

–delegate appropriately;

–respect confidentiality;

–manage risk;

–report concerns about safety;

–be open when things go wrong;

–be honest and trustworthy; and

–keep records of their work.

The standards

1. Promote and protect the interests of service users and carers

Treat service users and carers with respect

1.1 You must treat service users and carers as individuals, respecting their privacy and dignity.

1.2 You must work in partnership with service users and carers, involving them, where appropriate, in decisions about the care, treatment or other services to be provided.

1.3 You must encourage and help service users, where appropriate, to maintain their own health and well-being, and support them so they can make informed decisions.

Make sure you have consent

1.4 You must make sure that you have consent from service users or other appropriate authority before you provide care, treatment or other services.

Challenge discrimination

1.5 You must not discriminate against service users, carers or colleagues by allowing your personal views to affect your professional relationships or the care, treatment or other services that you provide.

1.6 You must challenge colleagues if you think that they have discriminated against, or are discriminating against, service users, carers and colleagues.

Maintain appropriate boundaries

1.7 You must keep your relationships with service users and carers professional.

2 Communicate appropriately and effectively

Communicate with service users and carers

2.1 You must be polite and considerate.

2.2 You must listen to service users and carers and take account of their needs and wishes.

2.3 You must give service users and carers the information they want or need, in a way they can understand.

2.4 You must make sure that, where possible, arrangements are made to meet service users' and carers' language and communication needs.

Work with colleagues

2.5 You must work in partnership with colleagues, sharing your skills, knowledge and experience where appropriate, for the benefit of service users and carers.

2.6 You must share relevant information, where appropriate, with colleagues involved in the care, treatment or other services provided to a service user.

Social media and networking websites

2.7 You must use all forms of communication appropriately and responsibly, including social media and networking websites.

● **Work within the limits of your**

knowledge and skills

Keep within your scope of practice

3.1 You must keep within your scope of practice by only practising in the areas you have appropriate knowledge, skills and experience for.

3.2 You must refer a service user to another practitioner if the care, treatment or other services they need are beyond your scope of practice.

Maintain and develop your knowledge and skills

3.3 You must keep your knowledge and skills up to date and relevant to your scope of practice through continuing professional development.

3.4 You must keep up to date with and follow the law, our guidance and other requirements relevant to your practice.

3.5 You must ask for feedback and use it to improve your practice.

4 Delegate appropriately

Delegation, oversight and support

4.1 You must only delegate work to someone who has the knowledge, skills and experience needed to carry it out safely and effectively.

4.2 You must continue to provide appropriate supervision and support to those you delegate work to.

5 Respect confidentiality

Using information

5.1 You must treat information about service users as confidential.

Disclosing information

5.2 You must only disclose confidential information if:

– you have permission;

– the law allows this;

– it is in the service user's best interests; or

– it is in the public interest, such as if it is necessary to protect public safety or prevent harm to other people.

6 Manage risk

Identify and minimise risk

6.1 You must take all reasonable steps to reduce

the risk of harm to service users, carers and colleagues as far as possible.

6.2 You must not do anything, or allow someone else to do anything, which could put the health or safety of a service user, carer or colleague at unacceptable risk.

Manage your health

6.3 You must make changes to how you practise, or stop practising, if your physical or mental health may affect your performance or judgement, or put others at risk for any other reason.

7 Report concerns about safety

Report concerns

7.1 You must report any concerns about the safety or well-being of service users promptly and appropriately.

7.2 You must support and encourage others to report concerns and not prevent anyone from raising concerns.

7.3 You must take appropriate action if you have concerns about the safety or well-being of children or vulnerable adults.

7.4 You must make sure that the safety and well-being of service users always comes before any professional or other loyalties.

Follow up concerns

7.5 You must follow up concerns you have reported and, if necessary, escalate them.

7.6 You must acknowledge and act on concerns raised to you, investigating, escalating or dealing with those concerns where it is appropriate for you to do so.

8 Be open when things go wrong

Openness with service users and carers

8.1 You must be open and honest when something has gone wrong with the care, treatment or other services that you provide by:

– informing service users or, where appropriate, their carers, that something has gone wrong;

– apologising;

– taking action to put matters right if possible; and

– making sure that service users or, where

appropriate, their carers, receive a full and prompt explanation of what has happened and any likely effects.

Deal with concerns and complaints

8.2   You must support service users and carers who want to raise concerns about the care, treatment or other services they have received.

8.3   You must give a helpful and honest response to anyone who complains about the care, treatment or other services they have received.

9   Be honest and trustworthy

Personal and professional behaviour

9.1   You must make sure that your conduct justifies the public's trust and confidence in you and your profession.

9.2   You must be honest about your experience, qualifications and skills.

9.3 You must make sure that any promotional activities you are involved in are accurate and are not likely to mislead.

9.4   You must declare issues that might create conflicts of interest and make sure that they do not influence your judgement.

**Important information about your conduct
and competence**

9.5   You must tell us as soon as possible if:

– you accept a caution from the police or you
have been charged with, or found guilty of, a criminal
offence;

> – another organisation responsible for
> regulating a health or social-care profession
> has taken action or made a finding against
> you; or

> – you have had any restriction placed on your
> practice, or been suspended or dismissed by
> an employer, because of concerns about your
> conduct or competence.

9.6   You must co-operate with any investigation
into your conduct or competence, the conduct
or competence of others, or the care, treatment
or other services provided to service users.

10   Keep records of your work

Keep accurate records

10.1 You must keep full, clear, and accurate records for everyone you care for, treat, or provide other services to.

10.2 You must complete all records promptly and as soon as possible after providing care, treatment or other services.

Keep records secure

10.3 You must keep records secure by protecting them from loss, damage or inappropriate access.

Fitness to practise

When we say someone is 'fit to practise', we mean that they have the skills, knowledge, character and health they need to practise their profession safely and effectively.

We can consider concerns which members of the public, employers, professionals, the police and other people raise about a registrant's fitness to practise. When we are deciding whether we need to take any action against a registrant to protect the public, we look at whether the registrant has met these standards.

You can find out more information about our fitness to practise process in our brochures 'How to raise a concern' and 'What happens if a concern is raised about me'. You can download these from our website at www.hcpc-uk.org, or you can phone us on 020 7840 9806 to ask for a copy.

Appendix B: Code of Professional Conduct and Ethics for Social Workers – Republic of Ireland.

Overview of the Code

This Code specifies the standards of ethics, conduct and performance expected of registered

social workers. You have a duty to always protect the health and well-being of people who use

your services. To protect the public, you must comply with this Code of Professional Conduct and

Ethics.

The social work values informing this code are:

Respect for the inherent dignity and worth of persons

Pursuit of social justice

Integrity of professional practice

Confidentiality in professional practice

Competence in professional practice.

Note: The term "service user" is used throughout this document. It includes all those who access social work services,

whether they are adults, children and patients in hospital or attending services voluntarily or involuntarily.

Your particular duties are listed below:

1. Uphold human rights in your practice

2. Respect the rights and dignity of people

3. Respect service users' relationships

4. Promote social justice

5. Comply with the laws and regulations governing your practice

6. Carry out your duties professionally and ethically

7. Demonstrate ethical awareness

8. Demonstrate professional accountability

9. Act in the best interest of service users

10. Communicate with service users, carers and professionals

11. Seek informed consent

12. Keep accurate records

13. Deal appropriately with health and safety risks

14. Delegate and manage appropriately

15. Teach and assess students fairly

16. Undertake research ethically

17. Make sure your advertising is truthful and accurate, does not mislead and complies with

legislation

18. Maintain high standards of personal conduct

19. Address health issues in regard to fitness to practise

20. Provide information about your conduct and competence

21. Treat information about service users as confidential

22. Act within the limits of professional knowledge, skills and experience

23. Keep professional knowledge and skills up to date.

Respect for the inherent dignity and worth of persons

1. Upholding human rights in your practice

You should uphold human rights in your practice, by:

respecting the right to self-determination;

promoting the right to participation;

treating each person in a caring and respectful fashion.

2. **Respecting the rights and dignity of people**

You must show through your practice and conduct, a respect for the rights and dignity of people regardless of:

gender;

family status;

marital status;

age;

disability;

sexual orientation;

religion;

race;

membership of the Traveller community, as identified under the Equal Status Acts, 2000-2008.

3. **Respecting service users' relationships**

In your practice, you should respect service users' relationships with their families and other caring relationships. You should also show respect for colleagues and others working to help service users.

Pursuit of Social Justice

4. **Promoting social justice**

You should promote social justice in your practice, through:

challenging negative discrimination and unjust policies and practices;

recognising and respecting diversity;

demonstrating cultural competence;

advocating for the fair distribution of resources based on identified levels of risk/need;

working towards social inclusion.

Integrity of professional practice

5. Complying with the laws and regulations governing your practice

You must be familiar with and work within the laws and regulations governing your practice and keep up with any changes in legislation or regulation.

6. Carrying out your duties professionally and ethically

a) To protect the public you must:

carry out your duties and responsibilities in a professional and ethical way;

always behave with integrity and honesty.

b) Your practice should benefit and not harm others. Often difficult decisions must be made that may be perceived as harmful by a service user. If there is a conflict of interests between the service user and the safeguarding of children or other vulnerable people, safeguarding should take precedence.

7. Demonstrating ethical awareness

a) You must make sure you read and understand this Code of Professional Conduct and Ethics.

b) You must not enter into any agreement or contract or accept any gift that might cause you to act against the terms of this Code of Professional Conduct and Ethics.

c) You must take particular care when ethical issues arise. Please see Appendix A for a suggested way of dealing with ethical dilemmas.

d) If there is a conflict between this Code of Professional Conduct and Ethics and a registrant's work environment, the registrant's obligation is to the Code.

e) Subject to your duty to act in the best interests of your service users, you have a responsibility to engage and advocate with the relevant authorities to promote the provision of appropriate resources and facilities.

f) You have a duty to assist in the efficient and effective use of resources and to give advice on their appropriate allocation. While balancing a duty of care to the individual service user, you should be aware of the wider need to use limited resources efficiently and responsibly. Such awareness should inform decision making in your practice.

g) Written records of advocacy on behalf of services or service users should be kept on file, demonstrating the registrant's efforts to address concerns.

8. Demonstrating Professional accountability

You must be prepared to explain and account for your actions and decisions.

9. Acting in the best interests of service users

a) You are responsible for acting in the best interests of service users.

b) You must:

treat service users as individuals;

respect diversity, different cultures and values and not condone, facilitate or collaborate with any form of discrimination;

respect and, where appropriate, promote or advocate the views and wishes of service users and carers;

support service users' rights to take part in all aspects of the service and to make informed choices about the service they receive;

help service users to reach informed decisions about their lives and promote their autonomy.

Any action which diminishes service users' civil or legal rights must be ethically,

professionally and legally justifiable;

do nothing, and as far as practicable allow nothing to be done, that you believe would risk the health or safety of service users;

make service users aware that their interests may be overridden in circumstances where the service user's interest is outweighed by the need to protect others;

when working in a team, be responsible for your professional conduct, for any service or professional advice you provide and for your failure to act;

protect service users if you believe that they are threatened by a colleague's conduct,

performance or health. The safety of service users must always come before any personal and professional loyalties;

discuss the matter with an appropriate professional colleague if you become aware of any situation that puts a service user at risk;

work in line with the principles of human rights and social justice. You may be required to support service users to take risks to allow them to reach their full potential and well-being.

You should be mindful of the effect these risks may have on the service user and on others, particularly children and vulnerable adults;

avoid conflicts of interest.

c) You must not:

transfer public service users to your private practice for commercial gain;

knowingly work with a service user with whom you have or have had a personal relationship that may compromise your professional practice.

10. Communicating with service users, carers and professionals

a) You must make sure that you communicate properly and effectively with service users, their carers and their family.

b) You must also co-operate, communicate effectively and share your knowledge and expertise with other professionals and with students for the benefit of service users.

11. Seeking informed consent

a) You must explain to the service user the assessment or intervention that you plan to carry out, the implications involved and any other possible interventions. You must also take account of the service user's capacity to understand the information and to give their consent.

b) Every effort must be made to seek the service user's informed consent for any intervention before it is carried out. In the event that a service user cannot give informed consent, every effort must be made to ensure that any actions taken are in the service user's best interests.

c) You must record the service user's views with regard to any proposed intervention. The decisions they make with regard to their cooperation or opposition to any such proposed intervention must be shared as appropriate with members of the health or social care team involved in the service user's care.

d) In emergencies, you may not be able to explain assessments or interventions, get consent or pass on information to other members of the team. You should at all times act in the best interests of the service user.

e) If a service user refuses assessment or intervention and you believe it is necessary for their well-being, you must make reasonable efforts to persuade the service user, particularly if there is a significant or immediate risk to their life.

f) If you are working with people under a legal mandate, you must respectfully and clearly state your legal responsibilities and the consequence of non-cooperation. You must also clarify those matters which are open to negotiation and agreement.

g) You must follow your employer's procedures on consent and you must also be aware of any guidance issued by appropriate authorities.

12. Keeping accurate records

a) You must keep clear and accurate records according to the policies and procedures in your workplace.

b) You must keep records for each person who asks for or

receives advice or services.

c) All records must be:

complete;

legible (if handwritten);

identifiable as being made by you;

dated;

prepared as soon as practicable following intervention;

clear and factual.

d) If you supervise students, you must review each student's entries in the records and record that you have done so.

e) When records are reviewed, you must update them and should note any arrangements for the service user's continuing care.

f) You must make every effort to protect information in records against loss or damage and against access or use by anyone who does not have permission to access or use the records.

g) When you update records, you must not erase information that was previously there or make that information difficult to read. Instead, mark the old information in some way.

h) Social work records should be based on professional assessment which is regularly reviewed and updated.

i) You must hold and use records according to relevant legislation.

j) You have a duty to maintain accurate and up to date service users' records either in manual or electronic form. You are expected to be aware of your obligation under the Data Protection Acts in relation to secure storage and eventual disposal of such records as well as relevant published Codes of Practice.

13. Health and safety

a) You must follow risk assessment policies and procedures to assess potential risks in the workplace and area of practice.

b) If you identify a risk, you must take the necessary steps to minimise, reduce or eliminate the risk in line with relevant legislation such as the Safety, Health and Welfare at Work Act 2005 and your employer's policies, for example, Policy, Procedure, Protocol and Guidelines (PPPGs).

c) You must tell relevant colleagues and agencies about the outcomes and implications of risk assessments.

14. Delegation and management

People have the right to assume that the person who provides a service to them has the knowledge and skills to do so.

a) When you delegate tasks to someone else, you must be sure that they have the knowledge, skills and experience to carry out the tasks safely and competently.

b) You must not ask another person to perform any task that is outside their knowledge, skills and experience unless they are under the direct supervision of an experienced practitioner.

c) You are accountable for any task you delegate to another practitioner and responsible for any task you delegate to students or others.

d) If a person is unwilling to carry out a task because they do not think they are capable of doing so safely and competently, you must not force them to carry out the task. If their refusal raises a disciplinary or training issue, you must deal with this separately. The service user must not be put at risk.

15. Teaching and assessing students

If you are responsible for teaching and assessing social work students you must do so fairly and respectfully and on the basis of agreed criteria.

16. Undertaking research ethically

You must undertake research ethically. Please see Appendix B for a suggested way of dealing with research projects.

17. Truthful advertising

You must make sure that any advertising you do is accurate, does not mislead and complies with relevant legislation.

18. Maintaining high standards of personal conduct

a) You must not:

abuse, harm or neglect service users, carers or colleagues;

exploit or discriminate unlawfully or unjustifiably against service users, carers or colleagues;

form inappropriate personal relationships with service users;

condone unlawful or unjustifiable discrimination by service users, carers or colleagues;

put yourself or other people at unnecessary risk;

behave in a way that would call into question your suitability to work in health and social care professional services; or

engage in conduct that is likely to damage the public's confidence in you or in your profession.

b) You must:

work openly and co-operatively with colleagues in the workplace; recognise and respect the roles and expertise of practitioners from other agencies or professions and work in partnership with them.

Social Workers Registration Board

19. Addressing health issues in regard to fitness to practise

You must take action if health issues are harming your fitness to practise. For example, you may need to limit your work or stop practising if health issues are affecting your conduct, performance or judgement.

20. Providing information about your conduct and competence

a) You must raise concerns with the appropriate authority if policies, systems, working conditions or the actions, professional performance or health of you or of others compromise service user care or public safety.

b) You must co-operate with any investigation or formal inquiry into your professional conduct.

Confidentiality in Professional Practice

21. Treating information about service users as confidential

a) You must treat information about service users as confidential and use it only for the purpose for which you obtained it unless to do so would put the service user or others at risk.

b) You must not knowingly release any personal or confidential information to anyone who is not entitled to it except if the law or your professional practice obligations require you to do so.

You must also check that people who ask for information are entitled to it.

c) You must only use information about a service user to provide service to that person or if the service user has given specific permission to do so.

d) You should consult service users about their preferences regarding the use of information about them.

e) You must keep to the conditions of any relevant data protection legislation and follow best practice and relevant agency guidelines for handling confidential information relating to individuals at all times. Best practice is likely to change over time, and you must stay up to date with developments.

Disclosure of Information to other relevant Professionals

f) Information may need to be shared with other relevant professionals to provide safe and effective care. If disclosure of a service user's information is necessary as part of their care, you should take reasonable steps to ensure that you make such a disclosure to an appropriate person who understands that the information must be kept confidential.

Competence in Professional Practice

22. Acting within the limits of your knowledge, skills and experience

a) You must act within the limits of your knowledge, skills and experience.

b) You should only practise in fields in which you have education, training and experience. When accepting a service user, you have a duty of care. This duty includes the obligation to refer the service user for further professional assessment or intervention if it becomes clear that the task is beyond your knowledge, skills or experience.

c) A service user has the right to a referral for a second opinion for assessment or intervention at any time. If a service user asks for a second opinion/review, you must refer them promptly to another professional.

d) If you receive a referral from another health or social care professional, you must make sure that you fully understand the request. You should only assess or intervene if you believe it is right to do so. If this is not the case, you must discuss the matter with the practitioner who made the referral and the service user before providing any service.

e) You must meet relevant standards of practice and work lawfully, safely and competently.

Supervision Expectation for Social Workers

f) You should seek and engage in supervision in professional practice on an on-going and regular basis.

g) You must seek support and assistance from your employer if you do not feel competent to carryout any aspect of your work or if you are unsure about how to proceed in a work matter.

23. Keeping your professional knowledge and skills up to date

a) You must make sure that your knowledge, skills and performance are of a high quality, are up to date and are relevant to your practice.

b) You must:

Maintain and develop your professional competence by undertaking relevant education and training to improve your knowledge and skills;

Keep up to date with relevant knowledge, research methods and techniques so that your service, research activities and conclusions will help and not harm others. You can do this, for example, by reading relevant literature, consulting with peers and taking part in continuing education activities;

Take part in continuing professional development (CPD);

Keep clear and accurate records of CPD.

HIS HONOUR JUDGE CLIFFORD BELLAMY

DESIGNATED FAMILY JUDGE FOR LEICESTER

PRACTICE GUIDE: THE USE OF SECTION 20 OF THE CHILDREN ACT 1989 IN THE CONTEXT OF CHILD PROTECTION

- This Practice Guide has been agreed between the Designated Family Judge for Leicester, Leicester City Council and Leicestershire County Council. It sets out best practice to be followed in the use of section 20 of the Children Act 1989 as a child protection measure for the safeguarding of children in Leicester and Leicestershire. It should be read alongside the Leicester and Leicestershire Pre-Proceedings Protocol.

Preamble

- It is acknowledged that when a child is accommodated before care proceedings are issued:

  - the court has no jurisdiction to scrutinise the local authority's interim care plan for the child[cx] or to control the planning for the child and prevent or reduce unnecessary and avoidable delay;

  - the court has no power under section 34 of the Children Act to determine issues relating to parental contact with the child;

  - the child will not have the benefit of the appointment of an independent Children's Guardian to represent and safeguard his interests;

  - the child is not entitled to legal aid and is therefore unlikely to have legal representation[cxi]; and

  - unless a pre-proceedings meeting has been

convened, the parents have no entitlement to legal aid and are, therefore, unlikely to have legal representation.

These factors clearly give rise to scope for unfairness in the use of section 20.

- In the last three years the use of section 20 has been the subject of judicial scrutiny and criticism in a number of cases. This has led to judicial guidance on the proper use of section 20.[cxii] This Practice Guide reflects on that judicial guidance.

- The misuse of section 20 has in the recent past led to awards of damages under section 7 of the Human Rights Act 1998. A key objective of this Practice Guide is to ensure that in their use of section 20 local authorities treat children and families fairly and act in accordance with the law.

Guidance

- Accommodation of a child under section 20 is frequently referred to as 'voluntary accommodation'. This description highlights the absolute importance of recognising that a child can only be accommodated under section 20 if a parent with parental responsibility consents to his or her child being accommodated.

- In this context, 'consent' means informed consent. This requires the social worker obtaining the parent's consent to satisfy herself that the parent has a clear understanding of what she is being asked to consent to and that she is capable of giving consent. It has been said that consent 'must not be compulsion in disguise'.[cxiii]

- Particular issues arise when seeking to obtain parental consent to the accommodation of a newborn baby immediately after birth. Where the local authority's interim plan for such a child is to remove the child from her mother immediately following birth and it seeks to do so with parental consent under section 20, it is of the utmost importance that the guidance given by Hedley J in *Coventry City Council v C, B, CA and CH [2013] 2 FLR 987* is complied with. That guidance provides that, 'i) Every parent has the right, if capacitous, to exercise their parental responsibility to consent under Section 20 to have their child accommodated by the local authority and every local authority has power under Section 20(4) so to accommodate provided that it is consistent with the welfare of the child.

ii) Every social worker obtaining such a consent is under a personal duty (the outcome of which may not be dictated to them by others) to be satisfied that the person giving the consent does not lack the capacity to do so.

iii) In taking any such consent the social worker must actively address the issue of capacity and take into account all the circumstances prevailing at the time and consider the questions raised by Section 3 of the 2005 Act, and in particular the mother's capacity at that time to use and weigh all the relevant information.

iv) If the social worker has doubts about capacity no further attempt should be made to obtain consent on that occasion and advice should be sought from the social work team leader or management.

v) If the social worker is satisfied that the person whose consent is sought does not lack capacity, the social worker must be satisfied that the consent is fully informed:

a) Does the parent fully understand the consequences of giving such a consent?

b) Does the parent fully appreciate the range of choice available and the consequences of refusal as well as giving consent?

c) Is the parent in possession of all the facts and issues material to the giving of consent?

vi) If not satisfied that the answers to a) – c) above are all 'yes', no further attempt should be made to obtain consent on that occasion and advice should be sought as above and the social work team should further consider taking legal advice if thought necessary.

vii) If the social worker is satisfied that the consent is fully informed then it is necessary to be further satisfied that the giving of such consent and the subsequent removal is both fair and proportionate.

viii) In considering that it may be necessary to ask:

a) what is the current physical and psychological state of the parent?

b) If they have a solicitor, have they been encouraged to seek legal advice and/or advice from family or friends?

c) Is it necessary for the safety of the child for her to be removed at this time?

d) Would it be fairer in this case for this matter to be the subject of a court order rather than an agreement?

ix) If having done all this and, if necessary, having taken further advice (as above and including where necessary legal advice), the social worker then considers that a fully informed consent has been received from a capacitous mother in circumstances where removal is necessary and proportionate, consent may be acted upon.

x) In the light of the foregoing, local authorities may want to approach with great care the obtaining of Section 20 agreements from mothers in the aftermath of birth, especially where there is no immediate danger to the child and where probably no order would be made.

- As a matter of good practice, unless it is not practicable to do so legal advice should normally be obtained before inviting a parent to consent to his or her child being accommodated under section 20.

- If a parent objects to his or her child being accommodated under section 20 the local authority may only lawfully remove the child from parental care with the authorisation of a court. Such authorisation may take the form of an Emergency Protection Order or an Interim Care Order.

- There is in law no requirement for consent under section 20 to be obtained in or evidenced by writing.[cxiv] However, it has been said that 'a prudent local authority will surely always wish to ensure that an alleged parental consent in such a case is properly recorded in writing and evidenced by the parent's signature'.[cxv] In future, obtaining written consent should be regarded as standard practice.

- There is no prescribed form to be used for recording

consent under section 20. As a minimum, written consent should contain the following information:

- the name or names of the parent(s) giving consent;

- the name(s) and date(s) of birth of the child(ren) in respect of whom consent is being given;

- the name and status of the professional obtaining parental consent;

- the date, time and place at which the consent form is completed and signed;

- details of the arrangements for parental contact with the children (or a reference to the local authority's care plan if one has been prepared).

- If written consent is recorded in a handwritten document it is important that the document is legible.

- Section 20(8) provides that 'Any person who has parental responsibility for a child may at any time remove the child from accommodation provided by or on behalf of the local authority under this section.' A written form of consent must make it clear that the parent can 'remove the child' from the local authority accommodation 'at any time' and should not seek to impose any fetters on the parent's right under section 20(8).

- Whether handwritten or typed the document must be clear and precise as to its terms and drafted in simple and straight-forward language which the parent can readily understand.

- In any case in which the first language of the parent is not English it is important that:

    - a parent is assisted by an appropriately qualified interpreter in any discussions leading to parental consent being given;

    - a translation of the form of consent is provided to the parent concerned at the time it is signed or, if that is not possible, within three working days thereafter;

    - if it is not possible for a translation of the form of consent to be prepared at the time consent is

653

given, the original form of consent should contain a statement confirming that the form of consent has been read over to and explained to the parent in his or her first language;

- when available, the parent should sign the translated version of the form of consent, adding, in the parent's language, words to the effect that 'I have read this document and I agree to its terms.'

- When consent is obtained orally and is not evidenced in writing the social worker must ensure that she makes a note in the child's records of the circumstances in which consent was obtained and the reasons why consent was not obtained in writing. In such circumstances the fact that the parent has consented, an explanation of the effect of that consent and confirmation of the parent's rights under section 20(8) should be communicated to the parent concerned (translated into the parent's first language if necessary) within five working days.

- Whether a child is accommodated under section 20

prior to or during the course of care proceedings there is no power to require that a parent must give a period of notice if she wishes to withdraw his or her consent. Nothing should be said to the parent to suggest the contrary and no statement to the contrary should be contained in the written form of consent.

- The ability to accommodate a child under section 20, with parental consent, is not intended to be a long-term alternative to care proceedings. It is intended as a short-term measure pending the commencement of care proceedings. The point has been made that 'Section 1 (2) Children Act 1989 makes clear the general principle that any delay in determining any proceedings in which any question with respect to the upbringing of a child arises is likely to prejudice their welfare. That principle applies as well in the context of any delay in issuing proceedings in circumstances such as this case.'[cxvi]

- If it is likely to be necessary for the Family Court to make findings concerning the causation of injuries sustained by an accommodated child, 'short-term' means no longer than is necessary to enable the local authority to prepare and issue an application for a care order. In such circumstances it is imperative that care proceedings are issued promptly, particularly if there are complex medical issues as a result of which the court is likely to give permission for the instruction of independent medical evidence.

- In any case in which a child has been accommodated under section 20 for more than three months the case should be reviewed by senior management. Processes should be put in place to ensure that this occurs in a timely way.

29 January 2016

Appendix D: Articles of the United Nations Convention on the Rights of the Child

Article 1: Definition of a child

Article 2: Non-discrimination

Article 3: Best interests of the child

Article 4: Implementation of rights

Article 5: Parental guidance and the child's evolving capacities

Article 6: Survival and development

Article 7: Name and nationality

Article 8: Preservation of identity

Article 9: Separation from parents

Article 10: Family reunification

Article 11: Illicit transfer and non-return

Article 12: The child's opinion

Article 13: Freedom of expression

Article 14: Freedom of thought, conscience and religion

Article 15: Freedom of association

Article 34: Sexual exploitation

Article 35: Sale, trafficking and abduction

Article 36: Other forms of exploitation

Article 37: Torture and deprivation of liberty

Article 38: Armed conflicts

Article 39: Rehabilitative care

Article 40: Administration of juvenile justice

Article 41: Respect for existing standards

Appendix E: Template Judicial Review

No. 13

STATEMENT REQUIRED TO GROUND APPLICATION FOR JUDICIAL REVIEW:

of the decisions and actions by TUSLA–Child and Family Agency to apply for removal of my child under Section 13 (1) of the Child Care Act 1991 and to seek and obtain an Interim Care Order under Section 17(1) of the Child Care Act 1991 without due diligence and assessments as required under the Child Care Act 1991 and Children First working protocol- and xxxx District Court in the granting of the said order without ensuring that all correct procedures had been applied and adhered to.

(a) **Applicant's name**:

xxxxxxxxxxxxxxxxx

(b) **Applicant's address:**

xxxxxxxxxx

xxxxxxxxxx

xxxxxxxxxx

xxxxxxxxxx

(c) **Applicant's description:**

Mother to Child: xxxxxx d.ob. xx-xx-20xx

(d) **Relief sought:**

(I)   An order of certiorari in respect of the issuance of an Interim Care Order on xx [month] 20xx by xxxx District Court, whereby the said child was removed from the custody of his natural parent without the application of fair procedures laid down in Statute and best practice.   Tusla-Child and Family Agency have acted beyond the limits of their authority.

(ii) Interlocutory Mandatory Injunction in respect of the Interim Care Order of [date] by xxxx District Court, returning the child to the care of the parent under Tusla-Child and Family Agency supervision.

(iii) Interlocutory Mandatory Injunction in respect of daily access to the child to enforce the right of child and Mother to breast feed and bond.

(iv) Enforcement of the Child's rights under Articles

2,3,4,5,7,8,9,10,16 & 18 of the United Nations Convention of the Rights of the Child.

(v) Enforcement of the parent's and child's Human Rights under Articles 5,6,7,8 and Article 9 of the European Convention of Human Rights.

(vi) Damages in respect of the violations of the European Convention of Human Rights and the violations of the United Nations Convention of the Rights of the Child.

(e) **Grounds upon which such relief is sought:**

1.1 My child was removed from the care of her natural parent by a mis-application of Sections 13, 17 (1) and 18 of the Child Care Act 1991 through the issuance of an Interim Care Order granted to Tusla whilst breaching Articles 5 & 6 of the European Convention of Human Rights. *"In the determination of his civil rights and obligations or of any criminal charge against him, everyone is entitled to a fair and public hearing within a reasonable time..."* This was a draconian measure without any just cause and denied the Mother the right to make any representations or given an adequate opportunity to present her case. xxxx Child and Family Agency expected her to leave hospital, having given birth just over 16 hours earlier to attend Court for a contested hearing. She had neither been discharged nor had xxxx Child and Family Agency verified with any Medical Professional at xxxx General Hospital that it was safe or desirable for her to do so. She was not given a chance to comment on the material put forward by Tusla – Child and Family Agency prior to its presentation to the District Court. This is a breach of Articles 5 & 6 of the European Convention of Human Rights.

1.2 Her father attended on her behalf, whereupon, although he was allowed to put forward a hastily written statement by herself and evidence to substantiate it, he was excluded from the Court and an *ex-parte* hearing constituted, despite the pressure and harassment the Mother had endured from the Social Worker from xxxx Tusla-Child and Family Agency throughout that morning over the telephone, whilst she was breast-feeding her child, to attend Court. Thus the judge allowed her Article 6 Rights to be violated as she was left un-represented to contest the hearing.

1.3 Tusla–Child and Family Agency did not act with due proportionality in regard to its decision to seek an Interim Care Order.

The 1991 Child Care Act requires that *18.—(1) Where, on the application of a health board with respect to a child who resides or is found in its area, the court is satisfied that—*

(a) the child has been or is being assaulted, ill-treated, neglected or sexually abused, or

(b) the child's health, development or welfare has been or is being avoidably impaired or neglected, or

(c) the child's health, development or welfare is likely to be avoidably impaired or neglected,

and that the child requires care or protection which he is unlikely to receive unless the court makes an order under this section,

There is no evidence to suggest that a or b can be met. C is based on the likely and again there is no evidence to suggest that this will be the case as Tusla Child and Family Agency failed in their Statutory duty to undertake any pre-birth assessments, despite having the opportunity to do so. They relied upon un-corroborated information received from xxxxx Metropolitan Borough Council in the UK, which consisted of historic issues that no longer have any relevance upon the Mother's life. There was no assessment of the current circumstances.

1.4 Tusla–Child and Family Agency have failed in their duty to carry out their assessments as per the Children First National Guidance 2011, which is going to be afforded statutory footing, which means that she as a parent, has not been given the opportunity to prove her ability to parent or to be assessed for any support services that may be given to help with any concerns that may remain. Tusla only met with the Mother to tell her that they had taken the decision to remove her child at birth without undertaking any necessary assessments. This decision was based purely upon inaccurate and unchecked information received from UK authorities where the applicant used to reside. There has been a failure to hold case conferences or to seek the views, wishes and feelings of her as a parent.

Under Section 1 - the Principles aims and use of national guidance of the Children First document 2011 *"The key principles that should inform best practice in child protection and welfare are:*

(I) The welfare of children is of paramount importance.

The Child's welfare has not been given paramount importance

as it is clearly in the best interests of the child to be with natural parents as recognised by the Constitution and Supreme Court rulings. The Supreme Court has taken the view that in cases in which the actions of the parent are at issue *"it is presumed that his or her actions are in accordance with the best interests of the child."* The courts have made it plain that welfare implications of a parent's conduct unless some *"positive evidence [is] produced that it would not serve [the child's] best interests."* McK. V Information Commissioner [2006] 1.1 R. 260, at 267 & 268. As there is no evidence that she has, or would harm any child, let alone her own bar, third-party hearsay presented as a fact, it clearly is apparent that Tusla-Child and Family Agency have acted beyond authority.

(ii) A proper balance must be struck between protecting children and respecting the rights and needs of parents/carers and families. Where there is conflict, the child's welfare must come first...

Parents/carers have a right to respect and should be consulted and involved in matters that concern their family.

There has been no consultation, only the presentation of a *fait accompli* that her child was to be taken into care at birth.

*(iii) Children should only be separated from parents/carers when alternative means of protecting them have been **exhausted**. Re-union should be considered in the context of planning for the child's future.*

There has been no consideration to alternative means of 'protecting' her child, let alone an exhaustion of them. No proportionality has been applied, the removal of her child clearly goes against the principles of the Constitution, the Child Care Act 1991, the Children First: National Guidance 2011 and the child's and the Mother's Human Rights.

Furthermore, a Practice Direction issued by Dolphin House for the Dublin Metropolitan area (DCO5) indicates that best practice should:

'2.2   The Child and Family Agency (CFA) should in advance of instituting proceedings have regard to the Principals of Best Practice in Child Protection contained in paragraph 1.1.1 of the Children First National Guidance for the Protection and Management of Children (2011) and evidence of such compliance should be available as set out in Appendix 1.

2.3   The parties should have an opportunity of entering into productive discussions at the earliest possible opportunity.

Where proceedings under Part III section 13 of the Act are brought the application shall be grounded on an affidavit sworn by the appropriate CFA personnel, or on information on oath and in writing sworn by the appropriate CFA personnel. A copy of the affidavit or information shall be served on the respondents with the application.

6.9   Where proceedings under Part III section 13 are brought ex parte application pursuant to section 13 (4)(c) to have the application heard ex parte and the application shall be grounded on affidavit sworn by the appropriate CFA personnel, or on information on oath and in writing sworn by the appropriate CFA personnel. A copy of any order (including an order to dismiss), shall be served on the respondent(s) as soon as practicable. A note of evidence given by the CFA during the said application shall be prepared as soon as practicable by the CFA or their solicitor and approved by the judge and a copy of any affidavit or information and of the note of evidence shall be available to the respondents on application to court.

6.10 The CFA shall on request provide the solicitors for the respondents with access to all reports and documentation or records relied upon by the CFA or to which it has had regard in forming the opinion that the relevant statutory threshold under section 13 of the Act has been met or exists so as to require them to initiate proceedings. Unrepresented parties shall be provided with access to such documentation in accordance with clause 11.4 of this practice direction.

*6.11 Notice of the hearing of an application for an emergency care order under section 13 shall be served at least **two days prior** to the date fixed for hearing the application unless in the urgency of the matter requires the matter to be heard ex parte.*

8.3 Content of social work reports and Guardian ad Litem reports to court should be:

- *As short and focused as possible;*

- *Be clearly set out using numbered paragraphs, headings and sub-headings and numbered pages;*

- *Balance description and background chronology with evaluation, summary and assessment;*

- *Differentiate fact from opinions;*

- *Unsubstantiated allegations should be highlighted as such;*

- *Only facts which will be substantiated by evidence at hearing should be contained in final reports;*

- *Present the information with sensitivity and in a way which does not exacerbate the relations between the parties;*

- *Be fair to the parties and demonstrate balance;*

- *Avoid unnecessary repetition of material which is available in other or earlier documents before the court.*

All of which Tusla-Child and Family Agency and the District Court failed to correctly apply.

1.5 In Tusla–Child and Family Agency -V- CG & anor (Care Order Proportionality) 2014 IEDC 06, the issue of proportionality is firmly set in its legal context:

"The evidential threshold to be established is a high one. Article 42.5 of the Constitution (pre amendment) confirms that the State may only intervene to supply the place of a parent in "exceptional" situations where there has been parental failure. Any interference considered necessary to protect the

rights of the child must be implemented by appropriate means but always with due regard to the natural and imprescriptible rights of the child. Of course it is necessary under the Constitution, it is necessary to have regard to the rights of the parents whether under the Constitution or otherwise; otherwise includes the European Convention of Human Rights and the European Charter of Fundamental Rights....

Even where such circumstances have been established evidentially it is necessary for the Agency to establish that the child requires care or protection which he/she is unlikely to receive unless the court makes an order under this section."

There is no evidence that the threshold has been crossed. The Mother has not failed in her parenting, having not even been given the opportunity to prove her ability and capability at this juncture. As can be seen in Exhibit 1. She was granted unsupervised contact with her children from my previous relationship. Exhibit 2. Demonstrates that she was granted custody of her son and Exhibit 3 shows that xxxx Metropolitan Borough Council assessed that she was more than capable of providing care, warmth, emotional security and excellent parenting.

She has never harmed a child.

The Mother strongly protests that the information provided by xxxx Metropolitan Borough Council Children's Services contains misleading, inaccurate and spurious allegations, the veracity of which have not been investigated or proved by the social workers and is presently being solely relied upon by Tusla–Child and Family Agency.

Secondly, the key principle governing the application of Article 6 is fairness. In cases where an applicant appears in court not withstanding lack of assistance of a lawyer and manages to conduct his or her case in the teeth of all the difficulties, the question may nonetheless arise as to whether this procedure was fair (see, for example, no. 46311/99, McVicar v. the United Kingdom, judgment

of 7 May 2002, to be published in ECHR 2002.

There is the importance of ensuring the appearance of the fair administration of justice and a party in civil proceedings must be able to participate effectively, inter alia, by being able to put

forward the matters in support of his or her claims. Here, as in other aspects of Article 6, the seriousness of what is at stake for the applicant will be of relevance to assessing the adequacy and fairness of the procedures

She has been denied the information relied on by Tusla in the court prior to the hearing. The affidavits used in the ex-parte application fell short of the information supplied to the District Court upon the application for the interim care order, not only that but she contests that the Affidavit of the Social Worker relied upon by the District Court in the making of a Section 13 Emergency Care Order and upon which the furtherance of keeping her child in Care under the Interim Care Order, did not and does not constitute the facts or reality of the situation and contains factual inaccuracies that raises serious questions as to the reliability of the Social Worker's grounds and evidence and also raises the question whether her reliance upon un-assessed and un-checked 'evidence' presented as fact to the District Court constituted perjury.

The District Court relied upon Tusla's Social Worker's Affidavit and the District Court judge refused to read the Mother's sworn Affidavit at the Interim Care hearing. Again the Child and Family Agency failed to provide any material to the Respondent upon which they sought to rely in the above

673

application. As *"procedural standards are one important way in which fairness is protected. In civil cases, for example, parties are required as a general principle to disclose documents that they will rely on in court, as well as documents in their possession, even if these are detrimental to their case. They should also exchange the statements of the witnesses they wish to call in advance. These requirements ensure that both parties know the facts of the case and can respond effectively to allegations against them."* xxxx Metropolitan Borough Council sent a Social Worker to this hearing, yet what they intended to 'disclose' or 'allege' as a witness has not been provided. There was no 'official' confirmation of this attendance, no Affidavit nor any prior service of what they sought to rely upon in the court. This is a serious violation of the Applicant's rights and one has to ask as to why this subterfuge was undertaken?

'The fact that the person is unlikely to know the case against him or her will almost certainly breach the right to a fair trial. One of the core principles of natural justice and one of the fundamental parts of the right to a fair trial under Article 6 is the right to know the case against you. Any use of closed material that prevents a person from knowing the case against them is therefore highly likely to lead to that person having an

unfair trial and risks breaching Article 6.

1.6 Case Law

B.

The Court's assessment

1.

General principles

113. The mutual enjoyment by parent and child of each other's company constitutes a fundamental element of family life, and domestic measures hindering such enjoyment amount to an interference with the right protected by Article 8 of the Convention (see, amongst others, the <u>Johansen v.Norway judgment of 7 August 1996,Reports of Judgments and Decisions 1996- III, § 52</u>). Any such interference constitutes a violation of this Article unless it is "in accordance with the law", pursues an aim or aims that are legitimate under paragraph 2 of Article 8 and can be regarded as"necessary in a democratic society".

114. In determining whether the impugned measures were "necessary in a democratic society", the Court will consider whether, in the light of the case as a whole, the reasons adduced to justify these measures were relevant and sufficient for the purpose of paragraph 2 of Article 8 of the Convention

(see,inter alia, the Olsson v. Sweden (no. 1) judgment of 24 March 1988, Series A no 130, § 68)

116.The margin of appreciation so to be accorded to the competent national authorities will vary in the light of the nature of the issues and the seriousness of the interests at stake. While the authorities enjoy a wide margin of appreciation in assessing the necessity of taking a child into care, in particular where an emergency situation arises, the Court must still be satisfied in the circumstances of the case that there existed circumstances justifying the removal of the child, and it is for the respondent State to 28 P., C. AND S. v. THE UNITED KINGDOM JUDGMENT

establish that a careful assessment of the impact of the proposed care measure on the parents and the child, as well as of the possible alternatives to taking the child into public care, was carried out prior to implementation of a care measure (see K. and T. v. Finland, no. 25702/94, [GC], ECHR 2001- VII, § 166; Kutzner v. Germany, no. 46544/99, § 67, judgment of 26 February 2002, unreported). None of this was addressed or considered.

117. Following any removal into care, a stricter scrutiny is called for in respect of any further limitations by the authorities, for example on parental rights of access, as such further restrictions entail the danger that the family relations between the parents and a young child are effectively curtailed (the above-mentioned judgments, Johansen, § 64, and Kutzner, § 67). The taking into care of a child should normally be regarded as a temporary measure to be discontinued as soon as the circumstances permit, and any measures of implementation of temporary care should be consistent with the ultimate aim of reuniting the natural parent and child (Olsson (no. 1) judgment, p.36, § 81; Johansen judgment, p. 1008, § 78; E.P. v. Italy, no. 31127/96, § 69, judgment of 16 September 1999, unpublished). In this regard a fair balance has to be struck between the interests of the child remaining in care and those of the parent in being reunited with the child (see the above mentioned Olsson (no. 2) v. Sweden judgment, pp. 35 -36, § 90; the Hokkanen v. Finland judgment, p. 20, § 55). In carrying out this balancing exercise, the Court will attach particular importance to the best interests of the child which, depending on their nature and seriousness, may override those of the parent (the Johansen judgment, p. 1008,

§ 78)

119. The Court further recalls that whilst Article 8 contains no explicit procedural requirements, the decision-making process involved in measures of interference must be fair and such as to afford due respect to the interests safeguarded by Article 8:

"[W]hat has to be determined is whether, having regard to the particular circumstances of the case and notably the serious nature of the decisions to be taken, the parents have been involved in the decision-making process, seen as a whole, to a degree sufficient to provide them with the requisite protection of their interests. If they have not, there will have been a failure to respect their family life and the interference resulting from the decision will not be capable of being regarded as 'necessary' within the meaning of Article 8." (see the W. v. the United Kingdom judgment of 8 July

1987, Series A no. 121-A, pp. 28-29, §§ 62 and 64).

120. It is essential that a parent be placed in a position where he or she may obtain access to information which is relied on by the authorities in taking measures of protective care or in taking decisions relevant to the care and custody of a child. Otherwise the parent will be unable to participate effectively in the decision-making process or put forward in a fair or adequate

manner those matters militating in favour of his or her ability to provide the child with proper care and protection (see the McMichael v. the United Kingdom judgment of 24 February 1995, Series A no. 307-B, p. 57, § 92, where the authorities did not disclose to the applicant parents reports relating to their child, and T.P. and K. M. v. the United Kingdom, no. 28945/95, [GC] ECHR 2001-

V, where the applicant mother was not afforded an early opportunity to view a video of an interview of her daughter, crucial to the assessment of abuse in the case; also Buchberger v. Austria, no. 328

99/96,judgment of 20 December 2001).

124. The applicants have argued that these measures were not necessary for S.'s protection and were disproportionate, pointing inter alia to P.'s weakened state, the draconian step for both mother and baby of removal so soon after birth and the possibility that S. could have remained in the

hospital with her mother under supervision. They have also criticised the decision-making process before the birth, alleging that they were not properly involved or informed and that it should have been possible to take the matter before a court for a fair examination of the issues before the birth.

131. It has nonetheless given consideration as to the manner of implementation of the order, namely, the steps taken under the authority of the order. As stated above (paragraph 116), the removal of a baby from its mother at birth requires exceptional justification. It is a step which is

traumatic for the mother and places her own physical and mental health under a strain, and it deprives the new- born baby of close contact with its birth mother and, as pointed out by the applicants, of the advantages of breast -feeding. The removal also deprived the father, C., of being close to his daughter after the birth.

133. The Court concludes that the draconian step of removing S. from her mother shortly after birth was not supported by relevant and sufficient reasons and that it cannot be regarded as having been necessary in a democratic society for the purpose of safeguarding S. There has therefore

been, in that respect, a breach of the applicant parents' rights under Article 8 of the Convention.

The Mother asserts that the taking of her baby at 23 hours old and the severity of the measures applied for and intended are not proportional and breach her family's Human Rights under Article 8.

1.7 Although the UK courts are a different jurisdiction, decisions in those Courts have been referred to in the Irish jurisdiction and the principles followed. Hence I make reference to the following and hope his Honour is of a similar mind:

<u>Re K D [1998] 1 AC p.812</u> letter B Lord Templeman stated; *'The best person to bring up a child is the natural parent. It matters not whether the parent is wise or foolish, rich or poor, educated or illiterate, provided the child's moral and physical health are not endangered. Public authorities cannot improve on nature.'*

Hedley J in <u>Re L (Threshold Conditions) [2007] 1 FLR 2050</u>:

"Many parents are hypochondriacs, many parents are criminals or benefit cheats, many parents discriminate against ethnic or sexual minorities, many parents support vile political

parties or belong to unusual or militant religions. All of these follies are visited upon their children, who may well adopt or 'model' them in their own lives but those children could not be removed for those reasons."

Having never harmed any child or even the victim of such an allegation, how can Tusla-Child and Family Agency determine that they have met any threshold or criteria for the action of removing the applicant's child? She suggests that support not proceedings would and should have been the most effective use of Tusla-Child and Family Agency's time and money in the case of her child.

2. A further breach of the Mother's and her child's Human Rights has been perpetrated through the limited contact afforded to her with her new born child and the denial of a proper breast feeding regime, which is contrary to the best advice given by the HSE and World Health Organisation that *breast is best.*

*In the matter of unborn baby M; R (on the application of X and another) v Gloucestershire County Council.

http://www.bailii.org/ew/cases/EWHC/Admin/2003/850.html

Citation: BLD 160403280; [2003] EWHC 850 (Admin). Hearing Date: 15 April 2003 Court: Administrative Court. Judge: Munby J.

Abstract.

"Per curiam. If the state, in the guise of a local authority, seeks to remove a baby from his parents at a time when its case against the parents has not yet even been established, then the very least the state can do is to make generous arrangements for contact, those arrangements being driven by the needs of the family and not stunted by lack of resources. Typically, if this is what the parents want, one will be looking to contact most days of the week and for lengthy periods. Local authorities also had to be sensitive to the wishes of a mother who wants to breast-feed, and should make suitable arrangements to enable her to do so, and not merely to bottle-feed expressed breast milk. Nothing less would meet the imperative demands of the European Convention on Human Rights..."

She wishes to exercise those Human Rights on behalf of her child and breast feed. It is not simply a case of breast milk is best, as clearly the message put forward by the HSE, but the bond between mother and baby is one furthered by breast

683

feeding. Indeed to deny the right to breast feed could be classed as an abuse of the child, as important antibodies and protections are afforded by breast feeding. The rights of the baby being paramount, "Who is this baby supposed to bond with?" Babies can "fail to thrive" and feel rejected, this is not an object but a human being and by removing him and keeping him from his Mother, could have a detrimental effect on him.

2.1 Relevant case law:

KEEGAN v. IRELAND - *16969/90 [1994] ECHR 18 (26 May 1994) paragraph 50.*

According to the principles set out by the Court in its case-law, where the existence of a family tie with a child has been established, the State must act in a manner calculated to enable that tie to be developed and legal safeguards must be created that render possible as from the moment of birth the child's integration in his family (see, mutatis mutandis, the Marckx v. Belgium judgment of 13 June 1979, Series A no. 31, p. 15, para. 31, and the above-mentioned Johnston and Others judgment, p. 29, para. 72). In this context reference may be made to the principle laid down in Article 7 of the United Nations Convention on the Rights of the Child of 20 November

1989 that a child has, as far as possible, the right to be cared for by his or her parents. It is, moreover, appropriate to recall that the mutual enjoyment by parent and child of each other's company constitutes a fundamental element of family life even when the relationship between the parents has broken down (see, inter alia, the Eriksson v. Sweden judgment of 22 June 1989, Series A no. 156, p. 24, para. 58).

Section 13 removal and orders only allowed if danger is actually established.

This danger was patently not there, there was no reason why mother and baby could not have been kept together in the hospital in those crucial first days.

HAASE v. GERMANY - 11057/02 [2004] ECHR 142 (8 April 2004) at paragraph 99 The Court observes moreover that, before public authorities have recourse to emergency measures in such delicate issues as care orders, the imminent danger should be actually established. It is true that in obvious cases of danger no involvement of the parents is called for. However, if it is still possible to hear the parents of the children and to discuss with them the necessity of the measure, there should be no room for an emergency action, in particular when, like in the present case, the danger had already existed for a long period.

There was therefore no urgency as to justify the District Court's interim injunction. Section 12 removal only in extreme cases North Western Health Board v. W. (H.) [2001] IESC 90 (8th November, 2001) at paragraph 230. It would be impossible and undesirable to seek to define in one neat rule or formula all the circumstances in which the State might intervene in the interests of the child against the express wishes of the parent. It seems however to me that there must be some immediate and fundamental threat to the capacity of the child to continue to function as a human person, physically morally or socially, deriving from an exceptional dereliction of duty on the part of parents to justify such an intervention. And if application is made for an Emergency – or Interim Care Order: The parents must be served with notice of the hearing (notwithstanding the ex parte allowance) and served with evidence in summary: X and Y, R (on the application of) v Gloucestershire County Council [2003] EWHC 850 (Admin) (15 April 2003) paragraph 44 (iii) Save in wholly exceptional cases parents must be given adequate prior notice of the date, time and place of any application by a local authority for either an emergency protection order or an interim care order. They must also be given proper notice of the evidence the local authority is relying upon. About quality of evidence: X and Y, R (on the application of) v Gloucestershire County Council [2003] EWHC 850 (Admin) (15 April 2003) paragraph 44 (ii) At the risk of unnecessary repetition I emphasise that the removal of a child from his mother at or shortly after birth is a draconian and extremely harsh measure which demands "extraordinarily compelling" justification.

The fullest possible information must be given to the court. The evidence in support of the application for such an order must be full, detailed, precise and compelling.

The sources of hearsay evidence must be identified. Expressions of opinion must be supported by detailed evidence and properly articulated reasoning.

And if an Emergency-or Interim Care Order is granted Access and breast-feeding: X and Y, R (on the application of) v Gloucestershire County Council [2003] EWHC 850 (Admin) (15 April 2003) paragraph 44 (iv) If a baby is to be removed from his mother one would normally expect arrangements to be made by the local authority to facilitate contact on a regular and generous basis. It is a dreadful thing to take a baby away from his mother: dreadful for mother, dreadful for father and dreadful for the baby. If the state, in the guise of a local authority, seeks to intervene so drastically in a family's life–and at a time when, ex hypothesi, its case against the parents has not yet even been established–then the very least the state can do is to make generous arrangements for contact. And those arrangements must be driven by the needs of the family, not stunted by lack of resources.

Typically, if this is what the parents want, one will be looking to contact most days of the week and for lengthy periods. And local authorities must be sensitive to the wishes of a mother who wants to breast-feed and must make suitable arrangements to enable her to do so–and when I say breast-feed I mean just that, I do not mean merely bottle-feeding expressed breast milk. Nothing less will meet the imperative demands of the Convention. Contact two or three times a week for a couple of hours a time is simply not enough if parents reasonably want more.

*Work towards reunification compulsory **JOHANSEN v. NORWAY** - 17383/90 [1996] ECHR 31 (7 August 1996) at paragraph 78 and more. The Court considers that taking a child into care should normally be regarded as a temporary measure to be discontinued as soon as circumstances permit and that any measures of implementation of temporary care should be consistent with the ultimate aim of reuniting the natural parent and the child*

*Proportionality:- The actions of the social worker should be proportional to the alleged threat to the child. **de Freitas v. The Permanent Secretary of Ministry of Agriculture, Fisheries, Lands and Housing and Others (Antigua and Barbuda) [1998] UKPC 30 (30th June, 1998)** para 25: "whether: (i) the legislative objective is sufficiently important to justify limiting a fundamental right; (ii) the measures designed to meet the legislative objective are rationally connected to it; and (iii) the means used to impair the right or freedom are no more than is necessary to accomplish the objective." ... The matter must be investigated adhering to relative guidelines, (today "Children First"). Case law: (although referenced to previous guidelines, now replaced by "Children First" in a sexual abuse allegation, it is still* *applicable in all cases) G.H. v A.F., District Court 11, Dolphin House, 18 October 1995, Unpublished, Judge William Early, Last paragraph: The contents of these publications should be known and adhered to by all persons involved in the investigation and assessment of cases of child sexual abuse. Efforts must be made to prevent taking the child unnecessary into care – Regular contact – Decision making -* **Moser v Austria - 12643/02 [2010] ECHR 381** *(4 March 2010) paragraph 73. Having regard to the authorities' failure to examine all possible alternatives to transferring custody of the second applicant to the Youth Welfare Office, their failure to ensure regular contacts between the applicants following their separation and the first applicant's insufficient involvement in the decision making process, the Court considers that although the reasons relied on by the domestic courts were relevant, they were not sufficient to justify such a serious interference with the applicants' family life.*

Notwithstanding the domestic authorities' margin of appreciation, the interference was therefore not proportionate to the legitimate aims pursued. The mutual enjoyment by parent and child of each other's company constitutes a fundamental element of family life KEEGAN v. IRELAND -

690

16969/90 [1994] ECHR 18 (26 May 1994) paragraph 50. According to the principles set out by the Court in its case-law, where the existence of a family tie with a child has been established, the State must act in a manner calculated to enable that tie to be developed and legal safeguards must be created that render possible as from the moment of birth the child's integration in his family (see, mutatis mutandis, the Marckx v. Belgium judgment of 13 June 1979, Series A no. 31, p. 15, para. 31, and the above-mentioned Johnston and Others judgment, p. 29, para. 72).

In this context reference may be made to the principle laid down in Article 7 of the United Nations Convention on the Rights of the Child of 20 November 1989 that a child has, as far as possible, the right to be cared for by his or her parents. It is, moreover, appropriate to recall that the mutual enjoyment by parent and child of each other's company constitutes a fundamental element of family life even when the relationship between the parents has broken down (see, inter alia, the Eriksson v. Sweden judgment of 22 June 1989, Series A no. 156, p. 24, para. 58). Section 12 or other removal and orders only allowed if danger is actually established HAASE v. GERMANY - 11057/02 [2004] ECHR 142 (8 April 2004) at paragraph 99

*Work towards reunification compulsory JOHANSEN v.
NORWAY - 17383/90 [1996] ECHR 31 (7 August 1996) at
paragraph 78 and more. The Court considers that taking a
child into care should normally be regarded as a temporary
measure to be discontinued as soon as circumstances permit
and that any measures of implementation of temporary care
should be consistent with the ultimate aim of reuniting the
natural parent and the child (see, in particular, the above-
mentioned Olsson (no. 1) judgment, p. 36, para. 81).
HOKKANEN v. FINLAND - 19823/92 [1994] ECHR 32 (23
September 1994) 61. From the foregoing it cannot be said
that, bearing in mind the interests involved, the competent
authorities, prior to the Court of Appeal's judgment of 21
October 1993, made reasonable efforts to facilitate reunion.
On the contrary, the inaction of the authorities placed the
burden on the applicant to have constant recourse to a
succession of time-consuming and ultimately ineffectual
remedies to enforce his rights. KOSMOPOULOU v. GREECE
- 60457/00 [2004] ECHR 58 (5 February 2004) 44.As to the
State's obligation to take positive measures, the Court has
repeatedly held that Article 8 includes a right for parents to*

have measures taken with a view to their being reunited with their children, and an obligation for the national authorities to take such measures. This applies not only to cases dealing with the compulsory taking of children into public care and the implementation of care measures, but also to cases where contact and residence disputes concerning children arise between parents and/or other members of the children's family (Hokkanen v. Finland, judgment of 23 September 1994, Series A no. 299, p. 20, § 55). Regarding fair hearings: Parent had to be informed of evidence during "Child Protection Conferences" and other "Tribunals" and should have been allowed to answer Mantovanelli v France (1997) 24 EHRR 370 paragraph 32 ".. each party must in principle have the opportunity not only to make known any evidence needed for his claims to succeed, but also to have knowledge of and comment on all evidence adduced or observations filed with a view to influencing the court's decision (see, mutatis mutandis, the Lobo Machado v. Portugal and Vermeulen v. Belgium judgments of 20 February 1996, Reports of Judgments and Decisions 1996-I pp. 206-07, para. 31, and p. 234, para. 33, respectively, and the Nideröst-Huber v. Switzerland judgment of 18 February 1997, Reports 1997-I, p. 108, para. 24).

In this connection, the Court makes it clear at the outset that, just like observance of the other procedural safeguards enshrined in Article 6 para. 1 (art. 6-1), compliance with the adversarial principle relates to proceedings in a "tribunal"; no general, abstract principle may therefore be inferred from this provision (art. 6-1) that, where an expert has been appointed by a court, the parties must in all instances be able to attend the interviews held by him or to be shown the documents he has taken into account. What is essential is that the parties should be able to participate properly in the proceedings before the "tribunal" (see, mutatis mutandis, the Kerojärvi v. Finland judgment of 19 July 1995, Series A no. 322, p. 16, para. 42 in fine)." The court should construe the pleadings liberally and expansively, affording the plaintiffs all opportunity in obtaining substance of justice, over technicality US case law: Maty v. Grasselli Chemical Co., 303 U.S. 197 (1938); Picking v. Pennsylvania Railroad Co., 151 F.2d 240 (3rd Cir. 1945); Jenkins v. McKeithen, 395 U.S. 411, 421 (1959); Haines v. Kerner, 404 U.S. 519, 520-21, 92 S.Ct. 594, 596, 30 L.Ed.2d 652 (1972); Cruz v. Beto, 405 U.S. 319, 322, 92 S.Ct. 1079, 1081, 31 L.Ed.2d 263 (1972); Puckett v. Cox, 456 F. 2d 233 (6th Cir. 1972); and, etc., etc., practically ad infinitum. Extracts not available – just the reference mentioned Circumstances must be confirmed and alternatives to taking in care must be exhausted impact on parents and children must be assessed P, C and S v United Kingdom (2002) 35 EHRR 31, [2002] 2 FLR 631 para 116 "116. The margin of appreciation so to be accorded to the competent national authorities will vary in the light of the nature of the issues and the seriousness of the interests at stake. While the authorities enjoy a wide margin of appreciation in assessing the necessity of taking a child into care, in particular where an emergency situation arises, the Court must still be satisfied in the circumstances of the case that there existed circumstances justifying the removal of the child, and it is for the respondent State to establish that a careful assessment of the impact of the proposed care measure on the parents and the child, as well as of the possible alternatives to taking the child into public care, was carried out prior to implementation of a care measure (see K and T v Finland [2001] ECHR 25702/94 at para 166; Kutzner v Germany [2002] ECHR 46544/99 at para 67).

Furthermore, the taking of a new-born baby into public care at the moment of its birth is an extremely harsh measure. There must be extraordinarily compelling reasons before a baby can be physically removed from its mother, against her will, immediately after birth as a consequence of a procedure in which neither she nor her partner has been involved (K and T v Finland [2001] ECHR 25702/94 at para 168)." Judge must consider human rights of children and the family Proportionality other options.

2.2 What is clear from the above case law is that the applicant has suffered contrary to the established European and domestic precedents, has been subject to arbitrary decisions by the Tusla - Child and Family Agency who have failed to follow procedure, protocol, and the law, have breached the mother's and the child's human rights and acted ***ultra vires*** in their actions at obtaining an Emergency Care Order and Interim Care Order, with the threat of returning the child to a country it has never set foot in contrary to European jurisprudence, the Irish Constitution, the Human Rights Convention of the European Union, the European Charter of Fundamental Rights and contrary to the basis of the Child care Act 1991 and the Children First: National Guideline 2011.

2.3 In the best interests of the child and pursuant as to her rights as a Mother she would respectfully ask why the District

Court Judge in the ICO hearing did not consider the alternative order of a Supervision Order. This would have restored the child to her and allowed her to prove to the Social Workers that she is a loving, caring and able parent. It would have allowed time for assessments, support and for the child to be where he belongs with his family.

2.4 Having never harmed her child, or any child, and only ever acted in his best interests she avers that removing xxxx is a punishment without a crime–Article 7 of the European Convention of Human Rights. "Concern" is not evidence, even to the standard of Balance of Probabilities. She has been threatened by the UK social workers with non consensual adoption of her child without any assessments or her views, wishes or feelings taken into account. She strongly suggests that this attitude is being continued by the local social services in Ireland and as a result abusing the rights of both her child and the applicant parent.

2.5 Key issues that have been cited are seriously misrepresented and of great concern is that the Threshold information that xxxx Metropolitan Borough Council Children's Services and by default Tusla are relying upon is un-evidenced and consists of social workers opinions and conjectures-not facts. The President of the Family Division (UK)–Judge Munby was highly critical of a local authority's lack of evidential clarity when seeking to establish their case, pursuant to s31 of the Children Act 1989. RE A (2015).

The President provided guidance in three distinct areas:

i. Prove the Assertion!

The President first deals with a perceived failure of local authorities to properly establish the matters upon which they rely (emphasis added):

"The local authority, if its case is challenged on some factual point, must adduce proper evidence to establish what it seeks to prove. Much material to be found in local authority case records or social work chronologies is hearsay, often second- or third-hand hearsay. Hearsay evidence is, of course, admissible in family proceedings. But, and as the present case so vividly demonstrates, a local authority which is unwilling or unable to produce the witnesses who can speak of such matters first-hand, may find itself in great, or indeed insuperable, difficulties if a parent not merely puts the matter in issue but goes into the witness-box to deny it.

It is a common feature of care cases that a local authority asserts that a parent does not admit, recognise or acknowledge something or does not recognise or acknowledge the local authority's concern about something. If the 'thing' is put in issue, the local authority must both prove the 'thing' and establish that it has the significance attributed to it by the local authority." (Para 9).

ii. Plead Threshold Properly!

The second matter the President takes issue with is the pleading of the threshold findings sought (emphasis added):

"*...The schedule of findings in the present case contains, as we shall see, allegations in relation to the father that "he appears to have" lied or colluded, that various people have "stated" or "reported" things, and that "there is an allegation". With all respect to counsel, this form of allegation, which one sees far too often in such documents, is wrong and should never be used.* **It confuses the crucial distinction, once upon a time, though no longer, spelt out in the rules of pleading and well understood, between an assertion of fact and the evidence needed to prove the assertion. What do the words "he appears to have lied" or "X reports that he did Y" mean? More important, where** does it take one? **The relevant allegation is not that "he appears to have lied" or "X reports"; the relevant allegation, if there is evidence to support it, is surely that "he lied" or "he did Y".** *(Para 10)*

The second fundamentally important point is **the need to link the facts relied upon by the local authority with its case on threshold,** *the need to demonstrate why, as the local authority asserts, facts A + B + C justify the conclusion that the child has suffered, or is at risk of suffering, significant harm of types X, Y or Z...* **the linkage may be very much less obvious where the allegation is only that the child is at risk of suffering emotional harm or, as in the present case, at risk of suffering neglect.** *"* (Para 12).

iii. Are Local Authorities/Courts Setting the Bar Too High?

Lastly, the President restates and approves various authorities on the standard of care expected of parents. The President asserts that it is "vital always to bear in mind in these cases" and to recognise the "diverse standards of parenting" that must be tolerated by society. The President cites Baroness Hale in Re B at para 15 (emphasis added):

"We are all frail human beings, with our fair share of unattractive character traits, which sometimes manifest themselves in bad behaviours which may be copied by our children. **But the State does not and cannot take away the children of all the people who commit crimes, who abuse alcohol or drugs, who suffer from physical or mental illnesses or disabilities, or who espouse antisocial political or religious beliefs."**

The President also agreed with the somewhat controversial remarks of His Honour Judge Jack in *North East Lincolnshire Council v G & L* [2014] EWCC B77 (Fam) (emphasis added):

"...The reality is that in this country there must be tens of thousands of children who are cared for in homes where there is a degree of domestic violence (now very widely defined) and where parents on occasion drink more than they should, I am not condoning that for a moment, but the courts are not in the business of social engineering. The courts are not in the business of providing children with perfect homes. **If we took into care and placed for adoption every child whose parents had had a domestic spat and every child whose parents on occasion had drunk too much then the care system would be overwhelmed and there would not be**

enough adoptive parents. *So we have to have a degree of realism about prospective carers who come before the courts."*

It can clearly be seen that the documents produced to the District Court on behalf of xxxx Children's Services do not meet the President's ruling and procedural interpretation of the statute, hence the granting of an Interim Care Order would not be sanctioned by a UK court and by default it should not be relied upon in the Irish Courts to grant any draconian order separating a baby from his parents.

2.6   Further, the threatened attempt to 'return' an Irish born child- made by both UK and Irish social services as well as xxxx District Court by its consideration of 'jurisdiction' is contrary to established case law, viz: **ZA & Anor v NA [2012] EWCA Civ 1396 (26 October 2012)**

Lord Justice Rimer:

- *I have had the advantage of reading in draft the judgments of Thorpe and Patten LJJ. I respectfully agree with them, for the reasons they give, that there is no question of the three older children having ceased to be habitually resident in England and Wales at the time of the order of Parker J or of the earlier order of Peter Jackson J.*

- *As regards the youngest child, H, the position is different. He was born in Pakistan and has never set foot in England and Wales. In respectful disagreement with Thorpe LJ, I agree with Patten LJ, for the reasons he gives, that it follows that H cannot be said to have been habitually resident in England and Wales at the date of either order. The decisions of this court in Re M (Abduction: Habitual Residence) [1996] 1 FLR 887 and Al Habtoor v. Fotheringham [2001] 1 FLR 951 show that the question of whether a person is habitually resident in a particular country is one of fact. They further show that an essential ingredient in the factual mix justifying an affirmative answer is that the person was at some point resident in that country; and that it is not possible to become so resident save by being physically present there. If there has been no residence there, there can be no habitual residence there.*

Habitual residence in a particular country is not, therefore, a status in the nature of a legal concept that can, in the case of a child who has never resided there, be attributed to him at birth merely by virtue of his association with a parent who is habitually resident there. I consider, with respect, that it follows that the decision of Charles J in B v. H (Habitual Residence: Wardship) [2002] 1 FLR 388 was, as regards child H, wrong. Charles J found that H was habitually resident in England and Wales, but the child had never been there and so the essential factual ingredient of physical presence there was missing.

- *The judge in the present case should, I consider, also have held that H was not habitually resident in England and Wales. The guidance as to 'habitual residence' in the decisions of the Court of Justice to which Patten LJ refers, if applicable to the present case, neither requires nor justifies a different conclusion.*

- *I agree with Patten LJ that the appeal against the judge's order should be allowed to the extent that he indicates in his judgment.*

Lord Justice Patten:

- *As Thorpe LJ has explained, the facts of this case are*

both disquieting and not unfamiliar. But, as Parker J herself recognised, the court's jurisdiction to make return orders in respect of these children in wardship proceedings depends upon their being habitually resident in this jurisdiction. Although the courts at every level have emphasised that habitual residence is a question of fact to be determined in the light of all relevant circumstances and is not as such a legal construct as in the law of domicile, there are necessarily limits to what is capable of amounting to residence. In this case, that question arises in an acute form in relation to the youngest child (H) who was born in Pakistan and has never left that country. The judge (in reliance on the decision of Charles J in B. v H. (Habitual Residence: Wardship) [2002] 1 FLR 388) has held that H acquired at birth habitual residence in England and that the habitual residence of the three older children (which it is common ground was in England prior to their arrival in Pakistan) could not have been and was not changed by their retention in that country contrary to the wishes of their mother.

- *The grounds of appeal challenge the judge's findings in respect of all the children and also criticise the judge for failing to take account of or to apply the UK-Pakistan Judicial Protocol on Children Matters 2003 ("the Pakistan Protocol") and the principles of comity. It is said that the judge wrongly presumed that the English court should determine jurisdiction notwithstanding that the children are physically within the jurisdiction of the Pakistan court; are already subject there to an order for custody in favour of the father obtained in proceedings which pre-date the mother's English wardship application; and are the subject of an on-going dispute about jurisdiction based on habitual residence. But in a refinement of these criticisms not advanced before the judge, Mr Setright QC also submits that Parker J failed properly to apply the provisions of s.2 of the Family Law Act 1986 by not determining whether the court had jurisdiction to entertain the mother's application under article 8 of Council Regulation (EC) No. 2201/2003 ("Brussels II Revised"). He submits that this Regulation is the first stop jurisdictional framework for all cases involving parental*

706

responsibility in England and Wales regardless of whether the other countries concerned are themselves subject to the Regulation. For this he relies on the decision of the Supreme Court in Re I (A Child) (Contact Application: Jurisdiction) [2010] 1 AC 319. The practical effect of this argument (if correct) is that the judge should have considered the question of habitual residence by reference to the jurisprudence of the ECJ as recently expounded in the cases of Re A (Area of Freedom, Security and Justice) [2009] 2 FLR 1 and Mercredi v Chaffe [2011] 1 FLR 1293.

- *Had the judge followed this course she would, it is submitted, have reached the conclusion that a child must be physically present in a particular country before he or she can become habitually resident there. This would mean that H is not habitually resident in England and Wales and that the judge was wrong to base her decision to the contrary on the decision of Charles J in B. v H. But the appellants also contend that even if the question of habitual residence falls to be determined by reference to the English authorities decided prior to the application of Brussels II Revised, the same conclusion should have been reached. We are therefore invited to hold that B. v H. was wrongly decided.*

- *If the right view is that not only H but also the three older children were no longer habitually resident in England and Wales when the mother made her application for a return order then the judge's order cannot stand. But even if she was only wrong about H, the question is raised as to whether the English court should decline jurisdiction on forum conveniens grounds given that the only courts who can exercise jurisdiction over all four children are those in Pakistan where the children are physically present even if not habitually resident. Again the judge was not asked to consider this question and, in the light of her findings on habitual residence, it did not arise.*

Habitual residence

- *Habitual residence rather than domicile is now the internationally accepted test for determining jurisdiction in family cases. In relation to children, it was adopted as the jurisdictional test in the 1980*

Hague Abduction Convention and serves the same purpose in matrimonial and parental responsibility proceedings under Brussels II Revised. In domestic law it features in the Matrimonial and Family Proceedings Act 1984; the Child Abduction and Custody Act 1985; and the Family Law Act 1986. This is not, of course, an exhaustive list.

- *As a consequence, English courts have had since the 1980's to consider what constitutes habitual residence and the correct approach to its determination. As part of this process a number of boundaries have been defined:*

(1) habitual residence is primarily a question of fact to be determined by reference to all the relevant circumstances. It is not to be treated as a term of art nor is it a legal concept in the sense of a set of pre-determined rules designed to produce a particular legal result in given circumstances: see J (A Minor) (Abduction: Custody Rights) [1990] 2 AC 562;

(2) consistently with this, a child does not automatically take the habitual residence of its parents or custodial parent and there is no mandatory coincidence between them: see Re M

*(Abduction: Habitual Residence) [1996] 1 FLR 887 at p. 891;
Al Habtoor v Fotheringham [2001] 1 FLR 951. For the same
reason, it is also possible for a person (child or adult) to have
no place of habitual residence at any given point in time.
Although justifiable concern has been expressed (particularly
in the context of international abduction) about a child having
no habitual residence in a case where jurisdiction to make
protective orders is in general based upon that condition, the
law has yet to reach the stage where every child is deemed to
be habitually resident somewhere (see Nessa v Chief
Adjudication Officer [1999[1 WLR 1937 at p. 1942) and the
contrary has not been argued on this appeal;*

*(3) the acquisition of habitual residence in any country
requires the adult or child in question to be physically present
there. In Re M (supra) (where the wardship and return order
had been made in respect of a child who remained in India)
Sir John Balcombe (at p. 895) said:*

> *"Before a person, whether a child or
> an adult, can be said to be habitually
> resident in a country, it is clear that
> he must be resident in that country.
> Of course, residence does not*

necessarily require physical presence at all times. Temporary absence on holiday, or for educational purposes (as in Re A) will not bring to an end habitual residence. But here the Judge found as a fact, and on ample evidence, that K became habitually resident in India. He has never to this day come back to England. As a matter of fact, he has not been resident in England since he went to India in February 1994. Bracewell, J held that the mother's change of mind both brought to an end K's habitual residence in India and gave him an habitual resident in England.

I have the gravest doubts whether the first proposition is correct. Clearly, the mother's change of mind could not alter the fact that he was, and is, physically resident in India. Whether her change of mind could alone alter the 'habitual' nature of that residence I very much doubt, but in any event it is not necessary finally to decide that point on this appeal, since the one thing about which I am quite clear is that the child's residence in India could not become a residence in England and Wales without his ever having returned to this country. As I said before, the idea that a child's residence can be changed without his ever leaving the country where he is resident is to abandon the factual basis of "habitual residence" and to clothe it with some metaphysical or abstract basis more appropriate to a legal concept such as domicil."

In his judgment Millett LJ said that:

"Three principles must be borne in mind:–

(1) The question whether a person is or is not habitually resident in a particular country is a question of fact; Re J (a Minor) (Abduction: Custody Rights) [1990] 2 AC 562, 578, sub nom C v S (A Minor) (Abduction) [1990] 2 FLR 442, 454 per Lord Brandon. The concept of habitual residence is not an artificial legal construct.

(2) While it is not necessary for a person to remain continuously present in a particular country in order for him to retain residence there, it is not possible for a person to acquire residence in one country while remaining throughout physically present in another.

(3) Where both parents have joint parental responsibility, neither of them can unilaterally change the habitual residence of the child by

> *removing the child wrongfully and in breach of the other party's rights; Re J at 572 and 449 respectively per Lord Donaldson, MR."*
>
> *(4) In Al Habtoor (at p. 966) Thorpe LJ affirmed the authority of these passages and the point is not open for argument in this court.*

Hence not only would it be wrong to attribute habitual residence of the child to the jurisdiction of the UK, but it would not be in his 'best interests' to 'return' a child to a place where he has never been and where he faces the strong possibility of non-consensual (or forced) adoption, a truly draconian measure, but also face a life where those subjected to the care system face poorer life outcomes than those who have not been subject to care. Just a couple of simple outcomes should suffice to demonstrate:

13% of children leave care with five good GCSE's compared with 58% of others,

7% of under 18's in care have a criminal conviction against 2% of all under 18's and

80% of care leavers are unemployed after 2 years.

A system that has such poor outcomes can never be justified in the child's best interests.

2.8 The Mother avers that she left the UK freely, legally and exercised her rights under Article 45 of Charter of Fundamental European Rights. There were no court orders, proceedings or child protection measures in place in the UK. Her child was born in Ireland, it is by law entitled to Irish citizenship, which she claims for him, and all the attendant protections of the Constitution. A foetus cannot be abducted, neither can an Irish born child said to be habitually resident in a country it has never been to, and equally it is not conferred that habitual residency by virtue of its parents habitual residence (RE F (Abduction: Unborn Child) [2006] EWHC (Fam) UK] (see attached case law Exhibit 4). Therefore neither the UK has a right to involvement in this case, make a Brussels II application, nor the District Judge the authority to make an Article 17 Declaration.

(g) **Applicant's address for service within the jurisdiction (if acting in person):**

xxxxxx

xxxxxx

xxxxxx

Dated this ....day of …....…..... 2016

(Signed)

Applicant:

Sworn before me by the said

  on the   day of   20

in the city/county of

before me a Commissioner for Oaths /

Practicing Solicitor and the deponent

  is personally known to me / is identified to

me by   who personally known to me /

whose identity has been established by

reference to a relevant document

containing a photograph

_____

Commissioner for Oaths/Practising Solicitor

No. 14

THE HIGH COURT

JUDICIAL REVIEW BETWEEN

 XXXXXX [APPLICANT]

AND

TUSLA - CHILD AND FAMILY AGENCY

XXXXX DISTRICT COURT [RESPONDENTS]

I, [Name], applicant in these proceedings, make oath and say as follows:

(a) I have read this statement;

(b) so much of this statement as relates to my own acts and deeds is true, and so much of it as   relates to the acts and deeds of any and every other person I believe to be true.

Statement:

1. I left the United Kingdom lawfully and freely, exercising my Article 45 right under the Charter of Fundamental European Rights of the European Union.

2. There were no proceedings in any court, no pre-birth assessments, no child protection plans nor any lawful reason why I should not choose to leave the UK and establish a life in the Republic of Ireland. I chose to leave and exercise my fundamental rights to escape the people and situations that had caused me issues in the past and to begin a new life. This is a right that I lawfully exercised. XXXX Metropolitan Council have no claim against my Irish born child other than to pass the case over to Ireland as is the procedure under the 'Working Together' guidelines (UK).

2. It is now clear that XXXX Metropolitan Council's Children's Services sent the untrue, inaccurate and defamatory information to XXXX Child and Family Agency. Who then, without due diligence, corroboration or independent assessment and contrary to the Child Care Act 1991 and the Children First National guidance held a strategy meeting on xx/xx/20xx, whereupon they decided to take the information provided by XXXX Metropolitan Council as prima facie and apply for an ex-parte Emergency Care Order. The CFA did not: engage with me beyond a meeting to tell me they intended to remove my child at birth (which they did at 23 hours old), seek my views, present the information provided to them with transparency or integrity or respond to my attempts

719

at contesting the information provided to them.

3. Without any due diligence and procedural adhesion a decision was taken by a Team Leader that XXX XXX should be taken at birth into care. XXXX social workers have no evidence, proof or verification of matters passed to them by XXXX Metropolitan Council as they have failed in their duty to undertake their own assessments or cooperation in working with me. XXX XXX was removed from our care on xx-xx-20xx and an Interim Care Order granted xx-xx-20xx.

4. I contest that the actions taken by XXXX Social Workers on behalf of Tusla-Child and Family Agency were not proportional either under the constitution nor relevant statutes/guidance. The measure taken was draconian in the extreme, without threshold and the Social Workers had failed to professionally evaluate all other options available, such as support for the family, a supervision order or independent evaluations.

5. Since taking XXX XXX - Social Workers have limited my contact with her to two times a week for one and a half hours and denied my child and my rights to bond and breast feed her, contrary to well established European and Irish Court rulings. This I contest is a major breach of XXX XXX and my own

Human Rights. Indeed I would go further and suggest that there is a deliberate policy to destroy the bond between mother and child.

6. Social Workers are failing in their professional requirements and I believe will continue to do so in order to remove my child permanently from my care, hence my decision to apply for leave for a Judicial Review.

7. Further, XXXX Child & Family Agency are clearly conspiring with XXXX Metropolitan Council's Children's Services to 'return' my child to a jurisdiction where she has never set foot, contrary to both UK law and international law. A Brussels II application has been threatened by the Social Worker, yet there is no legal basis for this. XXX XXX is an Irish born baby that cannot be attributed with any UK nationality or habitual residence, even by virtue of the nationality or previous habitual residence of his parents. [RE F (ABDUCTION: UNBORN CHILD)[2006] EWHC 2199 (Fam) UK].

8. I believe that there was therefore no urgency as to justify Section 13 or 18 (1) removal : only in extreme cases : *North Western Health Board v. W. (H.) [2001] IESC 90 (8th November, 2001) at paragraph 230. There was no immediate*

and fundamental threat to the capacity of the child to continue to function as a human person, physically morally or socially, deriving from an exceptional dereliction of duty on the part of parents to justify such an intervention. If application is made for an Emergency – or Interim Care Order: The parents must be served with notice of the hearing (notwithstanding the ex parte allowance) <u>and served with evidence in summary:</u> X and Y, R (on the application of) v Gloucestershire County Council [2003] EWHC 850 (Admin) (15 April 2003) paragraph 44 (iii) Save in wholly exceptional cases parents must be given adequate prior notice of the date, time and place of any application by a local authority for either an emergency protection order or an interim care order. They must also be given proper notice of the evidence the local authority is relying upon. This was not done.

9. Article 7 of the United Nations Convention on the Rights of the Child of 20 November 1989 that a child has, as far as possible, the right to be cared for by his or her parents. It is, moreover, appropriate to recall that the mutual enjoyment by parent and child of each other's company constitutes a fundamental element of family life even when the relationship between the parents has broken down (*see, inter alia, the Eriksson v. Sweden judgment of 22 June 1989, Series A no.*

722

156, p. 24, para. 58). Section 13 and18 removal and orders are only allowed if danger is actually established. I would strongly argue that upon Social Workers and Garda arriving to take the child that there was no basis for attributing any danger to the child from me or any other. I believe that the removal was an abuse of process and that the safety and security of the child could have been maintained in the hospital environment and that there was no basis to remove my child at 23 hours old.

10. I contest that the granting of an Interim Care Order without hearing from all parties is a gross violation of our Human Rights, not just Articles 5 and 6 but also Article 7 No Punishment Without Crime. I have committed no crimes, there is no actual evidence or proof that I have neglected, ill treated or assaulted my child in any way, yet the order is based upon this. At the hearing in the District Court on <u>XXX date</u> my sworn Affidavit was refused to be read by the judge and he relied entirely upon Tusla's submissions. I have not been able to defend the accusations against me, and now my child is suffering contrary to Article 40.3 which guarantees to protect the "personal rights of the citizen from unjust attack". I would contest that if my child can be taken under Irish law and jurisdiction, then she and I should be afforded the rights

conferred in the Constitution. The family's right to autonomy from State interference is established in strident and expansive terms in the constitutional text. Hence the constitutional rights afforded to the family have been breached in our case. We further submit that both, my parental and my child's rights under Article 8 have been violated.

12. As a litigant in person I respectfully request that where I may have erred in procedure or application that the court may grant guidance to help us ensure we meet the courts requirements to successfully be granted leave to apply for a Judicial Review.

Signed and sealed this _____ day of
_____ 20____

By: _____

Sworn before me by the said

on the   day of   20

in the city/county of

before me a Commissioner for Oaths /

Practicing Solicitor and the deponent

is personally known to me / is identified to

me by   who personally known to me /

whose identity has been established by

reference to a relevant document

containing a photograph

Commissioner for Oaths/Practising Solicitor

725

Appendix F: Template Letter before Claim, Defamation

Name

Address 1

Address 2

Address 3

[DATE]

By Post [and by Email]

Name of individual [Social Worker, Health Visitor etc]

Address1

Address 2

Address 3

Letter before claim under the pre-action protocol for defamation.

Our claim

Outline what your complaints are -

Material complained of:

Be specific listing everything you believe is defamatory, where it appears (i.e. social workers report, child protection conference minutes, etc) with dates.

The issue

These are the allegations which will be the subject of a

possible action.

Under the law of England and Wales, a defamatory statement is one which tends to lower the claimant in the estimation of right thinking members of society generally (*Sim v Stretch [1936] 2 All ER 1237*). The words are defamatory, identify or refer to the claimant and are published and spoken by you to third parties.

Legal proceedings

In order to protect our interests we are considering proceedings against you in the High Court. These proceedings would seek remedies including but not limited to the following:

substantial damages;

an injunction to restrain you from publishing the same or similar statements in the future; and costs.

Next steps

We are not against freedom of speech and recognise the value of fair comment. At this stage we have no desire to issue legal proceedings against you and we are keen to do all we can to avoid litigation where possible.

However, in accordance with the pre-action protocol for defamation, we will desist from issuing legal proceedings provided within 14 days of the date of this letter you agree to do the following:

- produce an apology and a declaration that the allegations referred to are false and defamatory and cause such apology and declaration to be published to all persons and organisations who have had an involvement with this case. (such apology to be approved by us prior to publication);

- provide details of recipients of advice or comments made of this nature, together with contact details for each recipient;

- make proposals for the payment to us of damages for the harm caused to our reputation; and

- undertake to actively ensure that no further defamation is perpetrated by yourself or anyone you have repeated these defamatory claims to.

If the above undertakings are not complied with by 4.00pm GMT on [DATE – 14 days from date of their receipt of your letter] we shall revert to taking steps towards the swift issue of proceedings without further notice.

We draw to your attention the terms of Section 2 of the Defamation Act 1996, under which you have the right to offer to make amends.

We await your response by return. In the meantime we reserve our rights, in particular the right to produce this letter to the Court when it comes to consider costs under CPR 44.3.

Yours faithfully

Appendix G: Useful Case Law.

This is by no means a definitive list, but these are examples of key cases that you should be aware of and look closely for references to other key judgments noted in them. Do not forget that a number of judgments are referred to and the key sections noted in the main text above. I have given examples of recent important cases, but there is no substitute for spending time on http://www.bailii.org/ which is an easy to navigate site containing published judgments. Equally, judgments from the Irish Republic can be found on bailii or at http://www.courts.ie/Judgments.nsf/FrmJudgmentsByCourtAll?OpenForm&l=en

European jurisprudence may be found at: http://www.echr.coe.int &

https://europa.eu/european-union/about-eu/institutions-bodies/court-justice_en

What you may find interesting is that you can use international judgments in your case especially where the country operates a common law jurisdiction.

In the matter of B (a Child) 2013 UKSC 33

Summary

Application of the criteria for making a care order under section 31 of the Children Act 1989 when the risk is of future psychological or emotional harm.

Key points:

74. A care order in a case such as this is a very extreme thing, a last resort, as it would be very likely to result in Amelia being adopted against the wishes of both her parents.

75.As already mentioned, it is clear that a judge cannot properly decide that a care order should be made in such circumstances, unless the order is proportionate bearing in mind the requirements of article 8.

76.It appears to me that, given that the Judge concluded that the section 31(2) threshold was crossed, he should only have made a care order if he had been satisfied that it was necessary to do so in order to protect the interests of the child. By "necessary", I mean, to use Lady Hale's phrase in para 198, "where nothing else will do". I consider that this conclusion is clear under the 1989 Act, interpreted in the absence of the Convention, but it is put beyond doubt by article 8. The conclusion is also consistent with UNCRC.

77. It seems to me to be inherent in section 1(1) that a care order should be a last resort, because the interests of a child would self-evidently require her relationship with her natural parents to be maintained unless no other course was possible in her interests. That is reinforced by the requirement in section 1 (3)(g) that the court must consider all options, which carries with it the clear implication that the most extreme option should only be adopted if others would not be in her interests. As to article 8, the Strasbourg court decisions cited by Lady Hale in paras 195-198 make it clear that such an order can only be made in "exceptional circumstances", and that it could only be justified by "overriding requirements pertaining to the child's welfare", or, putting the same point in slightly different words, "by the overriding necessity of the interests of the child". I consider that this is the same as the domestic test (as is evidenced by the remarks of Hale LJ in Re C and B [2001] 1 FLR 611, para 34 quoted by Lady Hale in para 198 above), but it is unnecessary to explore that point further.

78.The high threshold to be crossed before a court should make an adoption order against the natural parents' wishes is also clear from UNCRC. Thus, Hodgkin and Newell, Implementation Handbook for the Convention on the Rights of the Child, Unicef, 3rd ed (2007), p 296, state that "there is a presumption within the Convention that children's best interests are served by being with their parents wherever possible". This is reflected in UNCRC, which provides in article 7 that a child has "as far as possible, the right to know and be cared for by his or her parents", and in article 9, which requires states to ensure that

"a child shall not be separated from his or her parents against their will, except when competent authorities subject to judicial review determine, in accordance with applicable law and procedures, that such separation is necessary for the best interests of the child".

82.What the Strasbourg jurisprudence requires (and, I would have thought, what the rule of law in a modern, democratic society would require) is that no child should be adopted, particularly when it is against her parents' wishes, without a judge deciding after a proper hearing, with the interests of the parents (where appropriate) and of the child being appropriately advanced, that it is necessary in the interests of the child that she is adopted.

104.We were not addressed on this Article or on those two cases. However, they all give added weight to the importance of emphasising the principle that adoption of a child against her parents' wishes should only be contemplated as a last resort – when all else fails. Although the child's interests in an adoption case are "paramount" (in the UK legislation and under article 21 of UNCRC), a court must never lose sight of the fact that those interests include being brought up by her natural family, ideally her natural parents, or at least one of them.

130. Whether or not article 8 has any part to play in the threshold decision, it certainly comes into full flower at the disposal stage. Lady Hale and Lord Wilson have both referred to emphatic statements by ECtHR in such cases as Johansen v Norway (1996) 23 EHRR 33, K and T v Finland (2001) 36 EHRR 255, R and H v United Kingdom (2011) 54 EHRR 28, [2011] 2 FLR 1236 and YC v United Kingdom (2012) 55 EHRR 967 concerning the stringent requirements of the proportionality doctrine where family ties must be broken in order to allow adoption to take place. I agree with Lady

Hale's statement (in para 198 of her judgment) that the test for severing the relationship between parent and child is very strict and that the test will be found to be satisfied only in exceptional circumstances and "where nothing else will do". I also agree with what Lord Wilson has said in para 34 of his judgment, that "a high degree of justification" is required before an order can properly be made.

198. Nevertheless, it is quite clear that the test for severing the relationship between parent and child is very strict: only in exceptional circumstances and where motivated by overriding requirements pertaining to the child's welfare, in short, where nothing else will do. In many cases, and particularly where the feared harm has not yet materialised and may never do so, it will be necessary to explore and attempt alternative solutions. As was said in Re C and B [2001] 1 FLR 611, at para 34,

"Intervention in the family may be appropriate, but the aim should be to reunite the family when the circumstances enable that, and the effort should be devoted towards that end. Cutting off all contact and the relationship between the child or children and their family is only justified by the overriding necessity of the interests of the child."

Re W (Fact Finding: Hearsay Evidence) [2013] EWCA Civ 1374

Appeal by parents as to findings of fact made within care proceedings in which hearsay evidence had been adduced.

Summary

The local authority's evidence in relation to the sexual abuse findings was hearsay. The principal source of evidence was reports from a child to a social worker and they reported to the court. The judge ordered evidence to be given by an elder child, but that statement was never produced. The judgment made useful note of the authorities on hearsay evidence.

7. This case gave rise to no general arguments of principle. There is a great deal of authority on the subject of hearsay evidence in cases concerning children. I will list below the authorities that were cited to us as of particular relevance to the issue but we were not asked to revisit them or to venture any general guidance, the appeal being approached with commendable practicality on the basis that the judge erred in the way in which she treated the evidence in this particular case. The authorities were: Official Solicitor v K [1965] AC 201; Re W (Minors)(Wardship: Evidence) [1990] 1 FLR 203;

R v B County Council, ex parte P [1991] 1 FLR 470; Re N (Child Abuse: Evidence) [1996] 2 FLR 214; Re D (Sexual Abuse Allegations: Evidence of Adult Victim) [2002] 1 FLR 723; Re B (Allegation of Sexual Abuse: Child's Evidence) **[2006] EWCA Civ 773**; *H v L* **[2006] EWHC 3099 (Fam)**; *B v Torbay Council [2007] 1 FLR 203; W (a child)* **[2007] EWCA Civ 1255**; *JFM v Neath Port Talbot Borough Council* **[2008] EWCA Civ 3**; *Enfield LBC v SA (By her Litigation Friend, The Official Solicitor) [2010] EWHC 196 (Admin); Re W (Children)(Abuse: Oral Evidence)* **[2010] UKSC 12** *[2010] 1 FLR 1485; Surrey County Council v M, F and E* **[2013] EWHC 2400 (Fam)**.

R(AB and CD) v Haringey London Borough Council [2013] EWHC 416 (Admin)
http://www.bailii.org/ew/cases/EWHC/Admin/2013/416.html

Judicial Review in respect of a decision to initiate and undertake a Section 47 enquiry.

Summary

Judicial review proceedings that asserted that a decision to abandon an initial assessment and raise the case to a section 47 enquiry was unlawful. That such a decision was never in fact taken, and even if it had then it was a decision without adequate grounds. The parents, who were social workers themselves claimed that the process was so fundamentally flawed and lacking in the essential minimum requirements that it was unlawful. Found for the parents.

G (A Child) [2013] EWCA Civ 965

Second appeal against decision to make final care order placing a child into long term foster care.

Summary

The ground of appeal in both appellate courts was that the Judge had failed to carry out a balancing exercise to identify the risks of separating J from M against the risks of returning home.

69.Secondly, for the reasons that I have already given, I consider that the district judge failed to conduct the necessary welfare balancing exercise and I therefore consider that HHJ Hughes was in error in holding that she was 'not willing to say that the judge has not conducted a balancing exercise'. Where, as here, a circuit judge accepts that the first instance judge has not expressly referred to the welfare checklist and has not expressly weighed up the harm of returning to the mother

against the harm if the child went into local authority care,
then, on the basis of the positive duty identified by the majority
in Re B, the judge must go on and herself review the
proportionality of the order that has been made to determine
whether that order is 'wrong'.

70.*For the reasons that I have given, I have therefore*
concluded that both the district judge and the circuit judge in
this case erred significantly in the manner in which they
discharged their respective roles in relation to these
proceedings. As a result I would allow the appeal, set aside
the care order and reactivate the interim care order that was
in force prior to the final hearing. The interim care order will
run initially for 28 days from the date of this judgment. In
consequence there must inevitably be a rehearing of the local
authority application for a care order. That hearing should be
conducted at circuit judge level by a fresh tribunal and I
would therefore direct that the matter is to be placed before
the Family Division Liaison Judge for London for allocation.

Re B-S (Children) [2013] EWCA Civ 1146

Appeal by mother against the refusal to grant her leave to
oppose the adoption of two of her children. Appeal dismissed.

Summary

This is an important ruling: President of the Family Division –
Munby J details the case law, including ECHR jurisprudence
and the case of *Re B (A Child)* [2013] UKSC 33, (above) and
reinforces the point that: the severance of family ties inherent
in an adoption without parental consent is an extremely
draconian step and one that requires the highest level of
evidence. The guidance that flows from this judgment is : The
courts are to adopt the least interventionist approach when
dealing with the upbringing of children.

*26.First (Re B paras 77, 104), although the child's interests in
an adoption case are paramount, the court must never lose
sight of the fact that those interests include being brought up
by the natural family, ideally by the natural parents, or at least
one of them, unless the overriding requirements of the child's
welfare make that not possible.*

*27.Second (Re B para 77), as required by section 1(3)(g) of
the 1989 Act and section 1(6) of the 2002 Act, the court "must"
consider all the options before coming to a decision. As Lady
Hale said (para 198) it is "necessary to explore and attempt
alternative solutions". What are these options? That will*

depend upon the circumstances of the particular cases. They range, in principle, from the making of no order at one end of the spectrum to the making of an adoption order at the other. In between, there may be orders providing for the return of the child to the parent's care with the support of a family assistance order or subject to a supervision order or a care order; or the child may be placed with relatives under a residence order or a special guardianship order or in a foster placement under a care order; or the child may be placed with someone else, again under a residence order or a special guardianship order or in a foster placement under a care order. This is not an exhaustive list of the possibilities; wardship for example is another, as are placements in specialist residential or healthcare settings. Yet it can be seen that the possible list of options is long. We return to the implications of this below.

28.Third (Re B para 105), the court's assessment of the parents' ability to discharge their responsibilities towards the child must take into account the assistance and support which the authorities would offer. So "before making an adoption order ... the court must be satisfied that there is no practical way of the authorities (or others) providing the requisite assistance and support." In this connection it is worth remembering what Hale LJ had said in Re O (Supervision Order) [2001] EWCA Civ 16, [2001] 1 FLR 923, para 28:

"It will be the duty of everyone to ensure that, in those cases where a supervision order is proportionate as a response to the risk presented, a supervision order can be made to work, as indeed the framers of the Children Act 1989 always hoped that it would be made to work. The local authorities must deliver the services that are needed and must secure that other agencies, including the health service, also play their part, and the parents must co-operate fully."

That was said in the context of supervision orders but the point is of wider application.

29. It is the obligation of the local authority to make the order which the court has determined is proportionate work. The local authority cannot press for a more drastic form of order, least of all press for adoption, because it is unable or unwilling to support a less interventionist form of order. Judges must be alert to the point and must be rigorous in exploring and probing local authority thinking in cases where there is any reason to suspect that resource issues may be affecting the local authority's thinking.

__Adoption__   –   __essentials__

33. Two things are essential – we use that word deliberately and advisedly – both when the court is being asked to approve a care plan for adoption and when it is being asked to make a non-consensual placement order or adoption order.

__Adoption__   –   __essentials:__   __(i)__   __proper__   __evidence__

34. First, there must be proper evidence both from the local authority and from the guardian. The evidence must address all the options which are realistically possible and must contain an analysis of the arguments for and against each option. As Ryder LJ said in Re R (Children) __[2013] EWCA Civ 1018__, para 20, what is required is:

"evidence of the lack of alternative options for the children and an analysis of the evidence that is accepted by the court sufficient to drive it to the conclusion that nothing short of adoption is appropriate for the children."

The same judge indicated in Re S, K v The London Borough of Brent [2013] EWCA Civ 926, para 21, that what is needed is:

"An assessment of the benefits and detriments of each option

for placement and in particular the nature and extent of the risk of harm involved in each of the options".

McFarlane LJ made the same point in Re G (A Child) [2013] EWCA Civ 965, para 48, when he identified:

"the need to take into account the negatives, as well as the positives, of any plan to place a child away from her natural family".

We agree with all of this.

35. Too often this essential material is lacking. As Black LJ said in Re V (Children) [2013] EWCA Civ 913, para 88:

"I have searched without success in the papers for any written analysis by local authority witnesses or the guardian of the arguments for and against adoption and long term fostering ... It is not the first time that I have remarked on an absence of such material from the evidence, see Plymouth CC v G (children) [2010] EWCA Civ 1271. Care should always be taken to address this question specifically in the evidence/ reports and that this was not done here will not have assisted the judge in his determination of the issue."

In the Plymouth case she had said this (para 47):

"In some respects the reports of the guardian and the social worker, and the social worker's statement, are very detailed, giving information about health and likes and dislikes, wishes and feelings. However there is surprisingly little detail about the central issue of the type of placement that will best meet the children's needs ... In part, this may be an unfortunate by-product of the entirely proper use, by both witnesses, of the checklist of factors and, in the case of the social worker's placement report, of the required pro forma. However, the court requires not only a list of the factors that are relevant to the central decision but also a narrative account of how they fit together, including an analysis of the pros and cons of the various orders that might realistically be under consideration given the circumstances of the children, and a fully reasoned recommendation."

36. Black LJ has not altered the views that she expressed on these earlier occasions and the other members of the court agree with every word of them. We draw attention in particular to the need for "analysis of the pros and cons" and a "fully reasoned recommendation". These are essential if the exacting test set out in Re B and the requirements of Articles 6 and 8 of the Convention are to be met. We suggest that such an analysis is likely to be facilitated by the use – which we encourage – of the kind of 'balance sheet' first recommended by Thorpe LJ, albeit in a very different context, in Re A (Male Sterilisation) [2000] 1 FLR 549, 560.

37. It is particularly disheartening that Black LJ's words three years ago in the Plymouth case seem to have had so little effect.

38. Consider the lamentable state of affairs described by Ryder LJ in Re S, K v The London Borough of Brent [2013] EWCA Civ 926, where an appeal against the making of a care order with a plan for adoption was successful because neither the evidence nor the judge's reasoning was adequate to support the order. It is a lengthy passage but it merits setting out almost in full (paras 22-26):

"22... what was the evidence that was available to the judge to support her conclusion? ... Sadly, there was little or no evidence about the relative merits of the placement options nor any evidence about why an adoptive placement was necessary or feasible.

23 The allocated social worker in her written statement recommended that [S] needed:

"a permanent placement where her on-going needs will be met in a safe, stable and nurturing environment. [S]'s permanent carers will need to demonstrate that they are committed to [S], her safety, welfare and wellbeing and that they ensure that she receives a high standard of care until she reaches adulthood

Adoption will give [S] the security and permanency that she requires. The identified carers are experienced carers and have good knowledge about children and the specific needs of children that have been removed from their families ..."

24 With respect to the social worker ... that without more is not a sufficient rationale for a step as significant as permanent removal from the birth family for adoption. The reasoning was in the form of a conclusion that needed to be supported by evidence relating to the facts of the case and a social worker's expert analysis of the benefits and detriments of the placement options available. Fairness dictates that whatever the local authority's final position, their evidence should address the negatives and the positives relating to each of the options available. Good practice would have been to have heard evidence about the benefits and detriments of each of the permanent placement options that were available for S within and outside the family.

25 The independent social worker did not support adoption or removal but did describe the options which were before the court when the mediation opportunity was allowed:

"Special Guardianship Order: This is the application before the Court and which would afford [S] stability, in terms of remaining with the same primary carer and the opportunity to be raised within her birth family. I do not consider that the situation within the family is suitable at present for this Order to be made.

Adoption: [S] could be placed with a family where she should experience stability and security without conflict. This may be the best option for [S] if current concerns cannot be resolved in a timely manner."

26 In order to choose between the options the judge needed evidence which was not provided. The judge's conclusion was a choice of one option over another that was neither reasoned nor evidenced within the proceedings. That vitiated her evaluative judgment which was accordingly wrong."

39. Most experienced family judges will unhappily have had too much exposure to material as anodyne and inadequate as that described here by Ryder LJ.

40. This sloppy practice must stop. It is simply unacceptable in a forensic context where the issues are so grave and the stakes, for both child and parent, so high.

Adoption – essentials: (ii) adequately reasoned judgments
41. The second thing that is essential, and again we emphasise that word, is an adequately reasoned judgment by the judge. We have already referred to Ryder LJ's criticism of the judge in Re S, K v The London Borough of Brent [2013] EWCA Civ 926. That was on 29 July 2013. The very next day, in Re P (A Child) [2013] EWCA Civ 963, appeals against the making of care and placement orders likewise succeeded because, as Black LJ put it (para 107):

"the judge ... failed to carry out a proper balancing exercise in order to determine whether it was necessary to make a care order with a care plan of adoption and then a placement order or, if she did carry out that analysis, it is not apparent from

her judgments. Putting it another way, she did not carry out a proportionality analysis."

She added (para 124): "there is little acknowledgment in the judge's judgments of the fact that adoption is a last resort and little consideration of what it was that justified it in this case."

42. The judge must grapple with the factors at play in the particular case and, to use Black LJ's phrase (para 126), give "proper focussed attention to the specifics".

43. In relation to the nature of the judicial task we draw attention to what McFarlane LJ said in Re G (A Child) [2013] EWCA Civ 965, paras 49-50:

"In most child care cases a choice will fall to be made between two or more options. The judicial exercise should not be a linear process whereby each option, other than the most draconian, is looked at in isolation and then rejected because of internal deficits that may be identified, with the result that, at the end of the line, the only option left standing is the most draconian and that is therefore chosen without any particular consideration of whether there are internal deficits within that option.

The linear approach ... is not apt where the judicial task is to undertake a global, holistic evaluation of each of the options available for the child's future upbringing before deciding which of those options best meets the duty to afford paramount consideration to the child's welfare."

We need not quote the next paragraph in McFarlane LJ's judgment, which explains in graphic and compelling terms the potential danger of adopting a linear approach.

44. We emphasise the words "global, holistic evaluation". This point is crucial. The judicial task is to evaluate all the options, undertaking a global, holistic and (see Re G para 51) multi-faceted evaluation of the child's welfare which takes into account all the negatives and the positives, all the pros and cons, of each option. To quote McFarlane LJ again (para 54):

"What is required is a balancing exercise in which each option is evaluated to the degree of detail necessary to analyse and weigh its own internal positives and negatives and each option is then compared, side by side, against the competing option or options."

45. McFarlane LJ added this important observation (para 53) which we respectfully endorse:

"a process which acknowledges that long-term public care, and in particular adoption contrary to the will of a parent, is 'the most draconian option', yet does not engage with the very detail of that option which renders it 'draconian' cannot be a full or effective process of evaluation. Since the phrase was first coined some years ago, judges now routinely make reference to the 'draconian' nature of permanent separation of parent and child and they frequently do so in the context of reference to 'proportionality'. Such descriptions are, of course, appropriate and correct, but there is a danger that these phrases may inadvertently become little more than formulaic judicial window-dressing if they are not backed up with a substantive consideration of what lies behind them and the impact of that on the individual child's welfare in the particular case before the court. If there was any doubt about the importance of avoiding that danger, such doubt has been firmly swept away by the very clear emphasis in Re B on the duty of the court actively to evaluate proportionality in every case."

46. We make no apologies for having canvassed these matters in such detail and at such length. They are of crucial importance in what are amongst the most significant and difficult cases that family judges ever have to decide. Too often they are given scant attention or afforded little more than lip service. And they are important in setting the context against which we have to determine the specific question we have to decide in relation to Re W (Adoption: Set Aside and Leave to Oppose) [2010] EWCA Civ 1535, [2011] 1 FLR 2153.

Adoption – the current reforms to the family justice system
47. First, however, we need to see how all this fits in with the current reforms to the family justice system and, in particular, with the revised Public Law Outline.

48. Our emphasis on the need for proper analysis, argument, assessment and reasoning accords entirely with a central part of the reforms. In his 'View from the President's Chambers' the President has repeatedly stressed the need for local authority evidence to be more focused than hitherto on assessment and analysis rather than on history and narrative, and likewise for expert reports to be more focused on analysis and opinion: see 'The process of reform: the revised PLO and the local authority', [2013] Fam Law 680, and 'The process of reform: expert evidence', [2103] Fam Law 816. What the court needs is expert opinion, whether from the social worker or the guardian, which is evidence-based and focused on the factors in play in the particular case, which analyses all the possible options, and which provides clear conclusions and recommendations adequately reasoned through and based on the evidence.

A-W & C (Children) [2013] EWHC B41 (Fam)

Mother's application (within care and placement proceedings) for declarations in relation to alleged breaches of her Human Rights by virtue of alleged inappropriate procedures by the Local Authority social work team relating to the removal of her youngest child shortly after birth

Summary

Misuse of police powers to effect removal of a baby after birth after parents refused to agree to a section 20 after taking legal advice.

The mother's application for declaratory relief in respect of alleged breaches of her rights under the Human Rights Act 1998

3. The mother, who I am going to refer to as CC, seeks declarations pursuant to section 7 of the Human Rights Act

*1998 that her rights pursuant to Article 6 and Article 8 of the European Convention on Human Rights have, by reason of the conduct of the social work team employed by Lancashire County Council on 18th February 2013, been breached. Lancashire County Council is the defendant to that claim. Her claim was initially issued on 19th February by way of Part 8 procedure and has been treated as consolidated within the care proceedings. That seems to me to be in accordance with the practice approved by the Court of Appeal in the case of Re S **[2010] EWCA CIV 1383**. I first dealt with this case on 18th February 2013 in the county court, on a first appointment in respect of A's case, and I transferred the matter to the High Court. Mr. Justice Cobb, therefore, dealt initially with the contested interim care order, gave directions for the declaratory proceedings) and conducted two hearings on 7th March and 21st March 2013. The case was thereafter released back to be heard by me sitting as a Deputy Judge of the High Court to deal with both the care proceedings and the consolidated Human Rights Act declaratory proceedings.*

4. At an early stage of the Human Rights Act proceedings it became clear that the local authority's case was that officers of the Lancashire Constabulary of Police had acted independently of the local authority in carrying out the acts complained of by the mother as the basis of her Human Rights Act action, and that raised serious criticism of those officers as well as of the social work team. Thus the Lancashire Police have attended and been represented and participated at relevant hearings both in front of Mr Justice Cobb and in front of me, although they have not been made defendants in the Human Rights Act proceedings and are not parties to either set of proceedings. No declaration has been sought against them. However, any survey of the events which form the basis of the mother's action under the Human Rights Act necessarily involved the scrutiny of the conduct of the officers involved and it was therefore appropriate and proper for the police to be invited to attend and to be represented. They have had the advantage of representation by Mr Dalal of counsel during the hearing before me.

5. As I have already set out, the approach of Lancashire County Council during the hearing which I have conducted has been to accept responsibility in general for the completely inappropriate procedures adopted on 18th February 2013 and to concede that declarations should be made and to apologise to the mother. It was the account of the Local Authority witness that the instigator of A being received into police protection on that day was DC K. DC K was the instigating officer of the section 46 process, to use the language of Home Office Circular 017/2008 which provides guidance to officers as to the proper use of that process.

6. Originally the mother's human rights action incorporated a claim for damages. This was compromised and withdrawn at the first hearing when Lancashire County Council made concessions as to the unlawfulness of their procedure and reimbursed the mother's solicitor the monies she had expended upon a modest hotel for the mother to stay at in order to remain close to A after the mother was discharged from hospital and before A was removed to foster care. I was concerned, therefore, only to consider whether to make declarations setting out that the local authority acted in breach of the mother's rights under the European Convention and how they had done so. The local authority conceded that such declarations could and should be made, and in very large measure conceded the terms of such declarations. They would not concede any declaration that the local authority should have sought an emergency protection order pursuant to section 44 of the Children Act 1989 when they erroneously believed that a contested ICO could not take place. The police have made no concessions at all as to the process adopted by their officers on that day.

7. The mother's case was, therefore, not brought to pursue monetary compensation but rather to achieve a scrutiny of what went on that day, and the hearing proceeded with evidence about the events which led to A being placed in police protection on 18th February in order for me to determine what had happened that day. This was despite the substantial concessions of the local authority at the suggestion and with the agreement of all parties before me with the possible exception of the police who, in any event, raised no objection to the evidence being heard. Indeed Mr. Dalal of counsel was enthusiastic that I should hear the evidence of their witness, DC K.

The   **Law**

15. By section 46(1) of the Children Act 1989 :

"Where a constable has reasonable cause to believe that a child would otherwise be likely to suffer significant harm he may;

(a) remove the child to suitable accommodation and keep him there,   *or,*

(b) take such steps as are reasonable to ensure the child's removal from any hospital or other place in which he is then being accommodated is prevented."

Subsection (2) reads:

"For the purposes of this Act a child with respect to whom a constable has exercised his powers under this section is referred to as having been taken into police protection."

The subsequent subsections lay down the statutory obligations upon the police once a child has come into police protection to alert the relevant local authority, the child and the parents of the steps that have been taken. It is of note that section 46(7) enables the designated officer to apply for an emergency protection order whilst a child is in police protection. The designated officer is an officer appointed in accordance with section 46(3)(e) to enquire into cases where children have been taken into police protection. Home Office guidance, to which I have already referred, requires such an officer to be of the rank of Inspector or above. In A's case the designated officer was Inspector BL.

16. Section 44 of the Children Act 1989 enables emergency protection orders to be sought from the court when the criteria for them are made out.

Section 44(1) reads:

"Where any person ('the applicant') applies to the court for an order to be made under this section with respect to a child, the court may make the order if, but only if, it is satisfied that;

(a) there is reasonable cause to believe that the child is likely to suffer significant harm if;

(i) he is not removed to accommodation provided by or on behalf of the applicant; or (ii) he does not remain in the place in which he is then being accommodated."

17. Section 38 of the Children Act 1989 sets out the regime for making interim orders and the threshold criteria for interim care orders. Both section 44 and section 38 provide a court procedure whereby both threshold criteria and the need for removal can be judicially invigilated, with all parties having an opportunity to be heard on both aspects; that includes the child through his or her Children's Guardian and legal team. I pause to say that it must have been perfectly clear to all parties on 18th February 2013 that the parents' case was not as to the need for intervention or as to threshold, but as to the need or not and as to the proportionality of the separation proposed. Under section 38 in contested interim care proceedings the court has a duty to scrutinise and approve the local authority care plan, and in cases involving removal of children from their parents, particularly infants, the court will carefully examine the need for separation to manage any risk established, the principle being absolutely clear that in general the least intrusive intervention is always to be preferred. I do not propose to go through the long line of authorities which set out those principles. No party before this court disputes them. It is equally clear that the only forum for arguing how or what that intervention should be in is the Family Court, whether in the FPC, the County Court or the High   Court.

18. I turn now to the Human Rights Act 1998 and by section 1 of that Act a number of Articles of the ECHR were directly enshrined into UK law. The relevant Articles for these proceedings are Article 6 and Article 8. It is not often it is necessary in a case to read into a judgment the actual Article but I in this instance I do pause to read parts of Article 6 and Article 8 into this judgment. Article 6(1) reads as follows:

"In the determination of his civil rights and obligations or of any criminal charge against him, everyone is entitled to a fair and public hearing within a reasonable time by an independent and impartial tribunal established by law."

Article 8 reads as follows:

"(1) Everyone has the right to respect for his private and family life, his home and his correspondence.

*(2) **E+W+S+N.I.** There shall be no interference by a public authority with the exercise of this right, except such as is in accordance with the law and is necessary in a democratic society in the interests of national security, public safety or the economic well-being of the country, for the prevention of disorder or crime, for the protection of health or morals, or for the protection of the rights and freedoms of others."*

There is no question that the separation of an infant from her mother at birth engages both of those Articles absolutely and starkly. Section 6 of the Human Rights Act states:

"It is unlawful for a public authority to act in a way which is incompatible with a Convention right."

Section 7 of the Human Rights Act reads as follows. I will read only the relevant parts. Subsection (1):

"A person who claims that a public authority has acted or proposes to act in a way which is made unlawful by section 6(1) may;

(a) bring proceedings against the authority under this Act in the appropriate court or tribunal, or,

(b) rely on the Convention right or rights concerned in any legal proceedings, but only if he is or would be a victim of the unlawful Act."

The procedure therefore, adopted by the mother's legal team in pursuing an application for a declaration intended to be heard at the same time as the care proceedings seems to me to have been an appropriate procedure, as approved by the Court of Appeal in Re S.

19. I turn to the case law on section 46, which is helpfully derived from three Court of Appeal authorities. The first is the case of Langley –v- Liverpool City Council **[2005] EWCA Civ 1173**, [2006] 1 FLR 342. The Court of Appeal in that instance were Lords Justices Dyson, Thorpe and Lloyd. The decision

considered the interplay between emergency protection orders and section 46 in the context of an out of hours removal of a child from a family home by police after an EPO had been granted but not executed. The Court of Appeal were unanimous that section 46 could be exercised in respect of a child subject to an EPO but in coming to their conclusions about that particular case they surveyed the statutory scheme and the following paragraphs are of significance and relevance to A's case.

Paragraph 38 (from the judgment of Lord Justice Dyson): -

"In my judgment, the statutory scheme clearly accords primacy to section 44. Removal under section 44 is sanctioned by the court and it involves a more elaborate, sophisticated and complete process than removal under section 46. The primacy accorded to section 44 is further reinforced by sections 46(7) and 47(3)(c). The significance of these provisions is that they show that it was contemplated by Parliament that an EPO may well not be in force when a removal is effected under section 46, and that removal under section 46 is but the first step in a process which may later include an application for an EPO."

He goes on to say at paragraph 40:

"I would, therefore, hold that; (i) removal of children should usually be effected pursuant to an EPO, and, (ii) section 46 should be invoked only where it is not practicable to execute an EPO. In deciding whether it is practicable to execute an EPO, the police must always have regard to the paramount need to protect children from significant harm."

Paragraph 76 (from the judgment of Lord Justice Thorpe):

"It is to be emphasised that even in emergency the local authority must apply in the Family Proceedings Court for an order and prove the need for the order to the satisfaction of the court. This is a potent check on the local authority's powers of intervention in emergency."

20. The second Court of Appeal authority to which I have been referred by Mr Dalal is that of A –v- East Sussex County Council & The Chief Constable of Sussex Police. This is a decision of Lords Justices Carnwath and Jackson and Mr Justice Hedley reported at [2010] EWCA Civ 743. Mr Dalal referred me to this authority because he thought that the facts were similar to the facts in A's case. In that case the mother sought damages under section 7 of the Human Rights Act to compensate her for what she argued was an unlawful removal of her child from hospital and, therefore, her care. There was a suspicion that her presentation of her child was consistent with her demonstrating factitious illness syndrome. Section 46 was used to remove him to foster care after he had been in hospital for five days following a decision that he was ready for discharge medically. The mother in that case wished to take him home and there would have been nothing to stop her. Two days later at the FPC (Family Proceedings Court) a plan to place both in a mother and baby home was approved. The assessment of them was positive and the proceedings were eventually discontinued. The reported decision is upon the mother's separately brought Human Rights Act action. The first instance judge had decided that the mother's expressed intention not to co-operate and the risk that she might walk out of the hospital with the child justified the decision to remove the child from her by way of section 46. In that case the local authority had arranged an on notice hearing on 31st December and, therefore, correctly anticipated on 29th December, which is the day of the event complained of by the mother, that it would not be until two days later that a court decide whether such separation was justified. The mother's withdrawal of co-operation and the risk that she would move

the child from hospital was a precipitating factor in that case.
The Court of Appeal considered that the judge was entitled to
come to this conclusion and were not persuaded to overturn it.
I consider that the ultimate decision turned on its own facts
which are distinct from the facts in this case. However, there
are paragraphs in the judgments delivered which seem to me
to   be   relevant   to   A's   case:-

Paragraphs 22 and 23 (from the judgment of Mr Justice
Hedley)

"However, whilst I am satisfied that the judge was on the
evidence entitled to take the view that what occurred was in
the circumstances neither unlawful nor disproportionate, I am
left with the distinct impression that things could have been
handled rather better than was in fact the case. It may,
therefore, be helpful to indicate what sort of approach should
be taken in circumstances such as these which, though fairly
unusual, will be familiar to any experienced child protection
practitioner."

23. "It is essential to stress that even in an emergency it is
desirable, where possible, to work in partnership with a
parent. Parents can, with careful and sympathetic explanation,

be brought to agree to regimes of supervision or to the child remaining in hospital, or even to voluntary accommodation under Part III of the Act for a brief period. Where parents have access to a solicitor (particularly where, as here, he or she is available), then the solicitor should be apprised of the local authority's concerns and proposals and then be invited (if the solicitor thinks it proper to do so) to give advice to the parent. Even where emergency powers are obtained under section 44 or exercised under section 46, least interventions are best. For example, the police have power to prevent a removal from hospital. In the circumstances of this case it would have been surprising had the hospital, if pressed, refused to keep the child for an extra two days. The removal of the child to a known destination (e.g. a relative) is to be preferred to removal to a stranger. If, however, there is removal to a stranger, the parent should, in the absence of good reason (e.g. abusive or irrational behaviour) be informed of the fact and be allowed to pass relevant information to the carer and speedy arrangements be made for contact. If a court order has not been obtained or obtained ex parte, an inter partes hearing should be arranged as soon as possible. The learned judge described a hearing two days hence as 'creditable' but it should also be the norm. It goes *without saying that where practicable an order of the court should be sought in preference to the use of section 46 powers."*

24. He goes on to say at paragraph 25:

"Social workers in these situations are in a very difficult place. If they take no action and something goes wrong, inevitable and heavy criticism will follow. If they take action which ultimately turns out to have been unnecessary, they will have caused distress to an already distressed parent. On the other hand they are also invested with or have access to very Draconian powers and it is vital that, if child protection is to command public respect and agreement, such powers must be exercised lawfully and proportionately and that the exercise of such powers should be the subject of public scrutiny."

25. I consider that whilst A's case is in some ways similar to the East Sussex one, it is different on its facts significantly. The police and social services in the East Sussex case were faced with a mother who wanted to remove her baby from hospital. That was not the case in A's case. It was the hospital who wished the baby to leave. The mother was co-operative and indeed the father was co-operative. They were merely refusing to agree, pursuant to their own legal advice, to section 20 accommodation. The local authority knew the mother's wish was simply to remain with her child and that she was following advice in not agreeing to section 20. In all other respects she was willing to co-operate and work with them to secure the management of the risks they perceived. The crisis was not one of non-co-operation by her but by reason of the hospital wanting to discharge A on that day, although there is no evidence that they were pressing for discharge at the very point in time when the child was taken into police protection.

The third relevant case on section 46 is that of Re S to which I have already made reference in talking of the procedure adopted by the mother's team here. The Court of Appeal were Sir Nicholas Wall, the President of the Family Division, and Lady Justice Arden and Lord Justice Wilson (as he then was). In that case on the appeal of the local authority the Court of Appeal did overturn the findings of the first instance judge that the local authority had acted in breach of the mother's Article 6 and 8 rights. However, the following paragraphs set out the court's preferred approach to the circumstances in which section 46 should be operated.

Paragraphs 66, 67 and 68 (from the judgment of the President of the Family Division, Sir Nicholas Wall) :-

66 "It is also right to say, I think, that the separation of mother and child under an ICO in care proceedings is, for good reason, usually a judicial as opposed to an administrative decision. The court is the parent's safeguard against arbitrary or inappropriate action by a local authority. Thus in the overwhelming majority of the cases, it will be for the judge or magistrates to make the decision. I can thus readily understand Her Honour Judge Finnerty's view that both she and the Family Proceedings Court were, inappropriately, being presented with a fait accompli.

67. "For the local authority to succeed in this appeal, therefore, the facts have to be regarded as wholly exceptional."

The President goes on at paragraph 68, having dealt with some of the facts of that case:

68. "In anything other than wholly exceptional circumstances, the rule must be that it is for the court to make the relevant decision unfettered by events which effectively curtail its powers. The question, therefore, is whether or not the current case can be said to be 'wholly exceptional'."

He   went   on   to   find   that   it   was.

26. At this point it is useful to refer to the Home Office Circular 17/2008, to which I have already made reference, helpfully provided to me by Mr Firbank. That Circular issues guidance to the police in the use of their powers under section 46. There had been earlier guidance both in 1991 and 2003 and I suspect that the 2008 guidance was issued after the Liverpool case to which I have made reference to reflect the law as it emerged from that case. Paragraph 3 of the guidance reads as follows:

"The provisions of the Act aim to strike the proper balance between the provision of speedy and effective help to children at risk and unwarranted interference in family life. The underlying principle of the Act is that the welfare of the child is paramount."

The guidance goes on to say at paragraph 15:

"Police protection is an emergency power and should only be used when necessary, the principle being that wherever possible the decision to remove a child/children from a parent

should be made by a court."

It goes on to say at paragraph 16:

"All local authorities should have in place local arrangements (through their local Chief Executive and Clerks to the Justices) whereby out of hours applications for EPOs may be made speedily and without an excess of bureaucracy. Police protection powers should only be used when this is not possible."

27. During the evidence, which I am about to summarise, it became obvious that DC K had gone to the hospital on 18th February to assist ML, who was then the recently allocated social worker, to persuade the mother to agree to section 20 accommodation for A and to explain that the alternative would be section 46. It seems to me, however, that had they succeeded in the persuasion that they were about to undertake that also would have been open to criticism on the authorities, and I derive that conclusion from two first instance decisions to which I was referred.

The first is Re CA [2012] EWHC 27 a decision of Mr Justice Hedley in. which he said simply:

"The use of section 20 is not unrestricted and must not be compulsion in disguise."

The second is Surrey County Council –v- M, F & E [2012] EWHC [2400] a decision of Mrs. Justice Theis and at paragraph 60 she said this:-

"To use the section 20 procedure in circumstances where there was the overt threat of a police protection order if they did not agree, reinforced by the physical presence of uniformed police officers, was wholly inappropriate. By adopting this procedure the local authority sought to circumvent the test any court would have required them to meet if they sought to secure an order, either by way of an EPO or interim care order."

28. Although DC K and her colleague in A's case were not in uniform when they went to the hospital, the object here and the nature of the discussions that they were intending to have were exactly as discussed in those two paragraphs. Had the mother felt pressured to act against her solicitor's advice, it seems to me that the use of section 20 would have been open to parallel criticism and it would have amounted to an inappropriate coercion to co-operate in the local authority's care plan without that care plan having been properly scrutinised and approved in a hearing where all parties, including the mother

774

and A, could have had a say.

36. I heard oral evidence from DC K. I have already referred to her statement, but I have not yet read into this judgment the sentiments contained in that statement at the end, which I consider to be somewhat alarming. She says this:

"I can categorically state that I was in no doubt that a police protection order was absolutely essential in order to keep A safe. I came to that informed decision having paid great attention to the background of this family, in addition to my recent involvement with them. Basically if this child had been allowed to return home with the parents then I would have been neglecting my role as a police officer. I am a child protection officer and that is what I did on that day. My actions were not at the instigation of the local authority."

She did not draw back from that stance during her oral evidence. She is obviously a very experienced officer. She demonstrated pride in the role she holds in child protection. Her demeanour is pleasant and sensitive and I can well imagine that she has an excellent manner with both the parents and the children she encounters in the course of her duties. However, I consider her approach on 18th February in taking A into police protection at the point in time that she did to have been fundamentally flawed. It was plain that she went to the hospital with the intention, were mother not to agree to accommodation, of taking the child into police protection.

37. Euphemistic language was used during her evidence about encouraging parents to co-operate or engage with the local authority. However, it is plain that in DC K's mind the co-operation could only take one form, namely agreement to section 20. When the mother, acting on her solicitor's advice, refused to consent DC K encapsulated her was "We can't just go up there and be blocked". Later I repeated this in asking her questions myself and she seemed to think that the word "blocked" was one that I had used and not her. I am quite clear in my note that those were her words. She failed to weigh into the balance the fact that the parents were co-operating with the local authority in every regard except with regard to a separation pursuant to section 20. They were not threatening to remove A; they were responding to their own legal advice; they had cared for A well on the ward. Not only did DC K have a low threshold for the need for intervention, which to my mind did not arise at all unless or until the hospital was to insist upon discharge and at that point the parents sought to go home with A, but she also seemed to pay little or no heed

that the S46 route into to the care of the local authority is the one to be least preferred, affording, as it does, no right of argument or judicial scrutiny.

38. I refer again to the document that she wrote, as I said probably in advance of attending the hospital, countersigned by her Inspector. It seems to me that it would be strongly arguable, that, even had the decision to go by section 46 occurred out of hours, the justification set out in that document is insufficient. I know that DC K in evidence advanced a lot of other reasons in addition to those set out in the document, but it is very important that the documents to be kept as records of when an authority is to take an action of such consequence as this one contain full reasons even if in summary and note form. She and Inspector BL both took as read that there could be no court hearing until later in the week and that an EPO was not an available route. I consider that both DC K and Inspector BL as the designated officer had a separate duty from the local authority to ensure, not only that separation and protection were absolutely necessary, but also that this route to it was absolutely necessary and that there was no prospect that a separation could be scrutinised or, if necessary, endorsed by a court. She should have been

asking herself, "Why do I have to make this decision now?".
So, however impressive DC K was in terms of her commitment
and her demeanour, her failure in exercising such a draconian
power to establish that this route to protection was absolutely
necessary was unimpressive.

39. I, therefore, came to these conclusions in respect of the
Human Rights Act application. I remind myself of the irony
that I was considering the evidence in respect of this case on a
day when there were not one but two scandalous child death
cases reported in the press, and indeed I would not want
anything that I say in this case to discourage those involved in
protection of children from courageous intervention to protect
them. It seemed to me that everybody involved on 18th
February 2013 was doing their best to promote the safety and
welfare of A and to act professionally and appropriately. I do
not consider anybody was motivated by an improper desire to
circumvent proper procedure and the court process. The
social worker was working under enormous pressure. Police
and child protection authorities need to be ready to intervene
protectively. The officer in this case is clearly zealous and
confident of her ability to make the right decision, but the
consequence of what they did on that day was that a mother,
aged only 17 herself, was deprived of the opportunity of

arguing that she and her four day old baby should be kept together, and, importantly, deprived her of the opportunity to argue that they could be kept together safely. The local authority has conceded that that was the case and has apologised profusely to mother. Unfortunately the police will not make any such concession. It seems to me that the outcome on the day was unfair. Mother was engaging with the legal process. There was no suggestion that she was going to leave the hospital. She was acting on the advice of her solicitor and, as I have said, the question that the social worker and the police officer should have been asking themselves was whether there was any other route of protection open to them.

40. The separation of a parent and child by any authority is a most serious act and it must be necessary and proportionate. The gravity and importance of that principle is all the more acute where that child is a newborn and magnified when the mother of that child is herself a child. Protection of the child, of course, is a foremost priority but protection does not require in every case an enforced separation. There are a whole range of remedies before enforced separation, which is the absolute last resort. Decisions as to whether that protection is necessary should be made by a court, and decisions as to what course is the least interventionist necessary should be made by a court. There was a duty, it seems to me, not just on the social worker but on the police themselves to look at the route into protection. DC K did acknowledge in her evidence that separation is always the last resort. It did not seem to me there was any real acknowledgement that section 46 as the route of that separation is also the route of last resort. As I have said, the local authority has made concessions. The police are completely unapologetic. DC K was absolutely convinced of the need for intervention but she is ill equipped to look at the form of protection needed. Her assumption was that the local authority plan for separation was the only route and she made no or no sufficient effort to find out whether a court was available to weigh up the alternatives. She was far too ready to assume responsibility and take the decision without acknowledging that it was for a court to determine what was necessary and proportionate. That type of decision making is quite understandable late at night, at weekends, at Bank Holidays, in the context of parents determined to not work with the local authority, demonstrating violence or threatening to snatch a child from where that child is considered to be safe. None of those things applied here.

In the Matter of J (Children) [2013] UKSC 9

Supreme Court. Appeal by local authority concerning whether a child can be regarded as 'likely to suffer' harm for the purposes of s 31(2) of the Children Act 1989 if another child has been harmed in the past and there is a possibility that the parent now caring for him or her was responsible for the harm to the other child. The Supreme Court unanimously dismissed the appeal. Lady Hale gives the main judgment, Lord Wilson and Lord Sumption disagreeing on one point.

Summary : Supreme Court Press Summary.

Section 31 (2) of the Children Act 1989 imposes a threshold which must be satisfied before a care or supervision order can be made in respect of a child. First the child must have suffered or be likely to suffer significant harm; secondly, that harm must be attributable to the care given or likely to be given to the child. If the threshold is crossed then the court will treat the welfare of the child as its paramount consideration when deciding whether to make an order.

The issue in this case is whether a child can be regarded as 'likely to suffer' harm if another child has been harmed in the past and there is a possibility that the parent now caring for him or her was responsible for the harm to the other child.

The local authority in this case brought care proceedings in respect of three children who are cared for by DJ and JJ. The two oldest are the children of DJ and his former partner, and have always lived with DJ. The youngest child is JJ's daughter, her third child with her former partner, SW. The local authority submitted that the three children were likely to suffer significant harm because JJ's first child with SW, T-J, had died of non-accidental injuries in 2004. In earlier care proceedings relating to JJ and SW's second child, who was subsequently adopted, a judge had found that either JJ or SW had caused the injuries to T-J and the other had at the very least colluded to hide the truth. In the present proceedings the local authority sought to rely solely on the finding that JJ was a possible perpetrator of the injuries to T-J. It submitted that this was a finding of fact sufficient as a matter of law to satisfy the s 31(2) threshold in respect of the three children now cared for by JJ and DJ.

The High Court held on a preliminary issue that likelihood of significant harm can only be established by reference to past facts that are proved on the balance of probabilities. Mere possibility was insufficient. The Court of Appeal dismissed an appeal by the local authority but granted permission to appeal to the Supreme Court.

The Supreme Court unanimously dismisses the local authority's appeal. The main judgment is given by Lady Hale, with whom all the justices agree. Lord Wilson expresses disagreement on one point, which Lord Sumption shares. Lord Reed gives an additional judgment, with which Lord Clarke and Lord Carnwath agree. Lord Hope agrees with Lady Hale and Lord Reed.

It is a serious matter for the state compulsorily to remove a child from his family of birth. The section 31(2) threshold is an important measure to protect a family from unwarranted intrusion while at the same time protecting children from harm [1] [75]. The wording of Section 31(2) has been the subject of six appeals to the House of Lords and Supreme Court. Those cases have consistently held that a prediction of future harm has to be founded on proven facts: suspicions or possibilities are not enough. Such facts have to be proved on the simple balance of probabilities [36]. This approach is supported by the legislative history of section 31(2) [45-46] [96]. It would be odd if the first limb (actual harm) had to be proved to the court's satisfaction but the basis of predicting future harm did not [47].

Care cases in which the only matter upon which the authority can rely is the possibility that the parent has harmed another child in the past are very rare. Usually there will be many readily provable facts upon which an authority can rely [5]. Even in cases where the perpetrator of injuries could not be identified there may be a multitude of established facts from which a likelihood that this parent will harm a child in the future could be shown. However, the real possibility that the parent caring for the child has harmed a child in the past is not by itself sufficient [54]. In this case there were many potentially relevant facts found in the earlier proceedings against JJ which might have been relevant to an assessment of whether JJ would harm children in the future, such as the collusion with SW which prevented the court from identifying the perpetrator, the failure to protect T-J, and the deliberate failure to keep T-J away from health professionals [56]. Other relevant matters for the assessment would have been consideration of the household circumstances at the time of T-J's death and whether JJ's new relationship with DJ looking after much older children was different [53]. As the local authority had chosen not to rely on these facts, however, it would not be fair to the whole family to allow these proceedings to go on. JJ has been looking after these three children and a new baby for some time without (so far as the court is aware) giving cause for concern and, should the local authority wish to make a case that any of these children is likely to suffer significant harm in the future, it will be open to it to bring new proceedings [57].

Lord Wilson, while agreeing with Lady Hale for the most part and in the disposal of the appeal, identified an issue on which he differed from the majority. In his view, since the consignment of a person to a pool of possible perpetrators of injuries to one child could not constitute a factual foundation for a prediction of likely significant harm to another child in his or her care, then as a matter of logic, it could not become part of the requisite foundation in combination with other facts and circumstances [80]. Lord Sumption agreed [92].

Re F (A Minor) [2016] EWHC 2149 (Fam)

Judgment of Hayden J concerning the probity and reliability of a Court expert's evidence in public law care proceedings.

Summary

The Court appointed expert made findings against the mother, she appealed on the basis that the expert had misquoted and misrepresented her. She was able to back this with recordings of her sessions with the expert.

The judge examined the duties of a court expert and found:

- *"extensive parts of the report which purport, by the conventional grammatical use of quotation marks, to be direct quotations from the Mother, are in fact nothing of the kind. They are a collection of recollections and impressions compressed into phrases created by Dr Harper and attributed to the Mother" [15];*
- *"the report is heavy with apparent reference to direct speech when, in truth, almost none of it is" [15];*
- *to have covered thirteen topics which included the mother's sexual issues, childhood experiences and domestic abuse in an assessment meeting lasting no longer than fifteen minutes would have "required a degree of brutality or at least gross insensitivity" [24]; and*

- *"the overall impression is of an expert who is overreaching his material, in the sense that whilst much of it is rooted in genuine reliable secure evidence, it is represented in such a way that it is designed to give it its maximum forensic impact.That involves a manipulation of material which is wholly unacceptable" [26].*

Mr Justice Hayden found that the expert had "disregard for the conventional principles of professional method and analysis display[ed] a zealotry which he should recognise as a danger" to himself and his clients [32].

The judge found that the court could not accept the conclusions of the expert.
30. Finally, there has been much discussion at the Bar as to how I should characterise Dr Harper's professional failings. Ultimately I have come to the conclusion that the language or nomenclature is irrelevant. What matters is the substance of my findings and their impact on these children.

31. Ms Lee is right to emphasise the observations of Butler-Sloss (P) in Re U: Re B (serious injury;standard of proof) [2004] 2 FLR 263 at para 23iv:

"The court must always be on guard against the over-dogmatic expert, the expert whose reputation or amour-propre is at stake, or the expert who has developed a scientific prejudice"

Re A (A Child) [2015] EWFC 11

The President outlines the importance of three fundamental principles within s.31 applications. It deals with the factual basis that threshold criteria must be based upon. We have considered this extensively above, but I make no apology for its inclusion here:

Some   fundamental   principles
7. In the light of the way in which this case has been presented and some of the submissions I have heard, it is important always to bear in mind in these cases, and too often, I fear, they are overlooked, three fundamentally important points. The present case is an object lesson in, almost a textbook example of, how not to embark upon and pursue a care case.

8. The first fundamentally important point relates to the matter of fact-finding and proof. I emphasise, as I have already said, that it is for the local authority to prove, on a balance of probabilities, the facts upon which it seeks to rely. I draw attention to what, in Re A (A Child) (No 2) *[2011] EWCA Civ 12*, [2011] 1 FCR 141, para 26, I described as:

"the elementary proposition that findings of fact must be based on evidence (including inferences that can properly be drawn from the evidence) and not on suspicion or speculation."

This carries with it two important practical and procedural consequences.

9. The first is that the local authority, if its case is challenged on some factual point, must adduce proper evidence to establish what it seeks to prove. Much material to be found in local authority case records or social work chronologies is hearsay, often second- or third-hand hearsay. Hearsay evidence is, of course, admissible in family proceedings. But, and as the present case so vividly demonstrates, a local authority which is unwilling or unable to produce the witnesses who can speak of such matters first-hand, may find itself in great, or indeed insuperable, difficulties if a parent not merely puts the matter in issue but goes into the witness-

box to deny it. *As I remarked in my second View from the President's Chambers, [2013] Fam Law 680:*

"Of course the court can act on the basis of evidence that is hearsay. But direct evidence from those who can speak to what they have themselves seen and heard is more compelling and less open to cross-examination. Too often far too much time is taken up by cross-examination directed to little more than demonstrating that no-one giving evidence in court is able to speak of their own knowledge, and that all are dependent on the assumed accuracy of what is recorded, sometimes at third or fourth hand, in the local authority's files."

It is a common feature of care cases that a local authority asserts that a parent does not admit, recognise or acknowledge something or does not recognise or acknowledge the local authority's concern about something. If the 'thing' is put in issue, the local authority must both prove the 'thing' and establish that it has the significance attributed to it by the local *authority.*

10. The second practical and procedural point goes to the formulation of threshold and proposed findings of fact. The schedule of findings in the present case contains, as we shall see, allegations in relation to the father that "he appears to have" lied or colluded, that various people have "stated" or "reported" things, and that "there is an allegation". With all respect to counsel, this form of allegation, which one sees far too often in such documents, is wrong and should never be used. It confuses the crucial distinction, once upon a time, though no longer, spelt out in the rules of pleading and well understood, between an assertion of fact and the evidence needed to prove the assertion. What do the words "he appears to have lied" or "X reports that he did Y" mean? More important, where does it take one? The relevant allegation is not that "he appears to have lied" or "X reports"; the relevant allegation, if there is evidence to support it, is surely that "he lied" or "he did Y".

11. Failure to understand these principles and to analyse the case accordingly can lead, as here, to the unwelcome realisation that a seemingly impressive case is, in truth, a tottering edifice built on inadequate foundations.

12. The second fundamentally important point is the need to link the facts relied upon by the local authority with its case on threshold, the need to demonstrate why, as the local authority asserts, facts A + B + C justify the conclusion that the child has suffered, or is at risk of suffering, significant harm of types X, Y or Z. Sometimes the linkage will be obvious, as where the facts proved establish physical harm. But the linkage may be very much less obvious where the allegation is only that the child is at risk of suffering emotional harm or, as in the present case, at risk of suffering neglect. In the present case, as we shall see, an important element of the local authority's case was that the father "lacks honesty with professionals", "minimises matters of importance" and "is immature and lacks insight of issues of importance". May be. But how does this feed through into a conclusion that A is at risk of neglect? The conclusion does not follow naturally from the premise. The local authority's evidence and submissions must set out the argument and explain explicitly why it is said that, in the particular case, the conclusion indeed follows from the facts. Here, as we shall see, the local authority conspicuously failed to do so.

*13. In the light of the local authority's presentation of this case, it is important always to bear in mind, and again, I fear, it is too often misunderstood or overlooked, the point made by Macur LJ in Re Y (A Child) **[2013] EWCA Civ 1337**, para 7,* *in a judgment agreed by both Arden and Ryder LJJ:*

"(3) In upholding the criticism made of the judgment as to inadequate identification of risk and consequent evaluation of likelihood of that risk in subsequent analysis of measures which mitigate that risk, that is articulation of the proportionality of the order sought and subsequently made, the judge was not assisted by the dearth of relevant evidence which should have supplied, in particular by the local authority. Relevant evidence in this respect is not and should not be restricted to that supportive of the local authority's preferred outcome.

(4) I regret that quite apart from a lamentable lack of evidence which would have enabled the judge to conduct a rigorous analysis of options objectively compliant with the twins' Convention rights, whether favoured by the local authority and/or Children's Guardian or not, I consider the case appears to have been hijacked by the issue of the mother's dishonesty. Much of the local authority's evidence is devoted to it. The Children's Guardian adopts much the same perspective. It cannot be the sole issue in a case devoid of context. There was very little attention given to context in this case. No analysis appears to have been made by any of the

professionals as to why the mother's particular lies created the likelihood of significant harm to these children and what weight should reasonably be afforded to the fact of her deceit in the overall balance (emphasis added)"

14. The third fundamentally important point is even more crucial. It is vital always to bear in mind in these cases, and too often they are overlooked, the wise and powerful words of Hedley J in Re L (Care: Threshold Criteria) [2007] 1 FLR 2050, para 50:

"society must be willing to tolerate very diverse standards of parenting, including the eccentric, the barely adequate and the inconsistent. It follows too that children will inevitably have both very different experiences of parenting and very unequal consequences flowing from it. It means that some children will experience disadvantage and harm, while others flourish in atmospheres of loving security and emotional stability. These are the consequences of our fallible humanity and it is not the provenance of the state to spare children all the consequences of defective parenting. In any event, it simply could not be done."

15. That approach was endorsed by the Supreme Court in In re B. There are two passages in the judgments of the Justices which develop the point and to which I need to draw particular attention. The first is in the judgment of Lord Wilson of Culworth JSC where he said (para 28):

"[Counsel] seeks to develop Hedley J's point. He submits that:

'many parents are hypochondriacs, many parents are criminals or benefit cheats, many parents discriminate against ethnic or sexual minorities, many parents support vile political parties or belong to unusual or militant religions. All of these follies are visited upon their children, who may well adopt or "model" them in their own lives but those children could not be removed for those reasons.'

I agree with [counsel]'s submission".

The other is the observation of Baroness Hale of Richmond JSC (para 143):

"We are all frail human beings, with our fair share of unattractive character traits, which sometimes manifest themselves in bad behaviours which may be copied by our children. But the State does not and cannot take away the children of all the people who commit crimes, who abuse alcohol or drugs, who suffer from physical or mental illnesses

795

or disabilities, or who espouse antisocial political or religious beliefs."

16. I respectfully agree with all of that. It follows that I also agree with what His Honour Judge Jack said in North East Lincolnshire Council v G & L [2014] EWCC B77 (Fam), a judgment that attracted some attention even whilst I was hearing this case:

"I deplore any form of domestic violence and I deplore parents who care for children when they are significantly under the influence of drink. But so far as Mr and Mrs C are concerned there is no evidence that I am aware of that any domestic violence between them or any drinking has had an adverse effect on any children who were in their care at the time when it took place. The reality is that in this country there must be tens of thousands of children who are cared for in homes where there is a degree of domestic violence (now very widely defined) and where parents on occasion drink more than they should, I am not condoning that for a moment, but the courts are not in the business of social engineering. The courts are not in the business of providing children with perfect homes. If we took into care and placed for adoption every child whose parents had had a domestic spat and every child whose

parents on occasion had drunk too much then the care system would be overwhelmed and there would not be enough adoptive parents. So we have to have a degree of realism about prospective carers who come before the courts."

17. There is a powerful message in these judgments which needs always to be borne in mind by local authorities, by social workers, by children's guardians and by family judges.

The President also drew attention to the decision of the Court of Appeal in Re W (Children) [2014] EWCA Civ 1065, and the decision of Keehan J in Northamptonshire County Council v AS and Ors [2015] EWHC 199 (Fam) which highlighted the inappropriate use of s.20 Children Act 1989 by some local authorities, including the applicant authority in this case.

BH (A Child : Human Rights Act : Injunction) [2017] EWFC 15 (23 February 2017)

Involving parents in the decision making process.

Summary

As indicated by Munby J in In re G (Care: Challenge to Local Authority's Decision) [2003] 2 FLR 42, the local authority must fully involve the parents in its decision-making process.

Baker J set out the following:

[35] While this process is being carried out, the child should remain at home under the care order, unless his safety and welfare requires that he be removed immediately. This is the appropriate test when deciding whether the child should be removed under an interim care order, pending determination of an application under section 31 of the 1989 Act: In re LA (Care: Chronic Neglect) *[2010] 1 FLR 80. The same test should also apply when a local authority's decision to remove a child placed at home under a care order has led to an application by the parents to discharge the order and the court has to decide whether the child should be removed pending determination of the discharge application. As set out above, under section 33(4) of the 1989 Act, the local authority may not exercise its powers under a care order to determine how a parent may exercise his or her parental responsibility for the child unless satisfied it is necessary to do so to safeguard or promote the child's welfare. For a local authority to remove a child in circumstances where its welfare did not require it would be manifestly unlawful and an unjustifiable interference with the family's article 8 rights.*

[36] In submissions before the district judge, and before this court, it was argued on behalf of the local authority that its removal of D from the family home was lawful simply by reason of the care order. That submission is fundamentally misconceived. The local authority's removal of the child would only be lawful if necessary to safeguard or promote his welfare. Any other removal, or threatened removal, of the child is prima facie unlawful and an interference of the Article 8 rights of the parents and child. In such circumstances, the parents are entitled to seek an injunction under s.8 of the HRA.

The well-known interim removal test in Re LA [2009] EWCA Civ 822, [2010] 1 FLR 80 is this:

[A]t an interim stage the removal of children from their parents is not to be sanctioned unless the child's safety requires interim protection.

.The facts of the case before Baker J in Re DE were that the threatened removal was to have been of a child from his natural parents (both of whom held parental responsibility for him), in whose care he had been placed pursuant to a care order, into foster care with carers who were (presumably) unknown to him. In

those circumstances, as set out above, the learned judge was able to conclude that the removal, representing as it did an overt exercise of the local authority's qualified right to 'determine the extent to which a parent [...] of the child [...] may meet his parental responsibilities for him' (section 33(3), Children Act 1989), could be justified, and so lawful, only if satisfied that such action 'is necessary [...] in order to safeguard or promote his welfare' (section 33(4), Children Act 1989). 'Any other removal', the learned judge concluded, 'is prima facie unlawful and an interference of the Article 8 rights of the parents and child'.

The following are brief pointers to further case law:

<u>Y v United Kingdom (2012) 55 EHRR 33, [2012] 2 FLR 332, para 134:</u>

'family ties may only be severed in very exceptional circumstances and ... everything must be done to preserve personal relations and, where appropriate, to 'rebuild' the family. It is not enough to show that a child could be placed in

a more beneficial environment for his upbringing. However, where the maintenance of family ties would harm the child's health and development, a parent is not entitled under article 8 to insist that such ties be maintained.'

IMA (Care Proceedings: No Threshold) [2014] EWFC B110 (13 August 2014)

This is a set of care proceedings heard in Manchester County Court, but it raises some important issues of wider importance.

It was a case in which the Local Authority obtained an Emergency Protection Order removing IMA in August 2013, and after that Interim Care Orders sanctioning IMA remaining in foster care, up until the final hearing, which took place in August 2014 a year after the initial removal.

The Local Authority had been seeking a plan of adoption, supported by the Guardian, but this had changed to permanent placement with a relative. It is of note that the plan of adoption had been supported by the Agency Decision Makers (whose job it is to assess separately to social workers whether the circumstances of an individual case mean that adoption is the right plan)

The Judge at final hearing found that the threshold criteria were not made out, and thus the child would be going home and no statutory orders would be made.

The threshold criteria was based on the risk of the child being exposed to domestic violence (which is, on the revised wording of the Children Act 1989 a matter which on its own is capable of meeting threshold). That had two aspects really (i) Was father a risk of violence or violent behaviour and (ii) was the child in mother's care going to be exposed to the father.

The fact that the Judge found that threshold was not met therefore was significant. This wasn't a case with a suspicious injury which on full investigation was found to be an accident or a peculiar medical condition, but rather that the child ought never really to have been removed. The Judge was not saying that the threshold HAD been met but due to changes the risks had dissipated or become manageable, but that the situation of this family had NEVER crossed the section 31 threshold.

And the Judge had advised the Local Authority in a number of hearings that he was concerned that the section 31 threshold was not made out on the evidence that they had presented and was giving them the opportunity to flesh out their evidence if they had more information which was not before the Court. He told them that on 17th February 2014, 14th April 2014 and 23rd June, before making it official at the final hearing by ruling that threshold was not met.

RE F (ABDUCTION: UNBORN CHILD) [2006] EWHC 2199 (Fam)

Family Division

Hedley J

25 August 2006

Child abduction – Wrongful removal – Status of foetus – Habitual residence –

Stay of proceedings – Comity

The mother was pregnant when she went to Israel on 4 October 2002. The father alleged that he agreed to her going to Israel on the basis that she would return to resume family life in South Wales after the birth, but that her real intention had been to remain in Israel. The child was born in November 2002. On 3 October 2003 the mother announced her intention to remain in Israel, and she thereafter lived there with the

child. On 23 March 2005, Hedley J stayed all proceedings in

this jurisdiction in relation to the child. In proceedings in which the father participated, the Israeli court exercised a welfare jurisdiction in relation to the child on 9 June 2005 and in doing so found that she was habitually resident in Israel.

The father also applied to the Israeli court under the Hague Convention on the Civil Aspects of International Child Abduction 1980 for summary return of the child, and sought the assistance of the English court in those proceedings. Notwithstanding the stay, Hedley J permitted trial of a preliminary issue of whether there could have been a wrongful removal or retention of the child within the meaning of Art 3 of the Hague Convention.

Held – declining to make any declaration and refusing to disturb the stay –

(1) The law of England and Wales conferred no independent rights or status on a foetus and it was not possible in law to abduct a foetus so as to constitute a wrongful removal under Art 3 (see para [5]).

(2) Habitual residence was a question of fact. The child had

never been present in this country, and to say that she was habitually resident here in October 2003 would be wholly artificial (see para [9]).

(3) In any event, the question of habitual residence was for the requested and not the requesting State, and the Israeli court had already pronounced on the issue. It behoved the English court, on principles both of the Hague Convention and comity, to remain

silent on the subject. The English court had no role to play unless and until the child was present in this jurisdiction (see para [10], [13], [14])

Statutory provisions considered

Family Law Act 1986, s 41(1), (2)

Hague Convention on the Civil Aspects of International Child Abduction 1980, Arts 3,

Cases referred to in judgment

Al Habtoor v Fotheringham [2001] EWCA Civ 186, [2001] 1 FLR 951, CA

B v H (Habitual Residence: Wardship) [2002] 1 FLR 388, FD

M (Abduction: Habitual Residence), Re [1996] 1 FLR 887, CA

W and B v H (Child Abduction: Surrogacy), Re [2002] 1 FLR 1008, FD

Re T (Children) [2014] EWCA Civ 1369

This case was concerned with an appeal from a decision refusing a Father permission to apply to revoke placement orders in relation to his sons.

Summary

Care proceedings: accusations and counter-accusations were made by father and the mother. They failed to adhere to agreements of expectations regarding their conduct. The paternal grandparents took placement of the children until the grandmother felt she could no longer cope. Father agreed to local authority accommodation. Placement orders were made for T. The threshold criteria was not disputed. The local authority agreed that the children had not suffered significant harm; but the case was based on a risk of emotional harm due to father and mothers abusive relationship.

Father applied to revoke the placement order. He claimed a change in circumstances: namely that he and the mother had divorced and he had been in a relationship with another woman for two months. The judge found that father's assertion of a change in his circumstances was unproven and that there had been no material change in circumstances. He therefore appealed.

Russell J gave the lead Judgment in the Court of Appeal and, in allowing the appeal re-stated the two stage test for such applications, citing B-S: 'a. an application for leave involves a two-stage process;

b. first of all, the court has to be satisfied on the facts of the case that there has been a sufficient change in circumstances 'of a nature and degree sufficient, on the facts of the case, to open the door to the exercise of judicial evaluation'

c. the test should not be set too high, because parents should not be discouraged from bettering themselves or from seeking to prevent the adoption of their child by the imposition of a test that is unachievable;

d. whether or not there has been a relevant change in circumstance must be a matter of fact to be decided by the good sense and sound judgment of the tribunal hearing the application;

e. if there is no change in circumstances, that is the end of the matter, and the application fails;'

During the leave to appeal process the father denied and then admitted, that he could be the father of the unborn child of the mother of the children, who he had divorced.

The Court of Appeal held that the Judge was wrong to conclude that there had been no change of circumstances. The bar must not be set too high to such applications:

'The facts form the basis of where the bar is set. The height of the test or bar which a particular applicant must climb over must be considered by the judge with respect to the factual background of the case as a whole and will vary from case to case. The relevance of the change, referred to by Wall LJ at paragraph 32 reproduced above, while being in part a matter of fact to be decided by the good sense and sound judgment of the tribunal hearing the application, imports an element of judicial evaluation. The judicial consideration of the relevance or otherwise of the change in circumstance, and therefore the height of the test, in a particular case must be measured against the facts of that particular case when the placement order was made.'

The Judge failed to consider the second "change of circumstances" argument by the father that the behaviour of the boys had deteriorated since the making of the orders. That could only be done by comparing their behaviour then and now.

The sibling relationships between the two boys and their elder siblings were also important:

'The right of children to have contact with each other has been considered by this court in Re H (Children) [2010] EWCA Civ 1200 when an appeal by an elder sister for indirect contact was allowed. Lord Justice Thorpe held that the judge at first instance had insufficiently weighed the rights of the children to a wider family life. The rights of the older siblings subsist after the placement orders were made and are not extinguished by the making of such orders. The long-term affects of enforced separation from loved siblings and the importance of inter-sibling relationships have often taken second place to the perceived need to protect adoptive placements. In this case it is accepted by all that the three younger boys are close and have a positive and apparently lasting and important relationship....

...decisions of the Family Court should be proportionate in

their outcome for all siblings and in this case there is evidence that separation will cause long term distress and possible harm contained in the accepted evidence of the social worker. Thus when considering whether there has been a change in circumstances the effects on all the siblings is something that should properly be kept in mind.'

The Judge had also erred in giving primacy to the Father's circumstances as opposed to the circumstances of the children.

The Court of Appeal are setting out guidance on the first stage of the test, namely the change of circumstances that is required before leave can be granted. Russell J noted the paucity of such guidance in this area and it is to be noted that in this case the 'bar' was set lower as a result of the fact that the original threshold criteria related to a risk of harm as opposed to actual harm suffered.

In giving the lead Judgment in P (A Child) [2014] EWCA Civ 1174 McFarlane LJ noted that this was an opportunity to bring applications for adoption orders by step-parents into line with the Re B / Re B-S line of authority. The Court allowed the appeal against the refusal of the adoption order.

McFarlane LJ aligned the approach to such applications with

the recent jurisprudence of Re B / Re B-S in this way:

'46. In an adoption application the key to the approach both to evaluating the needs of a child's welfare throughout his or her life and to dispensing with parental consent is proportionality. The strong statements made by the Justices of the Supreme Court in Re B and taken up by judges of the Court of Appeal in subsequent decisions to the effect that adoption will be justified only where 'nothing else will do' are made in the context of an adoption being imposed upon a family against the wishes of the child's parents and where the adoption will totally remove the child from any future contact with, or legal relationship with, any of his natural relatives. Although the statutory provisions applicable to such an adoption (in particular ACA 2002, s 1 regarding welfare and s 52 regarding consent) apply in precisely the same terms to a step-parent adoption, the manner in which those provisions fall to be applied may differ and will depend upon the facts of each case and the judicial assessment of proportionality.

47. By way of example, in a child protection case where it is clear that rehabilitation to the parents is not compatible with their child's welfare, the court may be faced with a choice between adoption by total strangers selected by the local

811

authority acting as an adoption agency or adoption by other family members. There is a qualitative difference between these two options in terms of the degree to which the outcome will interfere with the ECHR, Art 8 rights to family life of the child and his parents; adoption by strangers being at the extreme end of the spectrum of interference and adoption by a family member being at a less extreme point on the scale. The former option is only justified when 'nothing else will do', whereas the latter option, which involves a lower degree of interference, may be more readily justified.

48. Where an adoption application is made by a step-parent, the approach of the ECtHR in Söderbäck v Sweden should be applied according to the facts of each case. In doing so the following central points from the judgment in Söderbäck are likely to be important:

a) There is a distinction to be drawn between adoption in the context of compulsory, permanent placement outside the family against the wishes of parents (for example as in Johansen v Norway) and a step-parent adoption where, by definition, the child is remaining in the care of one or other of his parents;

b) Factors which are likely to reduce the degree of

interference with the Art 8 rights of the child and the non-consenting parent ['Parent B'], and thereby make it more likely that adoption is a proportionate measure are:

i) Where Parent B has not had the care of the child or otherwise asserted his or her responsibility for the child;

ii) Where Parent B has had only infrequent or no contact with the child;

iii) Where there is a particularly well established family unit in the home of the parent and step-parent in which 'de facto' family ties have existed for a significant period.'

Appendix H : Appeals to Circuit Court in Ireland.

No. 101.1

0.101, r.1

Notice Of Appeal To The Circuit Court

(Civil Proceedings)

District Court Area of District No.

(Title of Proceedings)

TAKE NOTICE that (insert here, as appropriate, the Plaintiff/ the Respondent/the Applicant/(or) name the Third Party or other party appealing)

hereby appeals to the Judge of the Circuit Court at the next sitting of the Circuit Court at

from the *(Decree) *(Dismiss) *(Order(s)) made by the Judge of the District Court in the above-mentioned proceedings on the day of 19 .

(OR)

from so much of the *(Decree) *(Dismiss) *(Order(s)) made

by the Judge of the District Court in the above-mentioned proceedings on the day of 19 , as declared

(set forth the part complained of)

Dated this day of 19 .

Signed..............................

Appellant/Solicitor for Appellant

To (the opposing Party/Parties)

of ....

To the Clerk of the District Court,

at ....

Example of Notice of Appeal to High Court.

THE HIGH COURT

CIRCUIT APPEAL

CIRCUIT NO.

CIRCUIT

COUNTY OF

BETWEEN:

PLAINTIFF/APPLICANT

and

DEFENDANT/RESPONDENT

Take notice that the _____ hereby appeals to the High Court sitting in _____ at the first opportunity after the expiration of ten days from the date of service hereof from _____ given herein on the _____

Dated the

Signed: _____

To: To:
  Chief   Registrar

  _____

  Central   Office

  _____

  High   Court

  _____

  Four   Courts

  _____

  Dublin   7.

  _____

Example indorsement of service

I _____ did serve this Notice of Appeal on _____ at _____
on the __ day of _____ 20__.

Signed _____ this __ day of ___ 20__.

Form 3 Appeal to Appeal Court From the High Court

No. 2

O.86A,r.6(1)

COURT OF APPEAL

CIVIL

APPLICATION FOR LEAVE TO APPEAL

For Office use

Court of Appeal record number of this appeal .....

Subject matter for indexing .....

[Title and record number as per the High Court proceedings]

..... V .....

Date of filing .....

TAKE NOTICE that on .... 20 .... at .... or at the first available opportunity thereafter, ..., the intending appellant, intends to apply to the Court of Appeal pursuant to (*state statutory requirement for leave to appeal*) for leave to appeal from the *judgment *order of the High Court made on .... 20 .... in the proceedings before the High Court bearing the above record number that:

The grounds of the application for leave to appeal are:

*The reasons why it is alleged that the conditions for leave to appeal set out in (*state statutory requirement for leave to appeal*) are satisfied are: A draft of the proposed notice of appeal is attached.

Dated: ..... 20 ....

Signed: .....

(Solicitor for)(Intending) Appellant (*or as the case may be*)

To: Registrar of the Court of Appeal

Office of the Registrar of the Court of Appeal (Civil)

And to (Solicitor for)(Intended) Respondent

Form 4 – Expedited Appeal to the Appeal Court.

No. 4

O.86A, r. 8(1)

COURT OF APPEAL

CIVIL

Notice of expedited appeal

For Office use

Court of Appeal record number of this appeal .....

Subject matter for indexing .....

[Title and record number as per the High Court proceedings]

..... V .....

Date of filing .....

Name of Appellant(s) .....

Appellant's solicitors .....

Name of Respondent(s) .....

Respondent's solicitors .....

Has any appeal (or application for leave to appeal) previously been lodged in the Court of Appeal in respect of the proceedings?

Yes .....

No .....

If yes, give Court of Appeal record number(s) .....

Has any appeal (or application for leave to appeal) previously been lodged in the Supreme Court in respect of the proceedings?

Yes .....

No .....

If yes, give Supreme Court record number(s) .....

1. Return date for directions hearing

TAKE NOTICE that this expedited appeal is listed before the Court of Appeal for directions at the following date and time:

Date .....

Time .....

2. Decision that it is sought to appeal

Name(s) of Judge(s) .....

Date of order/Judgment .....

Neutral citation of the judgment appealed against if known e.g. High Court [2009] IEHC 608 .....

The relevant orders made in the High Court .....

Is it sought to appeal from

        (a) the entire decision .....

        or

        (b) a part or parts of the decision .....

        and if

        (b) set out below the specific part or parts of the decision concerned.

        ....

3. Category of expedited appeal

The appeal is an expedited appeal because it is (*mark appropriate box*):

        an appeal against the grant or refusal of relief under Article 40.4.2° of the Constitution .....

        an appeal against the making or refusal of an interlocutory order .....

        an appeal against the making or refusal of an order granting summary judgment .....

an appeal against the making or refusal of a winding up order .....

an appeal against the making or refusal of an order appointing a provisional liquidator .....

an appeal against the making or refusal of an order appointing a receiver .....

an appeal against the making or refusal of an order in the course of examinership proceedings .....

an appeal against the making or refusal of an adjudication in bankruptcy .....

an appeal against the making or refusal of an order under Chapter 3 (Debt Settlement Arrangements) or Chapter 4 (Personal Insolvency Arrangements) of Part 3 of the Personal Insolvency Act 2012 .....

an appeal against the making or refusal of an order in any proceedings to which Order 133 (Child Abduction and Enforcement of Custody Orders) of the Rules of the Superior Courts applies .....

an appeal against the making or refusal of an order making a determination as to the capacity of a person (including an order making or refusing to make a person a ward of court)

an appeal against the making or refusal of an order in proceedings under the European Arrest Warrant Acts 2003 and 2012 or in extradition proceedings .....

an appeal from the making or refusal of an order of prohibition in criminal proceedings .....

an appeal against the refusal of an ex parte order .....

an appeal designated in a statutory practice direction as an appeal to which Part IV of Order 86A of the Rules of the Superior Courts applies (in which case, specify the nature of the appeal in the row below) .....

4. Grounds of appeal

Please set out below the grounds of appeal (numbered as 1, 2, 3, etc).

....

Name of counsel or solicitor who settled the grounds of appeal (if the appellant is legally represented), or name of appellant in person:

....

5. Order(s) sought

Set out the precise form of order(s) that will be sought from the Court of Appeal if the appeal is successful:

....

What order are you seeking if successful?

set aside .....

vary/substitute .....

If a declaration of unconstitutionality is being sought please identify the specific provision(s) of the Act of the Oireachtas which it is claimed is/are repugnant to the Constitution

....

If a declaration of incompatibility with the European Convention on Human Rights is being sought please identify the specific statutory provision(s) or rule(s) of law which it is claimed is/are incompatible with the Convention

....

Are you asking the Court of Appeal to:

depart from (or distinguish) one of its own decisions?

Yes .....

No .....

If Yes, please give details below:

....

make a reference to the Court of Justice of the European Union?

Yes .....

No .....

If Yes, please give details below:

.....

Will you request a priority hearing?

Yes .....

No .....

If Yes, please give reasons below:

.....

6. Documents relied on

Please set out below a list of all of the documents on which the appellant intends to rely at the hearing of the appeal:

....

7. Appellant Details

Where there are two or more appellants by or on whose behalf this notice is being filed please provide relevant details for each of the appellants

Appellant's full name .....

Original status

Plaintiff .....

Defendant .....

Applicant .....

Respondent .....

Petitioner .....

Notice Party ....

.

Solicitor

Name of firm .....

Name of solicitor responsible for this appeal .....

Email .....

Address .....

Telephone no. .....

Document Exchange no. .....

Postcode .....

Ref.....

If the Appellant is not legally represented please complete the following

Current postal address .....

e-mail address .....

Telephone no. .....

8. Respondent Details

Where there are two or more respondents affected by this appeal, please provide relevant details, where known, for each of those respondents

Respondent's full name .....

Original status

Plaintiff .....

Defendant .....

Applicant .....

Respondent .....

Petitioner .....

Notice Party .....

Solicitor

Name of firm .....

Name of solicitor responsible for this appeal .....

Email .....

Address .....

Telephone no. .....

Document Exchange no. .....

Postcode .....

Ref. .....

If the Respondent is not legally represented please complete the following

Current postal address .....

e-mail address .....

Telephone no. .....

Please submit your completed form to:

Office of the Registrar of the Court of Appeal (Civil)
The Four Courts
Inns Quay
Dublin

Together with an attested copy of the Order and any written Judgment in respect of which it is sought to appeal not later than ten days from the perfecting of the Order appealed against.

Save in the case of a notice of appeal from a decision made otherwise than *inter partes*, this notice is to be served, within seven days after it has been issued, on all parties directly affected by the appeal. A respondent may consent in writing to late service of a notice of appeal.

Note: The appellant must not later than four days before the date fixed for the directions hearing, lodge with the Registrar and serve on each respondent affected by the expedited appeal an indexed and paginated directions booklet.

Appendix I: Key Articles of ECHR

ARTICLE 1 Obligation to respect Human Rights: The High Contracting Parties shall secure to everyone within their jurisdiction the rights and freedoms defined in Section I of this Convention.

ARTICLE 2 Right to life:

1. Everyone's right to life shall be protected by law. No one shall be deprived of his life intentionally save in the execution of a sentence of a court following his conviction of a crime for which this penalty is provided by law.

2. Deprivation of life shall not be regarded as inflicted in contravention of this Article when it results from the use of force which is no more than absolutely necessary:

(a) in defence of any person from unlawful violence;

(b) in order to effect a lawful arrest or to prevent the escape of a person lawfully detained;

(c) in action lawfully taken for the purpose of quelling a riot or insurrection.

ARTICLE 3 Prohibition of torture: No one shall be subjected to torture or to inhuman or degrading treatment or punishment.

ARTICLE 4 Prohibition of slavery and forced labour:

1. No one shall be held in slavery or servitude.

2. No one shall be required to perform forced or compulsory labour.

3. For the purpose of this Article the term "forced or compulsory labour" shall not include:

(a) any work required to be done in the ordinary course of detention imposed according to the provisions of Article 5 of this Convention or during conditional release from such detention;

(b) any service of a military character or, in case of conscientious objectors in countries where they are recognised, service exacted instead of compulsory military service;

(c) any service exacted in case of an emergency or calamity threatening the life or wellbeing of the community;

(d) any work or service which forms part of normal civic

obligations.

ARTICLE 5 Right to liberty and security:

1. Everyone has the right to liberty and security of person. No one shall be deprived of his liberty save in the following cases and in accordance with a procedure prescribed by law:

(a) the lawful detention of a person after conviction by a competent court;

(b) the lawful arrest or detention of a person for noncompliance with the lawful order of a court or in order to secure the fulfilment of any obligation prescribed by law;

(c) the lawful arrest or detention of a person effected for the purpose of bringing him before the competent legal authority on reasonable suspicion of having committed an offence or when it is reasonably considered necessary to prevent his committing an offence or fleeing after having done so;

(d) the detention of a minor by lawful order for the purpose of educational supervision or his lawful detention for the purpose of bringing him before the competent legal authority;

(e) the lawful detention of persons for the prevention of the spreading of infectious diseases, of persons of unsound mind, alcoholics or drug addicts or vagrants;

(f) the lawful arrest or detention of a person to prevent his effecting an unauthorised entry into the country or of a person against whom action is being taken with a view to deportation or extradition.

2. Everyone who is arrested shall be informed promptly, in a language which he understands, of the reasons for his arrest and of any charge against him.

3. Everyone arrested or detained in accordance with the provisions of paragraph 1 (c) of this Article shall be brought promptly before a judge or other officer authorised by law to exercise judicial power and shall be entitled to trial within a reasonable time or to release pending trial. Release may be conditioned by guarantees to appear for trial.

4. Everyone who is deprived of his liberty by arrest or detention shall be entitled to take proceedings by which the lawfulness of his detention shall be decided speedily by a court and his release ordered if the detention is not lawful.

5. Everyone who has been the victim of arrest or detention in

contravention of the provisions of this Article shall have an enforceable right to compensation.

ARTICLE 6 Right to a fair trial:

1. In the determination of his civil rights and obligations or of any criminal charge against him, everyone is entitled to a fair and public hearing within a reasonable time by an independent and impartial tribunal established by law. Judgment shall be pronounced publicly but the press and public may be excluded from all or part of the trial in the interests of morals, public order or national security in a democratic society, where the interests of juveniles or the protection of the private life of the parties so require, or to the extent strictly necessary in the opinion of the court in special circumstances where publicity would prejudice the interests of justice.

2. Everyone charged with a criminal offence shall be presumed innocent until proved guilty according to law.

3. Everyone charged with a criminal offence has the following minimum rights:

(a) to be informed promptly, in a language which he understands and in detail, of the nature and cause of the accusation against him;

(b) to have adequate time and facilities for the preparation of his defence;

(c) to defend himself in person or through legal assistance of his own choosing or, if he has not sufficient means to pay for legal assistance, to be given it free when the interests of justice so require;

(d) to examine or have examined witnesses against him and to obtain the attendance and examination of witnesses on his behalf under the same conditions as witnesses against him;

(e) to have the free assistance of an interpreter if he cannot understand or speak the language used in court.

ARTICLE 7 No punishment without law:

1. No one shall be held guilty of any criminal offence on account of any act or omission which did not constitute a criminal offence under national or international law at the time when it was committed. Nor shall a heavier penalty be imposed than the one that was applicable at the time the criminal offence was committed.

2. This Article shall not prejudice the trial and punishment of any person for any act or omission which, at the time when it was committed, was criminal according to the general principles of law recognised by civilised nations.

ARTICLE 8 Right to respect for private and family life:

1. Everyone has the right to respect for his private and family life, his home and his correspondence. 2. There shall be no interference by a public authority with the exercise of this right except such as is in accordance with the law and is necessary in a democratic society in the interests of national security, public safety or the economic wellbeing of the country, for the prevention of disorder or crime, for the protection of health or morals, or for the protection of the rights and freedoms of others.

ARTICLE 9 Freedom of thought, conscience and religion:

1. Everyone has the right to freedom of thought, conscience and religion; this right includes freedom to change his religion or belief and freedom, either alone or in community with others and in public or private, to manifest his religion or belief, in worship, teaching, practice and observance. 2. Freedom to manifest one's religion or beliefs shall be subject

only to such limitations as are prescribed by law and are necessary in a democratic society in the interests of public safety, for the protection of public order, health or morals, or for the protection of the rights and freedoms of others.

ARTICLE 10 Freedom of expression:

1. Everyone has the right to freedom of expression. This right shall include freedom to hold opinions and to receive and impart information and ideas without interference by public authority and regardless of frontiers. This Article shall not prevent States from requiring the licensing of broadcasting, television or cinema enterprises.

2. The exercise of these freedoms, since it carries with it duties and responsibilities, may be subject to such formalities, conditions, restrictions or penalties as are prescribed by law and are necessary in a democratic society, in the interests of national security, territorial integrity or public safety, for the prevention of disorder or crime, for the protection of health or morals, for the protection of the reputation or rights of others, for preventing the disclosure of information received in confidence, or for maintaining the authority and impartiality of the judiciary.

ARTICLE 11 Freedom of assembly and association:

1. Everyone has the right to freedom of peaceful assembly and to freedom of association with others, including the right to form and to join trade unions for the protection of his interests.

2. No restrictions shall be placed on the exercise of these rights other than such as are prescribed by law and are necessary in a democratic society in the interests of national security or public safety, for the prevention of disorder or crime, for the protection of health or morals or for the protection of the rights and freedoms of others. This Article shall not prevent the imposition of lawful restrictions on the exercise of these rights by members of the armed forces, of the police or of the administration of the State.

ARTICLE 12 Right to marry: Men and women of marriageable age have the right to marry and to found a family, according to the national laws governing the exercise of this right.

ARTICLE 13 Right to an effective remedy: Everyone whose rights and freedoms as set forth in this Convention are violated shall have an effective remedy before a national authority notwithstanding that the violation has been committed by persons acting in an official capacity.

ARTICLE 14 Prohibition of discrimination: The enjoyment of the rights and freedoms set forth in this Convention shall be secured without discrimination on any ground such as sex, race, colour, language, religion, political or other opinion, national or social origin, association with a national minority, property, birth or other status.

The full list of all Articles can be found at http://www.echr.coe.int/Documents/Convention_ENG.pdf

civ   http://www.nkmr.org/en/import/2521-the-rhetoric-case-by-linda-arlig

cv   http://www.nkmr.org/en/import/2521-the-rhetoric-case-by-linda-arlig

cvi   www.publications.parliament.uk Publications and Records – Commons Select Committees- Education. Session 2010-12.

cvii   https://www.theguardian.com/law/2016/sep/20/family-courts-face-imminent-crisis-over-huge-rise-in-care-applications

cviii   http://www.communitycare.co.uk/2016/05/24/five-things-social-workers-need-know-children-social-work-bill/

cix

http://www.legislation.gov.uk/ukpga/2017/16/introductio
n/enacted

ᶜˣ   Regulation 4(2) of the *Care Planning, Placement and Care Review (England) Regulations 2010* requires that where a child is accommodated under section 20 a care plan must be prepared by the local authority 'before C is first placed by the responsible authority or, if it is not practicable to do so, within ten working days of the start of the first placement'.

ᶜˣⁱ   The local authority will be required to appoint an Independent Reviewing Officer for the child – section 25A of the Children Act 1989.

ᶜˣⁱⁱ Particular regard should be had to the decision of the Court of Appeal in *Re N (Children)(Adoption: Jurisdiction)* [2015] EWCA Civ 1112 and in particular the review of the use of section 20 set out in the judgment of Sir James Munby P at paras 157 to – 171. It is particularly appropriate to highlight the warning given at para 171 that: 'The misuse and abuse of section 20 in this context is not just a matter of bad practice. It is wrong; it is a denial of the fundamental rights of both the parent and the child; it will no longer be tolerated; and it must stop. Judges will and must be alert to the problem and pro-active in putting an end to it. From now on, local authorities which use section 20 as a prelude to care proceedings for lengthy periods or which fail to follow the good practice I have identified, can expect to be subjected to probing questioning by the court. If the answers are not satisfactory, the local authority can expect stringent criticism and possible exposure to successful claims for damages.'

cxiii   Per Hedley J in *Coventry City Council v C, B, CA and CH [2013] 2 FLR 987,* para. 27

cxiv   See *R (G) v Nottingham City Council and Nottingham University Hospital* [2008] 1 FLR 1668, para 53

cxv   See *Re N (Children)(Adoption: Jurisdiction)* [2015] EWCA Civ 1112, para 166

cxvi   Theis J in *Medway Council v Mother & Ors* [2014] EWHC 308(Fam), Para 14.

NOTES

Lightning Source UK Ltd.
Milton Keynes UK
UKHW011434010219
336574UK00009B/529/P